Edward Said at the Limits

Ahmad Izmer, *Edward Said (No. 3)*, Charcoal & Clay on Board, 31 x 26 cm. © 2002.

Edward Said at the Limits

By
Mustapha Marrouchi

State University of New York Press

Published by

State University of New York Press, Albany

For information, address State University of New York Press,
90 State Street, Suite 700, Albany, NY 12207

Production by Christine L. Hamel
Marketing by Fran Keneston

Library of Congress Cataloging-in-Publication Data

Marrouchi, Mustapha, 1956–
      Edward Said at the limits / by Mustapha Marrouchi.
         p. cm.
      Includes bibliographical references and index.
      ISBN 0-7914-5965-9 (alk. paper) — ISBN 0-7914-5966-7 (pbk. : alk. paper)
      1. Literature, Modern—History and criticism—Theory, etc. 2. Said, Edward W.
   3. Criticism—History—20th century. 4. Power (Social sciences) in literature.
   5. Politics and culture. 6. Politics and literature. I. Title.

PN51.M275 2004
801.95'092—dc22

                                                                                    2003059007

10 9 8 7 6 5 4 3 2 1

For the women of
الإنتفاظه
(Intifada)

If you can force your heart and nerve
   and sinew
To serve your turn long after they
   are gone,
And so hold on when there is nothing
   in you
Except the Will which says to them:
   "Hold on!"

—Antonio Gramsci, *Selections from the Prison Notebooks*, 45.

If one is writing within and about an already "raced" milieu, advocacy and argument are irresistible. Rage against the soul murder embedded in the subject matter runs the risk of forcing the "raced" writer to choose among a limited array of strategies: documenting their seething; conscientiously, studiously avoiding it; struggling to control it; or, as in this instance, manipulating its heat. Animating its dross into a fine art of subversive potency. . . . In his portrait of [the Other] . . . , [Edward Said] . . . not only summoned a sophisticated, wholly . . . imginastic vocabulary in which to launch a discursive negotiation with the West, he exploited with technical finesse the very images that have served white writers for generations.

Toni Morrison, "On 'The Radiance of the King,'" 18.

For those of us who see the struggle between Eastern and Western descriptions of the world as both an internal and an external struggle, Edward Said has for many years been an especially important voice.

—Salman Rushdie, *Imaginary Homelands*, 166.

ظاهرة ثقافية عربية غير مسبوقة

محمد شاهين, "في فضاء ادوارد سعيد," القدس العربي, 6.

Edward Said's metaphors alone tell an interesting story: the wanderer, the road, textual space, the foundling, widowhood, the dynasty, molestation, the harried critic, the monstrous library, "the tumbling disorder of brute reality that will not settle down."

—Michael Wood, "Damaging Thought," xi.

Ghazal
For Edward Said

In Jerusalem a dead phone's dialed by exiles.
You learn your strange fate: you were exiled by exiles.
You open the heart to list unborn galaxies.
Don't shut that folder when Earth is filed by exiles.
Before Night passes over the wheat of Egypt,
let stones be leavened, the bread torn wild by exiles.
Crucified Mansoor was alone with the Alone:
God's loneliness—just His—compiled by exiles.
By the Hudson lies Kashmir, brought from Palestine—
It shawls the piano, Bach beguiled by exiles.
Tell me who's tonight the Physician of Sick Pearls?
Only you as you sit, Desert child, by exiles.
Match Majnoon (he kneels to pray on a wine-stained rug)
or prayer will be nothing, distempered mild by exiles.
"Even things that are true can be proved." Even they?
Swear not by Art but, O Oscar Wilde, by exiles.
Don't weep, we'll drown out the Calls to Prayer, O Saqi—
I'll raise my glass before wine is defined by exiles.

Was—after the last sky—this the fashion of fire:
Autumn's mist pressed to ashes styled by exiles?
If my enemy's alone and his arms are empty,
give him my heart silk-wrapped like a child by exiles.
Will you, Beloved Stranger, ever witness Shahid—
two destinies at last reconciled by exiles?
> —Agha Shahid Ali, "Ghazal 1: For Edward Said"
> 1998.

Contents

Preface

There are many possible ways to describe Edward Said, none of them adequate but some less misleading than others. One can begin on safe ground, surely, by saying that he holds an exemplary position in the world of letters, that he is the father of the (so-called) postcolonial discipline, and that he is the critic of the postimperial *trace*. Simply to point him out, Said *ipse*, would be to mistake the inquirer's meaning if he or she wanted to know who Said really is. For if writing leads to a deeper understanding of the *trace* and of the paradoxes surrounding the concept of 'presence,' then *Edward Said at the Limits* places Said in a privileged position of being the subject of the inquiry. It is an event that cannot be meaningful without having divided itself, since it always refers back to the one and the *other* by birth: "I was born in Jerusalem, so were my parents and grandparents" (*Out of Place*, 1999: 5). From this position of elevated dislocation, of studied self-removal, Said has produced the most complex and demanding body of work of any postwar cultural critic. His books, occupying an ambiguous space between the West and the Rest, are haunted by solitude, disciplined by a need to understand the anxieties of the exile as postmodern savage. To ask how he achieved that point of vantage is to be reminded that his work is a reflection of sheer اجتهاد (perseverance).

His life is uprooted in other ways, too. As a wanderer twice displaced, in sentences of great precision and balance, Said reanimates the dilemmas of the postcolonial experience—the pathos of marginality and inner exile, the fear of throwing oneself into a void, and the failure of the liberated "I" to remake its home elsewhere.

Edward Said at the Limits is the second volume in a trilogy of studies of postcolonial theory and practice, of which the first one was *Signifying with a Vengeance* (State University of New York Press, 2001). Unlike its predecessor, the present work concerns itself with a writer—namely, Edward Said—who, in his quest to reshape the world, resembles a blacksmith transforming a red-hot lump of iron into a worthy blade. Eschewing argument by assertion, he claims the right to intricacy, to nuance, to insinuation—claims that may have contributed to a persistent interpretation of the Colonized *Other* either as a simple race-inflected allegory or as dream-besotted mysticism. The focus of the book is on the extraordinary ferment of a critic's intellectual life, all the way from politics to literature, cultural history to music. In such a long span, any such treatment has to be selective, and the book has its fair share of skimmings and exclusions. But I have tried to register something of the wealth of intellectual preoccupations of this remarkable individual and to frame it theoretically with some reflections on the nature of intellectual work in general and its place in cultural life in particular. One example illustrates what I mean. Amid all the pallid postcolonial hybridity and the old and new postmodern anything-goes-ism, *Orientalism* endures like Paleolithic mammals, resisting the inevitability of extinction. A quarter of a century after it first appeared, it still wakes us to the sight and sounds of the downtrodden and the afflicted, the poor and the dispossessed, and in doing so, wakes us to our vanity, our greed, and our mortality, returning us, however reluctantly, to our shared humanity. In the process, it makes the insistent dreamers among us mad and the newly awakened glad, and it is precisely for this reason that we rush to celebrate its 25th anniversary of being *in* and *of* the world. In today's cultural climate, *Orientalism* is, more than ever, poised to invent "un peuple qui manque," to adapt freely from Deleuze, "un peuple à venir encore enfoui sous . . . [les] trahisons et reniements"—just what it was surely constructed to achieve. What was once rejected has become the cornerstone, and centuries of insult and odious patronage are accordingly being made up for in the most obstinate of ways. Said is right to that extent.

During the five years when the contents of the book were taking shape, numerous friends and colleagues gave me the benefit of their helpful criticism, suggestions, and interest. Others provided me with the occasion to present my ideas in public, and on each and every one of these occasions I profited greatly from advice and argument, often pursued in subsequent e-mail exchanges via electronic informants. I particularly want to thank my friends David Hoeniger, Kip Sumner, and Wayne Tompkins for graciously reading the manuscript in its entirety and for supplying me most generously with some good and insightful criticism and information. Ted Blodgett gave me the benefit of his erudition, criticism, and friendship. I was the undeserving beneficiary of freely given time from Fran Devlin, who helped immeasurably in putting the manuscript through the travail of proofreading. Sherbanu Mamujee helped me a great deal in the preparation of the manuscript: her patience and competence were of invaluable importance.

I have enjoyed a most cooperative relationship with my publishers. James Peltz, Jane Bunker, Kelli Williams, and Katy Leonard of State University of New York Press have been most solicitous and helpful editors. Their foresight has meant a great deal to me. I would also like to thank Christine L. Hamel, and Fran Keneston in the Marketing Department, who worked tirelessly to put the manuscript in its present form. In doing so, they helped set me up in an enviable position whereby I could say: This is a good piece of writing. To all of you who kept me going and sustained me during this arduous task, my heartfelt thanks.

Aïda Khouildi has been exemplary in her ability, over the years, to forge a shared critique through her subtle and sharp eye. It gives me particular pleasure to thank her for her enduring devotion, generosity, and constant support; her tolerance for telephone conversations and for insisting that the transcriptions of certain concepts in Arabic must be permeated with style are resonant even today. Beyond this book or any other, I thank Aïda for sharing in the writing from a distance.

It seems appropriate, too, to reflect with gratitude on all I owe my father and mother, who cannot read this book for multiple reasons, one of them the barrier of the language. It is to their own kindness and my mother's love of the arts that I owe my earliest interest in literature. Over the years she has always been interested in my exploring new venues, and together we have shared many literary experiences. I have left last my gratitude of the deepest bond, the most cherished indebtedness, to the person who has been essential in every way to meeting the challenges and sharing the pleasures of this project: Carolyn Bryson. She deserves both the gratitude of the daily grind and the feelings of love and affection.

Finally, some necessary acknowledgments. My dear gratitude goes most particularly to Kostas Myrsiades, Andi Hubbard, Emmanuel C. Eze, Bruce Janz, Ronald Huebert, Debra Castillo, and Bill Ashcroft, who helped to disseminate parts of this book. Thanks, too, to Agha Shahid Ali, who kindly gave me permission to reproduce his poem (Ghazal 7: For Edward Said), Monica Min Lee who photographed the Said painting, and Raymond Shapiro who graciously accepted my request to reprint the caricature of Edward Said by David Levine, which appeared in *The New York Review of Books* 3 (March, 1994).

Writing this book has been particularly difficult because, while I concur with Said in everything fundamental, I am also mildly critical of him; however, I do not include myself among the calumniating legions marshaled against him by conformists, sycophants, and pseudointellectuals inside and outside academia who spin enormous structures of falsehoods about a man who refuses to cave in to the lures of power; nor would I want to play into the hands of the politically motivated hostility that has been directed at Said over the years. Those who think my assessment is too laudatory may find compensation in a narrative that rings correct, puts things into perspective, and does justice to the contribution of a consummate public intellectual, who continues to speak on behalf of the oppressed and to call ruling elites back from their brutal power games to the path of justice and human decency. This book is suffused with the human and moral example of Edward Said, a fine teacher, a kind man, a good friend, and a gifted cultural critic.

The day Edward died in a New York hospital, the news was telephoned to me in Toronto. The message was short: "Edward is dead." I felt heavy-hearted and did not speak, just flung my arms out in a gesture as if saying "Gone!" "Ego silebam et fletum frenebam" [I remained silent and restrained my tears] while trying to address my loss. The grief was all the more palpable for being wordless. It has been nearly a week since I received the news that engulfed the world, and I very much doubt I have absorbed loss of a mind so fine. For every now and again in the pelting details of the day-by-day life, there is a pause during which one must respond at a determined time and place to an unrepeatable event—the death of the man who put the maintenance of poetic inspiration above every other personal consideration. To pay homage to the friend-teacher-author who gave a voice to Palestine is to point out the debt as well as pay it back. Even so, aware as I am of the sorrow at the loss of Edward, and in particular to his beloved family and immense close circle of friends, I simply cannot reconcile myself to a world where he is no longer part of the crowd, part of the *mêlée*, part of the storm. It is an unthinkable thought that has alas become all too thinkable now. But he was too individual, too fierce a writer to dissolve easily. Formal and outrageous, exquisite and coarse, precious and raunchy, amazingly human and vulnerable in his larger-than-life status to all the personal pain and doubts that beset ordinary mortals, and never too self-preoccupied to let you gain entry to his life, Edward had a kindness of heart beneath the roaring certitude. Through his stand against domination of any kind and his defense of Palestine, he had grown into the giant figure we rightfully mourn today.

As *Edward Said at the Limits* prepares to make its debut in the world, Edward, who was my inspiration, will not be there to see it. My most painful regret is that he died during its final preparation. Over the years he was a tower of strength and support for me: always present, always kind and accommodating, always ready with one comment or another that somehow found its way into my narrative. I am more sorry than I can say that he did not live to read my labor of love and tell me what he thought of it. However, I am comforted to a certain degree by the belief that my book is *supplementing* his unique corpus, *albiet* in a minor way. It is also my humble way of saying thank you, Edward, for showing me the way to the mountain top. Like Iqbal Ahmad before him, he died at the height of his powers: in mid-sentence, so to speak. For us (ex-colonials), this is the cruelest of deaths. His monumental work is the measure of our loss, but it is also our treasure, to savor and to hoard while he is *out there, out there* in Culture, in Politics, in Theory, in Literature, in Music, a Ray of the clear Fountain of Eternal Day.

EDWARD SAID AT THE LIMITS

The time has come for critics and artists of the new cultural politics of difference to cast their nets widely, flex their muscles broadly and thereby refuse to limit their visions, analyses and praxis to their particular terrains. The aim is to dare to recast, redefine and revise the very notions of "modernity," "mainstream," "margins," "difference," "otherness."

—Cornel West, "The New Cultural Politics of Difference," 36.

A great deal of history has followed from attempts to blow history to pieces. Hegel believed that the *Zeitgeist* had arrived at its final consummation inside his own head, but this simply provided a cue to Marx, Kierkegaard, Nietzsche, Foucault, and a range of others to keep it going by challenging Hegel's assumption. Marx's cavalier declaration that all previous history had been no more than "pre-history" was as modernist a gesture as Fauvism. Pronouncements of the end of history simply contribute another event to the history they declare over and done with, as Francis Fukuyama, the right-wing pontificator and philosopher, has no doubt been discovering from his postbag. They are self-disconfirming prophecies, Cretan Liar paradoxes that, like all appeals to make it new, add one more item to that venerable lineage known as the avant-garde. Besides, you can only break with history if you are already standing somewhere inside it, and the instruments with which you emancipate yourself from it must be fashioned from its own unpromising stuff. It is also hard to be sure that your power to transcend the past is not itself determined by it—that you are not the plaything of history in the very act of leaping free of it. Postmodernity is the era in which time speeds up because democracy and technology now allow us to fashion our own destinies instead of waiting on the *longues durées* of Nature and Providence, but the same technology comes to be felt as an implacable, quasinatural force of which we are the mere passive products (Eagleton, 1998).[1]

1

Or, to put it another way, with the celebrated demise of communism, the rise of tribalism, and the global adoption of the free-market model, we have come, some say, to the "end-of-ideology" (Fukuyama, 1999). The familiar use of this phrase suggests that the triumph of Western liberalism is quite uncontested, and the values of individualism have been universally affirmed. Accompanying such assertions is a narrative of global transformation that no longer sees change as part of the struggle between different systems of government embedded in the conditions of historical and philosophical specificity. The "end of ideology" argument has resulted in a peculiarly ahistorical and decontextualized approach to political "turning points" seen as emanating from the emancipatory temperaments of great leaders—Nelson Mandela comes to mind—rather than emerging from the sustained struggles and strategies that form the collective will of a people. In this moment, at the limits of history as we have known it (the much-vaunted moment of the postnational, the transnational, the "glocal"), we are witnessing the dawning of other ways of telling. Voices bestriding nations and cultures, these "moral" authorities of emancipation stand for the power of almost unmediated direct action (Anderson, 1998).

"Is there a right 'tone' for such an *inter*national conversation?" Homi Bhabha asks and answers with equal aplomb. "This is as much an historical as a rhetorical or ethical issue. The ravages of class and racial division in the world, the *de facto* segregation of populations who are more or less yoked together by the demography and demagoguery of 'democracy,' turns 'us-and-them-ism' into stark alternatives" (1998: 24). In this silhouette of desperate subjects, laid out in various dimensions, there is a need for a breath of new life: I have rarely seen this hope better captured than in the words of Edward Said, who writes as an Arab-American: "[W]e can read ourselves against another people's pattern, but since it is not ours . . . we emerge as its effects, its errata, its counternarratives. Whenever we try to narrate ourselves, we appear as dislocations in *their* discourse" (*After the Last Sky*, 1986: 140). The technique of Said is enviable to say the least in that he is able to illuminate even the stormiest of human prospects (counternarratives of all kinds do constantly enter "mainstream" culture) with a serene, often revelatory, light that shows us not only the obligatory two sides to every question but also the often-overlooked third dimension as well. These alternatives are present with force both in his person and in his work.

One of the most celebrated writers in the latter part of the twentieth century, Edward Said, with his fresh, irreverent approach to literature, criticism, and meaning itself, proposes nothing less than a reinvention of reading (works of art) from the ground up. In doing so, he brings to literature and critique not just a new style and method but a new consciousness, a new way of seeing and coming to terms with the life around us. Breaking decisively with all previous literary traditions and applied norms, he has forged a unique idiom—by turns abstract and down-to-earth, playful and subversive, philosophical and aesthetic—which is likely to influence generations to come. Reading through thousands of words of public statements, of reviews and interviews, of adulations and accusations, one is struck by the high price he has had to pay for being the Arab world's cultural critic of the West and its misrepresentations of the Oriental *Other*. This, to be sure, is an urgent enough claim, since nothing is more honorable than the attempt to define a corrective way of thinking about history.

Said tells an anecdote that has something of the literary and at the same time something that exceeds the literary, a narrative form and a pointed, referential access to what lies beyond or beneath that form.

> I remember one of my earliest experiences, which had a lot to do with the writing of *Orientalism*, when I was walking in the Gezira Club of which we were members. It was a famous enclave built by the British. The members were mostly foreign, although there were some local members. I was thrown out by the secretary, who was a friend of my father's. . . . He said, "Don't you know that Arabs are not allowed here?" And I said, "Yes, but we're members." And he said, "Don't argue with me boy, get out!" It was that sense of forbidden space that really sowed, I think, the seeds of my rebellion against the hieratic and the fetishistic and the ritualized and the idolatrous. I felt the need always to go against those prohibitions and those statutes and those forbidden places. The urge to enter those places usually cost me quite dear, going into places where I wasn't wanted, which is what I felt I was doing in *Orientalism* (*Edward Said: A Critical Reader*, 1998: 28).

This conjunction of the literary and the referential, Joel Fineman informs us, functions in the writing of history not as the servant of a grand, integrated narrative of beginning, middle, and end, but rather as what "introduces an opening" into that teleological narration: "The anecdote produces the effect of the real, the occurrence of contingency, by establishing an event as an event within and yet without the framing context of historical successivity, i.e. it does so only insofar as its narration both comprises and refracts the narration it reports" (1989: 49). However, what is crucial for the reader in this account is the insistence on contingency, the sense if not of a break then of a swerve in the ordinary and well-understood succession of events. The historical anecdote functions less as explanatory illustration than as disturbance, that which requires explanation, contextualization, interpretation. That is why Said insists on the notion of "de-idolizing," which has always been important for him.

I

The memorable writer creates a whole world—a rounded world with an open sky, populated by a credible range of humans and animals who live by turns in towns and countryside as they seek the fullness of every desire, every actual need. That claim is hardly news to inveterate readers, though its prime implication is seldom noticed by critics—the implication that the prime desire of the narrative reader is for some rich, or occasionally bleak, form of alternate reality. Habitual readers are in search of excursions into worlds different from their own but so masterfully summoned before their eyes that disbelief is never aroused. The challenge to a writer such as Said to produce such worlds is immense but is seldom met in a single work. That is because it can be satisfied only when the writer has built an imaginary world that displays, in explicit action or implicit thought, the major emotions and core situations of our daily lives on earth, however transformed by the writer's eye.

Universally regarded as the progenitor of modern postcolonial theory and practice, the author of at least one book (*Orientalism*) that is sure to remain part of the canon of modern Third World literature so long as it requires a canon, Said's stature is now greater even than that of his fellow Palestinian, the national poet Mahmoud Darwish. Anyone who has ever read Said knows that his fictional world is a multitude of narratives, events, and texts. Let someone commit transgression, let another evince a commendable sense of honor or courage, a third will immediately tell a story about an occurrence that took place in a world regrettably passed or about to pass away. For readers who are familiar with Said's background, it takes a little while to realize that from childhood his imagination has been shaped by a profusion of narratives and images.

[T]here were two very powerful visual experiences of my youth, and I remember them very well. One of them was the wax museum, to which we would go often because I was so fascinated by the scenes from Egyptian history. You know, the opening of the Suez Canal, the dynasties. This was the monarchical period. They were lifelike figures, and I remember looking at them—I was very small, five, six, seven at the time—and always expecting them to move and say something, and, of course, they didn't. But I kept going back. A close friend of my parents, a historian, who lived in Beirut, would come to Cairo once a year or twice a year. I remember one of the great pleasures of those days was to go to the wax museum with him and have him make the speech and make the figures seem to speak.

And the second visual experience that was fascinating to me were the exhibitions in the Agriculture Museum, which must have been built by the British, a series of three huge buildings in Giza. The central building had exhibits of all the various wheat, sugarcane, and agricultural products, and instructive displays about Egyptian ecology, as well as birds and animals, and so on. But what fascinated me the most were the glass cases with exhibitions of various diseases, not lifelike images but anatomical representations of the human body. I would go back to them time after time after time to look at bilharzia, elephantiasis, and things of this sort (*Edward Said: A Critical Reader*, 1994: 289).

In its lush understanding of the ways in which the personal, the social, and the spiritual realms twine and untwine, in its couplings and parturitions, its battles and truces, Said's narrative contains a world we could never have imagined on our own. Yet, once encountered, it seems as familiar to us as the world of our own childhood.

Saul Bellow has remarked with considerable accuracy that writers are either "large-audience" or "small-audience," sometimes by intent, sometimes accidentally (neither adjective implies aesthetic superiority).[2] Foucault is clearly a large-audience critic; Deleuze is small; *Of Grammatology* is large; *Playing in the Dark* is small; *The Wretched of the Earth* is minuscule, limited almost entirely to graduate seminars. And while the charged intensity of Said's first two books, *Joseph Conrad and the Fiction of Autobiography* and *Beginnings: Intention and Method*, may have seemed ideal for some readers, one can see in retrospect that the force of the controlling passion in those early books demanded the wide hearing that they later achieved. (A third edition of *Beginnings* was published by Granta in 1997). Moreover, Said's gifts for observing and transforming a spacious visible world into its matching mirror-world of *contrapuntal* reading had grown to the point of overflow (*Culture and Imperialism* is one of the many displays of a suddenly effortless power that not only can hold us but can promise to spread both in the reader's memory and in the writer's works to come).[3]

The startling pleasure the reader feels in reading Said is best described in the following passage by Eqbal Ahmad, which shows the uniqueness of his voice and the rightness of his vision.

> It was left to the African, Caribbean, and Asian writer to imagine the alternative and start writing back. Edward Said is foremost among those who pushed this quest forward beyond nationalism and post-colonial statehood, crossing boundaries to interpret the world and the text "based on counterpoint" as he would say, "many voices producing a history" (1994: xviii).

It is in the narrative fueled by political anger and frustration that we find Said's real brilliance. This is what makes him such a penetrating writer, and not merely for his own condition as an أديب (scholar). His work asks us to examine our own condition, political and existential, particularly here in the West where we choose not to look very long or very hard because outward pressures do not compel us to do so.

No American scholar has written more fondly about the Arab quest for identity or has more sharply accused the West of imperialism and racism than Said. Yet he sees in his beloved Arab Middle East the pathos of "an aggrieved and unfulfilled nationalism, beset with conspiracies." He warns against "the provincial and self-pitying posture that argues that a largely fictional and monolithic West disdains us. . . . There are many Wests, some antagonistic, some not." He warns too against "thinkers who want to start from scratch and zealously, not to say furiously, take things back to some pure, sacred origin. This has given all sorts of pathologies time and space enough to take hold." In other words, history as a weapon is an abuse of history. The high purpose of history is not the presentation of self nor the vindication of identity but the recognition of complexity and the search for knowledge. "We need odes not to blood and mythology or uprooted, mourned or dead plants," writes Said, "but to living creatures and actual situations" (1981: 72). Yet by responding in multitudes, readers have given their resounding answer to a question his work had posed from the start: "Have I made a whole world and led you through it toward a new comprehension of our life and time, maybe all human history?" For Said's aim by now is clearly that ambitious.

In a profoundly disturbing essay, "Palestinians under Siege," Said writes movingly and passionately about the injustice visited on Palestine, America's total control over the region and the Arab impotence. For Said, if biased reporting disguises the extent of the disparity, misrepresentation has made it almost impossible for the public to trust the Western media, completely cowed by the fearsome Israeli lobby, with commentators spinning distorted reports about "Palestinian violence" while ignoring the real fact that Israel is in military occupation.

> Consider the following: citing an Anti-Defamation League survey of editorials published in the mainstream US press, *Ha'aretz* on 25 October found "a pattern of support" for Israel, with 19 newspapers expressing sympathy for Israel in 67 editorials, 17 giving "balanced analysis," and only nine "voicing criticism against Israeli leaders (particularly Ariel Sharon), whom they accused of responsibility for the conflagration." In November, FAIR (Fairness and Accuracy in Reporting) noted that of the 99 Intifada stories broadcast by the three major US newsworks between 28 September and 2 November 2000, only four made reference to the "Occupied Territories." The same report drew attention to phrases such as "Israel . . . again feeling isolated and under siege," "Israeli soldiers under daily attack," and, in a confrontation where its soldiers were forced back, "Israelis have surrendered territory to Palestinian violence" (2000: 10).

Highly partial formulations of this kind are threaded through network news commentary, obscuring the facts of occupation and military imbalance: high-tech weapons ranging from missiles made by the Boeing company of America to British-supplied Cobra and Apache attack helicopters piloted by a professional army.

Elsewhere, Said has noted that the most demoralizing aspect of the Zionist-Palestinian conflict lies in the way its narrative unfolds: there is no common ground for a solution that may lead to a genuine reconciliation. We see nothing but intransigence and intolerance on both sides. No matter what one does or says, the two experiences are totally irreconcilable: one premised on the nonexistence of the other, and an inability to forget, or to surrender what was destroyed.[4] "We were dispossessed and uprooted in 1948," he evinces.

> They think they won independence and that the means were just. We recall that the land we left and the territories we are trying to liberate from military occupation are all part of our national patrimony; they think it is theirs by Biblical fiat and diasporic affiliation. Today, by any conceivable standards, we are the victims of the violence; they think they are. . . . Even the notion of a common life shared in the same small piece of land is unthinkable. Each of us thinks of separation, perhaps even of isolating and forgetting the other (2000, 14).

In such a conjuncture, the act of writing itself becomes a burden, a fate, an act of survival, even a retribution for the need to be recognized; when what at first was the joy of creation and self-realization turns into an affliction; when, in the Arab world in particular, the vocation of writing takes its revenge on those who have tasted the thrill of representing the drama of a vast, unwieldy, and refractory region—a drama of *becoming*. Said has not escaped this penance. There are few countries in the Near East that he can visit with a sense of security, never mind feeling that he is welcome. He is the favorite target of many. In 1985 a famous Israeli dove and philosopher compared him to Enoch Powell because he criticized Israeli immigration policy for favoring easy access to Israel for Jews but not for others.[5] Because of his forthrightness, coupled with his inability to look away, he was for a while banned from entering his spiritual homeland, and his works were seized from bookstores by Arafat's administration in the summer of 1995 ("In Arafat's Palestine," 1996: 6–7).

"The exposure comes with a price," Bayoumi and Rubin perceptively observe. "Said is routinely vilified in much of the popular press. He has been dubbed a 'professor of terror,' and 'Arafat's man in New York.' His Columbia University office has been ransacked, he has received numerous death threats, and the New York City Police Department once considered his life in sufficient enough peril to install a 'panic button' in his apartment. Yet he remains wedded to his principles and unseduced by authority" (2000: xii). There is no denying the force of Bayoumi and Rubin's argument, and I am stirred and astonished at their brilliance and by the imaginative sympathy with which they rekindle the arguments and emotions about a writer such as Said. But what needs to be resolved is the role of Said the intellectual figure as a vigilant *saboteur*, one who draws the fragmentary consciousness of those he represents into coherent, intellectually articulate form, equipping them with a "world view" definitive enough to match that of their political oppressors. The organic intellectual Said is a political dissident as well as a *specialist.* Lady Wilde, once a member of the organic intelligentsia of Young Ireland, articulated the point I am trying to make with precision: "The utterances of a people, though always vehement, are often incoherent; and it is then that men of education and culture are needed to interpret and formulate the vague longings and ambitions of the passionate hearts around them."[6] And Gramsci adds: "A human mass does not 'distinguish' itself, does not become independent in its own right without, in the widest sense, organizing itself; and there is no organization without intellectuals, that is without organizers and leaders . . . the existence of a group of people 'specialized' in conceptual and philosophical elaboration of ideas" (1971: 157). This is clearly true of the Palestinian nationalist intelligentsia from Darwish to Said. They represent a classic example of Gramsci's "national-popular" intellectuals, linking ideas and the common people, popular consciousness and the political state.

Although much of what Said writes about is peculiar to the Palestinian experience, many of the problems and concerns he sees among Palestinians have parallels in other parts of the Middle East and the rest of the Arab world. Regimes throughout the region have developed expertise in—if nothing else—the repression and control of their own people. A defenseless subservience has become an official way of life in the Arab world, with no moral or political principles to rectify it. Therefore, although no other Arab people has confronted Zionism and the state of Israel as directly and continuously as have the Palestinians, dislocation, degradation, and fear about the future are not uncommon in the experience of other Arab peoples as well. One marked difference, however, is that in the absence of a "center," the Palestinian narrative has been more varied than that of any other people inhabiting a single country—say, Malawi or Ulster. The post-1972 period has witnessed the growth of religious divisions among an urbanized class as Palestinians are forcibly scattered into communities throughout the West Bank and Gaza Strip, Lebanon and Jordan, and Europe and North America.

The pace of this brutal unfolding process is shrewdly captured in the artesian well of hatred spouting in the Holy Land as I write. It is a terrible reminder that deep national grievances never drain away but instead seep underground to await their moment. The recent scenes in Palestine are reminiscent not just of the very worst days of the occupation, but of the violence that was endemic when the Israeli state was founded, "destroying and depopulating 531 Arab villages in the process. Two thirds of the population were driven out: they are the four million refugees of today" (Said, 2000: 10).[7] It may well be that the two populations (Jews and Arabs) have indeed psychologically regressed half a century or more. Then was all the time and effort devoted to making peace a gigantic fraud, a process of self-deception for Palestinians and others who tried to sustain it? Those, like Said, who opposed Oslo root and branch, now feel justified, and rightly so. Yet it is arguable that it was not the Oslo process itself that led to this disaster but Israeli insistence on completely dominating and controlling the Palestinian future. Everything had to be arranged so that the Palestinian state could offer no threat, so that the Israeli settlements could be maintained and the lion's share of Jerusalem could be retained. Thus, for example, the peace process gives no considered attention to the immense Palestinian losses of land and goods, none to the links between past dislocation and present statelessness, while as a nuclear power with a formidable military arsenal, Israel nevertheless continues to claim the status of victim and demand restitution for genocidal anti-Semitism in Europe. In this climate of violence and counterviolence, Said comments pertinently:

> My guess is that some of the new Palestinian *Intifada* is directed at Arafat, who has led his people astray with phony promises, and maintained a battery of corrupt officials holding down commercial monopolies even as they negotiate incompetently and weakly on his behalf. Some 60% of the public budget is disbursed by Arafat to bureaucracy and security, only 2% to the infrastructure. Three years ago his own accountants admitted to an annual $400m in disappeared funds. His international patrons accept this in the name of the "peace process," certainly the most hated phrase in the Palestinian lexicon today.
>
> An alternative peace plan and leadership is slowly emerging among Israeli, West Bank, Gaza and diaspora Palestinians. No return to the Oslo framework; no compromise on the original UN resolutions (242, 338, and 194) mandating the Madrid conference in 1991; removal of all settlements and military roads; evacuation of all the territories annexed or occupied in 1967; boycott of Israeli goods and services. A new sense may actually be dawning that only a mass movement against Israeli apartheid (similar to the South African variety) will work. . . . Israel's supporters would be wise to remember that the question of Palestine concerns an entire people, not an aging and discredited leader. Besides, peace in Palestine/Israel can only be made between equals once the military occupation has ended. No Palestinian, not even Arafat, can really accept anything less (Ibid., 3).

This is why Said, who speaks with authority on the subject of dispossession and dislocation, remains the most courageous of Arab scholars. Those who, like Jonathan Freedman, accuse him of being a "rejectionist" will do well to think again, because Said writes about our inability—after more than half a century—to understand the injustice inflicted on Palestine, because he writes about a nation (Israel) that claims "purity of arms," but fires missiles at civilian apartment blocks and then asserts it is "restoring order." For Said, who believes that the peace process put an end to idealism and vision and that Arafat has not negotiated but surrendered *à la* Pétain, *pragmatic* is a nauseating word. His project is therefore far more heroic—the struggle of the Palestinians is not to establish a parochial little entity whose main purpose is to give the world another airline but to transcend themselves as a people and to fight for justice in the world. Wheeling and dealing in short-term nationalism is not an item on Said's agenda.

To which one should add, by way of admiration perhaps, that ever since the النكبه (1967 Defeat) Said seems to have entered the general imagination and stayed there. "Beginning in 1968," he writes in his introduction to *The Politics of Dispossession*, "I started to think, write, and travel as someone who felt himself to be directly involved in the renaissance of Palestine life and politics" (1994: xv). Contact with Palestinians in exile was followed by trips to Amman in 1969 and 1970 and an extended stay in Beirut from 1972 through 1973. In *After the Last Sky: Palestinian Lives*, his moving portrait of a people struggling to free themselves of domination, Said writes how his year-long stay in Beirut was crucial because it allowed him to re-educate himself in Arabic and Arab cultural traditions at a "time of Palestinian renaissance in politics and culture" (1986: 172). This change in direction gives us a strong sense of his personality and of the development of his ideas and arguments. It brings out the extent to which voicing his opinion was for him from the start a vehicle for resistance. It also reveals how much Said has relied on what he took to be his exceptional talent for getting *inside* the heads of past and/or present Zionists, to see their projects of expansionism and their worlds in their own terms.

Although fated to a career as an extraterritorial scholar, Said has always nurtured his ties to Palestine, returning to his people and land as often and for as long as possible. In his public life, he has been the most visible spokesperson for the Palestinian cause in the West. This has earned him death threats and caused him to face intimidation time and again. And yet he has never ceased to speak out against the excesses and arrogance of the colonial powers. During the Gulf War, for example, he attacked the misrepresentations of the media and emphasized the xenophobia and sheer bloody-mindedness of Western policies in Iraq, ignoring the dangers of expressing such views at a time when public opinion in America would brook no opposition to Operation Desert Storm. He served his turn in the Palestine National Council and played a crucial role in its deliberations. And when he was close to the highest echelons of the PLO and had direct access and regular contacts with Yasser Arafat, he retained an independent stance on Palestinian issues and did not hesitate to turn against Arafat when he felt that the "little dictator" and his cronies had opted for an easy and unjust settlement to the Palestinian problem in the Oslo agreement.

Said also writes regularly in Arabic and has thus striven to reach a worldwide Arab-speaking audience. In sum, he has taken up in real life what he has advocated as desirable to further the counterdiscourse of resistance to coercive powers and hegemonic systems; public and private interventions on behalf of his community and the cause of a dispossessed people; a critical and independent consciousness that works for national liberation but is not blinded by nationalism; scholarly work that exposes the links between Western culture and imperialism and upholds the scholarship that transgresses boundaries and celebrates hybridity. He has done all this while holding a consistently secular, democratic, and cosmopolitan position.[8]

"A lone individual, who might have done very well for himself either by keeping silent or by playing along, and who had moreover recently been diagnosed as being gravely ill, chose instead to place the emphasis on unwelcome truth, on what people do not want to hear" (1998: v). This is how Christopher Hitchens does justice to Said, who, in a life that reflects many of the distinctive features of the twentieth century, has made an outstanding contribution to debates on literature, theory, politics, history, music, and opera. The entire corpus of his output continues to be imitated in the twenty-first century wherein the new figure of the intellectual, created in the nineteenth century, plays a large role. Another onrush of modernization, which has come in the form of globalization, has helped produce a new scapegoat, the Arab, who replaces the old (but not forgotten) figure of the Jew. Said has become a university text for the Western classroom as he is for the Third World; whether in the original, in translation, or in adaptation, his work has had a significant effect on the development of any study and/or understanding of the relations between the metropolitan West and the decolonizing periphery. In large measure, thanks to him, we have become aware that all *reading*, all memories of reading, and all criticism are processes of fragmentation, a prey to (but also the beneficiaries of) the random, the contingent, the mediated. (The film *Mansfield Park* would have been impossible for instance without Said's analysis of Jane Austen's links to Caribbean slavery).

The roles Said plays are many: an outstanding representative of the poststructuralist Left in America, an original thinker, a central figure to the Third World, and a restless pilgrim between the West and its former colonial possessions. Said, whose life is emblematic of modern existence itself, deserves both the deep admiration and the searching criticism that this book offers. His work has helped us appreciate the implicit, and challengeable, assumptions that underlie conventional apologies: that there is an "original," "whole," seamless *oeuvre* that could be read or represented in a nonselective, unexcerpted, nonviolent way. As much as Joseph Conrad, Said is also a self-created and ambiguous figure. A Palestinian Christian, he was brought up in Jerusalem and Cairo but has built a formidable career in America, where he has assumed the position of the exiled literary man *in extremis*—an Arab critic of the West and the Arab world, a reader who is at home in Western literature but makes an active case for other literatures. Said loathes insularity and parochialism and has disdained the "flat-minded" approach to reading. Over the years, he has gained many followers, some of whom he has recently chastised for carrying his moral and political critiques of Western literature to the point of caricature.

Recalling Foucault's remark that *Discipline and Punish* was what he would call "*his book*," I asked Said in the winter of 1993 when he came to McMaster University in Canada to lecture in memory of Sir Bertrand Russell on peace in the Middle East, which of his works he would call "*his book*"? He replied: "unequivocally, *Culture and Imperialism*." This is significant as that book proved to be more mature, more free of the jargon and of the sweeping statements that marred *Orientalism*. *Culture and Imperialism* avoided polemicism and set out to examine the relationship between imperialism and British, French, and American literature. Said presented the resistance to European rule by analyzing works of Third World intellectuals who articulated the struggle for liberation and the assertion of new identities. His final section looks at the American drive for empire. The narrative sets the stage for critical attention to the "territorial, spatial, and geographical foundations of life," to adapt a phrase from Gramsci, whom Said admires. Said's analysis of a wide range of literary texts, which he uses as sources for understanding the dynamics of politics and culture in their connections with the whole imperialist enterprise, can be read as a fulfillment of the historical materialist premises outlined in fragmentary form in both the *Prison Notebooks* and the *Letters from Prison*. Unlike Gramsci, however, Said does not adhere explicitly to Marxism, nor does he identify himself with any one political current or movement. Nevertheless, underlying his work is a set of theoretical principles and practical stances that is certainly in harmony with a Gramscian world view.

The great achievement of *Culture and Imperialism* is not, however, expressed in the local solutions it proposes (Said falls short in his reading of Camus, for example),[9] but in its distance from a narrow national vision of the political processes that promise social and economic transformation. His real contribution lies in occupying the uncomfortable space between imperial domination and its negation by anticolonial forces. As a sequel to *Orientalism* and part of his intention (and method) to bring to account the great European writers of the nineteenth and twentieth centuries, examining and judging them as a way of combating the notion—still alive today—that Europeans and Americans have the right to govern the inhabitants of the Third World, *Culture and Imperialism* is meant as a *supplement* that challenges yet again the Western habit of constructing an "exotic" image of the East as a means of controlling it. It also writes back to the West with a vengeance.[10]

In refusing to accept the cloak of neutrality that most critics assume, Said has shown how theory can be applied to the most volatile of struggles for cultural hegemony. Theory's task is to illuminate in the sensuous phenomena the totality of all the characteristics and interrelations that have been realized through intensive study. The literary score is never identical to the work; devotion to the text means the constant effort to grasp what it hides. In this way, Said's performance becomes both a disclosure and a heightening, in which a particular kind of inventiveness in analysis is taken up by the performer and reformulated dialectically in modern terms. His method of analysis shows an amazingly prescient and almost instinctive understanding of the idea of creativity as manifested in a kind of polyphonic writing that is at the same time both virtuosic and intellectually discursive. "Such a method," Said maintains,

> relates to a rhetorical tradition going back to Cicero. *Inventio* has the sense of rediscovering and returning to, not of inventing as it is used now, e.g., the creation of something new, like a light bulb or transistor tube. Invention in this older rhetorical meaning of the word is the finding and elaboration of arguments, which in the literary realm means the finding of a theme and elaborating it contrapuntally so that all of its possibilities are articulated, expressed and elaborated. Much used by Vico, for example, *inventio* is a key term for his *New Science*. He uses it to describe a capacity of the human mind, the *ingenium*, for being able to see human history as something made by the unfolding capacity of the working mind (2000: 289).

For Said, too, invention in this sense is a form of creative repetition and reliving. The idea of both interpretation and narrative as invention can be given a literary extension by looking at the special quality of Said's polyphonic composition. His remarkable gift for تفسير و تحليل (explication and interpretation) is evident in his ability to draw out of a theme all the possible permutations and combinations implicit in it. To put it in simple terms, this is exactly the kind of Said I choose to deal with in *Edward Said at the Limits*, a writer whose compositions provide an opportunity for the thinking, intellectual virtuoso to try to interpret, revise, and rethink in his or her own way so that each performance becomes a matter that involves rhythm, color, tone, phrasing, voice, and inflection.

II

It was in 1994 that Said was awarded the Picasso Medal (UNESCO) for his lifetime endeavor and in 1998 the Owais Prize in honor of his body of work, composed during what he called "nearly four decades of turbulent life in exile" ("Living by the Clock," 1999: 11). In the same year, Said was invited to lecture at Le Collège de France and in 1999 at the Herbert von Karajan Centrum in Vienna. In 2002, Said and Daniel Barenboim were joint winners of Spain's Prince of Asturias Concord Prize for overcoming historical antagonism, promoting dialogue for peace. Said is also the subject of many learned books, and he keeps turning up in essays in quite unusual ways as in *Take Care of Things, Edward Said* (1991); *Edward Said: A Critical Reader* (1993); *Edward Said* (1999); *Edward Said: The Paradox of Identity* (1999); *Edward Said and the Work of the Critic* (2000); *Edward Said and the Religious Effects of Culture* (2000); *Edward Said* (2000); *Revisiting Culture, Reinventing Peace: The Influence of Edward W. Said* (2000); *The Edward Said Reader* (2000); *Edward Said and the Writing of History* (2001); *I Saw Ramallah* (2001); *Edward Said: An Intellectual Biography*

(2002). Those who are interested in his work draw solace from knowing that numerous attempts are now under way to grant him the intellectual recognition he deserves.

While Said continues to have many admirers, and while he has influenced and inspired readers worldwide, he is only now winning the larger readership that his work merits. As it becomes clearer over the next few years that Said's work is central to an understanding of our world, one can be certain that a great deal of scholarly research will be devoted to his legacy. It is by such probing that we can take the measure of the man and his achievements. As we make our global leap—a leap in technology as well as in globocracy—it is worth our while, I think, to explore his way(s) of telling and/or seeing and their pertinence to the matter of personal or historical experience, asking how his life-long association with politics, literature, culture, and music establishes a unique aesthetic space essentially meant to reveal how he came to discover both his voice and the subjects of his writing. What we must not lose sight of, however, is that first and foremost Said has always been able to communicate a high degree of pleasure not only in what he does as performer and personality but also in the kind of intellectual activity his life and *oeuvre* seem endlessly capable of stimulating.

Edward Said at the Limits sets out to chart his progress from a traditional philologist in *Joseph Conrad and the Fiction of Autobiography* (1975) to a critic of colonial discourse and a preeminent intellectual who has perhaps done more than any other to explore the West's misconceptions of the Orient. Possibly the best-known Arab-American intellectual of his generation, Said covers a wide range of subjects from aesthetics to opera, political commentary to groundbreaking research in modern theory and practice. His اجتهاد (perseverance) has touched a broad public both within the United States, his adopted home, and abroad. It is a perseverance in which readers can recognize profound family affections, eloquent landscapes, and vigorous social and/or political concerns. It tells an expressive story spanning Said's boyhood to his present age of nearly seventy, a story that encompasses a childhood with a Victorian father and a literate mother and relatives; an adolescence with schoolfellows and friends; an adulthood with a marriage and children; a displacement from the Middle East to the United States; travel, illnesses, deaths, and sorrows. Within its social autobiographical circuit, Said's corpus also projects a strong literary engagement, looking steadily and with eloquent force at what it means to be an exile in our postmodern constellation where the subject is bent on experimenting with his or her life. Said has forged one imaginative cast after another in an attempt to represent the almost unrepresentable collective suffering of his people, and he has tried, equally consistently, to bring intellectual reflection to the emotional attitudes that too often yield to the ambivalence of subalternity.

The purpose of this book is to grant Said serious attention and to accord his work the critical scrutiny to which it has to be subjected before one can begin to place him in proper perspective as the individual whom many have claimed as a centrally important twentieth-century figure. It explores the *specificity* of Said's difference (with an attitude), the literary, cultural, social, and aesthetic role(s) he has played as an academic intellectual and the nature of the intelligence and the authority he has managed to deploy in the press and the media from his base in the academy in New York. Of the essays and books written about him, not one offers a satisfactory inquiry into the entire complex body of his work. *Edward Said at the Limits* is meant precisely to serve that purpose. Its aim is to trace Said's development as a writer who fits easily into the world of clubs and establishment literature, where he feels completely at home (as he does in his very establishment Cairo, London, Paris, and New York digs), while at the same time fiercely lampooning it in his works. He is a mass of contradictions: a Protestant and a skeptic; an outwardly conventional "Arab" who seems most comfortable in exile from Palestine; an anti-American with scads of American friends; a leftist battling against a fierce internal and/or external Western misconception of "lesser races"; a man of almost eighteenth-century charm, sophistication, and wit, completely urbane yet always projecting the sense that somewhere underneath all of that is a hair shirt, a need to suffer; a grown man with a schoolboy's sense of fun—in short, a very complicated person.[11]

The first chapter looks at the intellectual as "cultural amphibian" in our post-political, liberal-permissive society: how Said, like Jean-Paul Sartre and James Baldwin before him, speaks truth to power; how he refuses to give in to its lures; how he negotiates an ideology of difference. Throughout his career as a witness, he has provoked strong reaction to his corrective way of thinking about politics, drawing an urgent and absolutely necessary line between individual responsibility and the authority of consensus. Like his admired models—Theodor Adorno, Julien Benda, Régis Debray, Michel Foucault, C. L. R. James, Frantz Fanon, Malcolm X—he is not just a theorist or a critic, but a highly public intellectual as well. In his sharp disagreement with Conor Cruise O'Brien, Said held to a radical distinction between the roles of intellectual and politician.[12] Both are honorable callings: the undertaking of the elected politician, he rejoins, is to work in "half-truth"—the best that can be hoped for in a competitive political system. But to try to combine the two, power and truth, is to serve neither. In a liberal state, a division of labor between independent intellectuals and professional politicians is essential. Having become minister of culture under Charles de Gaulle, André Malraux risked ceasing to be a serious intellectual as did Václav Havel, and Bronislaw Geremek most recently.[13] But why should sterling figures such as Malraux, Havel, and Geremek not try to raise the standards of public office? Said, who is both an intellectual and a political activist, would no doubt reply that as politicians they can no longer be the thinkers they once were. Two features stand out in the debate. Said's definition of the intellectual derives from a coinage of Gramsci, "living in truth," originally of quite general application, as a term for moral integrity under totalitarian rule. There is always a somewhat sententious pathos to the phrase, since truth is not an abode but at best a target, variable, and missable, in life. But if clandestine literature has its credo, the argument above needs to be more exact. Said's conversion of the term *living in truth* into a talisman of the intellectual as an individual with a specific public role to play rests on a confusion. Integrity can be found (or lost) in any occupation. Intellectualism is something else: its arena is ideas.

Values—ethical, epistemological, aesthetic—figure in the contests of this field, but they do not define it. Intellectuals are judged not by their morals but by the quality of their ideas, which are rarely reducible to simple verdicts of truth or falsity, if only because banalities are by definition inaccurate. "I want to insist," Said writes,

> that the intellectual is an individual with a specific public role in society that cannot be reduced simply to being a faceless professional, a competent member of a class just going about her/his business. The central fact for me is, I think, that the intellectual is an individual endowed with a faculty for representing, embodying, articulating a message, a view, an attitude, philosophy or opinion to, as well as for, a public. And this role has an edge to it, and cannot be played without a sense of being someone whose place it is publicly to raise embarrassing questions, to confront orthodoxy and dogma (rather than to produce them), to be someone who cannot easily be co-opted by governments or corporations, and whose *raison d'être* is to represent all those people and issues that are routinely forgotten or swept under the rug. The intellectual does so on the basis of universal principles: that all human beings are entitled to expect decent standards of behavior concerning freedom and justice from worldly powers or nations, and that deliberate or inadvertent violations of these standards need to be testified and fought against courageously (*Representations of the Intellectual*, 1994: 11–12).

Or, to put the matter differently, as bearers or originators of ideas, intellectuals have quite naturally participated in politics—with roles both in opposition and in power—ever since they first emerged as modern phenomena, in the epoch of the American and French Revolutions. Indeed, exemplars of intellectuals who lived in moral independence, free from the blandishments of political power, tell the same story, less gloriously. "We have George Orwell. We have Raymond Aron": the one supplying officialdom with a secret list of suspect acquaintances, the other keeping silent about the Algerian War and its aftermath for years, not to displease his employers at *Le Figaro*.[14] Neither will bear scrutiny as examples of intellectuals who had no truck with power. For Said, to seek to insulate intellectuals, even such cynosures, from the grime of politics is vain (Hitchens, 2000).

Although it is his prescription for the intellectual as hustler that attracted debate, perhaps the more significant aspect of Said's dichotomy has passed virtually undiscussed. Politicians could not be expected to speak the unvarnished truth; lies are part of their professional equipment, functional necessities of a successful career in any parliamentary democracy, where competition between parties typically requires the skills of advertising, rather than the pursuit of ideas or exercise of reflection. In other words, if norms for intellectuals are set at improbably high (unworldly) levels, expectations of politicians appear to be geared to indulgently low (all too worldly) standards, as if mediocrity and chicanery were intrinsic to the trade. This is not, however, Said's view. On the contrary, while usually scathing about the collective faults of politicians, he is respectful of those intellectuals who have compassion for the downtrodden and the oppressed. Absent though these qualities may be from our "official" intellectuals, they are present in force in his life and works. He articulates this point in *Representations of the Intellectual*, which brings together most of his ideas about the qualities he deems necessary for the intellectual in opposition. Said sees opportunities for him or her to intervene in the "clamorous antagonism between the powers of the national state and the disadvantaged populations locked inside, but unrepresented or suppressed by it" (*Representations*, 1994: 38). In the Arab world, he feels intellectuals can oppose the contention of fundamentalists that there is no such a thing as a "pure" and incontrovertible series of practices that constitute a way of life. Instead, Said invokes the complex, heterogenous history of Islamic practice and urges the intellectual "to face the challenges of non-Islamic minorities, women's rights, for modernity itself, with humane attentiveness and honest reappraisals, not dogmatic or pseudo-populist chants," mindful of the once-thriving Islamic tradition of اجتهاد (perseverance) or personal interpretation. Above all, Said argues, the intellectual in the world must exercise his or her critical sense in all public questions; yea-saying must give way to "critiques of the leadership, to presenting alternatives that are often marginalized, or pushed aside as irrelevant to the main battle at hand" (ibid., 40). That is why Nawal al-Saadawi, Iqbal Ahmad, Nasr Hamid Abu Zeid, and Ali Shariati are some of his *exemplary* intellectuals; they never clouded their critical sense with dogmatism, fundamentalism, or nationalism.

For Said, the model intellectual is one who questions the status quo and sees culture as a contest between orthodoxy and uncritical beliefs as well as being an oppositional figure who revels in transgressing official lines. Another no less impressive figure of dissent is to be found in the Egyptian-American intellectual Saadedin Ibrahim, professor of sociology at the American University in Cairo and director of the Ibn Khaldun Center. Ibrahim was sent to jail in a country whose political centrality and size guaranteed much commentary and, especially in the liberal West, a great deal of negative judgment against the system that seemed to be persecuting a man for his independent, if not always widely popular, opinions. The few Arabs who defended him almost uniformly began by saying that they found his views and his methods distasteful: he was known to favor normalization with Israel; he seemed to prosper financially because of what appeared to be his entrepreneurship; and his ideas in general circulated with more success outside, rather than inside, the Arab world (Said, "The Role of Public Intellectuals" 2001). Still, the Mubarak government wanted to make it clear to everyone that an example was being made of him; he therefore suffered unjustly despite his, on the whole, rather special way of life and success (Fisk, 2001: 4). In his opposition to tyranny and his public stand for justice, Ibrahim stood as the consummate oppositional intellectual in a monotonous, uniform society. One can also argue that Said, too, is the figure of the intellectual in opposition par excellence, who in his public life as well as in his writings has demonstrated the principles that will further the counterdiscourse of resistance and the struggle for justice.

The second chapter considers two exemplary readings—namely, Brennan and Prakash, who wrote on Said with great acuity. It also deals with the influence of Michel Foucault to whom Said was close and whom he found instrumental in writing *Orientalism*. Later, Said would reject Foucault, mainly because he "seems actually to represent an irresistible colonizing movement that paradoxically fortifies the prestige of both the lonely individual scholar and the system that contains him." He turned instead to Fanon, because he moves "from confinement to liberation." Although both Foucault and Fanon were influenced by Nietzsche and Heidegger, Said feels that only "Fanon presents that formidable arsenal into anti-authoritarian service" (1993: 278). Foucault, Said regretfully concludes, "takes a curiously passive and sterile view not so much of the use of power, but of how and why power is gained, used and held on to. . . . What one misses in Foucault," he adds, "is something resembling Gramsci's analysis of hegemony, historical blocks, ensembles of relationships done from the perspective of an engaged political worker for whom the fascinated description of exercised power is never a substitute for trying to change power relationships within society" (1983: 221–22). Clearly, Said is intent on burying Foucault whose Eurocentrism, he thinks, was almost total, as if history itself took place only among a group of French and German thinkers.

The chapter also concentrates on Said's *alternative* narrative as a politics of the underground part of identity: a lesson for justice. It is meant to capture his stubborn dedication to lost causes; his fierce quality of engagement; his genuine sympathy for the underdog; his continued interest in peaceful resistance; his restless need to keep moving; the sense that beneath the sharp intelligence, the occasional outbursts of anger, the mordant wit that sometimes wounds, there is a man of unusual kindness and old-fashioned dignity. Brought to life in this chapter are his taste in reading *contrapuntally*, his tangled relationship with the Zionist lobby that wanted to have him dismissed from Columbia University after thirty-eight years of teaching following an instance during which he was photographed without his knowledge pitching a tiny pebble in playful competition with members of his family in Southern Lebanon, his passionate interest in world affairs, and his occasional need to shock.[15] The reader may find that the Said that comes across in these pages is at times infuriating, crotchety, and sad but still hugely interesting, a man of enormous talent whose best work is behind him but who still feels the need to soldier on, writing those many words a day in tiny, cramped handwriting, a program that has been the major act of self-discipline of his adult life as he notes in *Beginnings: Intention and Method*:

> Beginnings inaugurate a deliberately *other* production of meaning—a gentle (as opposed to a sacred) one. It is "other" because, in writing, this gentle production claims a status *alongside* other works: it is *another* work, rather than one in a line of descent from X or Y. Beginnings, as I treat them, intend this difference, they are its first instance: they make a way along the road (1985: 13).

The essay ends with a close analysis of the concept of 'textual territory,' or what Deleuze aptly called "plateau." In *Culture and Imperialism*, a powerful paratactic text that loses nothing of its cutting edge against the exploiters, because it dares, in closing, to dissolve the line between the Margin and the Rest, Said reverses the relation between text and event and speaks of a Third Word held forever in check by a West (the U.S. in particular) even more greedy in its quest for empire building. (The ruthless invasion of Iraq is a grim reminder of America's intervention overseas). The book, which serves as the capstone to this achievement, exhumes hitherto buried documents and revives forgotten (or abandoned) histories and literatures. In the process, it involves a sense of the dramatic and of the insurgent, making a great deal of one's rare opportunities to tell, by some other way of telling, (to adapt freely from John Berger), of subjugation and its opposite, resistance.[16]

The third chapter follows Said's rootprints during a visit to his native Palestine after many decades of exile and ponders the management of displacement. Born in 1935 in Jerusalem into a family more or less "out of place" wherever they found themselves: Palestinian, Lebanese, but American on their passports; Anglican in their worship, but otherwise unconnected to England; Francophone, Anglophone, but Arabic-speaking among themselves—custom-built Levantines, in a word. Said maintains that it is "[b]etter to wander . . . , not to own a house, and never to feel too much at home anywhere" ("Which Country?" 1999: 294). This chapter also contains a section on his invisible, "imaginary homeland," inhabited by the likes of James Joyce, Vladimir Nabokov, Faiz Ahmad Faiz, Hannah Arendt, Salman Rushdie. The powerful allure of Said's remembrances of "home" is that, in their special construction of Palestine, they make it a metaphor for belonging, a "dwelling" in the sense that Heidegger yearned for in the homeless twentieth century.

Said praises exile, and the "process of intellectual discovery which relative rootlessness gives you," without ever glibly glossing over its pain or the cushioning effect of privilege. He no longer has the need to feel "at home." Although he enjoys living in New York as a "gateway city that's so much part of the world," he observes: "I still feel New York isn't home. I don't know where home is, but it certainly isn't here" (*Out of Place*, 1999: 294). His comments on the experience of multiplicity due to displacement as both gift and loss are wonderfully delicate and subtle and can be seen as offering an original reading of Marcel Proust's suggestion that true paradises are lost paradises. "Exile is predicated on the existence of, love for, and a real bond with one's native place; the universal truth of exile is not that one has lost that love or home, but that inherent in each is an unexpected, unwelcome loss. Regard experiences then as if they were about to disappear" (Said, 1993: xv). This is a truth for those who have lost their love and home and for those who have not and for those also who have returned to them. Exile, as Said suggests, can be a happy and an unhappy condition, a chance of belonging to more than one history, one narrative, one event. Or, what Jacques Derrida has termed "*ce 'je'-là est déjà multiple*" (*Le Monolinguisme de l'autre*, 2000: 78). Exile can be suffered or sought or imaginatively borrowed. It is a way of understanding loss and a way of knowing what there is to lose, the paradise that cannot exist until it is gone (Wood, 1993).

The fourth chapter examines Said's meditation on what Pierre Nora has aptly called "*milieux*" and "*lieux de mémoire*," which exist in an odd tension with the nostalgic celebrations of place (Jerusalem, Cairo, Alexandria, and Dhour), which in turn exert too great an influence over the shape of identity. The chapter attempts to recover the author's act of reinvention, a disobedient labor of remembrance. In creating this remembrance across time, it is place again that reveals the struggle to *relocate* the past. It emerges as an increasingly complex site in the dialectic of belonging and its opposite, unbelonging. Place is, as Said insists, crucial to the construction of one's identity. But it exists not only as a determining but as a determined cultural location, as a space of memory with respect to smells, colors, and forms that alters the identity of the person inhabiting, viewing, passing through, or writing about it as Said does in *Out of Place: A Memoir*. While this remembering might be attributed to any number of factors, I have found it to become most visible when remembrance, especially nostalgic remembrance, is regularly intimate with forgetting. The essence of this idea is captured with consummate skill in the following passage by Michel de Certeau, who writes:

> [W]hen political circumstances or the economic situation forces one into
> exile, what remains the longest as a reference to the culture of origin con-

cerns food, if not for daily meals, at least for festive times—it is a way of inscribing in the withdrawal of the self a sense of belonging to a former land. It is multi-secular experience, easily verifiable, that has been reproduced by the Maghreb Jews newly arrived in France at the end of the wars of independence: "We do 'our own style' of cooking, 'our' cuisine, the way we used to do 'over there,' in order to remember Algeria and the time before we left. Food thus becomes a verifiable discourse of the past and a nostalgic narrative about the country, the region, the city, or the village where one was born." Reserved for the day of the Sabbath and for big events, whether liturgical or stemming from family history (birth, marriage, etc), traditional food with its meticulous rites of composition (a certain dish for Passover or one for circumcision) and preparation becomes the support and the "narrative of difference, inscribed in the rupture between the alimentary time of the 'self' and the alimentary time of the other" (1998: 184).

Said goes farther afield than the displaced Jews of Algeria in that he draws on Palestinian food practices and the inventory of their ingredients, their diverse preparations, rituals, spices, smells, tastes. He also represents his entire *(mi)lieux* as a haunting place, an expanse that contains both joy and sadness. In the end, he recognizes that he cannot forget this terrifying space of memory, which he identifies as a space of productive translations and mergings. He compares it to an archaeological site that must be excavated so that we may have access to shards of its memory. It is to the dolor and poignancy of that remembering that this chapter responds.

The fifth chapter considers Said as a first-rate musicologist and musician and one of the leading commentators on music—opera in particular. An accomplished pianist, Said dares to read music against the grain. He discusses Umm Kalthum, Tahia Carioca, Bach, Mozart, Wagner, Rossini, Beethoven, Toscanini, Gould, Adorno, and others. His line of argument guides the reader through the complexities of the links between music and culture and between musical works and their social/political structures. It is through composers (Bach, later Beethoven, Wagner, Schoenberg, Boulez) and/or performers (Pollini, Barenboim, Yo-Yo Ma) and their works that Said establishes the right of music to be acknowledged as a moral and critical force in the development of a postmodern society that is short of all of them. By recovering music for nonmusicologists, the chapter hopes to add to our appreciation of this already talented cultural critic whose ideas on music require no reconciliation, no harmonizing. Said's ideas are off the edge and may be "out of place, but they are always in motion, in time, in place, in the form of all kinds of strange combinations moving about, not necessarily forward, sometimes against each other, contrapuntally, yet without one central theme," except for the experience of playing, listening to and/or critiquing musical performances (Said, *Out of Place*, 1999: 295).

Said loves music. He draws on the most important musical influences on his life—namely, Ignace Tiegerman, a small Polish pianist, conservatory director, and gifted teacher resident in Cairo since the mid-1930s, and his own mother, who inspired him throughout the years to read and/or play music in solitude. "I still remember her as my point of reference," he observes with a touch of pride,

> mostly in ways that I neither fully apprehended nor concretely understood. . . . That feeling I had of both beginning and ending with my mother, of her sustaining presence and, I imagined, infinite capacity for cherishing me, softly, imperceptibly, underwrote my life for years and years. At a time when I was myself going through radical change—intellectual, emotional, political—I felt that my mother's idealized person, her voice, her enveloping maternal care and attention, were what I truly could depend on (1999: 292).

His inclination to composers of the late classical and early romantic school—Beethoven, Wagner, Strauss, (but not Mozart so much, because the levity and ease of composition that characterized Mozart's work clashed with Said's instinctive conviction that artistic creation had to be difficult, requiring an effort that could be painful and filled with self-doubt)—is strong, to say the least. This may explain his choice of sound over silence, Beethoven's need for meaning and restlessness of mind over the stillness of Conrad's Marlow.[17] "More than any other composer," he writes, "it was Beethoven who informed my musical self-education most consistently" (*Out of Place*, 1999: 100). What makes Beethoven appealing are the heights and depths of his emotion along with the tremendous range of expression and ravenous articulation of feelings.

The sixth chapter concentrates on misunderstandings and misconceptions about Said, found among those who have attempted to vilify him as well as to degrade and to devalue his capacity as a man of letters (e.g., a notorious article in *Commentary*).[18] The essay "'My Beautiful Old House'" defines Said as a "liar" and a "fraud," who "has served up—and consciously encouraged others to serve up—a wildly distorted version of the truth, made up in equal parts of outright deception and of artful obfuscations."[19] Normally, of course, "critics" who identify themselves with this kind of critique are beneath contempt. But then, of course, stung by the fact that the world of common sense ignored them, their lies grow bolder, their noise more deafening. They quickly recognize their very excess as a marketable commodity especially in the page circuits of overkill, reactionary right-wing journals such as *Commentary*. I have selected among this school just one example, that of Justus Reid Weiner, which should serve, I believe, for all others yet struggling to attain their own level of notoriety. It would be unwise to ignore the defamation squad, just so long as they are quarantined, for the health of literature, in their own compound.

The chapter is in fact a response to "'My Beautiful Old House,'" the history of which is noteworthy. After being rejected as a contribution to the pro-Israel

New Republic, which misses no occasion to target Said with "invisible bullets," Weiner began to shop around for a journal that would accept his stillborn off-spring. It should be noted that the reason for this rejection according to the editorial collective was the essay's lack of sufficient evidence and its shoddy scholarship and language, which revolted even those who dislike Said intensely.[20] Embarrassed, Weiner was encouraged to rewrite his text in more acceptable language and re-present it for publication in *Commentary*. The result was an uneven, labored rehash (bits and snippets, rearrangements of contexts and changes of departure points, factual mistakes), with its polemics intact. In desperation, the editors invited a response from readers sympathetic to Said, which they published in the following issue of *Commentary* along with Weiner's masterpiece letter, which speaks of serious mistakes that merely demonstrate his encyclopedic ignorance on the subject of Said, the exile.

My concern is to situate Weiner's attack in its sociological actuality, an actuality little known outside a closed circle, a reality made up of those calculating, trite, opportunistic claims leading the "scholar" to abandon any genuine dispassionate concern for Said's literary corpus. To this end, I want to be instructive and announce at the outset that Weiner's accusations are no better than specious. The facts are: Said not only attended St. George School in Jerusalem where he was born (André Sharon, a Jewish schoolboy friend of Said from his Cairo days, attests to that), but has also set down a painstakingly factual account of his own past and of his family background with its hopes and impediments. Above all, in writing about his مِسِيرَه (plight) in *Out of Place* and *Reflections on Exile*, Said wanted to be the sole begetter of his life story, of the secret truth about how he came to be what he is. No one else but the subject and/or biographer can tell that story, and only the storyteller should have the right to narrate it (for us), as Said does in his memoir.

The seventh chapter deals with writing, intellectual life, and the public sphere in the Third World in general and the Arab world in particular. "There is some value to remembering," Said remarks, "that the triumph of the leadership's failure on nearly every front, its mediocrity and opportunism: the chorus of hand-clapping flatterers who decorate the royal and presidential courts and the corporate boardrooms with their unctuous, unremitting approval forces the dissident intellectual to provide honest analyses and indications of what is reasonable and just. This, instead of joining the first row—limousines, private planes, the unlimited power and privilege—which allow[s] leaders with no democratic constituency to behave ruthlessly" ("Enemies of the State" 2001: 5). In such circumstances, what does the Third World dissident who has witnessed years of crushing tyranny write about? Will a vision, a new role for him or her, rise from the ranks of the oppressed to project renewed hope and determination? What is the point of writing if it does not attempt carefully and attentively to understand psyche, society, and world? How can one care for the self while setting one's creative energy free?

Said recently described meeting Jean-Paul Sartre a year before he died in 1980, during which Sartre's stance on Israel disappointed Said, yet he remained a "great intellectual hero" to Said's generation because he invested his "insight and intellectual gifts" in the service of "nearly every progressive cause of our time" ("My Encounter with Sartre" 2000: 4). Sartre's notion of the dissident as someone whose learning and achievement in one field is applied elsewhere may be said to describe Said himself. An accomplished professional in the tenured academy, Said exults in the role of humanist gadfly, challenging the experts in their carefully guarded territories. Like C. L. R. James, the founder of the counternarrative, he is an independent and controversial critic, a prolific writer with broad intellectual interests in numerous cultures. Above all, he is a romantic nationalist and political maximalist. This, to be sure, is an urgent enough claim, since nothing is more time honored than the effort to define a corrective way of thinking about the man of letters. The chapter also situates Said among other Third World intellectuals and argues that if literary work is mired in personal circumstance, it is also unavoidably connected with the exercise of power and authority.

Finally, Said's writings—books, essays, chapters in various books, and interviews from 1964 to 2002—make up the substance of the database, which should prove useful to any reader of this book. Many of Said's books have been translated into several languages: *Orientalism*, for example, into Arabic, German, Spanish, Turkish, Persian, Japanese, Catalan, Serbo-Croatian, Dutch, Polish, Portuguese, Korean and Swedish. In 1993 it became a best-seller in Sweden. There are several editions (Greek, Russian, Norwegian, and Chinese) either under way or about to appear. Other translations are rumoured, including one in Hebrew. There have been partial translations pirated in Iran and Pakistan. Many of the translations (in particular, the Japanese translation) have gone through more than one edition. In this sense, *Orientalism* is a *Merz*: the translations are the sum of the ensemble of the fragments that make the original. It is a *mise-en-abime* par excellence. The upshot is that "*Orientalism*, almost in a Borgesian way, has become several different books," which raises the difficult problem of interpretation. "I begin with the notion that interpretation is misrepresentation." Said adds

> that there is no such thing as the correct interpretation. For instance, I recently got a letter from the publisher of the Bulgarian edition of *Orientalism*, asking if I would write a preface for it. I didn't know what to say. *Orientalism* is about to appear in Hungary, in Vietnam, and in Estonia. These are all places that I've never been to and I know very little about. So you can see how uncontrolled all these interpretations can be. In that respect, I think certain kinds of distortions and deviations are inevitable (*The Edward Said Reader*, 2000: 429).

Or, to put it differently, for each new audience and/or constituency Said acquires, there must be a new interpretation, a new experience, a new resistance. His role as a dissident voice is to make us aware of the attendant condition (of time, place, previous events) in profound ways—an exercise that requires a deep understanding of the world of which we are part.

III

Certain figures are so ineffably remote that even at a human distance—say, the distance at which one shakes hands—they remain unfamiliar or at any rate less familiar and approachable than their photographs. The closer you think you are, the more distant the person becomes when you start writing about him or her, as many of us have discovered. Writers, like actors, such as John Gielgud or Laurence Olivier, are hard to pin down on paper, since they live to some degree in their own writing, which is very often designed to create a quite different person from the one they actually, in real life, appear to be. It is doubtful, for example, whether meeting C. L. R. James would have told us as much about him as would reading his work—hence the disappointment that people often feel when encountering a famous writer. Those who have met Edward Said usually remember not only his tolerance, kindness, and generosity but also his sheer dislike of American foreign policy and the Zionist lobby. In the end, he is a foreign émigré with "a mind so fine that no idea could violate it," to adapt from T.S. Eliot, and a voice always . . . bent on speaking out against injustice of any kind. This attitude is most evident in the compassion and self-reflective wisdom that has moved him in book after book, sally after sally, cause after cause.

Said is, in his own way, an unknowable man, partly, indeed mostly, by design. There is about him, to begin with, a certain reticence (which is, in essence, an eccentric's pose), apt to make him seem from time to time like a remote and slightly lonely figure. Among family and friends, however, he is cheerful, convivial, much given to jokes and laughter, and pleasant company. The following example, which I will give in full, narrates a chance encounter in 1998 with Ahmad Hamed, the family butler in Cairo in the late 1940s and 50s. It is both moving and revealing of Said's human warmth.

While in Cairo during my November 1998 trip, I went to pay a call on our old neighbors Nadia and Huda, and their mother, Mrs. Gindy, who for many years lived three floors below us, on the second floor at 1 Sharia Aziz Osman. They told me that number 20, our old apartment, was empty and up for sale, but, having thought about it for a moment after they suggested buying it back, I felt no enthusiasm for reacquiring a place we had vacated almost forty years ago. A moment later Nadia and Huda said that before we had lunch, there was somebody waiting for me in the kitchen. Would I like to see him? A small, wiry man in the dark robe and turban of a formally dressed Upper Egyptian peasant came into the room. When told by the two women that this was the Edward he had patiently been waiting to see, he drew back, shaking his head. "No, Edward was tall, and he wore glasses. This isn't Edward." I had quickly recognized Ahmad Hamed, our *suffragi* (butler) for almost three decades, an ironic, fanatically honest and loyal man whom we had all considered a member of the family. I then tried to persuade him that it was indeed me, changed by illness and age, after thirty-eight years of absence. Suddenly we fell into each other's arms, sobbing with the tears of happy reunion and a mourned, irrecoverable time. He talked about how he had carried me on his shoulders, how he had chatted in the kitchen, how the family celebrated Christmas and New Year's, and so on.

Said concludes:

And then, as the past poured out of him, an old man retired to the distant town of Edfu near Aswan, I knew again how fragile, precious, and fleeting were the history and circumstances not only gone forever, but basically unrecalled and unrecorded except as occasional reminiscence or intermittent conversation (*Out of Place*, 1999: xiii).

The passage shows the sensation of the writer's specific materials, words, and syntax that ascend irresistibly into his work. The exercise enables Said to tell us as much as he can about how life was lived in those days as he recalls it. Memory, which summons forth only old perceptions, is obviously not enough to get away from lived perceptions; neither is an involuntary memory that reminds us of the present as it fades away. Memory plays a small part in narrative. It is true that every work of art is a *monument*, but here the monument is not something commemorating a past; it is a bloc of present sensations that owe their preservation only to themselves. The monument's action is not memory but fabulation. We write not with childhood memories but through blocs of childhood that are the becoming-child of the present. Music is full of them. It is not memory that is needed but a complex material that is found not in memory but in words and sounds: "Memory, I hate you." The telling, on the other hand, is experienced through language (English) even if the persona, Said, is torn about his multiple identity.

Thus it took me about fifty years to become accustomed to, or, more exactly, to feel less uncomfortable with, "Edward," a foolishly English name yoked forcibly to the unmistakably Arabic family name Said. True, my mother told me that I had been named Edward after the Prince of Wales, who cut so fine a figure in 1935, the year of my birth, and Said was the name of various uncles and cousins. But the rationale of my name broke down both when I discovered no grandparents called Said and when I tried to connect my fancy English name with its Arabic partner. For years, and depending on the exact circumstances, I would rush past "Edward" and emphasize "Said"; at other times I would do the reverse, or connect these two to each other so quickly that neither would be clear. The one thing I could not tolerate, but very often would have to endure, was the disbelieving, and hence undermining, reaction Edward? Said? (*Out of Place*, 1999: 3).

It is this refusal to look for any panacea that makes Said's work so powerful. His extreme honesty shames those who overstep the limits of decorum and see life as having no real meaning. Said sees no force guiding our destiny, and if he did, it would be malevolent in the Schopenhauerean sense of man as ruled by his own will.

Said's development as a writer is inexorably connected to the violent struggle that has racked Palestine since its annexation by Israel in 1948. Where other books on Said have dwelt chiefly on the political aspects of his writing, *Edward Said at the Limits* looks squarely at Said as a celebrated man of letters trying to understand situations and when necessary to supply solidarity to political causes and never to be condescending or evasive. A reading of the critic's development over the past thirty-five years, its narrative tells a story of aesthetic inventiveness, generosity of spirit, and ongoing experimentation in form and expression. It also attempts a nuanced portrait of the private as well as public life of a cultural critic, whose work has given a voice to our troubled times. A representation of the critic as exiled intelligence, the book shows how, from one narrative to the next, Said has maintained vigilant attention to finding a language of his time— "symbols adequate for our predicament," as he has said (*Out of Place*, 1999: 11). The worldwide response to his words suggests that their relevance extends far beyond this moment.

I hope it is not presumptuous to claim that *Edward Said at the Limits* belongs on the same shelf as the work of Michael Sprinker, Arif Dirlik, Timothy Brennan, Gyan Prakash, Bart-Moore Gilbert, Jonathan Arac, Terry Cochran, Abdirahman Hussein, Bill Ashcroft, Pal Ahluwalia, Lindsay Waters, Jim Merod, Kojin Karatani, and Rashid Khalidi, to mention a few of the better-known names. Unacknowledged similarities between these scholars' work and mine are proof that we are in the same camp. But I concentrate more on Said's life and work, an account of his intellectual, cultural, and aesthetic development. My use of his occasional essays and interviews and at times my avoidance of his better-known, magisterial works such as *Orientalism* and *Culture and Imperialism* is deliberate. Such a strategy is in keeping with my book's focus on the semiautobiographical and private aspects of his emotional and exilic life rather than on his more public, academic career. George Steiner has an eloquent comment that describes the motives behind this approach: "I speak about 'My Homeland, the Text'—this is where my passport is, and this is where Edward Said's passport is also. I had occasion to meet him recently, and was terribly moved when he said that he was now even more of an exile than myself, since he was now exiled from the Arab side as well as the Jewish side" (quoted in Vulliamy, 1999: 14). Surrounded by calumnies, Said may be the last Renaissance man of his time: a learned, charming, passionate advocate of justice for all and the most respected Arab intellectual even among Israelis. Yet there is no sentimentality in Said, this U.S. academic, who has had to defend himself against hate letters and death threats. He often portrays the selfish, the self-important, and the tyrannical and contrasts them to the weak and unfortunate, who have to live through their wits, but who know the value of sharing. Said can change people and never for the worse.

It is precisely this side of Said that *Edward Said at the Limits* intends to capture. It is an attempt at drawing a positive portrait of the world's most instantly recognizable and tenacious exponent of the Palestinian predicament and a living example of the maxim coined by Theodor Adorno: "For a man who no longer has a homeland, writing becomes a place to live" (1997: 135). Said has also become a figure of tragic dignity—fighting cancer, for which he undergoes regular treatment.

> During my last treatment—a twelve-week ordeal—I was most upset by the drugs I was given to ward off fever and shaking chills, and manifestly upset by the induced somnolence, the sense of being helpless, the helplessness that many years ago I had conceded as that of a child to my mother and, differently, to my father. I fought the medical soporifics bitterly, as if my identity depended on that resistance even to my doctor's advice (*Out of Place*, 1999: 295).

Said relishes the thought that he was treated "in a Long Island Jewish hospital, by an Indian doctor, where all the nurses were Irish." But holding up a three-page list of harrowing side-effects, he says: "I had 'em all. I was sick as a dog. I couldn't talk. I had temperatures of 104, 105, and shaky chills."[21] The course—"a treatment not a cure"—worked miraculously. His blood cell count returned to normal and the illness has since been in remission. But now, after nearly a decade, it shows signs of an insidious return. Said blanches at the prospect of further treatment. He makes it clear that the only consolation, short-lived but real, has to be in shared suffering: there is always someone worse off to comfort; misery is bearable if shared.

Said has lived as intensely as his work is intense. For him, artists create because they cannot stop themselves: it is an obligation and a compulsion. He has also worked in a space that he constantly fills with new ways of seeing things, of imaginatively stating what is obvious to him—but not to others until they encounter the result, nearly always with shock. Art for Said is not necessarily a means of expression but rather an admission and exploration of impotence, the inability of the artist to really change anything for the better. It is a Beckett-ian conception of art at best, even if at times he is quick to claim faithfully that art (music in particular) enhances life, comforts and awakens aesthetic apprecia-tion and pleasure.[22]

In the course of *Edward Said at the Limits*, I show just how the Said *story* articulates the ambiguity and the anguish—of being an intended victim—result-ing from competing demands to act in solidarity with the voiceless and/or dis-possessed and, at the same time, to create in solitude. There is also, it must be said, very little self-congratulation in Said or mere autobiography of the sort found in so much contemporary identity politics and a good deal of marketable academic writing. In Said, what is written about has a greater claim to his atten-tion than the manner of saying it, which is not a meditated response to the many identities that have been imposed on Said by others: too steeped in the challenge posed by the written and/or spoken word, too entranced by the charisma of liber-ated Palestine, too generous even to those who do not take to him easily. To be sure, few writers can be expected to encompass their own historicality the way Said does or to account finally for the kinds of culpability that might nowadays come with being a cultural critic, whether they are longstanding or presentist. This latter claim is symptomatic of cultural criticism, and surely part of its appeal is that we are allowed to be relatively free from anxiety about what we are doing when we speak or write on a subject such as the Said phenomenon.

Although I criticize Said, I hope my position is less reductionist, more nuanced with a certain complicity. As Gayatri Chakravorty Spivak perceptively put it: "I always attempt to look around the corner, to see ourselves as others would see us. Not, however, in the interest of work stoppage, but so that work is less clannish" (1999: xii–xiii). The Said who had written *Orientalism*, who is more at home in New York than he is in the desolate streets of Ramallah, and whose biting wit, immense sense of fun, and huge social energy which makes him that rarest of beings, a literary genius and *un homme du monde*—both a deeply serious man and the life of the resistance movement for a free and just Palestine—has become with illness a withdrawn figure, more deeply embedded in his habits, trying to keep his interest in life going by writing, frequent travel, and an involvement in music. It is tempting to add that, unsurprisingly, and in spite of his leukemia, which is taking a dreadful toll, Said still clings to the idea of *performance* as he makes clear in the following passage, which I quote at length.

> The greatest performances provide the invaluable restatements and forceful interpretations of the essay, a literary form overshadowed by the grander structures of epic and tragedy. The essay, like the recital, is occasional, recreative, and personal. And essayists, like pianists, concern themselves with givens: those works of art always worth another critical and reflective reading. Above all, neither pianist nor essayist can offer final readings,

however definitive their performances may be. The fundamental sportiness of both genres is what keeps them honest, as well as vital. But there is an irreducible romance to the pianist's art. It is suggested by the underlying melancholy in Schumann's *Humoresque* and Chopin's Ballade in F Minor; by the lingering authority of legendary pianists—Busoni, Eugen d'Albert, Franz Liszt, Leopold Godowsky—with magical names; by the sonorous power that can encompass the solidest Beethoven and the most slender Fauré; by the curious, almost audible mixture of dedication and money circulating through the recital's atmosphere (*Reflections on Exile*, 2000: 229).

A figure of dissent such as Said, who combines the style of the elegant essayist, accomplished pianist, and virtuoso performer, is becoming increasingly rare. There are few like that today, unless one considers the extraordinary Adorno who was throughout his life intent on incorporating every nuance, every twist, every harmony and rhythm. Said may have been fortunate in having Adorno as a precursor, and we are even more fortunate in having Said's own contribution to the world of *belles lettres* and musicology. He has made it with clarity and force.

In the end, it is not difficult to see why Said's work caught the world's attention, for it is steeped in dexterity, memory, and pitch. And if it appears to be involved in an existential مسيبة (plight), his tone has reached well beyond discomfort, impatience, or anger. He is in a hurry to overcome his illness but not before capturing the reader with the spectacle of his pyre. Said is not one to hedge his bets, and if his political dissent were not enough to trouble the world, the aesthetic content of his traveling narrative has raised eyebrows. For nearly all his texts seek to be inventive and subversive, though they are also often playful. Reading against the grain is, for him, the trigger, the touchstone, the lamp by which he sees and makes us see. In the process, his narrative flies in the face both of his native tradition and of the near monolithic tradition of symbolist literature in the twentieth-first century West, in which a candle is not just a candle or an apple just an apple, but rather a symbol of something else, something more significant. For Said, a candle is a candle, an apple is an apple, not to be observed and meditated on, Pongelike, for the essence of its candleness or appleness, but made use of as a prop or projectile, customarily in a text of guerilla assault, in what he ironically termed "permission to narrate" (1984). As to whether he has succeeded in presenting us with a salutary *alternative* to the usual sense of standing up for a worthy cause, or of reading and/or interpreting, only the reader (of Said and/or this book) can decide.

CHAPTER ONE

THE INTELLECTUAL WITH A MANDATE

> If Said's lifelong intellectual work has been a labor of love, excruciation, delicacy, deliberation, ascesis, pride, worry, commitment, and hope—and I think it exhibits such pressures all across its verbal landscape—it also has achieved tangible results in the world that few university intellectuals aspire to or accomplish.
>
> —Jim Merod, "*Sublime Lyrical Abstractions of Said*," 119.

The story of Edward Said's life reads like a fairy tale. The son of a prosperous Palestinian American businessman who headed an office equipment company and published books, by the time he graduated from Princeton, Said had already studied at Harvard and passed all examinations as a senior with the highest average in Mount Hermon School (Massachusetts) (Nairn, 1997: 169). A scion of the Arab *haute bourgeoisie*, Said is a tireless dissident figure but a learned entrepreneur, a sort of *homme de lettres* destined to become lord mayor of literary New York through the judicious deployment of quick-witted prose and decisive critical dicta. From *Beginnings: Intention and Method* (1975) to *Out of Place: A Memoir* (1999), he has disguised himself in what Virginia Woolf once termed a "four-piece suit," while arming himself with a remarkable talent and a mordant irony; accurate insights and revealing detail are his speciality. At the same time, to many, he is a profoundly hybrid writer who is never shy about his aspirations. Indeed, if Said resembles anyone, in his clean, combative prose and unfeigned heart, it is Raymond Williams.[1] And whereas Williams had a sense of social and emotional nuance, Said starts where society ends. Williams, in fact, was so close to his world that he was content merely to record it; Said, by contrast, continues to peel the surface or الظاهر (the outside) of any given text—what might be considered its once-and-for-all sense uttered for and during a specific occasion as opposed to its hidden meanings الباطن (the inside) (1983: 35). In the process, he does not try to satisfy our expectations; he simply takes us into the heart of the matter and—caught in his strange exile (he seems to live in constant displacement)—makes fewer compromises than any cultural critic around, except perhaps for Terry Eagleton.[2] If we consider the sheer weight of his ambitions, it seems that Tolstoy might almost have been running interference for him in *War and Peace*: "One step beyond the boundary line, which resembles the line dividing the living from the dead, lies uncertainty, suffering and death. . . . You fear and yet long to cross that line" (1950: 97). In this, he may show an inkling that Tolstoy's idea of causation is not the same as his. That Said's stance is so much more is a judgment that should be defended against simpler, more obviously appealing defenses of the oppressed, against sympathetic denials of the claim that they have often contributed to their own oppression.

In the days when Said was growing up, European genteel tradition held sway over all Cairo. Much of the city was captive to Western high art: an annual opera and/or ballet season; recitals; concerts by the Berlin and Vienna Philharmonics; regular visits of La Comédie Française and the Old Vic; all the latest American, French, and British films; cultural programs sponsored by the British Council and its continental equivalents (*Reflections on Exile*, 2000). Culturally speaking, then, he was the unfortunate, unwilling heir of European imperialism: the building of the empire had been sanitized for him by his schoolbooks, extracurricular activities, teachers, and language. Said wrote:

> The moment one became a student at VC one was given the school handbook, a series of regulations governing every aspect of school life—the kind of uniform we were to wear, what equipment was needed for sports, the dates of school holidays, bus schedules and so on. But the school's first rule, emblazoned on the opening page of the handbook, read: "English is the language of the school; students caught speaking any other language will be punished" (*Out of Place*, 1998: 3).

The factual fog was pretty thick. He knew that Napoleon Bonaparte led the first French expedition in 1798. This was enough to whet the French appetite for empire: Paris dispatched the army to Egypt, and an expedition turned into conquest. Later, in secondary schools run by the British, even the most liberal history masters underplayed the gruesome details of that and other conquests that followed as they evolved into full-scale colonization. Textbooks were apologetic and pious: on the one hand, the White European and American men behaved atrociously; on the other hand, roads and hospitals provided the natives with. . . . Well, even Marx saw some positive aspects to colonialism. If it could be "constructive" as well as "destructive" in India, why not in Egypt or anywhere else in the colonies?

In this context of Western high art on the one hand and imperialism on the other, it is quite extraordinary to come upon someone like Said, who, even though schooled in the foreign masters' classroom, remains fearlessly Arab at heart, right down to his scorn for the West and of some of its values. Of his relationship with Cairo's Victoria College, the supposed "Eton of the Middle East," Said merely notes that "it was a really mongrel atmosphere. . . . All the masters were English, and they treated us with contempt. . . . It was the last days of the British presence in Egypt and they were the last remnants of this rather scraggly empire."[3] Against this turbulent background, the British were free to apply their authority as they wished. Said confides to Eleanor Wachtel that "prefects in those schools were allowed the privileges of masters. There was a lot of beating, caning. I got caned the first day I was in school for talking in prayers or something equally horrendous" (Wachtel, 1977: 77). In the end, he found little difficulties in meeting the West on its own turf. Today he stands as one of a select band of superstar academic literary critics in the United States (The others are Stephen Greenblatt, Stanley Fish, Henry Louis Gates, Cornel West, Gayatri Chakravorty Spivak).

Said is the hero of quite another fairy tale—the kind of quest-romance in which the only son in a family of seven sets out as a traveler, rooted nowhere and moving endlessly on in order to disprove the illusion of home, seeking a prize he can barely define. Home for him is a metaphysical place—a meditation on space, a sermon on our estrangement. "Which country?" he once asked, and replied: "I've never felt that I belonged exclusively to one country, nor have I been able to identify 'patriotically' with any. . . . Thinking affectionately about home is all I'll go along with."[4] Yet the fact remains that in recent years his traveling has assumed more the aspect of a quest, and while remaining an observer, he is an increasingly shrewd witness. As he grows older, his pointed comments on literature, politics, music, theory, and culture acquire a greater sense of moral urgency, and his sympathy for embattled peoples including his own has turned into a voluble indignation on their behalf. In recent years, the focus of this anger has been aimed at the Palestine Liberation Organization (PLO) leadership. Said has always opposed injustice (the result, perhaps, of being the single skeptic in a Middle Eastern household of dictators and potentates, kings and sultans); and he does not conceal his frustration and disappointment.

> I regard Yasser Arafat as a Pétain figure who has taken advantage of his people's exhaustion and kept himself in power by conceding virtually everything significant about our political and human rights. What he did after he came to Gaza in July 1994 has worsened the effects of the twenty-nine-year occupation (which still continues), and over months I have reminded my readers, of whom he seems to have been one, that cronyism,

a huge security apparatus, kowtowing to the Israelis, buying people off and torturing, imprisoning or killing dissidents at will, are not the ways to establish a new polity for our people.

Arafat's view at present is, I believe, to rule without question and to try either to efface, humiliate or circumvent any challenge to his tattered authority ("Bookless in Gaza," 1996: 6–7).

What is fundamentally most damning, however, is that which is still probably the most intriguing dimension of the man: an outsider in the West, he is perhaps more aware of the boundaries and dynamics of actual communities, and he is no friend of the established order. Rejecting the division between "liberal" and "mechanic"—that is, between intellectual and practical knowledge—he refuses to set limits on the complex perceptual abilities of the prejudiced and unfair. The ordinary actions of life, Said once observed, contains "an infinitude of experiences that is impossible to retrace" (*After the Last Sky*, 1986: 111). His community is both organic and functional, not an abstraction held in the minds of an exclusive but passive body of people. For Edward Said is undeniably resolute, despite his famous gift for polemicism, his high spirits, his sense of the tragic. His oppositional criticism—ultimately his anticriticism—has sought in all seriousness to engage the chaos and pathos of the present without a single concession to the knowing smile of the postmodernism drawing room or the disaffected twitch of a Lyotardian eyebrow. True, it has been a postmodernism that knows how it would be received and dismissed, yet, even so, it reiterates a commitment to what D. H. Lawrence once called the "naivety that breaks the back of sophistication":

> Tell me, is the gentian savage, at the top of its
> coarse stem?
> Oh what in you can answer to this blueness?[5]

Perhaps most naive of all, postmodernism has produced a bloom of pallid performances and risks "at the top of its"—seemingly—"coarse stem," a postmodernism, more specifically, that confronts, transcribes, and seeks (with varying degrees of failure) to analyze "the sexual anxieties, cultural tensions, gender and racial conflicts most contemporaries burlesque, repress or suppress" (Žižek, 1999). Even as Said preens himself in "well-tailored suits," he is driven literally as well as allegorically around the world by the energy of his need to unveil the secrets buried in the West's cultural unconscious; the author of *Orientalism* (1979), *The World, the Text, and the Critic* (1983), *Culture and Imperialism* (1994), *Power, Politics and Culture* (2001) has often been an all too embarrassingly sincere archaeologist of what we now consider to be politically incorrect emotions. Even now, in a decade wearily marked by ironic post- (or even post-post-) modernism and righteous censoriousness, Said's impulsive postcolonialism might be seen as a critique that dare not speak its name.

The questions that most preoccupy those who take him seriously can therefore be put as follows: What made Said, the Palestinian American intellectual possible? What are the enabling conditions for this consummate intellectual, active on many fronts, as *agent provocateur*? These are typically anti-Saidian questions. Said, who created the intellectual, not as a Bohemian or a café philosopher, but as a figure representing many different kinds of concerns and constituencies, continues to assert his capacity for exhaustive knowledge of his own truth, as a citizen and as an intellectual. In doing so, he rules out, as reductive, any attempt to circumscribe the uncircumscribable, to classify the unclassifiable. More important, one wants to know: What if Said were only the ideologist of the intellectuals, confident that they would recognize themselves in the image he reflects back to them, that of the dissident intellectual, and at the same time someone of sufficient weight, practical exposure, and political acumen to be qualified to travel the world as an emissary for justice? What if Said, who reigns supreme, were dominated by what he dominates? What if the free intellectual were actually the most determinate of intellectuals, unaware as he is that the will to power attaching to his social position lies precisely in the illusion of the absence of will to power? Why does Said think serious damage has been done to the communication of the truth and to the expression of opinion? But before I deal with these issues, I want to discuss how Said has compiled a hermeneutics that attends to the stark violence and Manichean oppositions of imperialism (American in particular) by teasing out for examination the hesitancies and uncertainties that colonialism has produced.

I

It is too often the case that the dark smoulderings of the most impassioned artist are rewarded primarily by the pale fire of scholarship, and the treatment of Said by a number of essayists proves him no exception to this rule. While the subject matter of Michael Sprinker's meticulously researched *Edward Said: A Critical Reader* (1992) is enthralling, the interview with Said appended to the book tells us about the complexity of the man. The interviewers have scrupulously accumulated some fascinating details that illuminate for us the writer's life from his early days in Jerusalem and Cairo to his writing practices, from his infamous quarrels with his critics to the symptoms signaling the onset of his struggle with leukemia, but never manage to shape what seems like clinical data into a lively portrait. To be sure, the raw material the essayists have to work with is often so electrifyingly interesting that this book is a good read, at times even compelling. It ends with this insight: "I still feel," Said tells Jennifer Wicke and Michael Sprinker, "even with regard to the Palestinian movement, and certainly in the context in America in which I find myself—I still feel, finally, somehow *misplaced*." But this is not all. The interview as a whole has a narrative coherence that others lack. Said confides by way of explanation: "I don't feel that I really have found or can ever find a solid, unchanging mode in which to work. For me it's too shifting. That's a tremendous limitation, but one I'll have to live with" (Sprinker, 1992: 264). The upshot is that Edward Said plays a uniquely influential role in American intellectual life. Undaunted by normal constraints of time and energy, he simultaneously pursues three consuming careers, as a literary critic, political gadfly, and accomplished musician. Remarkably, he also teaches English, writes monumental books of cultural history (*Orientalism* was nominated for the National Book Critics Circle Award), and helps to salvage the rich but dying تراث (heritage) of an oppressed homeland—namely, Palestine, where two-thirds of the population live below the poverty level of two dollars a day.[6] In none of these realms does he make any concessions to political correctness or literary fashion.

In a period that sees a steady decline of the Left and an almost unanimous acceptance of market capitalism, Said persists in calling himself a man of the Left, not because he expects "Leftocracy," in Wole Soyinka's celebrated formula, to revive and succeed but because he wants to reiterate the urgent moral need for a fairer, more fraternal, more egalitarian society. He expounds:

> The net effect of "doing" Marxist criticism or writing at the present time is of course to declare political preference, but it is also to put oneself outside a great deal of things going on in the world, so to speak, and in other kinds of criticism.
>
> Perhaps a simple way of expressing all this is to say that I have been more influenced by Marxists than by Marxism or any other "ism." If the arguments going on within twentieth-century Marxism have had any meaning, it is this: as much as any discourse, Marxism is in need of systematic decoding, demystifying, rigorous clarification.[7]

This is the point to note, because it is based on the same logic that Said himself employs by writing and being politically active. Over the years, he has attracted a youthful following drawn to his tough-minded idealism, itself traceable to such incorruptible forebears as C. L. R. James and Raymond Williams, leftist intellectuals of a more innocent and hopeful age.

Quite apart from his remarkable range of political essays, letters, travel writings, and literary/cultural analyses, most by now the fodder for endless deconstruction, Said is a figure of extraordinary fascination, even for those sitting on the opposite side of the fence from him. "He has become," Bruce Robbins observes, "a public figure in a sense that would apply to very few literary critics, however respected" (1994: 2). Paradoxically, then, to contemplate works by the author of that famous critical maxim "*contrapuntal* reading" is more often than not to marvel at the "life-rapidity"—another Lawrentian phrase—of the vehement "distinguished appearance . . . [of the] . . . well-tailored" artist himself. Indeed, one might say of Said, as Keats said of Shakespeare, that he "leads a life of Allegory.

His works are the comment on it." (1992: 251). Except that Said transmutes Shakespeare, by contrast, into an avatar of his own antipathies toward the "State."

To the critic, Said's almost allegorical charisma is of special interest because both his popular and critical reputation have fluctuated dramatically since 1967, when the entire map of the Arab world changed. For the first time, Israel, which had been largely confined to the small boundaries of the 1948 state, had over-flowed into Jordan, taking the West Bank, Gaza, the Sinai desert and the Golan Heights. It came to be known as the النكبة (1967 Defeat) for it marked both a crushing defeat for the Arabs and a huge disaster in their Realpolitik. For Said, however, 1967 had one salutary effect: it heralded new beginnings.

> I remained in New York and continued teaching, but beginning in 1968 I started to think, write, and travel as someone who felt himself to be directly involved in the renaissance of Palestinian life and politics. Those of us who were concerned sought each other out across the oceans and despite years of silence. On the cultural and intellectual level, the appearance of an organized Palestinian movement of resistance against the Israeli occupa-tion began as a critique of traditional Arab nationalism whose ruins were strewn about the battlefields of 1969. Not only did Palestinian men and women take up arms on their own behalf for the first time, but they were part of a national experience that claimed primacy in modern Arab discourse by virtue of openness, honesty, realism. We were the first Arabs who at the grass-roots level—and not because a colonel or king commanded us—started a movement to repossess a land and a history that had been wrested from us (*The Politics of Dispossession*, 1994: xv).

The whole idea of being an Arab and then beginning to discover for himself what that meant, as a Palestinian, all really came to the fore in 1968. "That was," Said continues, "the great explosion and it had a tremendous effect on my psy-chological and even intellectual processes because I discovered then that I had to rethink my life and my identity, even though it had been so sheltered and built up in this completely artificial way. I had to rethink it from the start and that was a process that really is continuing. It hasn't ended for me" (Ibid., 43). In some respects, indeed, the heart of the matter is that an author has a self out of which he or she writes, a private self, a self that no one sees and that he or she keeps jealously to himself or herself unless he or she chooses to write about it. It is a self, by definition, very different from his public face, just as my face, lost in this sentence, is different from the one I put on as soon as someone enters the room. In 1968 Said recovered his other self. Yet even those authors who like him know how to reclaim their identity become its victims. Too often, reality cannot keep pace with the imagination. To be sure, the embattled author of *Orientalism* is not alone among writers in having been labeled a Palestinian polemicist, an anti-Western and anti-Semite, an élitist (and no doubt in a range of other formulations it would be better not to recall), a paradigmatic bad boy. And that Said has been at one time or another, in one way or another, most of these things, besides being in some sense "*un*-English," "*un*-American," "*un*-Western," is not irrelevant to any discussion of his long-term ascendency as a man of letters. As the appearance of a number of essays and books attests, he continues to enthral readers and writers alike. Perhaps it is precisely his intellectual as well as his political incorrectness that intrigues us; perhaps—as scholars of his life along with his art—we are bemused, even bewitched, by the ways he *does not* fit into our current systems of interpretation. He remains "out of place," as he aptly put it in his memoir *(Out of Place*, 1999: iv).

Said is the critic of the present in what has become a kind of cultural afterward, an era of postmodernity. He is the godfather of the discipline called "postcolonial theory and practice" in an age when late capitalism is pervaded with spectacular crises and catastrophes: world wars and revolutions, including counterrevolutions (the failure of the socialist projects in the former Soviet Union and China, among others), tribal warfare, the rise of nationalism. Said is also the priest of spontaneity in an era of irony and parody; the acolyte of intuition, of blood wisdom, of Sufi-like "lapsings" from consciousness—the impassioned enemy of wholesale knowledge—in a thought-tormented, digitized, hypertextual, capital-driven *début du siècle*. And most important of all, he is the paradigm of authorial energy, the proponent of authorial *authority*, in an age when that mystical being once known as the "author" has sickened, failed, faded, been pronounced dead, and been buried with considerable deconstructive fanfare. It is what Žižek, writing about the postmodern superego, calls the "world turned upside down" (1999: 3). As we all know, postmodernism is a series of arguments, not a way of life or a recipe for action.

It could be said that I have summarized here the negative and unpleasant features of postmodernism, without mentioning the well-nigh irrepressible virtues of survival and resistance that characterize the various communities of authors. This is because I want to emphasize that the absence of a historical consciousness or collective memory is no longer tenable. What is decisive is the way historical and humanistic discourses are fashioned—either to reproduce hegemonic racial politics or to subvert it. Since I have already dealt with *Edward Said: A Critical Reader*, I now want to reflect on the scholarly mapping of the Said *story*. To do so is definitely to avoid postmodernist indeterminacy and aporia and to emphasize instead the historical determinations of the subaltern's passage from an intransitive to a transitive consciousness on the way to full awareness. The pivotal meditation between one stage and another is praxis, the authentic union of action and reflection.

In his insightful *Letters to Cristina*, Paulo Freire reads the world as an integration of multiple objects and events in social existence. This dialectical epistemology synthesizes object and subject, means (technique) and ends (value): "In the education and training of a plumber, I cannot separate," he observes, "except for didactic purposes, the technical knowledge one needs to be part of the polis, the political knowledge that raises issues of power and clarifies the contradictory relationships among social classes in the city" (1996: 115). Ethics, pedagogy, and politics are joined in the practice of socially accountable freedom. In this, Freire echoes Gramsci's elevation of human work as the fundamental educational principle that can equip every citizen with the skills of governing:

> The discovery that the relations between the social and natural orders are mediated by work, by man's theoretical and practical activity, creates the first elements of an intuition of the world free from all magic and superstition. It provides a basis for the subsequent development of an historical, dialectical conception of the world, which understands movement and change, which appreciates the sum of effort and sacrifice which the present has cost the past and which the future is costing the present, and which conceives the contemporary world as a synthesis of the past, of all past generations, which projects itself into the future (Gramsci, 1978: 52).

Instead of exacerbating the fragmented, schizophrenic condition of the subaltern, Said, like his *maître à penser*, Gramsci, employs a radical critique of the ideological mechanisms (schooling being one of the most crucial) that reduce the hybrid, exotic "Other" to repetition or silence. In this enterprise, he charts the limits of the possible on the uncertainty of what is practical, committed to challenging a Euro-American hegemony "forged in the crucible of patriarchy and white supremacy" (McLaren, 1995: 34). Thinking about the West and its intellectual rapacity Said finds it impossible to return to clarifying first principles.

II

It is doubly fitting that some of the fairest words on Said are those by Michael Sprinker himself, praising Said's intellectual legacy: "No single volume can do full justice to the rich and voluminous treasure of Edward Said's intellectual endeavor. [*Edward Said: A Critical Reader*] is an interim balance sheet drawn up to assess a career whose future may hold even more brilliant accomplishments than those to date" (1992: 4). In another no less handsome tribute, introducing Edward Said in 1986 at the Institute of Contemporary Art in London, Salman Rushdie announced that Said "reads the world as closely as he reads books" (1991: 166). Orphaned by Israel's annexation of what was Palestine, Said is the minority Christian whose fate has become nomadic because it cannot accommodate itself to the exclusionism that the Christians share with other minorities in the Cairo-Jerusalem-Beirut triangle. That process of instability is summarized in the following excerpt:

I didn't spend a huge amount of time in Palestine or, for that matter, anywhere really, we were always on the move. We would spend part of the year
in Egypt, part of the year in Palestine and another part of the year in
Lebanon where we had a summer house. In addition to the fact that my
father had American citizenship, and I was by inheritance therefore American and Palestinian at the same time, I was living in Egypt and I wasn't
Egyptian. I, too, was this strange composite (1977: 75).

In 1948, Said's family moved to Cairo, "a city of innumerable adjustments and
accommodations made over time; despite an equal number of provocations and
challenges that might have pulled it apart" ("Cairo and Alexandria," 1990: 3).
But Cairo proved to be *not* the place; in fact, the Saids never belonged there in
the true sense of the word, even though they were, and remained, close to the city.
In 1963, the Saids relocated to Lebanon where they lived the rest of their lives.

Said has undoubtedly dominated his generation of cultural critics and has no
successor. Those victims of their adolescent dreams who are now canvassing to
succeed him as the preeminent Third World intellectual, fail to see that the historical and structural conditions that made a Said possible are now disappearing.
The pressures of globalism and professionalism, governmental bureaucracy and
the glittering prizes of the media, the cultural goods market and consumerism
are combining to reduce the autonomy of the figure of the intellectual. They are
threatening what is perhaps the rarest and most precious element in the Saidian
model and the element most truly antithetical to traditional attitudes of mind—
namely, the refusal of worldly power and privilege and the affirmation of the
strictly intellectual daring of saying *no* to all its airs and graces, charms, and
witcheries. Said sums up the argument thus:

> Several times . . . I have been asked by the media to be a paid consultant.
> This I have refused to do, simply because it meant being confined to one
> television station or journal, and confined also to the going political lan-
> guage and conceptual framework of that outlet. Similarly I have never
> had any interest in paid consultancies to or for the government, where you
> would have no idea of what use your ideas might later be put to. Sec-
> ondly, delivering knowledge directly for a fee is very different if, on the
> one hand, a university asks you to give a public lecture or if, on the other,
> you are asked to speak only to a small and closed circle of officials. That
> seems very obvious to me, so I have always welcomed university lectures
> and always turned down the others. And, thirdly, to get more political,
> whenever I have been asked for help by a Palestinian group, or by a South
> African university to visit and to speak against apartheid and for aca-
> demic freedom, I have routinely accepted (*Representation of the Intellec-
> tual*, 1994: 87).

In this sense, Said echoes Sartre, who went so far as to refuse *La Légion d'honneur* given to him by the then President de Gaulle, the Nobel Prize or to enter *Le Collège de France* or any other *grande école*, maintaining that a writer should not be turned into a monument.[8]

Or, to put it another way, it is the intellectual's intention and method as scholar and critic to resist the lures of power that other intellectuals have consistently side-stepped or simply embraced with open arms. Said makes the point with force.

> Politics is everywhere; there can be no escape into the realms of pure art and thought or, for that matter, into the realm of disinterested objectivity or transcendental theory. Intellectuals are *of* their time, herded along by the mass politics of representations embodied by the information or media industry, capable of resisting those only by disputing the images, official narratives, justifications of power circulated by an increasingly powerful media—and not only media but whole trends of thought that maintain the status quo, keep things within an acceptable and sanctioned perspective on actuality—by providing what Mills calls unmaskings or alternative versions in which to the best of one's ability the intellectual tries to tell the truth (Ibid., 21–22).

While Said reads writers in order to voyage toward community, his critics harp on about a writer who is difficult to reconcile with what is known of his life. He is complex. Anyone who tries to describe him finds themself stringing together a number of seemingly incompatible labels and phrases. He is a Protestant, Palestinian Arab whose father served in the American army during World War I. An academic who has lived in the United States for the past fifty years, Said is also a political activist, yet he mistrusts nationalism, criticizes Arab dictators, and defends Salman Rushdie. A professor of English and comparative literature, a talented pianist and music critic for *The Nation*, Said teaches us to look below the surface so that we may discover the folly of a Bernard Lewis or a Daniel Pipes, who have traditionally tended to imagine the rest of the world as a checkerboard sprawl of underworld sinners. He can, in fact, be seen to be spinning out a vision, a vision of how literature can change lives, and vice versa. Thus the dialectic goes on, as Said seeks out a course between traditional conventions and cutting-edge clichés. On the one hand, he is an omnivorous intellectual whose writing spins effortlessly from *Aida* to poststructuralism to Tayib Salih (as a postmodern Conrad); on the other hand, he is a man of the people seeking a literature in which abstract ideas are as beside the point as they are in lovers' talk or prayer. Sprinker sums up the point with epigrammatic forcefulness: "We are far from having seen the end of the 'Said phenomenon'" (1992: 4). This is his verdict in *Edward Said: A Critical Reader*. It is not for me to agree or disagree with the finding; I must take the verdict for what it is, that is, an indisputable *social fact*, and to endeavor to account for it, to make it intelligible.

III

Much the best way to convey appreciation of Said's rousing and combative critique is to be aware of his darting, brash, and unsparing wit. It shines brilliantly from the pages of his books, in learned journals and periodicals like *The Guardian, The New York Times, London Review of Books, Harper's Magazine, Le Monde Diplomatique,* الحياة, week after week. But few people have the courage to accumulate enemies the way Said has. Starting with the political leaders, whom he twists remorselessly, he has been on the wrong side of the entire U.S. establishment, of *The New Republic*, of *Commentary*, of the Ajamis, the Lewises, the Pipes, the Makias, the Safires, the Huntingtons, the Lipmans, of nearly every journalist of note, Left, Right, and Center, of the *Lehrer Report*, of most academics, and of all TV networks, of the rich and the famous, of the State Department, the military, of Israel, the Jewish League, of Kissinger, Mubarak, Arafat, and many other Arab and non-Arab leaders. Instinctive suspicion of authority has been his dominant trait as a writer, and books such as *Orientalism, Culture and Imperialism*, and *Out of Place* miss no opportunity for settling accounts with the powerful, great and small: Miss Clark, a teacher who sided against him at the Cairo School for American Children; Michael Chalhoub, head boy at Victoria College, a dashing and utterly sadistic older student who grew up to be famous as Omar Sharif; Harry Truman, who had the effrontery to favor the establishment of a Jewish homeland; Jim Murray, a counselor at Camp Maranacook in Maine, who upbraided young Edward for sneaking an extra hot dog at a cookout; Eleanor Roosevelt, who excluded the Palestinian refugees from her wide embrace; Martin Luther King Jr., for expressing too great a satisfaction at the outcome of the Six-Day War; Sartre for siding with the Jewish State and ignoring the Palestinian quest; I. A. Richards, who had the bad grace to lose his marbles before Said arrived at Harvard for graduate school—all these get their due.

There is, however, another side to the Edward persona, and since it is an essential characteristic of what distinguishes Said in the United States from so many intellectuals, columnists, pundits, and media personalities, it should be spelled out: he is a committed intellectual, not simply a man of letters or a witty writer. It is difficult to imagine an intellectual today sounding an equally electrifying call to justice. In the Anglo-American world, the very word *intellectual* arouses among the general public at best a faint sense of irony. Outrage has otherwise retreated to the academy, whose alchemy produces professors with transgressive discourses. I think there is something to be learned from Said's stance on restoring honor to the profession of the engaged intellectual as represented by Zola, Russell, and Sartre before him and by the late Pierre Bourdieu. Said has the intellectual's restlessness, an eager erudition, a delightfully fresh and innovative style, a learned knowledge of history, and a commitment to social change. The single thing one cannot get from him, however, is a blueprint or a master theory. The subordination he critiques is not an object, or in the strict Marxist sense an ideology, but a collection of modes of deceit and cruelty presided over by experts in manipulation. Against these people, Said's method is the essay, the short article, the biting phrase: hit-and-run tactics rather than a war of position.

Said, has, it should be added, his softer side, which emerges occasionally in commendatory remarks about family, friends, figures of stoic calm and moral truthfulness (Eqbal Ahmad), poetry (Mahmoud Darwish), politics (Noam Chomsky), music (Glenn Gould), literature (Raymond Williams), friendship (Pierre Bourdieu and Ibrahim Abu Lughod). Paying homage to Bourdieu, he writes:

> I was always struck by his unassuming manner, and the cordiality of his regard for a potential friend and ally. Always serious, he was never solemn, and quite charmingly he rarely resisted the chance to say something witty or deflating. He never posed or took on airs. Directness and sincerity were the hallmarks of his intellectual presence, even though he could be scathingly ironic in his attacks on imposture and fraud (2002: 1).

There is nothing pro forma about the feelings of affection, admiration, and kindness Said has for his friends. As the passage above shows, he gratefully acknowledges individual talent and generosity of heart when he sees them in a person as humane, warm, and inspiring as Bourdieu.

Edward Said may be the last of a special breed of wide-ranging literary-political-aesthetic New York intellectuals, who are grouped around *Raritan*, one of America's most prestigious and influential voices of high culture. Its special tenor is provided by a small group of regular contributors. They include avant-garde intellectuals such as Marina Warner, Jane Miller, David Bromwich, Michael Fried, Stanley Cavell, Frank Kermode, George Kateb. However, no one has been more relentless in his analyses of topics varying from literature to history, politics to music, and none more celebrated of the group than Said, an early comer and postmodern savage. In a sense, he epitomizes the portrait Irving Howe drew of the New York intellectual in the 1950s. The New York intellectual "[has] a fondness for ideological speculation; [he] write[s] literary criticism with a strong social emphasis; [he] revel[s] in polemic; [he] strive[s] self-consciously to be 'brilliant'" (1979: 211). Said lives up to the expectations of the New York intellectual that Howe describes. In a way, these expectations could be seen in the two conflicting impulses of his own literary career. As I indicated in my introduction there are at least three Saids. For my purpose here, I want to consider two of the three. One is a literary scholar and critic, cultivated, knowledgeable, urbane, and, despite his interest in the literature of the Third World, a traditionalist in taste.

The other is a spokesman for the Palestinian cause and an adherent of the PLO for about two decades, polemical and sometimes, as happens in political disputes, strident. There is not necessarily a contradiction here, it ought to be possible for one person to pursue two or even three or more callings. But in the bruising course of actuality, it is often hard to avoid confusion and the blurrings of roles (Howe, 1994).

On the one hand Said strives for a tone of high moral seriousness and an ele-vated language that earlier legitimized his ambition to be accepted as a signifi-cant critic. On the other hand, he wants to avoid academic stuffiness and to preserve elements of the blunt style of polemic, sardonic, fast-paced, at times merciless criticism—that he has mastered in the sectarian alcoves of New York City. I cite two examples to elucidate. The first from *Beginnings: Intention and Method*, an essay that delves heavily into poststructuralism language games, pas-tiche, fragmentation, textuality, and difference; the second aimed at Russell Jacoby for his narrow and chauvinistic view of American culture that does not take account of the interesting role played by ethnic, nonnative intellectuals who have lived and worked in the country.

> For in isolating *beginnings* as a subject of study my whole attempt was pre-cisely to set a beginning off as *rational* and *enabling*, and far from being principally interested in logical failures and, by extension, ahistorical absurdities, I was trying to describe the immense effort that goes into his-torical retrospection as it set out to describe things from the beginning, *in history* (1985: xi–xii).

> Today, according to Jacoby, whose book [*The Last Intellectuals*] has been much celebrated by the Right (even though he is himself a sort of Left intellectual), intellectuals are highly specialized, jargon-mongering acade-micians, who eschew public debate for the cushy world of highly-paid and insulated academic discourse. The curious thing about Jacoby's book is that he not only excludes non-native-born Americans from his assessment (as if you can't be born in Ireland or Pakistan and still become an American intellectual), but also non-literary critics, and people who, while part of the Academy, still function outside it as public figures—Chomsky, for instance, or Christopher Lasch . . ., José Marti, C. L. R. James, Alexander Cock-burn and others ("Alexander the Brilliant," 1988: 17).

This association of apparent opposites—poised and meditative on the one hand and polemical and combative on the other—intrigues Said. The two Saids alter-nate and sometimes fuse throughout his *oeuvre*, even if at times they seem a little uncomfortable with one another. This is pertinent, but it would be more so had Said acknowledged that the values he espouses are essentially those of the Enlight-enment, a historical contribution of the very West that he seeks to censure.

Notwithstanding his reflexivity, I find Said's limitations much less severe than the anarchy of his *bien pensant* Noam Chomsky with whom he claims affinity. Said's espousal of the idea of "liberation" following independence in those territories that were once under Western tutelage seems attractive in this time of soured expectations. It presents a nourishing and serviceable example, despite his apparent conversion to a merely discursive articulation of Marxist theory, because he deals with institutions and concrete practices of domination, subordination, and racism within specific historical formations and plateaus. His sense of place, or misplacement and repertoires of cultural positions where identities are enunciated, is rooted in the reality of the Palestinian diaspora. Precisely because Said emphasizes the structural determinants of historical *un*-belonging, he cannot be associated with a ludic, performative post-age stamp obsessed with dismantling the intelligibility of modernity. Speaking of exile, he announces that it "is predicated on the existence of, love for, and a real bond with one's native place; the universal truth of exile is not that one has lost that love or home, but that inherent in each is an unexpected, unwelcome loss" (*Culture and Imperialism*, 1994: 336), a reality one cannot disagree with no matter how hard one tries.

Said's Marxism (or its articulatory version), his implicit compromise with the Left, refutes the metaphysics of liminality, the sterile formalism and aestheticism that can only reinforce the status quo in a saturated center. What is at stake in his counternarrative is the future—justice for the oppressed, equality for the deprived, liberation for the subaltern whether they be "Black in South Africa . . . , Asian in Europe . . . , Chicano in San Ysidro . . . , Palestinian in Israel . . . , Mayan Indian in the streets of San Cristobal . . . , artist without gallery or portfolio . . . , pacifist in Bosnia," or "housewife alone on Saturday night in any neighborhood in any city" (San Juan Jr., 1998: 19). For Said, out of necessities and limited possibilities, oppressed people the world over must endeavor to shape a future freed from the nightmare of colonial history. Such endeavors are central, not marginal, to any attempt to renew humanist learning. He calls for a rupture of the "centrality of imperial culture," which has insinuated itself into the postcolonial claim to speak for the subordinate, who is languishing to find the stable and set his or her energy free. This is how he outlines his view:

A huge and remarkable adjustment in perspective and understanding is required to take account of the contribution to modernism of decolonization, resistance culture, and the literature of opposition to imperialism. Although the adjustment has still not fully taken place, there are good reasons for thinking that it has started. Many defenses of the West today are in fact defensive, as if to acknowledge that the old imperial ideas have been seriously challenged by the works, traditions, and cultures to which poets, scholars, political leaders from Africa, Asia, and the Caribbean have contributed so largely. Moreover, what Foucault has called subjugated knowledges have erupted across the field once controlled, so to speak, by the Judeo-Christian tradition; and those of us who live in the West have been deeply affected by the remarkable outpouring of first-rate literature and scholarship emanating from the post-colonial world, a locale no longer "one of the dark places of the earth" in Conrad's famous description, but once again the site of vigorous cultural effort (*Culture and Imperialism*, 1994: 243).

Said knows that we are at the crossroads of tradition and modernity in the far-flung margins of the empire. Obviously this trope of a journey insinuates a meta-narrative biased against fixity and stasis, a "totalising" figure suspect to postcolonial theorists. But what is the alternative? For Said, mapping the contours of the recent past may help prefigure the shape of what is to come in the controversy over the internationalization of late capitalism, which, with the help of neoclassical economic theory, seeks to break down nation-state barriers (or what remains of them) to the encroachment of capital—in fact, the most widespread myth is that market forces released by uninhibited trade have made nation/nationality obsolete, residual, or inutile. One may ask: Are Japan, Germany, and the United States no longer enjoying nation-state sovereignties?

At this point, I can think of no better illustration of what Eqbal Ahmad says about the necessarily ethicopolitical function of the Third World intellectual than Said's life-long engagement in the cultural and political transformation of the Third World consciousness, which presents itself as a complex of narratives juxtaposing movements of empowerment, resistance, rupture, and convergence. "Dedication to universalism in politics, culture, and aesthetics serves for Said as a counterpoint to sectarian options. It is a question, he once asked, of whether you enter history with open arms or a tight fist. The roots of his universalist beliefs lie, I think, in Arab civilization; in his upbringing in Jerusalem and Cairo; in the Western tradition of Enlightenment; and in the Palestinian experience" (Eqbal Ahmad, 1994: 19). There is no doubt that the Saidian mode of critical inquiry challenges the official paradigm that divides "us" from "them." Its criterion of social practice unsettles the colonialist stereotype, made not to pause, always impelled to *further* action. In the process, Said deconstructs concepts such as "Arabs are rapacious" or "Blacks are lazy," which have been constructed by the West over the past five hundred years. He has performed this operation of untwining by faithfully and generously acknowledging his predecessors, from C. L. R. James to Frantz Fanon, from Baldwin to Malcolm X. To be genuinely marginal, out of place, his own person and alive, is what drives Said forward.

IV

Contemporary emphasis on the participation of literature in the social matrix balks at acknowledging how important the essay remains as "a comparatively short, investigative, radically skeptical form—the principal way in which to write criticism" (1983: 26). For Said, the essay is the antigenre that mimes the performance of the mind in solitary speech. In its normative form it deliberately strips away most social specification (age, location, sex, class, even race). In the meantime, the soul of the writer that is Said becomes a subject woven—more or less obviously—throughout the fabric of the subject of the essay itself. And if the essay can be encouraged to shed its penal associations, it can, paradoxically, suggest exactly the opposite: an enterprise taken up at leisure, a moment of peace, of the absence of strife, words set down by the writer in the solitude of his or her room, far from (or maybe because of) the pressure of the outside world, with its demands, its hatreds, and its rages. No one brings this aspect of the essay so to mind as does Said, who writes from the seclusion of his apartment in New York's Upper West Side. But he writes in a troublesome period, a period torn apart by religious wars in the Middle East, distorted by fanaticism, the lineaments of which he dislikes intensely, and by nationalism, which can quite easily degenerate into chauvinism and xenophobia.

Said also writes in an America that is more and more fragmented. For despite the media's unending stream of patriotic talk about "America," one occasionally has a sense of the country's immensity, its unmanageable extremes. "There is," Said intones, ". . . a stratum of monotonous sameness in the country, of regimented, mass-produced uniformity, of a pervasive unchanging pallidness . . . , which communicates a tremendous loneliness and anonymity to be found in American life" ("Miami Twice," 1987: 3). For Said, the nightmare of America today is the substitution of public relations for civil rights. It is the trend of not discussing serious issues and artificially imposing happy endings. If you have a problem, it must be *your* problem—everything is reduced to personal psychology. If you have a "dysfunctional psychology," you are not allowed to suggest that it may, in fact, be a systemic problem. "Above all, ['we'] cannot go on pretending that 'we' live in a world of our own," he writes; "certainly, as Americans, our government is deployed literally all over the globe—militarily, politically, economically. So why do we suppose what we say and do is neutral, when in fact it is full of consequences for the rest of the human race?" (Said, 2002: 74). Said wants us to move beyond personal psychology in order to address and look for the expression of *different* kinds of human experience and to equip society so that it can begin to discuss the structures that determine the lives within it. He seems to be hinting that in the United States, with their highly sophisticated techniques, they intentionally keep people structurally illiterate—they are not interested in educating them about the structural forces that are shaping their lives. And that, of course, is the glory of capitalism—as long as you keep celebrating individuals, you can say that some people are lucky, and some people are not—whereas the fact that 12 percent of Americans own 78 percent of the wealth of the country may be a structural question, not just an accident (Hitchens, 1999).

Since the 1960s, we have seen the failure of the melting pot ideology, which suggested that different historical, cultural, and socioeconomic backgrounds could be subordinated to the larger ideology or social vision which is "America." This concept obviously did not work, paradoxically because the United States encourages a politics of contestation. (The recent Inspector Clouseaulike performance of Bush and his psychopathic team over President Chavez of Venezuela shows, perhaps paradoxically, that the confidence of the establishment in such methods has not yet been regained.) We saw this during the civil rights struggles, where the prevailing notion of the state was contested by a group that had been oppressed, marginalized, and largely forgotten. This was an attack on the concept that Black history could be disregarded and suppressed. The melting pot metaphor suggested that Blacks could put their history behind them and become part of the larger society. Of course, that did not happen. Blacks had to fight to change laws, social practices, patterns of perception, and ideological structures. Their struggle encouraged other marginalized voices—women, ethnic minorities, and subaltern groups, gays and lesbians—who are now fighting for their rights.

Said praises this America, the one he calls the "New America," which is a great deal less provincial and regimented than the "Old" one. Much of this is, of course, due to the emergence of a mass counterculture of the Left in the sixties, a counterculture whose affiliation with non-American currents of thought, "lifestyles of radical will," in Susan Sontag's phrase, has continued well beyond that now excoriated decade. When he describes this "New America" and its people, Said is really dealing with subjects such as ethnicity, education, the university, the curriculum, and more challenging ideas such as inequality, injustice, and racism, most of which seem to defy ordinary conceptions of what a nation is or what time and space are. Take the "empire within the empire" in Miami, for example, where there is a Cuban Miami, an Anglo Miami—a considerably less interesting place—and finally the "volcano that is Black Miami," seething with unsettled social and economic problems. In the end, Miami often turns out to be what David Rieff calls an "anthology"—a word suggesting coexistence but not unity (1987: 147).

Said gives examples of ghetto gatherings in cities such as New York, Chicago, and Miami and discusses how each minority plays its part. Miami stands at the pinnacle of massive migratory movements. It is, in Said's words, "a mirror city to Havana." In bringing their "old" lives with them, the new instant exiles also dislocate the previous inhabitants. Thus the more Miami comes to house Chicanos—London (Indians) or Paris (Arabs)—the more the process dislodges and discomforts the (White) American, English, and French population respectively. Hanif Kureishi, another no less dislocated writer, put it in mordant terms: "If someone says, 'You fuck off home, you Paki,' you have to laugh about it. The levels of irony—you would get lost in them" (Quoted in Wilson, 1994: 102). This stringent reality of the uprooted experiences is captured in an even more profound way by Homi Bhabha in the following passage.

I have lived that moment of the scattering of the people that in other times and other places, in nations of others, becomes a time of gathering on the edge of "foreign" cultures; gathering at the frontiers; gatherings in the ghettos or cafés of city centres; gathering in the half-life, half-light of foreign tongues, or in the uncanny fluency of another's language; gathering the signs of approval and acceptance, degrees, discourses, disciplines; gathering the memories of underdevelopment, of other worlds lived retrospectively; gathering the past in a ritual of revival; gathering the present. Also the gathering of the people in the diaspora: indentured, migrant, interned; the gathering of incriminatory statistics, educational performance, legal statutes, immigration status—the genealogy of that lonely figure that John Berger named the seventh man (1990: 291).

For Said, there is now a precarious balance in American society between the so-called melting pot, with all its ideological, economic, and social appurtenances, and the disruptive flooding into the pot of new arrivals from abroad, whose purpose is to find prosperity and to form a functioning unit within America.

In New York City, for example, most of the fruit and vegetable shops are Korean, the news-stands Indian or Pakistani, hot-dog carts and small luncheonettes Greek, street pedlars Senegalese; a large population of Dominicans, Haitians, Ecuadorans and Jamaicans have made inroads into proletarian domains once populated by Blacks and Puerto Ricans, just as Japanese, Chinese and Vietnamese children play the role once reserved for bright, upwardly-mobile and professionally-inclined Eastern European Jews ("Miami Twice," 1987: 3).

There is, of course, value in pointing this reality out. New ages need new displacements, and writing on immigration, itself often, but not always, a function of America's overseas policy intervention, is as urgent a task as critiquing the culture that receives the immigrants. This would not be the only time that Said influences the way we look at Western culture: the invention of typography alone, as Neil Postman writes in *Amusing Ourselves to Death*, "created prose but made poetry into an exotic and élitist form of expression" (1985: 76–77). Karl Marx, no less a cultural figure, once pointed out that the *Iliad* would not have been composed the way it was after the invention of the printing press (1975: 23).

Said, however, is one who accepts the responsibilities of being a critic of cultures. "Were I to use one word consistently along with *criticism*," he writes,

[i]t would be *oppositional*. If criticism is reducible neither to a doctrine nor to a political position on a particular question, and if it is to be in the world and self-aware simultaneously, then its identity is its difference from other cultural activities and from systems of thought or of method. In its suspicion of

totalising concepts, in its discontent with reified objects, in its impatience with guilds, special interests, imperialized fiefdoms, and orthodox habits of mind, criticism is most itself and, if the paradox can be tolerated, most like itself at the moment it starts turning into organized dogma (1983: 29).

Yet none of this is enough to suggest that Said wants to do away with America. As Joseph Maguire has noted, "cultures and peoples are responsive and active in the interpretation of the global flow of people, ideas, images and technologies" (1993: 310–11). Said, the last person anyone can call an apologist for cultural imperialism, makes the same point (and with a sly allusion to Marx and Engels): the "history of all cultures is the history of cultural borrowings" (1993: 217). His point is—as even White Americans have learned to say—"right on," even if the United States is now carrying the narrative of imperialism in many different forms into the twenty-first century. Think of the brutal invasion of Iraq and the idea will be clear enough.

A good illustration of the way globalism, having transformed the structure of social dominance, operates is provided by the following instances. Take the public image of Bill Gates, who has been described not only as "a genius just like Edison or Ford" but also as a "terrorist that doesn't use bullets,"[9] and the matter will be quite obvious.

Gates is not a father-master, nor even a corporate Big Brother running a rigid bureaucratic empire, surrounded on an inaccessible top floor by a host of secretaries and assistants. He is instead a kind of Small Brother, his very ordinariness an indication of monstrousness so uncanny that it can no longer assume its usual public form. In photos and drawings he looks like anyone else, but his devious smile points to an underlying evil that is beyond representation. It is also a crucial aspect of Gates as icon that he is seen as the hacker who made it (the term "hacker" has, of course, subversive/marginal/anti-establishment connotations; it suggests someone who sets out to disturb the smooth functioning of large bureaucratic corporations). At the level of fantasy, Gates is a small-time, subversive hooligan who has taken over and dressed himself up as the respectable chairman. In Bill Gates, Small Brother, the average ugly guy coincides with and contains the figure of evil genius who aims for total control of our lives. In early James Bond movies, the evil genius was an eccentric figure, dressed extravagantly, or alternatively, in the grey uniform of the Maoist commissar (Žižek, 1999: 5).

In the case of Gates, this ridiculous charade is no longer needed—the genius turns out to be the boy next door.

Another aspect of this process of U.S. domination lies in the charged status of the narrative that followed the events of September 11 and that reminded us once again of the imperialist legacy in its interdependent aspects on both sides of the great cultural divide between the West and its nemesis—the Arab and/or Islamic world. Domination of Arabs by Whites simply did not end, and it will not go away with decolonization or independence. It persists with extraordinary tenacity, and with much generosity it animates all those institutions designed for naked aggression, violence, and forgetfulness. The Arab world, however, is busy waiting for the bits and pieces to fall from the West's groaning board. That what we now call "9/11" should become an event in the culture wars is a telling sign of the times. The context and framework of discussion and writing about Islam since the terrorist attack on New York and Washington is too inflamed, too urgent, too locked up in questions of defense, war, invasion (to say nothing of such equally fractious issues as American values, freedom, and righteousness, and the crusade on behalf of the "West"), for anything that could be considered an adequate understanding of Islam's huge complexity and its basic resistance to reductive formulae. Suddenly a rush of what appeared to be respectably expert material spouted up in the periodical press, most of it purporting to link "Islam" as a whole to such absurdly reductive passions as rage, antimodernism, anti-Americanism, antirationalism, violence, and terror. Quite unsurprisingly, when Samuel Huntington's vastly overrated article on the clash of civilizations appeared in 1993, the core of its belligerent (and dishearteningly ignorant) thesis was the battle between the "West" and "Islam" (which he sagely warned would become even more dangerous when it was allied with Confucianism. For the reader, it is in their very boldness, and their transcendence of trendy, op-ed thinking—their ability to show how political issues are personal and too difficult for dogma—that writers such as Said dazzle and liberate. Heir to a multitude of cultures, he refuses to be hemmed in by any one of them. One has only to look at the table of contents of some of his books to get a sense of the hybridity, spaciousness, and calm intake of breath that originates from the idea that the proper domain of the inquiring mind is, precisely, everything human, from cultures to manners, from eating habits to neighborhoods, from domination to resistance, from peace to pleasure. Here are some of his chapter titles: "Overlapping Territories, Intertwined Histories," "Freedom from Domination in the Future," "Beginning with a Text," "Memory and Forgetfulness," "Emergence," "Past and Future," "Performance as an Extreme Occasion," "Melody, Solitude, and Affirmation," "Intellectual Exile: Expatriates and Marginals," "Speaking Truth to Power," "The Palestinian Experience," "An Ideology of Difference," "Return to Palestine-Israel," "'Our' Lebanon." In "Winners and Losers," he leads us, as if we were entering a particularly musical conservatory, to the inevitable conclusion that discrimination against his people is a tyranny that is vicious and death dealing, causing, in one case, the killing of his kinsman the poet, Kamal Nasser, connected, in another, to the Zionism that turned out all of the lights of Palestine.

What Said has accomplished is not just the invention of a counterdiscourse, a dialogic performance, but a way of reading and/or interpreting. It is a reaffirmation of the theme of resistance against domination, the pervasive fragmentation and reification of life in late capitalism. In the wake of the demise of Soviet "state socialism" and globalized capitalism's commodification of the whole planet, his reconstruction of the subaltern dialectic valorizes three motifs in his analysis of culture and society: contradiction as the basis of historical motion, the agency of the subaltern as creative and transformative force; and the practice of freedom as the embodiment of universal justice. Of these three, the agency of the subaltern and how it cannot negotiate a change for the better because on the one hand the West strives to keep the Third World in check and on the other the native bourgeoisie continues to hijack the revolution and its aims becomes pivotal to Said's cultural politics of difference. It informs the narrative of complex dynamic forces in all his writings. It also enables Said to avoid the perils of empirical determinism when he reflects on the intellectual as the record of the mores and experience of his or her society as well as the voice of vision in his or her own time. Transported to the metropolis, the immigrant (in this case Said himself) discovers the Third World subtext in the palimpsest of world resistance while he—even he, the critic of imperialism—labors under Western skies as Mudimbe and Jewsiewicki would have it (1994: 34).

V

Said's uniqueness consists in the fact that, by a *coup de force* that presupposes a deal of rupture (of the letter), he brought together a set of hitherto separate ways of performing the role of the intellectual. One would need to go deep into social history to show that all the components of the social figure of the intellectual in opposition were in existence well before the concentration of capital operation whereby Said combines them in his own person. What can be briefly outlined is the logic of the process of accumulation (of capital) by which he makes himself the point of convergence of being a cultural critic invented and established in the course of the world's intellectual history. By crossing the invisible frontier that divides professors, critics, and political activists from writers—petty bourgeois "scholarship boys" from bourgeois "inheritors," science from genius, the profoundly conceptual from the subtly literary—Said has created a new figure: the writer-critic and aesthete-performer. His critical revolution against systems of knowledge is inseparable from a "revolution" in cultural writing. The application of Michel Foucault's theory of power/knowledge, which led him to abandon the closed world of the self-knowing consciousness for the open world of an oppositional consciousness, as represented by his other *maître à penser*, Frantz Fanon whose exploding toward things, toward the world, toward *other* people, entails the eruption into cultural discourse of a whole universe of new objects that had previously been excluded from the rather stuffy atmosphere of "academic" knowledge and left to writers. It also requires a new, openly literary, way of talking about these objects. Cultural critique takes to the streets, and the critic, like the literary man, brash, encyclopedic, mercurial, writes about urgent matters like dispossession, injustice, exile, the curriculum, and so on, disseminated to the reading public in learned journals such as *Critical Inquiry, Raritan, Diacritics, New Left Review*, and others. Moreover, by his choice of publishing houses like Pantheon, Vintage, and Verso, Said abolished the frontier between literary criticism and cultural criticism, between the literary effects encouraged by structuralist analysis and the *contrapuntal* analyses of such classical novels as *Mansfield Park, Heart of Darkness*, or *Kim*.[10]

Criticism, traditionally assigned to academics, is the indispensable accompaniment of this cultural revolution. Said exemplifies the fulfilment and fantasy of this revolution most vividly, bringing together in his work the professional roles of formalist critic, professional historian, committed polemicist for the Palestinian movement, and autobiographical recorder of the experience of exile. He combines the traditional role of man of letters with the new figure of the academic, radical, chic superstar, writing in a style that owes as much to Roland Barthes and Adorno as it does to Lionel Trilling and Antonio Gramsci. In his apprentice years, analyzing the authors he admired, some of whom stand outside the academic pantheon, was no doubt a (somewhat academic) way of identifying and assimilating the techniques that define the avant-garde writer, one who then integrates the innovations of Fanon, C. L. R. James, and Raymond Williams among others into the literary essay that is immediately, and rightly, recognized as inimitably his. But neither in literary criticism nor in cultural criticism, where he remains closer to Fanon than to Foucault, does Said achieve the formal revolution he demands in *contrapuntal* reading, which is not itself narrative, but rather, as suggested by its musical meaning, a technique of theme and variations. Yet counterpoint must be established by different narratives, and if the narrative as a whole (a book, for example) does not make a narrative, it makes a pattern of narrative challenged by the resistances of counternarrative. Critical discourse, being by nature normative, or rather performative, serves to disguise what is in fact a bid to establish a monopoly of literary legitimacy as the analytical conclusions of the critic, by imposing a new definition of the writer-critic "to narrate, or to block other narratives from forming and emerging" (Said, 1993: xiii). So when Said writes, à propos of Swift, for example, that a narrative technique implies a *strategy* (*of reading*), he establishes himself, rather than Paul de Man, Stanley Fish, Harold Bloom and others, as holding the monopoly of essayistic legitimacy, since he is its sole accredited strategist.

The distance from established positions and their occupants is what defines the free intellectual and his transfiguration in the *Pour-soi, En-soi*, to borrow Jean-Paul Sartre's serviceable formula. In fact, it could be shown that the fundamental categories of Said's ontology, the *For-itself* and the *In-itself*, are a sublimated form of the relationship between the "intellectual," who is constantly subject to the demands of his or her society, and the withdrawn philosopher-king who cares about nothing except his ivory tower. In other words, the intellectual, an unjustified "bastard," a lack of "being," a thin film of nothingness, freedom, and consciousness, moves between the materialistic, *les salauds* of La Nausée, and the people, who have in common the fact that they are fully what they are, and nothing more; while the intellectual in opposition is distant from himself or herself, separated from his or her being, and from all those who are only what they are, by the infinitesimal yet unfillable gap that is the source of both his wretchedness and his greatness. The typically Pascalian reversal wretchedness, and therefore greatness lies at the heart of the ideological transfiguration that, from Sartre to Said, has enabled the intellectual to make it a spiritual point of honor to transmute his exclusion from worldly power and privilege into something freely chosen. The "desire to be God," the imaginary reunion of the In-itself and the For-itself, which Sartre saw as part of the universal human condition, may ultimately be only a transfiguration form of the intellectual dream that Flaubert expressed more naively: "to live like a bourgeois and think like a demi-god" (i.e., like an intellectual) (in Bouillet, 1996: 151).

Thus, even in his life, divided between his desk and the public arena, between artistic manifestos and political stands, Said expresses and realizes the cultural unconscious of the Third World intellectual. But he pushes to its final limit the illusion of self-transparency, of adequate self-consciousness, which gives rise to the desperate refusal of all determination and the pathetic struggle to rescue the intellectual from every kind of reduction to the general, to type or class. Said takes the example of James Baldwin and Malcolm X, who define the kind of work that has most influenced his own representations of the intellectual's consciousness. He comments with precision:

> It is a spirit in opposition, rather than in accommodation, that grips me because the romance, the interest, the challenge of intellectual life is to be found in dissent against the status quo at a time when the struggle on behalf of underrepresented and disadvantaged groups seems so unfairly weighted against them. My background in Palestinian politics has further intensified this sense. Both in the West and the Arab world the fissure separating haves and have-nots deepens every day, and among intellectuals in power it brings out smug heedlessness that is truly appalling (*The Politics of Dispossession*, 1994: xvii).

Hence, the intellectual, a "spirit in opposition," who is capable of rejecting his or her class to fight at the side of the dispossessed, will be rejected by those who have not chosen, because he or she *has* chosen. He or she is a privileged figure—

privileged to be a figure—and cannot escape the curse, which is also a privilege, of consciousness and of a radical freedom vis-à-vis their condition and his or her conditioning. It is understandable that this message should strike a chord with the intellectual public that has gone far beyond mere intellectual agreement with Said, especially at a time when the political and social situation in the world inclines that audience to anxious self-questioning.

The self-legitimizing function of Said's criticism is therefore most evident in those cases where it borders on polemicism and is applied to his closest competitors (Terry Eagleton and Frederic Jameson come to mind), all of them aspirants to the dominant position where there is only room for one and to the corresponding emblems and attributes, such as the right to lay claim to the heritage of Raymond Williams, the great cultural critic. But the strategies that criticism makes possible would be nothing if they were not based on a "complete" oeuvre that entitles its author to mobilize in each field of intellectual inquiry the arsenal of the technical and symbolic *capital* he has acquired in others. By claiming in book after book, sally after sally, cause after cause that the rank of committed intellectual is the only legitimate intellectual, Said negatively defines his rivals as partial, even stunted intellectuals. Russell Jacoby, despite a few excursions into criticism, is only a chauvinist; Michael Walzer, having naively exposed his lack of critical expertise on Camus and Benda, is only a social critic and faux leftist; Walter Lippman is merely a pundit.[11] These insiders, experts, coteries, professionals, who mold public opinion, make it conformist, encourage a reliance on a superior little band of all-knowing men in power. They continuously engage in promoting special interests and lobbies, but intellectuals, such as Noam Chomsky, Alexander Cockburn, Christopher Hitchens, Eqbal Ahmad and others, are the ones who question patriotic nationalism, corporate thinking, and a sense of class, racial, or gender privilege.

VI

Said's monumental corpus has already elevated him to the ranks of Matthew Arnold, I. A. Richards, William Hazlitt, R. P. Blackmur, and a tiny number of other critics who by the range, power, and sheer continuity and resourcefulness of their work are placed where literature and commentary approach each other most closely. To us, emergent peoples of the world, the long list of Said's works always seems astounding. Here is a Columbia University professor of English and comparative literature who not only writes about the entire scope of literature but who reestablishes postcolonial literature and culture at the pinnacle of humanistic research. For Said also writes about opera, music, belly-dance, film, theory, television, tennis, exile, state terrorism, politics, society, and history with prescient authority and is both politically committed as an unwavering man of the Left and seriously involved with literature as an astute reader. To add to these qualities the fact that Said is a great teacher whose students people the world academy is to begin to indicate how important his work is. Bart Moore-Gilbert summarizes the point with dash and wit:

> I, like most others now working in this academic field [i.e., postcolonial theory], am greatly in his debt. I wish, then, to conclude by strongly endorsing the importance which many other critics have attributed to his work. Said's influence has been evident in a number of disciplinary fields, to an extent matched by only a handful (at most) of other contemporary cultural critics. In comparative literature, anthropology, sociology, area studies and political science, as well as English literature, Said's ideas have aroused widespread interest and excitement and enabled a very considerable amount of subsequent work (1997: 72).

He quotes Michael Sprinker as saying: "Specialists in these fields have often been critical of his interventions, but they have on the whole not been able to ignore or dismiss him out of hand." "This attests," Moore-Gilbert continues, "to the importance of many of the questions that Said has asked in his long and distinguished career" (1997: 72). A fact with which one can hardly disagree.

I met Said for the first time in 1986. Although I had heard about him, I never expected the kindness he showed me when I became a student of his in the fall of that year. From the first moment that I was introduced to him in Toronto, I was struck by his unassuming manner and the cordiality of his regard for a potential friend and ally. He had an encyclopedic grasp of literary, social, and political schools and movements, and in objectifying them both with unequaled mastery he was also able from there to rise to a theoretical vision that was incomparably elegant and stirring. I will always remember his extraordinary gifts as a teacher. Tough and tender, rigorous and beguiling, impatient and generous, he made you fear and love him. It was an education for me. I was flattered later that he seemed to consider me a "friend"; and in the intervening years he complemented my work. There was in all our interaction much sharing and dialogue, the least of which was his entrusting me with his curriculum vitae, which I needed for writing *Sä-ēd'* Data Base.[12] Not surprisingly, Said is the first to recognize in his own writing the authority of several other students of his, "for whom any teacher would have been grateful," he notes. "These young scholars and critics gave me the full benefit of their exciting work, which is now both well published and well known: Anne McClintock, Rob Nixon, Suvendi Perera, Gauri Viswanathan, and Tim Brennan" (1993: xxviii). This sentiment of gratitude is mutual between the teacher and his students as shown in the following excerpt where Viswanathan shows acknowledgment of kindness received: "Finally," she writes, "to Edward Said, who inspired me to write this book, I offer my warmest appreciation. The most encouraging of teachers, he deepened the excitement of intellectual inquiry. His friendship, kindness, generosity, and enthusiasm hold these pages together" (1989: x). I, too, have always felt that I was in the presence of a great teacher, whose disquisitions on the history of cultural representation, of education, and of literature in the post–Henry Ford age always deliver new insights and new perspectives. My essays are deeply indebted to these exchanges, and my own version of writing has been particularly shaped by Said, who taught and lectured in Toronto in the mid-1980s, when he held the Northrop Frye Chair of Literature, and early the 1990s, when he spoke at McMaster and York. And although there had been other powerful encounters along the way with the work, for example, of Michel Foucault, Jacques Derrida, Stephen Greenblatt, or Henry Louis Gates Jr., none equals my encounter with Edward Said. But the intellectual course of which I speak points less to a doctrine, cobbled together out of a set of what an English publishing house calls "modern masters," than to a shared life experience.

The distinguishing mark of Said's massive and multifarious work is that he thought and wrote about literature and culture in steady conjunction with other social actualities, from the metropolitan West to the decolonizing world to the reading public and the ownership of means of communication, in a way that has permanently altered, even dismissed, the model that disfigured cultural thought more or less from the beginning. That no scholar today considers culture to be an aftereffect of the economy is largely due to Said's efforts, summed up in a comment by Raymond Williams: "It is a pleasure to read someone who not only has studied and thought so carefully but is also beginning to substantiate, as distinct from announcing, a genuinely emergent way of thinking."[13] True, insofar as Said goes a good deal further than disproving a hopelessly mechanical theory of culture. He invented a whole series of fundamental refinements to our way of considering the relationships among texts, events, and the world. Thus he distinguishes between "dominant, residual, alternative and emergent" literary practices, in Williams's totemic phrase, and sees these together as constituting a basic contest within every culture, in which writers and readers (whose intention Said always respects) can make choices, endow their experiences creatively with imaginative forms, belong with greater or lesser loyalty to ethnic groups and ideological formations.[14] So dynamic is Said's perspective that he usually speaks of texts as practices, rather than as reified objects. And he never disregards the fact that since the historical world is made by men and women, the culture of those men and women is inherent in what they are as living, breathing social beings and not in a disembodied formalistic element called "textuality."

There is, of course, a place for filiation, as there is one for affiliation. An even closer kinship links the former to the latter. An accurate illustration of this relationship can be found in "Secular Criticism," which posits that if Orientalism is a form of "system," narrative is closely tied to "culture," as one of the modes of "affiliation" by which the human order is represented as if it were a natural chain of filiation, growth, and development ("Secular Criticism," 1984: 1–31). In the most literal sense, that is, displacement tampers with narrative, and human secularity challenges our inventiveness. Moreover, it is obvious that Said is at cross-purposes: he is thrown into strangeness between القدس (Jerusalem), laden with history, and mongrel New York steadied by Old World leanings. This being abroad at home is what Hélène Cixous aptly calls "*entredeux*" (1997: 10). Said's cosmopolitan voice is precisely that of the modern polyglot city, New York, a ferocious mishmash of "savages" and nobles. Beneath this multiplicity of selves, however, is another voice that is beginning to remake the contours of the "glocal" village, and it is one I would call "Said the nomadologue": a writer obsessed with the desire never to sink roots into his ancestral earth. For him, the "entire world is [indeed] a foreign place" (Hugo of St. Victor, 1961: 101).

Like his outer- and intermappings of the globe, Said's mythic *bricolage* is based in Palestine but expands beyond it. Reading *contrapuntally* may be his lasting contribution to the study of literature whereby he amalgamates many narratives to a vision—namely, humanism. "What I was trying to do in *Culture and Imperialism*," he writes, "was not to *narrate*; it's impossible to narrate so many narratives, even contrapuntally—even Glenn Gould couldn't do it. You are not talking about five voices, but eight hundred voices. You talk about Africa, and then there is a question about Latin America, in addition to Australia, New Zealand, and other parts of the world" (1994: 13). In other words, the counter-point goes beyond conventional attitudes, ideas, theories of the text to establish a valid argumentation. A *contrapuntal* reading is therefore uniquely carried by literature in which the ideology of a period is transformed into a new historicist way by the imagination, forming new and surprising wholes such as emancipation, enlightenment. Even when discussing ideas and concepts related to domination, as is the case in many novels he deals with, Said never loses sight of what we enjoy and experience in a great literary work. This, I have always felt, is the profound mark of his undeniable humanity. He allows himself neither the unconvincing celebratory cant of the Blooms nor the unrelenting rigor of the fully fledged deconstructionist skeptic. More important, perhaps, he seeks to develop alternative attitudes and developing resistances to the dreadful politics of the world in which we live.

VII

The pre-Intifada critical writings and political manifestoes—and indeed *Orientalism*, which was immediately hailed as a "masterly" fusion of reading literary texts as historical and theoretical events, and his cross-hatching scholarly monographs with political tracts—prepared the ground for Said's concentration of all forms of intellectual *capital*. This was achieved shortly before the 1982 Israeli invasion of Lebanon and the expulsion of the Palestinians. The invasion cost more than 17,500 lives, including those of the thousands of Palestinians who were murdered at the Sabra and Chatila camps. The murderers, who were Christian Lebanese militiamen, had been sent by the Israelis. Officially, the Palestinian link with Lebanon was severed in late August 1982, when the PLO, led by Yasser Arafat, evacuated the city of Beirut where they had been besieged by the Israeli army for three months. The following excerpt encapsulates Said's anger and frustration at the Israeli state's behaving like an murderous bully: "No television watcher could have had any doubts that the Israelis were savage and ruthless during the siege of Beirut" (1994: 255). Said's principal role here is that of a warning bell against the abuses of power and state terrorism. His relentless attack upon power, usually as embodied in the figures of speech and/or lies of American foreign policy, is Swiftian, though without Swift's Tory values. These instances of wit applied to superior power hint at an almost encyclopedic range of topic and detail gathered together in *The Politics of Dispossession*. From the book there arises a mordant portrait of America, the Arab world, and Israel with their flim-flam, vulgarity, cruelty, and rotten prose. Such a position stands him in good stead when he presents "terrorism," Libya, Iran, Iraq, and now Afghanistan as objects created by the U.S. government and the media (whose role in America is not to supply news but to manufacture consent) for the public, and for bullying the weak or unpopular "foreign devil."[15] The predictable experts (the likes of Judith Miller and Steven Emerson come to mind) pontificate and throw around generalities without context or real history. Why no one thinks of holding seminars on Christianity (or Judaism for that matter) and violence is probably too obvious to ask.

It is no accident that Said's ambition, the intellectual expression of the will to authority and transgression, is most clearly asserted in his magnum opus, *Culture and Imperialism*, which perfectly captured the *bien pensant* wisdom of the day. The sheer bulk of the book, which is that of a summa or treatise, the range of subjects it covers—emotion, domination, perception, imagination, aesthetics, music, memory, dispossession, exile, history, literature, politics; the seigneurial manner (signaled, inter alia, by the absence of references) of its confrontations with the most prestigious authors, from Jane Austen to Kipling to Conrad, from C. L. R. James to Fanon to Aimé Césaire; and above all, perhaps, the endeavor to out-think and subsume almost everything starting with the objects of rival systems of thought such as deconstruction or postmodernism—in fact, every aspect of the work testifies to the will to exercise the critic's traditional claim to be the ultimate founding authority and to do so, unchallenged, in every realm of existence and thought. Said's most reliable annexation strategy is to set himself up as a vigilant consciousness, capable of supplying the person or institution to which he addresses himself with a self-truth of which that person or institution has been dispossessed. All this leads to "*Culture and Imperialism* [which] maps out a possible idiom of 'us' as a cultural amalgam," Sara Suleri informs us, "one illustrated by the breadth and variety of Said's points of reference." She quotes Said as saying:

> *The voyage in*, then, constitutes an especially interesting variety of hybrid cultural work. And that it exists at all is a sign of adversarial internationalization in an age of continued imperial structures. No longer does the logos dwell exclusively, as it were, in London and Paris. No longer does history run unilaterally, as Hegel believed, from east to west, or from south to north (1993: 32).

Few readers may share Said's insistence on such an irreversible improvement in the intellectual texture of the times. Most, however, will draw sustenance from the implicit burden of the book, in which the voyage in is only another way of articulating the difficult similarity between it and a voyage out.

In order for us to begin to understand this mode of branching between the voyage in and the voyage out, we must pause to examine Said's relationship to the politics of the Middle East, a privileged site of origin and return not just for Judaism and Christianity but for Islam as well. This may begin to explain why Said has never really come to terms with the central problem of the whole region—namely, that the bulk of its hopes and impediments, defeats and victories—or victims—are not just common people or upper-class matrons but well-educated professionals, who have everything to lose by giving up the world for the mere idea of a homeland. This does not seem to be the same for Said, who opines: "I would find it very hard to live there, I think: exile seems to me a more liberated state, but, I have to admit, I am privileged and can afford to experience the pleasures, rather than the burdens, of exile" (1992: 55). Thus, in some sense, he always writes from the position of the privileged *outsider*. And by keeping his distance from the events he writes about, he virtually guarantees that neither he nor his readers will fit in, at least in the Arab world where nationalism has become the excuse for many evils: mismanagement of resources, the abrogation of personal freedoms, the one-party state, the dictatorship of the army, the cult of the leader, and various forms of extreme xenophobia. Frantz Fanon said that the important thing about the nationalism of an oppressed people is that once it realizes its goals, it should develop a social consciousness that is very different from a national consciousness. The necessity of national consciousness on the way to liberation that appears in Fanon's work as an immediate historical necessity, however, appears in Said's thinking also as tragedy: "It's the tragedy," Said tells Wicke and Sprinker, "the irony, the paradox of all anti-imperial or decolonizing struggles that independence is the only alternative to the continued horrors of the Israeli occupation, whose goal is the extermination of a Palestinian national identity" (*A Critical*, 1992: 236–37). This fateful conversion is very difficult; there are few examples of it in the Arab world today where, interestingly enough, the dismal reception of the epochal *Orientalism, Culture and Imperialism,* and Said's other books,[17] copies of which cannot be found, few of which have even been translated into Arabic, is an accurate indication of the decades of stagnation, frustration, and the absence of democracy that have afflicted intellectual and cultural life. This "structure of attitude" is what Abdallah Laroui has aptly called the "crisis of the Arab world" and/or mind (1976: 100).

Said's prime example of "vision based on no vision" is the upgraded bullock cart. The improvements provided by intermediate technology to this unwieldy vehicle would, he reckons, cost more than a harmless little engine. Instead of using technology and funds provided for it from the rich world, for a great leap forward, they use it on expensive modifications to the bullock cart, conniving at poverty and indulging in sentimentality imported from the West, with its romantic doubts about industrialism. Among other perversities this nonsense gives Arab poverty a certain glamor, but the glamor is spurious and hateful, and the poverty, terrible. And "the poverty of the land is reflected in the poverty of the mind" as V. S. Naipaul (1997: 36) would have phrased it.

In Said, too, you will find no postmodernist distrust of such things as first principles, which is why, even when one wants to disagree, even when one emphatically does so, he or she has such a powerful moral presence. So far as his own life and work are concerned, he has clarified first principles. The inability of others to accept them irritates him and can sometimes goad him into tetchiness or absurdity, nowhere more so than in the clinical details which he provides for his readers: he assembles data with a cool and clean hand, remaining quietly engaged in the cause of liberation even if at times it looks like a lost cause. Having become the embodiment of the dissident intellectual, who could claim moral authority as it was assumed by Zola, Russell, and Sartre before him, Said was bound to be confronted with the murky politics of the Middle East, which meant involvement in the struggle to liberate Palestine. He had to face a mass of demands, and the strategy of radical out thinking was the perfect means of giving a theoretically acceptable form to the relationship of mutual legitimation that the Palestinian intelligentsia had established with the Palestine National Council (PNC) in the pre-Intifada years.[18] For Said, the free alliance between the "fellow traveler" and the PNC of which he was a member from 1973 to 1991 had nothing in common with the unconditional surrender of the self that some have seen in it. It was what enabled the committed intellectual that is Said—along with Mahmoud Darwish and others—to constitute himself as the founding consciousness of the council, to situate himself, vis-à-vis the council and the people, as Pour-soi to En-soi, and while obtaining a certificate of "revolutionary virtue," retaining an undiminished freedom in his strictly intellectual activity.

To perceive the significance and force of the "Said phenomenon" more fully would therefore require an analysis of the social demand for intellectual *engagement* and an account of the conditions of the time, the sense of breakdown, anxiety, and tragedy associated with both the collective and the individual losses stemming from the النكبة (1967 Defeat), Oslo I, and Oslo II, as well as from personal tragic moments, and more especially of the structural defeats of exile and its trauma, which sees "things both in terms of what has been left behind and what is actually here and now; there is a double perspective that never sees things in isolation" (Said, 1994: 60). Or, to put it differently, there is in existence an autonomous intellectual world with its own institutions for reproduction capable of sustaining an independent "aristocracy of the intelligence," in Benda's phrase, cut off from political power and even in a state of insurrection against it. Benda also reminds us of the definition of the intellectual's accomplishment, recognized and sanctioned by these institutions, the university especially (1969). Said speaks of the latter as the "utopian space, which I believe must remain a place where such vital issues are investigated, discussed, reflected on" (1993: xxvi). It was the university that stood by him in July 2000 in defending his right to his opinions and actions. This is a view rooted in the very places that produced him, with his attitudes of mind and his qualifications, that is, with all the symbolic *capital* that was invested in the formation of his individual talent.

The brightest and most finely educated child of parents with the cultural capital, Said went through demanding *grande portes* to establishments such as Harvard and Princeton. In the process, he pursued knowledge by accumulating "capital" in the "fields" of literature, music, and politics. Today, no critic commands more attention, in the Anglophone world at least; no one is closer to the center of the local "field of power" as he would describe it, that is New York intellectual life, than Edward Said, who admits that he, like Peter denying Christ or a Jew trying to assimilate in nineteenth-century Europe, has been so demoralized that he pretended not to exist (Glass, 1994). As a young man, he distanced himself from his people, "admitting that [he] . . . was from Lebanon which was as cowardly as saying nothing, since it meant saying something that was intended to be deliberately not provocative." The truth was:

> I was born in Jerusalem; so was my father, his father, and so on; my mother was born in Nazareth. The facts were rarely mentioned. I earned my degrees, I became a professor, I wrote books and articles on European literature. And, as the jolts of Near Eastern politics dictated, I occasionally saw my family on vacations: sometimes in Egypt, in Jordan, finally in Lebanon. In 1967 I was "from" Lebanon (1985: 34).

Yet, in time, his true identity reasserted itself, particularly after the 1967 Arab-Israeli war, when the Palestinians turned their backs on the defeated Arab states and took up arms on their own behalf. This identity crisis forced him to become a fully fledged insider who is not afraid to speak his mind. "It is very, very hard," he writes, "to espouse, for five decades, a continually losing cause" (1996: 75). It is clear now what Said means: 9/11 put aside the Palestinian question and provided enough room for rallying behind the United States in its quest to bomb Afghanistan while Israel got carte blanche to rape and kill Palestinians with impunity.

Although Said has been an important intellectual in the broad sweep of the twentieth century, one cannot analyze him outside the context of his own history and that of the Middle East. When in 1972 and 1973 as a visiting professor from Columbia University in New York he went to Beirut to spend his sabbatical year, it seemed to be the apex of Beirut's intellectual development, before the corruption of oil wealth and the disillusionment of civil war set in. Said generated excitement in small seminars and large auditoriums, rousing graduate students from dogmatic slumber. He trampled over the academic boundaries that separated literature, philosophy, politics, religion, and, just as easily, crossed Lebanon's cultural divides, lecturing fluently in English, French, and Arabic to those whose political outlook was tied to each language.

In 1972 I had a sabbatical and took the opportunity of spending a year in Beirut, where most of my time was taken up with the study of Arabic philology and literature, something I had never done before, at least not at that level, out of a feeling that I had allowed the disparity between my acquired identity and the culture into which I was born, and from which I had been removed, to become too great. In other words, there was an existential as well as a felt political need to bring one self into harmony with the other, for as the debate about what had once been called "the Middle East" metamorphosed into a debate between Israelis and Palestinians, I was drawn in, ironically enough, as much because of my capacity to speak as an American academic and intellectual as by the accident of my birth. By the mid-Seventies I was in the rich but unenviable position of speaking for two, diametrically opposed constituencies, one Western, the other Arab (1998: 5–6).

His resonant voice and playful humor earned him a better reception for his ideas (most of them unpopular in Beirut's political and academic circles) than he might otherwise have expected. One evening at Beirut College for Women, he addressed a large assembly on a prize work of the Orientalist canon, Lawrence Durrell's *Alexandria Quartet*. Many of the Westerners in the room imagined themselves Durrellian heroes in a latter-day Alexandria of intrigue and romance. Said attacked the novel's triviality, its incomprehensible metaphors, its meaningless plot. He managed to persuade some of his listeners, but one university lecturer protested that Durrell's images were compelling. "Compelling?" Said asked. "When he needs an image for human communication, he reaches for the telephone" (1975: 234). As an almost doctrinaire secularist, Said is hardly swayed by an argument or hobbled by a rigid approach. Unlike other critics, he is always interested in concrete aspects of cultures and literatures, and there he is worth reading.

Beirut was not then the cultural backwater that a long war and botched reconstruction have since made it. It was the only heterogeneous and heterodox capital in the Arab world, a place where intellectuals flourished amid the risk of assassination by the Israelis, Arab governments, and fanatics. It was home to political and intellectual exiles from all over the world. It had more than forty daily newspapers, functioning theaters in five languages, and four universities. Undergraduates at the American University came from more than seventy countries, and the professors ranged from the usual displaced Captain Grimes types to the outstanding scholars in their field. Said was an exciting ingredient in an already well-spiced mix, but he was more than an academic gadfly. He brought his ideas to a real and brutal world that he would later describe as a place "of staggering violence and unpredictable resilience." Said compared "Beirut's relentlessly detailed self-dismantling—much of it performed on prime-time television—" to "a large scale version of the Laurel and Hardy film about two men vengefully destroying each other's car and house piece by piece, tit for tat, and while they glower and puff through many 'take thats,' the world around them gets wiped out." He warned, "If the struggle for power and territory continues unchecked in Beirut, very little of either will be left when, and if, a final victor emerges" (1985: 169). To put the matter differently: Can a country undergo collective therapy? Lebanon, where many of Said's immediate family still live, has always been intended as a place where an abusive past can be abandoned and the self made new. Not any more, Said maintains, insofar as what had been Lebanon is indeed a mournful place. That hatred can perpetuate itself in Beirut, a city of mixed geographies and mythologies, is beyond human understanding (Glass, 1994).[19]

Decades of colonial exploitation in countries such as Lebanon have produced the oddest, the most severe distortions in the historical consciousness and communal foundations of the peoples and societies left after the Europeans exited; and the new order brought to the fore not only young officers in power but new politically opportunistic transnational companies, eager for fabulous profits and expanding markets. This is an unwholesome blend, especially as it left the colony to fend for itself: for the natives an unappeased sense of retrospective injustice, for the Whites a resentful anger and contempt. The periodic revivals of nationalism in the postcolonial Third World have taken religious and secular forms, but whatever else these revivals afford—and they contain a great deal of undirected nativism and atavistic religious sentiment, as well as daring, often brilliant ideas—they are almost always full of the sense that the Europeans and now Americans have not sufficiently atoned for their past and present interventions. Such a sense of grievance cares little for the empty shelves, the rusty factories, the barely functioning armed forces. Much more emphasis is placed on the symbolic dimension whereby the Arabs, for example, are now so humiliated as to replicate their earlier colonial subjugation. Somewhere in all this colonial and postcolonial violence and counterviolence, a beleaguered community is evolving, but at what cost? It is this disabling legacy, especially the notion of the impossible coexistence of different kinds of right, that weighs on Lebanon today. Said voices anger and frustration over an animosity that dates from colonial times. In order to avert the danger of Lebanon being torn apart by rival militia gangs (Druz, *Shi'ite*, Sunni, Phalangist, Christian), who define themselves boldly according to their own credo and against one another, an ancient blood claim is exacted once again, with a tragic lack of logic. Seen from afar, at least, Lebanon is an infernal place with tremors rumbling beneath its feet.[20]

Palestinian commandos and thinkers, exiled from Jordan by the late King Hussein, had arrived in Lebanon to challenge the traditional establishment with their ideas as much as with their kalashnikovs. Debate rather than gossip or drug taking was the common social activity. The politics of nationalism and sectarianism, decolonization, the wars in Vietnam and South Lebanon, as well as Wittgenstein, Luis Buñuel, and Thomas Pynchon were discussed late into the night. The Israeli occupation of Gaza and the West Bank had lasted five years, longer than seemed possible. Arabs were questioning the moral premises of their nation-states, probably the most important development to emerge from their convincing military defeat in June 1967. This time of profound self-questioning gave birth to some of the best literature in the Middle East, what Said termed the "early years of the Palestinian Renaissance"—the poetry of Mahmoud Darwish and Samih al-Qassim; novels and short stories by Ghassan Kanafani, later murdered by the Israelis; and essays by Marxists such as Mohammed Sid-Ahmed and free-marketeers such as Ghassan Tueini (Said, 1994: 133). Political discussions harked back to the questions asked by Plato and Machievelli. The choice for Palestinians seemed either between an independent state in the West Bank and Gaza or a secular, democratic state in the entirety of what had become Israel—although neither was, in fact, likely (Gilsenan, 1995: 187–88; Glass, 1994).

Said favored the creation of two states in Palestine. To achieve that Israel would have to sacrifice land it had occupied in 1967, and most Palestinians, including Said's own family, would have to abandon their dream of returning home. A majority of Palestinians in Lebanon at that time favored the democratic, secular state, which was also the official goal of the Palestine Liberation Organization. Only Said and a few other Palestinians such as Mahmoud Darwish were courageous enough to stand against the tide on which Yasser Arafat was then riding. Two of the others, Said Hammami and Issam Sartawi, were assassinated by fellow Palestinians based in Syria. In such a situation, Said argues, the writer necessarily has several imperatives to respond to, chief among them being the raising of national consciousness, the carefully realistic rendering of particular circumstances, and perhaps less important, the discovery of adequate norms of aesthetic performance. In his credo as an intellectual published in 1994, *Representations of the Intellectual*, Said, paradoxical, ironic, mercilessly critical, defines the role of the intellectual in society in the following terms: "[T]he intellectual does not represent a statue-like icon, but an individual vocation, an energy, a stubborn force engaging as a committed and recognizable voice in language and in society with a whole slew of issues, all of them having to do in the end with a combination of enlightenment and emancipation or freedom" (1994: 73). The scale of Said as an intellectual in opposition can be praised on another level. In this context, Ahmad's homage is pertinent.

> In real life, his courage is palpable and a source of inspiration and comfort to family and friends. I am reminded of an incident some years ago. Three friends dined in Beirut with Faiz Ahmed Faiz, the Pakistani poet who had taken, from the U.S.-supported tyranny of Mohammed Ziaul Haq, a refuge of sorts in war-torn Lebanon. Said was fully engaged as Faiz recited a poem—"*Lullaby for a Palestinian Child*." Just then a violent fire fight started nearby; the waiters scurried inside leaving us the only diners in the courtyard. Instinctively, I stopped translating from Faiz's Urdu into English, and looked inquiringly at Nubar Hovsepian, who knew Beirut and its warriors well. "Go on," urged Said as if nothing unusual was happening. We went on[21] (*The Pen and the Sword, 1994*: 8).

One night in April 1973 in Beirut, Said discussed the Palestinian future with Kamal Nasser, his distant relative and a well-regarded poet. The next night, Israeli soldiers murdered Nasser in his bed. Years later, in the ostensible safety of New York, Jewish Defense League fanatics threatened to kill Said, too.

In the summer of 1973, Said left Beirut for his home in New York's Upper West Side. In October of that year, Egypt and Syria launched the October War against Israel to reclaim the territory they had lost in 1967. To the Arab states, the war had an additional, domestic objective: to reinforce the discredited style of government by soldiers, dictators, and sheikhs. The illusion of victory in the Golan Heights and Sinai stopped the political questions and the free exchange of ideas. Arab military dictators tightened their hold on the instruments of power, on speech, and on the press. Partial success on the battlefield was matched by a similar, sham victory in the economic warfare of the oil embargo. Until the Civil War of 1975 Lebanon stood for accommodation, tolerance, and, especially, representation. It is no accident, for example, that such disparities as the ideas of Arab nationalism, the renaissance of Arabic as a modern language, the foundations of the Egyptian press, the living possibility and continuity of the good life and commercial entrepreneurism (at least for the twentieth-century Arab) originated in Lebanon. Yet the crisis developed out of the lack of suitable Lebanese mechanisms to extract the best possible combination for Lebanon's destiny. "For if past, present and future are all readily negotiable with most interests," Said makes clear, "as I felt they were in Beirut, then crisis ensues. Call it equilibrium, and it still remains critical. As I saw it, Beirut was a victim of its openness and its true cultural virtuosity, as well as of the absence of an articulable foundation upon which to draw" (1994: 6). When civil war began in 1975, Lebanon felt the effect of the October War, of the wrath of Arab regimes and the need to end political dissent. In 1977, the year Anwar Sadat went to Jerusalem, Said returned to Beirut to visit family and friends. He wrote at the time: "Almost as much as by the terrible scars of war in downtown Beirut one is struck by relatively insignificant changes. Nearly everyone seems to be wearing either an oversized cross or a replica of the Koran around the neck—ostentatiously announcing not a religious conviction but a political assertion" (1977: 20). Beirut, like the rest of the Arab world, had separated itself into tribal and sectarian camps—the better for feudal, clerical, and foreign élites to control them. This destruction, Darwish would later describe as جنون بيروت (the madness of Beirut).

Said remained in contact with developments in Lebanon, not for its contributions to literature and philosophy, but because he was part of the vibrant exile community that was fighting to return to a homeland from which the Israeli settlers had driven them in 1947 and 1948 when Israel was established and Palestine, as a consequence, shattered. Israeli as well as Palestinian historians now accept that up to 750,000 Palestinian Arabs, fearful of being massacred, fled their homes in what is now Israel. Today, these refugees and their descendants number at least 3 million, 350,000 of whom still live in Lebanon, a few in modest comfort, most in squalid camps. Those Palestinians who stayed behind have been subjected to years of restrictions but at least are now citizens of Israel. This makes the tragedy of Said's exile all the more painful insofar as his family, too, had to abandon their home in Talbiya in late 1947, when a majority of the indigenous population became refugees.[22] In the excerpt that follows Said gives a poignant account of a visit to his native القدس (Jerusalem) in 1992, where he could not bring himself to enter the old family house, which the Israeli government had let to a group of fundamentalist American Christians.

It took almost two hours to find the old family house, and it is a tribute to my cousin's memory that only by sticking very carefully to his map did we finally locate it. . . .

It bore the name plate "International Christian Embassy" at the gate. To have found my family's house now occupied not by an Israeli Jewish family but by a right-wing fundamentalist Christian and militantly pro-Zionist group, run by a South African Boer no less! Anger and melancholy overtook me, so that when an American woman came out of the house holding an armful of laundry and asked if she could help, I could not bring myself to ask to go inside.

More than anything else, perhaps, it was the house I did not, could not, enter that symbolized the eerie finality of a history. It seemed to stare down at me from behind its shaded windows. Palestine as I had known it was over (Ibid., 50).

Realizing the subtlety of Said's reminiscences of things past, to adapt freely from Proust, one begins to imagine a critical account of his work that would jettison all earnest *explication de texte*—meaning, paraphrasable content, social and historical situation—and concentrate entirely on emotion, memory, cadence, rhythm, form. A critical study that would be true to Yeats's dictum "words alone are certain good" (1987: 163).

Said is consistently critical of Arabs, especially the Palestinians, and of the West, especially the United States. He is both a Palestinian and an American and finds virtues and faults in both peoples. He is also indignant about recurrent themes that he detects in the modern history of relations between the Palestinians and the West. One is the complete disregard for the Palestinians' right to express their wishes, a disregard that has lasted from Arthur Balfour's 1917 Declaration to the 1993 secret accords in Oslo and even more so today. Balfour admitted in 1919 that Britain had deceived the Arabs and that Zionism, "be it right or wrong, good or bad, is rooted in age-long tradition, in present need, in future hopes, of far profounder import than the desires and prejudices of the 700,000 Arabs who now inhabit that ancient land" (Said, *The Politics of Dispossession*, 1994: 166). Their desires and prejudices are of no more relevance, Said believes, to Arafat and his policemen than they were to Lord Balfour. He labors to make clear the case against corruption, injustice, and censorship. His greatest contempt is reserved for Yasser Arafat.

Arafat, I know, has been greatly angered by my persistent critique not only of the Oslo accords and what I believe to have been a fraudulent (so far as Palestinians are concerned) peace process, but also of his increasingly dictatorial, profoundly corrupt and visionless attempt to rule his people. I always point out that he is not president but, in effect, the Israeli enforcer of the military occupation by other means (Said, *Peace and Its Discontents*, 1996: 6).

Said laments the fact that there has been no census among the Palestinians and, consequently, no referendum on the PLO-Israel Agreement. The 1996 elections that put Arafat at the helm were confined to Gaza and the West Bank and thus excluded the vast majority of Palestinians who do not live in Arafat's Palestine, an area Said calls "a shabby undemocratic Palestinian protectorate under Israeli rule [that is] proclaimed as the fulfillment of our aspirations" (Ibid., 69). Said's criticism of Arafat extends to other Arab rulers. In the Arab world, the West has always adopted the comfortable policy of assuming that local dictators, kings, and generals are loved by their people if those leaders do what the West wants (Hosni Mubarak/King Abdullah/possibly Bachar Assad, though this will depend on his desire to make peace on Israel's terms) but hated by their people if the leaders oppose the West (Saddam Hussein/Colonel Ghaddafi/the Mullahs).

This dictatorial style of government is all the more true in the case of states such as Saudi Arabia, Kuwait, Bahrain, Qatar, Oman, essentially family companies, America's close allies in the Middle East and vital links between the West and its oil supplies. And whereas in the Gulf states anger increases daily, fed by everyday frustrations: bankrupt leadership, overcrowded hospitals, sporadic water supplies, daily powercuts, chaotic schools, low salaries, growing unemployment and recession; in some other parts of the Arab world (Algeria and Egypt come to mind), fundamentalists step in where the state fails: they provide meat for the poor on feast days, loans and white wedding dresses for young people who cannot afford to marry. Reticent and laconic, the masses have always tended to keep criticism to themselves. Now, however, frustration and anger have persuaded a handful of a new breed of intellectuals who, unlike the old ones, are not always the government's pawns, to break the silence. Some are highly educated, well-intentioned reformers, but they have to go abroad to speak out; at home, even bedrooms are bugged. The usual price for uttering any criticism is torture, which includes flogging, burial in burning sand, or beheading in a public place such as Riyadh's "chop-chop square," where the executioner swings his sword and hacks off the heads of public enemies, making fast work of sticky problems. Those who go abroad to criticize their leaders are sometimes kidnapped in style by private plane.[23] It is in this context that Said puts the following question to his fellow Arabs: "In what Arab capital is it possible to write or say what one wishes, to say the truth, to stem the tide of repressive central state authority, intolerant of everything except its own fantasies and appetites?" (*Peace and Its Discontents*, 1996: 94). Such questions are quite legitimate, but they are asked by Arabs who, like Said, reside *outside* the Arab world or by those who read Western newspapers and watch satellite television.[24]

Nevertheless, for Said, conversion to, and belief in, a political god of any sort is unfitting behavior for the intellectual. At the same time, he underlines the importance to the intellectual of passionate engagement, risk, exposure, commitment to principles, vulnerability in debating and involvement in worldly causes. He examines the aesthetics of political conversion and political recantation, providing examples precisely from the Arab world, where intellectuals reversed their position, praising political regimes that were once their hated enemies. He maintains that real intellectual analysis forbids one from taking sides and that the notion of a side is highly problematic where cultures are at issue, since most cultures are not homogeneous. Said's example of the intellectual as committed intelligence in revolt is the late Egyptian academic, Nas Hamid Abu Zeid. Because of his merciless analysis of "Islamic discourse," he was demoted, branded, cast aside, more or less constantly in hiding, and finally murdered by extremist assailants in June of 1992.[25]

Said also pays tribute to Jewish scholars such as Israel Shahak, Jakob Talmon, Yehoshua Leibowitch, Zev Sterhell, Uri Avneri, Ilan Pappe, and Noam Chomsky, who have written critically of Israel and its oppression of the Palestinians. He finds few Arab equivalents who dare to criticize their leadership. Of Chomsky, in particular, he writes that "even allowing that he neglects unduly the Arab side of things, we must note that he deals with societies and cultures that are his own and deals with them critically, harshly, truthfully: We cannot as Arabs say the same for ourselves" (*The Politics of Dispossession*, 1994: 329). As an Arab, Said has, in fact, done precisely that, to his cost. He was, of course, for a while on the hit list of Meir Kahane's extremist Jewish Defense League and subject to disgraceful attacks by sympathizers of Israel, such as Edward Alexander in "Professor of Terror" (1989: 49–50) and Justus Weiner in "'My Beautiful Old House,'" (1999: 23–32). Much of this violence against Said has taken its toll. He explains: "My family and I lived with death threats; my office was vandalized and sacked; I had to endure libelous abuse about my people and cause—not only was I a terrorist but also a professor of terror, an anti-Semite, an accomplice to murder, a liar, a deranged demagogue, etc." (*The Politics of Dispossession*, 1994: xix). In Palestine, Said's books have been confiscated by order of Minister of Information Yasir Abed Rabbo. He is now banned in the country of his birth for having dared to speak against Arafat. Arafat publicly condemned Said, whose advice he once sought (and always ignored), and the PLO bureaucracy has demanded that he stop criticizing them for ruling their little territory in Gaza and the West Bank as tyrannically as they once did West Beirut. Yet Said will not keep quiet. "Why should we," he asks, "be required not only to give up what we have lost to military occupation and pillage but in addition to apologize for having made the claims in the first place?" (*Peace and Its Discontents*, 1996: 142). He resigned from the Palestine National Council, the parliament in exile, in 1991, following the medical diagnosis of chronic leukemia, which has slowed him down considerably. It also revealed to him his own mortality prompting him to attempt to make sense of his own life as its end approaches. "All of a sudden," he writes, "then, I found myself brought up short with some though not a great deal of time available to survey a life whose eccentricities I had accepted like so many facts of nature" ("Between Worlds," 1998: 3). As illness imposes a more rigid time table, Said finds himself shifting his priorities to finally settle on his "deux amours": family and music.

Let me acknowledge here that Said continues to impose a narrative on a life marked not only by a fatal illness but by un unforgiving time table as well. He has not stopped writing critically of Israel, the United States, the Arab world, and all those who collude in the suppression of Palestinian rights, the denial of Palestinian history, and the deception that the September 1993 White House ceremony consecrated as peace with justice.[26]

> I am convinced that it is what we diaspora Palestinians need to do, despite the difficulty and unpleasantness of confronting die-hard Israeli nationalists in their intellectual sanctuaries, where the whole question of Palestine is now simply a matter of separation (as the relation between blacks and whites had been in apartheid South Africa), of Israeli security, of tactical fixing. The injustice done to us as a people has yet to be taken up as part of the history of postwar and post-Holocaust politics. And unless we bring it up, as my children's generation constantly do, refusing to hide behind the historical forgetfulness espoused by Arafat and his tiny band of true believers, we will continue to live through its agonies. This is as true for Israelis as it is for us. The consequences of 1948 just won't go away, partly because our conflict with Zionism is so specific, partly because our situation during the last fifty years has festered beneath a number of cosmetic changes, and remains unrectified, underanalyzed, morally and politically unacknowledged by most Israeli liberals and Israeli supporters. More significant, however, is the impression I had that beneath the official and institutional status quo, a healthy disorder bubbles away among young people who are very close to total impatience with the manifest failure of the present generation ("On Writing a Memoir," 1999: 7).

For Said, this is as much a historical as an ethical issue. The ravages of wars in the Middle East and its religious divisions, the de facto segregation of Palestinians *inside* and *outside* Israel who are nevertheless yoked together by the demography and demagoguery of "peace" turn Arabs and Jews into stark alternatives. In this silhouette of desperate subjects, laid out in two dimensions, there is a need for a breath of new life. Said models the intellectual vocation as a state of constant alertness, as perpetual willingness not to give in to half-truths or received ideas. Such a stand involves a steady realism, a rational energy, and a complicated struggle to balance the problems of selfhood against the constant demands of speaking out in the public sphere.

Even so, exactly what Said is doing in works of culture is a question worth raising. Pitched adroitly in style between academia and the general reader, his writings stitch together the topics of domination, resistance, the text, the world, the critic, power, representation, and its opposite, misrepresentation. In today's cultural climate, it is hard to see how he can fail to win a wider readership—exactly what his work is surely constructed to achieve. He is an intellectual who has achieved his stature largely by focusing on his inner and outer experiences of exile, by standing for the truth, by stripping away the integuments of recognizable reality in an increasingly rigorous aesthetic of diminution, concentration, and withholding. A truth in art, Oscar Wilde once remarked, is one whose contradiction is also true; and much the same could be said of Edward Said's own brilliant, distinguished career. Like Wilde, we remember Said as much for what he is as for what he writes. The English love a "character" rather as they love a lord, and if Said is certainly the one, he also dabbles in passing himself off as the *Other*. If he is the flamboyant *porte parole* for justice who takes fashionable London, Paris, and New York by storm, he is also the reviled target of the Anglo-American and/or Arab establishment. Everything about him is doubled, hybrid, ambivalent. He is leftist and liberal, bourgeois and underdog. It is the contrast between the brittle wit of his writings on literature, music, and the stark, plangent rhythms of his reflections on exile and politics that invite and justify further inquiry.

CHAPTER TWO

THE *OLD/NEW IDIOT*:
REREADING THE POSTCOLONIAL SIGN

> The *old idiot* wanted, by himself, to account for what was lost or saved;
> but the *new idiot* wants the lost, the incomprehensible, and the absurd to
> be restored to him. This is most certainly not the same persona; a muta-
> tion has taken place. And yet a slender thread links the two idiots, as if
> the first had to lose reason so that the second rediscovers what the *other*,
> in winning it, had lost in advance.
> —Deleuze and Guattari, *What Is Philosphy?*, 63. [Emphasis added]

Postcolonial theory was a 1980s' thing, a literary critical movement that took
shape on the East Coast, becoming established there and elsewhere as something
one could talk about after having talked too long about feminism, deconstruction,
and postmodernism. The term may have been coined by Edward Said in an essay
of 1979; if so it was already a restrike, minted from a prototype used by Abdallah
Laroui in the 1960s or perhaps by Albert Memmi in the 1950s. Said himself
came to prefer the term *emergent* theory and practice. But by the time he proposed
this, nominal territory had already been claimed: *post colonial theory* it was going
to be and has been ever since in the anthologies and commentaries published to
represent and explain this recent evolution in Anglo-American literary criticism.[1]

The critics associated with postcolonial theory (Hall, Said, Spivak, Bhabha)
have been exceptionally unwilling to stand together for a group photograph—the
mark of the movement is the disavowal of movements. So postcolonial theory
resisted systematization and became rather good at slipping through theoretical
nooses. Much like new historicism, in its enduring modern form as a hands-on
intellectual occupation that subsists by not being theory, philosophy, history, or
any other discipline bedazzled by the false promises of systems, structures, and

73

upper-case designations. Others produce their intellectual abstractions while postcolonial writers *avant la lettre*, represented by writers as apparently different as Aimé Césaire and Léopold Sédar Senghor (although they, too, were across the hall in another town in another time), remind us of the urgencies of real life. "In its initial, more or less literal, temporal sense," Arif Dirlik perceptively writes, postcolonial theory

> referred to newly liberated colonies, and was quite radical in its social, eco-
> nomic and political implications: breaking with the colonial past to create
> new societies economically, politically and culturally. Integral to the post-
> colonial vision of this early period (peaking in the 1960s) were ideologies
> of national liberation that sought national autonomy in all realms from the
> colonial past as well as the neo-colonial present (2001: 4).

There is much of this sort of language in most post colonial narrative, which describes and commends a total immersion in practice and close, detailed engage-ment with specific instances.

Postcolonial theory's opponents have not been slow to find fault with this commitment to peculiarities, seeing in it a symptom of leftist disillusionment, an evasion of the challenges posed by feminism and the women's movement, and a head-in-the-sand attitude to the movement's own historical identity as, for example, the purveyor of a history of the British Empire (Austen and all) that had remained incurious about the doings of the American empire of the present day, even if Said renders it careful consideration in the last section of *Culture and Imperialism*. (I will come back to this point later in the chapter). Postcolonial theory's preference for Said over Spivak, discourse over class and ideology (the latter again criticized by Robert Young as a sort of fetish), metaphors of circula-tion and exchange—"social energies"—over those of cause and effect, and almost anything over Derrida and the challenge of radical deconstruction seemed to many to be a rather too comfortable rehabilitation of old pleasures in the face of what came to be known as theory. At the same time, there was and is a foxiness to postcolonial theory, which threatens its critics with the hint (sometimes more than a hint) that all this practice has been thought about and dismissed for good reason, or already taken care of. Is this truth or just finesse? Who might tell, and how? Can we have devices of doubt along with the pleasures of real presence without creating hermeneutic turmoil? Can we enjoy our acts of postcolonial reading, and the colonial "pastness" we meet with in them, without suffering too much anxiety? To this set of questions one feels impelled to add yet another one: How important is *Orientalism* and its iconography to postcolonial theory? Does it risk the judgment of posterity by contamination from the Foucauldian method? To what extent, we ask, is the *concept* not paradigmatic but *syntagmatic*; not projective but *connective*; not hierarchical or *linear* but *variational*; not referential but *consistent*? What are we to make of Tim Brennan's reading of *Orientalism*, a reading that opened a gate and sponsored an escape? Above all, it bankrolled a break-out from tired narratives about the subject. What Brennan brought forward is that by being on the periphery, one knows where the center is.[2] Or, does one? And finally, can the inequalities of power and wealth between the First and Third World allow us to celebrate the "global" as if we were all participants in the same local festival? How can we remedy the profound anxiety in which we (the ex-subject people) see ourselves not as primitive and backward but rather as part of a shared history of human civilization?

I

There is no easy or ready-made method for discussing the life and/or works of a writer like Edward Said, whose art in its essence is so different, so remote from his everyday chores or even his career. The occasions for his *petits récits* and music writings are connected to the aesthetic texts of Sartre, Benda, Adorno, Gould, and others. But when it comes to such long-term projects, or *grands récits* such as *Orientalism* and *Culture and Imperialism*, which together form a mighty ensemble, he is majestic (what little he says is always full of insight). *Orientalism*, not surprisingly, is a book that meditates on the necessity "to reverse oneself, to accept thereby the risks of rupture and discontinuity" (1975: 34). Said makes clear how one can recast inherited texts and/or read them in revisionist ways.

> To make explicit what is usually allowed to remain implicit; to state that which, because of professional consensus, is ordinarily not stated or questioned; to begin again rather than to take up writing dutifully at a designated point and in a way ordained by tradition; above all, to write in and as an act of discovery rather than out of respectful obedience to established "truth"—these add up to the production of knowledge, they summarize the method of beginning about which this book turns (1979: 379).

But if *Orientalism* gestures unambiguously toward a political view of intellectual activity, it only occasionally reveals itself as "a profoundly American book" (Brennan, 2000: 560). No one who read the book would mistake it for the work of a dispossessed Arab American critic eagerly resolving to combat the wrongs done to his constituency by imperial powers, ever willing to accept duels in interpretation and virtuosity.

The book is also cannier than Brennan appears to think, for it wages struggles on behalf of the truth—not only the truth of usually unrecorded suffering but also the truth about the institutional obduracy that lurks insidiously beneath the surface of things and (a persistent theme of its author's early years) the callous posturing of so-called realistic or pragmatic intellectuals. Power has never fazed or impressed Said: he took on its many contemporary forms with undaunted courage. Brennan shrewdly points out that to make a topic of one's own development demands the most careful management of narrative. Its greatest exponent in this regard was Said, himself a colonial, and his project took the sweetly satisfying form of a whole life lived as a kind of revenge. Brennan also makes abundantly clear that *Orientalism*

> could not have been written anywhere else, and its legacy is fused, or confused, with an American national culture that is particularly impervious to what the book is saying. To call the book American is also, of course, to raise the issue of the authentic Third World dimension of the postcolonial intellectual as a way of probing the sensitive issue of metropolitan spokesmanship (Ibid.).

I can understand the appeal of this argument to an assiduous critic such as Brennan, who undertook to demonstrate that in certain provinces of thought or writing, a theory such as Orientalism and an actual experience (writing in exile) are interchangeable because they are directly adjacent.

According to Brennan, *Orientalism* has had at least two salutary types of pernicious effect, the *first* on its readers generally, and the *second* on those professionally involved in area studies. But his biting way of viewing the book does not explain his reluctance to engage in a critique of the discipline of Orientalism itself. Brennan avoids the ultimate question: Does the Said model in fact encourage or discourage people from understanding what would be a legitimate and constructive critique of Orientalism, from both within and without the community in the field? Insofar as Said's account of Orientalism is compatible with extensive public control over the funding of research and the application/dissemination of knowledge, his method of writing back to the center with a vengeance allows for radical change. Brennan's answer to this finding is that the Saidian model leaves no room for another critique.

> The late millennial *episteme*, if we are to take the concept seriously, may only be said to have provided a setting of a linguistic will to truth from which Said vainly sought to extricate himself. The logic of intertextuality dictates, in advance, that a Foucauldian *Geist* haunts *Orientalism*'s every line according to a historical grammar, rendering heroic improvisation a self-deluding exercise. Said himself, I believe, would not try to deny the inescapability of such a riposte to the argument I'm laying out here, provided the terms of Foucault's own theories were accepted *sui generis*. It would not then be the unyielding logic of the *episteme* but an ideological movement that was at issue and as such a contestable one. As Said himself repeatedly argues, one simply has to deny the terms to evade them. For

him, evidence still matters. One does not have to bow to Nietzsche's great epistemological step from evidence to self-reflection (the will to truth as a truth that one wills to be true). For this essay the evidence is of two types: what Said is on record as saying about this work and what the work internally shows (Ibid., 570).

This is meager. Revolutions in thinking are cognitively complex, but one of Said's central ripostes is that the Brennan method of interpreting concepts such as 'latent/manifest' (ظاهر / باطن) are of the nature not of culture but of theory, not a failure to meet one imaginary standard of tidy evaluation. The idea is a complex one, with many aspects, as can be seen already from the use to which it is put by structuralists.[3]

There is also a sense in which Brennan proves inadequate in dealing with Said's *organic* lived experience, for it is necessary to distinguish between, on the one hand, the accomplished in a relation with the self; and on the other the *event* (of writing *contrapuntally* and against the grain), that its own reality cannot bring to completion. In this respect, the procedure of theme and variation that Brennan ponders over, which maintains the harmonic frame of the theme of *Orientalism*, gives way to a sort of "framing" as Deleuze would have it. The Saidian method of تحليل و تفسير (deconstruction and disputation) therefore gives birth to much freer compounds, to almost complete or loaded aggregates, in permanent equilibrium. Increasingly, it is the intention of the composition that matters. This is how Said puts it: "In writing *Orientalism*, I see myself as an Oriental *writing back* at Orientalists, who for so long have thrived upon our silence. I am also *writing to* them by dismantling the structure of their discipline, showing its meta-historical, institutional, anti-empirical, and ideological biases" (1976: 47; emphasis added). It is at this point that a major lacuna arises in Brennan's otherwise mercilessly witty essay: the failure to note that *Orientalism* has a reference, one that is *plurivocal* (Palestinian by birth, Arab by race, French-German-English-American and possibly Arabic by methodology, English by language, American by location). Certainly, it is not defined by an external resemblance, which remains prohibited, but by an internal tension that relates it to the whole of thought. Put differently, *Orientalism* makes a signal contribution to our understanding of how the discipline works and what it has achieved. Orientalists may be good at running such a discipline, but few of them understand very well how it works. A model such as that of Bernard Lewis, whose scholarship Said examines with a fine-tooth comb, of how he tests and applies his theory to the Middle East, has had absurd conclusions and consequences—the idea, for example, that every observation is evidence for every theory—and his account of where that theory comes from in the first place is inchoate at best. The possibilities Said articulates and the arguments he makes are a crucial resource for improving our feeble understanding of the Arab region and its people (1999: 47–52).

What I resist in "The Illusion of a Future" is the move from the *transitive* to the *intransitive* model, and the reasons Brennan provides do not seem provocative or exacting enough to establish a genuinely alternative reading. His ardent and at times balanced narrative gives a diachronic structure to *Orientalism*, as it attempts to put the luminous details together into a suggestive protohistory of modernity. Motifs of this kind are both arresting and convincing, but they fall short in understanding a hybrid text that was fathered at a time of extreme tension between the West and its nemesis (i.e., the Arab world). Brennan cheerfully admits that the connections he adduces do not truly make a single empirical discourse. They are, however, loosely historicist: they suggest that significant things happen in the light of other things that have happened.

> Without Said's prominence, his prolific writing, and (not least) his effective personal presence as a speaker, the process of breaking from an Anglocentric parochialism and moving towards more unsettling and linguistically diverse kinds of intellectual influence would not have proceeded as inexorably as it did. Obviously, what produced the theoretical turn, on the one hand, and the postcolonial moment, on the other (not to mention the conflation of the two), involved much larger and more complicated forces than those entailed by one man's career. Indeed, that is the point of this essay. But given Said's combined authority as literary amateur *and* proponent of anticolonial liberation in Palestine, this fictional Foucauldian Said did provide reasons for talented and resourceful younger scholars with a taste for the political to see a side of the French theorist that Said, somewhat tendentiously, sought to emphasize in his own early writing: one that popularized critiques of the West and placed literary critics themselves as credible arbiters of political value by virtue of the role of language in power (Brennan, 2000: 568).

The model of modernity implied here is as relatively familiar as the one formed around "Traveling Theory" and real presence. But the derivation of the details is not familiar, indeed, it is unfamiliar enough to be breathtaking and to invite that willing suspension of disbelief that constitutes poetic faith, as Coleridge memorably put it. The pity of it is that from time to time Brennan does not have much that is penetrating to say about the author himself. His scattered comments on the constant pummeling Said has received amount to less than one instance.

> The finesse of scholarship is, as it were, made naked here; its very formidability and grandeur bears an inversely proportional relationship to the more basic questions that prejudice makes elusive: why is one only an "Oriental" in the West, but never in the Orient itself? Why have the subjects never been given (as Said was to put it in a later essay) "permission to narrate"? (Ibid., 582).

The question raised above demands an answer in the form of another question—namely, How are we to conceive of a practical distinction between the writer as writer and the person who has a personality, suffers, and has a psychology? To my mind, the condition of the writer and what he or she writes about go hand in hand; they suggest an unconscious desire to belong, a feeling that grows more apparent in Said's late style.[4] Unfortunately, because he takes Said's almost adopted home at face value, Brennan does not even entertain the possibility of rebelliousness. Said, whose directness and sincerity of approach are the hallmarks of his intellectual presence, even though he can be scathingly ironic in his attacks on imposture and fraud, is well aware of his power to generate provocative and expressive ideas that seem now and then to escape America's dominion entirely, and to assume the outlines of a separate world altogether. In objectifying cultural movements whose currents and transformations he has chronicled with unparalleled mastery, he was able from there to rise to a theoretical vision that is incomparably elegant and stirring still.

I would like to take Brennan further than he is willing to go, although the analogy with *authorization* is his, not mine. "The Illusion of a Future" declares itself to be a belated recognition that something should or could have been said about the intention and method of writing *Orientalism,* the greatness of which is measured by the nature of the events to which its concepts summon us or upon which it enables us to ponder. So the unique, exclusive bond between Orientalism as a creative discipline and *Orientalism* as a great book must be tested in its finest details. Great in what way? is the question. If it is nearly a quarter of a century too late to be a manifesto, then it is rather too soon to look like a summa, given that postcolonial theory's exponents are still in productive midcareer. "Said perceives his work as heir to," Dirlik shrewdly notes, "and continuous with, the critique of colonialism by an earlier generation of intellectuals who played seminal roles in articulating the tasks of anti-colonial politics and culture in the process of national liberation" (2001: 10). The matter of influences is rehearsed in the narrative and debts acknowledged to some of the familiar fellow spirits, such as Frantz Fanon, Walter Rodney, Amilcar Cabral, and C. L. R. James. There is also Raymond Williams, to be heard most obviously in Said's predilection for "lived experience," and E. P. Thompson, whose determination to remember the overlooked figures of the past is affirmed (though with qualifications) by Said as a formative model for his own work. Commenting on the role culture has played in the spread of imperialism, Said writes,

> If it is embarrassing for us to remark that those elements of a society we have long considered to be progressive were, so far as empire was concerned, uniformly retrograde, we still must not be afraid to say it. When I say "retrograde" I speak here of advanced writers and artists, of the working class, and of women, whose imperialist fervor increased in intensity

and perfervid enthusiasm for the acquisition of and sheer bloodthirsty dominance over innumerable niggers, bog dwellers, babus and wogs, as the competition . . . also increased in brutality and senseless, even profitless, control. What enables us to say all of those things retrospectively is the perspective provided for us in the twentieth century by theoreticians, militants, and insurgent analysts of imperialism like Frantz Fanon, Amilcar Cabral, C. L. R. James, Aimé Césaire, Walter Rodney, plus many others like them, on the one hand, and on the other hand, by the great nationalist artists of decolonization and revolutionary nationalism, like Tagore, Senghor, Neruda, Vellejo, Césaire, Faiz, Darwish . . . and Yeats (1990: 72–73).

There are also, appropriately, some surprises. One might not have thought of Memmi and Laroui as exemplary precursors, but here they are; and the appearance of Auerbach took me even more by surprise, though as with the best of Said's conjuring tricks, the outcome is perfectly obvious once he has performed it. Auerbach seems right, especially after he has been cloned with Faiz Ahmad Faiz and acquired a hold on the world that his more purely literary conjurings might not otherwise attain. It is Auerbach's presence that anchors the pervasive question of displacement, which is seen as common to his exile to Istanbul during the war, his act of homage to the texts of a literary tradition from which he had been exorcized (his "cultural catholicity").[5]

Just as with Auerbach, all the evidence we have about Said the exile and Said the reader-interpreter is that he has an uncanny power with individual phrases or themes whose combined potential he can understand at a glance. "*Orientalism* Now," a brilliant study by Gyan Prakash, reveals how Said's creative powers derive from his capacity for finding (*inventio*), fetching out, and knowing how to use all the combinations of which a given phrase is capable. In his deliberate, patient, overwhelmingly plotted, and elaborated text, Prakash is Brennan's exact opposite. If Brennan is to be admired for his normativity, Prakash is to be lauded for his eccentricity. His critique of Said ought to be fleshed out so that we may appreciate the scientific basis of his thesis, given the way that postmodern life, with its brittleness of response, noisy disruptions, and drastic impoverishment of experience, has thrown us out of kilter.

Like a mathematician with a rare insight into the heart of natural numbers, what their basic properties are, the way they cohere, combine, and behave in groups, Prakash sees into the Oriental system, discerning the articulation of its language as well as its potential for concentration, expansion, expression, and elaboration. He is most perceptive in demonstrating that, taking an almost random selection of notes in a given discipline, say, anthropology, Said is able to put the selection through every permutation and also to keep those combinations occurring together according to a rigorous set of rules over which he has complete mastery.

Edward Said's *Orientalism* has lived a seditious life. Since 1978, when it launched an audacious attack on Western representations of the Orient, the book has breathed insurgency. Its history is now inseparable from the several condemnations it provoked from some and the high praises it elicited from others. Denounced as an uncharitable and poisonous attack on the integrity of Orientalist scholarship, it opened the floodgate of postcolonial criticism that has breached the authority of Western scholarship of Other societies. The hallowed image of the Orientalist as an austere figure unconcerned with the world and immersed in the mystery of foreign scripts and languages has acquired a dark hue as the murky business of ruling other peoples now forms the essential and enabling background of his or her scholarship. The towering and sagely images of men like William ("Oriental") Jones have cracked and come tumbling down from their exalted spaces. This iconoclastic effect of Orientalism remains one of its most enduring influences, arousing some to an unrelenting hostility to the book while inciting others to mount further assaults on the authority of Western scholarship of the Other (Prakash, 1995: 24).

The magnificence of Said's narrative, as Prakash amply shows, its polyphonic ingenuity, and its steady way with counterargument square with his awareness of the problem of representing another culture. One cannot help but notice how abundantly they demonstrate Said's sense of responsibility to the public, his affiliation with a cause, a unified position he maintains in the midst of conflicting posts. Whether it be poststructuralism, postmodernism, postcolonialism, or postanything, they all represent a sort of spectacle. Those hoping for a weightier, more incisive input may find solace in the narrative of *Orientalism*. Prakash makes the point with flair:

> More than anything else, what counts for the extraordinary impact of *Orientalism* is its repeated dissolution of boundaries drawn by colonial and neo-colonial Western hegemony. The book ignited an intellectual and ideological conflagration by its insistent undoing of oppositions between the Orient and the Occident, Western knowledge and Western power, scholarly objectivity and worldly motives, discursive regimes and authorial intentions, discipline and desire, representation and reality, and so on. Violating disciplinary borders and transgressing authoritative historical frontiers, *Orientalism* unsettled received categories and modes of understanding. Its persistent and restless movements between authorial intentions and discursive regimes, scholarly monographs and political tracts, literature and history, philology and travel writings, classical texts and twentieth-century polemic produced a profound uncertainty (Ibid.: 21).

Like Raymond Williams, Said uses logic and paradox to diagnose and subvert, but unlike Williams, he has managed at last to come in from the cold. As a result, it is scarcely surprising that his engaging narrative has more than a touch of "mission accomplished" about it, the suggestion of a gate finally wide open.

However, neither Brennan nor Prakash is sufficiently concerned with the nature of the concept of 'Orientalism as reality'. They have preferred to think of it as a given knowledge or representation that can be explained by the faculties able to form it (abstraction or generalization) or employ it (judgment). They both teeter between different affirmations without redefining the concept of Orientalism that is not given; it is created; it is to be created. It is not formed but posits itself in itself—it is self-positing.[6] It would be pleasant to linger over these and other cases and tease out the doctrines they illustrate, but what finally interests me about them is their link to the pattern I have been describing, the pattern of demonizing the particularism of the *Other* (either social or anthropological) in favor of a general perspective that claims to be universal and that has the advantage of disturbing no one because it is at once safe and empty. What this means is that Brennan and Prakash fail to understand how creation and self-positing mutually imply each other because what is truly created, from the living being to the work of art, say, from Delacroix to *Femmes d'Alger dans leur apartement*, thereby enjoys a self-positing, as an aesthetic characteristic by which it is recognized. The concept of Orientalism as analyzed by Said posits itself to the same extent that it is created. In this sense, *Orientalism* is not post-Kantian—that is, it is not an *encyclopedia*—but stands for a modest task of a *pedagogy* of the concept. It contemplates, reflects, and communicates its findings to the members of its constituency and to those sitting on the outside of the fence. Take one meaning of *Orientalism* as a linguistic index: Arabia is a possible world, but it takes on a reality as soon as Arabic is spoken or Arabia is spoken about within a given field of experience, say, perfume or belly dance or terrorism.[7] This is very different, Said tells us, from the situation in which Arabia is realized by becoming the field of experience of domination and/or misrepresentation itself. Here, then, is a concept of the '*Other*' that is distorted and deliberately deformed by the West so that it may appear inferior. It is in this sense that Said thought anew the discipline of Orientalism. It is also in this sense that *Orientalism* resembles the (*new*) *idiot* as conceived by Nicholas de Cusa.[8] "The *new idiot* will never accept the truths of history. The *old idiot* wanted to account for what was or was not comprehensible, what was or was not rational, what was lost or saved; but the *new idiot* wants the lost, the incomprehensible, and the absurd to be restored to him. The *old idiot* wanted truth, but the *new idiot* wants to turn the absurd into the highest power of thought"—in other words, to create, to invent in Vico's sense of the word.[9] The old idiot wanted to be accountable only to reason, but the new idiot, closer to Job than to Socrates, wants account to be taken of "every victim of History." To adapt freely from Deleuxe and Guattari, these are not the same concepts insofar as the *new idiot* will never accept the truths of history.[10] That in essence is Said's critical attitude and position vis-à-vis the discipline of Orientalism, which, interestingly enough, totally eludes both Brennan and Prakash. Neither of them sees the death of experience or the spread of Western hegemony in the region during the global era, which Said sets up not only for the sake of analytic clarification but also for distancing himself from the old school that sees the Orient as a static block, frozen in time.

Certainly, there is a sense in which Said was struck by the consensus among those working in the field of Orientalism during periods of what Thomas Kuhn came to call "normal science."[11] It is not just that they accept the same theories and data, but they also have a shared conception of how to proceed in their research, a tacit agreement about where to look next. There is agreement about which new problems to tackle, what techniques to try, and what count as good solutions. It is rather as if the practitioners in a particular discipline, say, Oriental studies, are covertly given copies of a book of rules, the secret guide to research in their field. But no such rulebooks exist. Said, like Kuhn before him, wanted to find out what does the job of the rules that are not there in the first place. In the process, what he found was that the so-called experts on the Orient learned to proceed by example rather than by rule. They are guided by what Kuhn terms their "exemplars," or certain shared solutions to problems in their speciality, like the problem sets that science students are expected to work through. (*Exemplar* captures the most important sense of Kuhn's famous multivalent term, *paradigm.*) The function of problem sets is not to test students' knowledge, Kuhn adds, but to engender it. Similarly, exemplars guide research scientists in their work, for although, unlike rules, they are specific in content, they are general in their import. (Arabs are lazy, tricky, bloodthirsty, vindictive, irrational, antimodernist.) Those so-called scholars will choose new problems that seem similar to the exemplary ones, will deploy techniques similar to those that worked in the exemplars, and will judge their success by the standards the exemplars exemplify.

The idea of the coordinating and creative power of exemplars provided Said with the basis for his general model of how Oriental studies developed. Any new inquiry into the discipline must, he says, do without exemplars to start with and hence without coordination of normal science. If suitable exemplars are eventually found, normal science can proceed. But exemplars sow the seeds of their own destruction, since they will eventually suggest problems that are not soluble by the exemplary techniques. This leads to a state of crisis and in some cases to a scientific revolution, where new exemplars replace the old ones, and another cycle of normal science begins.

This finding brings us back to the original claim: What scientific truth is not, according to Kuhn, is an accurate representation of the world as it is in itself. Scientific theories represent a world, but one partially constituted by the activities of the scholars themselves. This is not a commonsensical view, but it has a distinguished philosophical pedigree, associated most strongly with Kant. The Kantian view is that the truths we can know are truths about a "phenomenal" world that is the joint product of the "things in themselves" and the organizing, conceptual activity of the human mind. Where Kant held that the human contribution to the phenomenal world is invariant, Said's view is that it changes fundamentally across scientific investigations. This is what he meant by his statement that, after his inquiry into Oriental studies, the discipline changed. The relevance of *Orientalism* to the student of the colonial encounter is thus proclaimed: it is Said's view that Western scholars have for a long time been putting their knowledge to the service of power and been involved in a discourse for "dominating, restructuring, and having authority over the Orient" (Said, 1997: 3). Scholarship of this kind enabled the colonization of the Orient, and Western writers and artists (Flaubert, Delacroix, Gide, Kipling, and others) were implicated, willingly or unwillingly, in an act of appropriation and subjugation. To take one example: Delacroix's *Femmes d'Alger* illustrates the point all too well.

The painting shows the gaze as it relates to the Other of the *Other*, the detritus of social strata, the leftovers, the nameless Arab females bathing in their private quarters. In their literal embodiment, these women are placed *inside* their *(mi)lieu* where they are constantly under surveillance from a central male vantage point: that of the artist. Said makes the point with force:

> [I]n the works of Delacroix and literally dozens of other French and British painters, the Oriental genre tableau carried representation into visual expression and a life of its own (which this book unfortunately must scant). Sensuality, promise, terror, sublimity, idyllic pleasure, intense energy: the Orient as a figure in the pre-Romantic, pretechnical Orientalist imagination of late-eighteenth-century Europe was really a chameleonlike quality called (adjectivally) "Oriental." But this free-floating Orient would be severely curtailed with the advent of academic Orientalism (1978: 118–19).

In such an arrangement, those under observation are literally scrutinized in detail and, at the psychological level, made constantly aware of the ever-present, unverifiable possibility that they are being gazed at all the time. This spatial arrangement, Foucault once argued, merely concretized a more diffuse societal practice in which the dominant watched the dominated. These types (Delacroix and others) belonged to a system, a network, an enterprise of representations. Thus "all designation must be accomplished by means of a certain relation to all other possible designations. To know what properly appertains to one individual is to have before one the classification—or the possibility of classifying—all others" (Foucault, 1970: 138).[12] Intermediate to these essentially panoptical variants is what ought to be identified as the internalization of the gaze—the disposition to make of oneself an object that can be observed without detrimental consequences—in a counter-logic of affirmative self-display.

Seeing is dependent on looking, which is itself an act of choice. The objects of our looking in *Femmes d'Alger* are not simply things but the relationships that exist between things, and between things and ourselves. Every look establishes a particular relationship between ourselves and the world we inhabit, and it is at the same time highly personal, reflecting the concerns of the viewer, the bearer of the look. There is an implicit affinity between Said's interpretation of the look and Sartre's in *L'Être et le néant*, a look that is dialectical, going with the assumption that we (the natives), too, are looked at, that we, too, become objects of the gaze of others.[13] In Franz Hals's portrait of the *Old Men's Almshouse in Harlem*, the Regents, as John Berger perceptively notes, look back at the painter, whom they see as a social inferior, even a pauper. However, he must strive to see them as objectively as he can, to avoid the temptation of seeing them as a poor man might naturally see them: eyes fixed on his rich clients with envy, contempt, or flattery. The same cannot be said of Delacroix in *Femmes d'Alger*. For the painting stresses the representation of the native nude, the naked Algerian woman as a recurrent subject for painting, which reflects the imbalance of power between the Western White male, master of the gaze, and the dominated native female, object of the gaze, an imbalance accentuated by the probability that the future owner of the painting would also be Western and White and male (and clothed). Berger goes on to argue that, because an oil painting is typically a commodity, it transforms "the look of the thing it represents" into a commodity. Hence there is an analogy between "possessing" and "the way of seeing which is incorporated in oil paintings" (2002: 322). He cites Levi-Strauss as observing that "it is this avid and ambitious desire to take possession of the object for the benefit of the owner or even of the spectator which seems to me to constitute one of the outstandingly original features of the art of Western civilization" (ibid., 411). Berger himself suggests that the norms of oil painting—"its own way of seeing"—were not established until the sixteenth century, remaining unchallenged until they were undermined by Impressionism and then, at the beginning of the next century, overthrown by Cubism. If this were true, however, Cubism should have changed not only the concept of 'painting' but also the relationship of art to property and possession. It would be more accurate, perhaps, to say that cubism changed an entrenched way of seeing and thus created a new way of looking, as a complex and multifaceted image was conceptually integrated by the viewer.[14]

Representing female form in paint is not just creating an image based on what Fraunhofer calls the "laws of anatomy" (1991: 21). It is also the painter's attempt to steal nothing less than God's secret, to master a sexuality posed as radically Other, as a mysterious essence and metaphysical ground of being; or, to return to the terms of Lacan's "Dieu et /la/Jouissance de la femme," the artist is in thrall to the mystery of sexual difference; God's secret is that "face of the female Other," the God face as supported by feminine *jouissance* around which male (Western artist and spectator) fantasy hopelessly turns in pursuit of an ever-elusive knowledge (it will be recalled that one of Lacan's illustrative examples in *La sexualité féminine* is a work of art, Bernini's sculpture of St. Teresa).[15] Closer to home, this may also remind us of Baudelaire's confession of artistic "impotence" in the poem "Un fantôme": "Je suis comme un peintre qu'un Dieu moqueur / Condamné à peindre, hélas! sur les ténèbres."[16] *Femmes d'Alger* is thus a painting in which Western White male artistic and Eastern erotic interests converge in a scopic regime of *pouvoir-savoir-plaisir*. It is a domain of violence and transgression in that it poses a challenge to all laws of anatomy and in that it is beyond the pleasure principle. Indeed, the relation of the (White) male artist to the Algerian (female) nudes is not just one of sexually interested looking (wanting what he paints) but also of looking at sexuality (wanting a knowledge and aesthetics he can put into paint). It is in this sense that the painter is said to be a painter and nothing but a painter, with color seized as if just squeezed from a tube, with the imprint of each hair of his brush, with this blue that is not an aqua blue but a liquid paint blue. Female nakedness is, of course, another figure in the representation of the female's sexuality; it torments the artist by virtue of being a visual *zero*.

Here then is a painting about a crisis of representation, where the essential, attempted move by the artist is not in fact beyond the figure toward abstraction but rather deep into the figure and its "secret" life, from the surface forms of "anatomy" to the *inside* of flesh, to the pulse and rhythms of blood felt by the male artist. The painting is also a strong marker of the disparate carnality of vision itself in that it bespeaks a message about a brutal colonial regime and the oppositions that criss-cross it.[17]

Of course, as Lacan points out, the viewer's eye is another sphere caught in this crossfire.[18] It is not that the viewer, seeing the painting from the same space, has absorbed a different aspect of the work (a portrait of Arab women taking a bath). The space of spectatorship itself has become transformative and contradictory. The work of art is caught in a double historical frame with contending focal points. As the painting circulates, the culture of France becomes a palimpsest of the colonial destruction of another culture—namely, the Algerian. Where the male viewer's gaze and the females' downcast look cross, there is no parallelism, no equidistance. We are at the critical point of contesting histories and incommensurable subjects of humanity (Bhabha, 1992). Or, to put it differently, the gaze of the master comes to be reinscribed in terms of, or in connection with, the enslaved or the colonized. The artist, in attempting to appropriate the private stare at the Algerian female, renders his gaze a public duplication of the divine glance. And by so doing, he establishes himself as ultimately different from all the rest of us viewing the painting. Delacroix is *sui generis*. It is this unmarked, privileged, and private, in Derrida's wording, "différAnce qui écarte le sujet de l'objet" that marks the artist's special stare.[19] It does not, however, make him a private person, even if it means that in public he also bears another body, his invisible body, the body of his gaze.

There is very little consent to be found in the fact that the Western artist's encounter with the naked body of the Oriental female produced a widely influential model of Arab women who never spoke of themselves; they never represented their emotions, presence, or history. *He* spoke for and represented them. *He* was White, male, colonizer, outsider, and these were historical facts of domination that allowed him not only to possess the women artistically but to tell his Western constituency in what way they were "typically Arab": soft, mellow, mysterious, voluptuous, devious, easy to penetrate (Said, 1979).

Men like Delacroix, however, suffer not just from distress at the strength of their own passions but from an endemic dread of regressing into infantile vulnerability. The danger of the sexual woman is that she is the same creature whose body bore and nurtured the male child, who having dragged himself away from her apron strings must now reencounter her. His fear of being engulfed or consumed is a terror of returning to helpless dependence, a fear, when it comes right down to it, of oblivion and death. We are just a hop and a skip here from Freud's Oedipus, and only a triple jump from Klein's object relations theory. Either way, psychoanalytic theory indicates to Delacroix that men like him need to wrench themselves from the power of maternally and sexually nourishing women in order to run the world. After all, maleness is a developmental afterthought. We all begin as female, and only some of us develop into males. By analogy, social maleness is a cultivation that needs to be protected from rampantly natural femaleness. "Maleness can be seen as a fragile pose, an insecure facade, something made up, frangible, that men create beyond nature" (Diski, 2001: 12). Here men, valiant but feeble, are fending off entropy itself, standing against extinction in the form of their own innate inner femaleness.

The upshot is that *Femmes d'Alger* is not an isolated instance in the drive to dominate Algeria; it clearly stands for the pattern of relative power between North/South, male/female, us/them that was enabled in the first place. The painting also bears the debris of a culture of domination: its presence in the Western museum today reflects not only the intrusion of a foreign artist into an "exotic" *milieu* but also turns the painting from being a sign in a sensation into a symbol of high art. And although it is independent of its creator through the self-positing of the created, it is nevertheless a bloc of emotions caught on the canvas. "The work of art is a being of sensation and nothing else: it exists in itself," Deleuze and Guattari inform us.

> The material is so varied in each case (canvas support, paint brush or equivalent agent, color in the tube) that it is difficult to say where in fact the material ends and sensation begins; preparation of the canvas, the track

of the brush's hair, and many other things besides are obviously part of the sensation. . . . This is why those who are nothing but painters are also more than painters, because they "bring before us, in front of the fixed canvas," not the resemblance but the pure sensation of a "tortured flower, of a land-scape slashed, pressed, and plowed," giving back "the water of the painting to nature" (1994: 166–67).

In this respect, the painter's position is no different from that of the writer, archi-tect, or anthropologist. They are all part of a system: colonial knowledge gathering, whether ethnography, compilations of lexicons and grammars, or physical surveys.

As we enter the last phase of the exhibition, the tragic history of French domination in Algeria becomes more apparent and the need for the parallax more pertinent, since in the very conventions of presentation, the painting reminds us of a past that knew all too well the colonial violence (of the brush). Said articu-lates the point: "The Orient was Orientalized not because it was discovered to be 'Oriental' in all those ways considered common-place by an average . . . Euro-pean, but also because it *could be*—that is, submitted to being—made Oriental" (1978: 5–6). But more compelling than the logic of anxiety, to be gazed at is to be imprisoned in *le lieu* and/or *milieu* where the encounter between the subordi-nate native and the artist took place. It is from this perspective of unveiling the secret of intrusion that Said's work assumes a monumental importance. This is indeed the new meaning of reference as a form of the proposition and its rela-tion to a system of domination. The operation is a complex variable that depends on a *rapport de force* between the subject/object represented here by the native female and the master artist represented by Delacroix. We may note the anonymity of the subject/object (femmes d'Alger) just like "l'Arabe" in Camus's *L'Étranger*, and the proper name (Eugène Delacroix) standing for a signature placed inside the painting so that an act of authorship may be fully established.[20]

Neither Prakash nor Brennan addresses this perspective of "*double interdit*" even if "The Illusion of a Future" marks out as noteworthy "the view that the imperial absurdities of the high nineteenth century—relatively easy to ridicule in retrospect—live on in the supposedly enlightened technologies of the contempo-rary [world]" (Brennan, 2000: 582). True. For let us not be persuaded, with all the goodwill in the world, that *Orientalism* is just a simple celebration of cultural borders and boundaries collapsing before the transcendence of the neoliberal and "global" vision—an international coterie of the inspired arguing well for the mul-ticultural millennium. The last time such an assumption was made, by Aziz, in E. M. Forster's *Passage to India*, his carefully laid plans to host what he called an "international picnic" at the Marabar Caves went, as we are aware, badly wrong (Bhabha, 1992).

There are of course links among territory, tradition, and peoplehood that serve certain functions of state and governance and bestow an important sense of belonging. But the strong, global version of this relationship can lead to a limiting collusion that returns to the dominant sociocultural paradigms of colonialism. For as we make our global leap—a leap in technology as well as globocracy—we must return to that early form of globalization that the periphery had known for at least 250 years in its different phases as the histories of European expansionism, colonialism, and paternalism (Bhabha, 1993). Much of the scholarly work on the new political and economic order, or what Harry Magdoff has described as "globalization," a system by which a small, financial Western elite expanded its power over the whole globe, inflating commodity and service prices, redistributing wealth from lower-income sectors (usually in the Third World) to the higher-income ones, is compelling to say the least. Along with this, as discussed in astringent terms by Said in the last chapter of *Culture and Imperialism*, there has emerged a new transnational order in which states no longer have borders, labor and income are subject only to global managers, and colonialism has reappeared in the subservience of the south to the north. The global perspective in 1830 as in 2002 was the purview of power. The globe shrinks for those who own it. For the displaced or the dispossessed, the migrant or refugee, no distance is more awesome than the few feet across borders or frontiers (Bhabha, 1992: 88). And in addition to the serendipity of domination, the common enemy is not the kind of oppressor that will acknowledge defeat, not least because it has no properly constituted representatives to sign the treaty on its behalf. Anyway, it already has feet in too many camps. Said goes on to show how the interest of Western academics in a subject such as multiculturalism and postcoloniality can in fact be a cultural and intellectual retreat from the new realities of global power. What we need, he is hinting, is a rigorous political and economic scrutiny rather than a gesture of pedagogic expediency, exemplified by the "liberal self-deception" contained in such new fields as cultural studies and multiculturalism.[21]

Contrary therefore to what Prakash and Brennan maintain in their otherwise compelling and persuasive investigations, *Orientalism*, in its journey round the back of theory—(of misrepresenting the Other as in the case of the Algerian woman), identified itself with the revolt against the sorts of wholeness called "totality" and "totalisation" and associated in the 1980s with perhaps a (mis)reading of Fredric Jameson, Marxism, and Sartre—against the belief, that is, in the accessibility of a social-historical whole determining individual lives or events. Resistance to this notion came from the conviction either that no such wholeness exists (the liberal autonomy position) or that even if it did, we could not know it as such (the hermeneutic instability lobby) and sometimes by both at once. Said himself became well known for wanting "to speak against the market forces and with the deprived, the disadvantaged, and the peripheral" (2000: 442): postcolonial theory, in its early days, emphasized the cinematic bringing to life of the colonial past—avowedly "representational," but giving the effect of the real—while standing against the postmodernist idea that coherent and complete patterns in the past could be determined and articulated. Like a clip of movie footage, the new postcolonial past was wholly there and yet not there and not implicated in any pattern beyond that of its own telling, except by loose association with something in the teller's own place and time that was itself resistant to full knowledge. Colonial history, in this way, became *synchronic*: events were conjured up in densely contextual detail but cut loose from what came before or after. Some said that this was as much of colonial history as we could have in an age that had forgotten how to think historically; others found only another incarnation of "slice-of-life" criticism, now in a mode more fully cinematic than ever.

There is yet another layer of brain-subject that is no less creative than the ones I have been discussing—notably, knowledge as neither a form nor a force, but a function clearly showing the persistence of the maxim: "I function."[22] The subject of Orientalism now appears as an "eject," because it extracts other disturbing elements I want to consider in the next section. The third section of *Orientalism* suggests that Said is not merely dissecting a body of colonial history and knowledge that has become a thing of the past; he contends that the discipline persists into the future as an influential academic tradition that, indeed, affects Western policy and attitudes to the Eastern world even now. If anything, Orientalism as an essential enabling cause of imperialism was—as the title of the relevant section of the book has it—"in full flower" between the wars and had been reincarnated as Middle Eastern studies in Anglo-American universities after World War II. From this vantage point, Orientalist discourse was still perpetuating imperialist doctrines even as the world was fast decolonizing itself. Or, as Said phrased it toward the end of the book: "The fact is that Orientalism has been successfully accommodated to the new imperialism, where its ruling paradigms do not contest, and even confirm, the continuing imperial design to dominate Asia" (1979: 322). One can hardly disagree with such a finding insofar as globalism (another scourge) is meant to be a consciously and conspicuously mediated response by the West to the many identities that sit Janus-faced on the boundary of cultural difference, agonizing over what it means to be subjugated and exploited for copper, uranium, coffee, sand, sun, sex, and other precious commodities. Moreover, 9/11 launched a postmodern warfare that keeps belching so much smoke, sound, and fury, signifying very little apart from the ignorance of those (R. Scott Appleby, Andrew Sullivan, Edward Rothstein, and company) who continue to produce it (Fish, 2002).

II

Said's concept of *Orientalism* as discourse, his view that with all its disciplinary apparatus it creates a relentless systemic pressure on all Orientalists, implies a rigorous determinism. Nowhere in the text is Said explicit about Western opposition or Eastern resistance to the domineering structures erected by Orientalism. And yet within the narrative itself he offers the case of Louis Massignon, who was guided by humanistic impulses, suggesting an alternative to scholarship that blindly or blithely carries on as if it had no concerns except to serve power. Was Said, then, being theoretically inconsistent? And was he oblivious to the narratives of resistance evident often even at the culmination of imperial power? Said dealt with the first question by declaring that he had deliberately designed *Orientalism* not in a linear but in a *contrapuntal* and therefore subversive mode so that it could point to the deterministic nature of Orientalist discourse. Even Foucault, Said pointed out, had described the intellectual's role as fighting "against the forms of power" and had suggested the possibility of "a discourse of struggle," although ultimately and inevitably Foucault allowed himself to be remembered as the "scribe of domination" (1975: 378–79). In *Orientalism*, Said implies that a Massignon was possible because the "determining imprint of individual writers" could never be ruled out (1979: 23). Unfortunately, because he takes Foucault's almost tedious piety at face value, Said does not even entertain the possibility of the archive. Foucault would have been well aware of his power to generate what one critic termed "strange, new, expressive and beautiful ideas" that must seem now and then to assume the outlines of a separate world altogether.

About Said's answer to the second question, I am less sure. In the years that followed the publication of *Orientalism*, Said became even more explicit in his critique of Foucault and confidently asserted his view that resistance has always been and will always be possible. In what is surely one of his most mercilessly biting essays written on poststructuralism—namely, "Criticism between Culture and System," he criticizes Foucault for "more or less [eliminating] the central dialectic of opposed forces that still underlies modern society" (1983: 221). In another widely admired essay, "Traveling Theory," Said takes Foucault to task not only for lending himself to the dictum that "power is everywhere" but also for overlooking the "role of classes, the role of economics, the role of insurgency and rebellion in the society he discusses" (ibid., 244). Even more outspoken is his critique of Foucault in his 1986 "Foucault and the Imagination of Power." Here Said arraigns the French intellectual for his "singular lack of interest in the force of effective resistance" to power and for being "unwilling to grant the relative success of . . . counter-discursive attempts first to show the misrepresentations of discursive power, to show, in Fanon's words, the violence done to physically and politically repressed inferiors in the name of an advanced culture, and then afterwards to begin the difficult, if not always tragically flawed, project of liberation" (Said, 153). In moving away from Foucault, in borrowing from such revolutionary intellectuals as Fanon, Gramsci, and Williams, in taking cognizance of the history of resistance in Africa, Asia, and the Caribbean, in celebrating the resistance literature that originated in the ex-colonies, Said is, in essence, carving a niche for himself and thereby charting a course that would make him not only a leading critic of colonialism but also the champion of the counterdiscourse of theory that Michel Foucault pioneered.

There is another compelling reason for Said's rejection of Foucault. At their meeting in 1979 at Foucault's apartment in Paris, Foucault did not want to participate in a seminar or say anything on Middle Eastern politics. He, instead, spoke of Iran and the revolution there, qualifying it as "very exciting, very strange, crazy." As the years went by, Said would amass facts and quasi-facts about the Palestinian question that would distance him from Foucault. "Finally," he writes, "in the late '80s, I was told by Gilles Deleuze that he and Foucault, once the closest of friends, had clashed fatally because of their differences over Palestine, Foucault expressing support for Israel, Deleuze for the Palestinians. No wonder then that he hadn't wanted to discuss the Middle East with me" ("My Encounter with Sartre," 2000: 14). Foucault, in Said's opinion, would have done better to deal with these matters candidly, instead of blindly siding with Israel. Much more is at work here, and this is why Said is correct to add that last, slightly dissonant observation.

Said's provisional beginning or point of incision in *Orientalism* is not therefore so much a reinscription of the motivations of European mercantile capitalism as the emergence of a new field of knowledge known as Orientalist studies. The concept of a 'field', a 'plane', a 'ground' and an 'utterance' is the fundamental organizing principle in Foucault's writings, and at the simplest level of resonance, Foucault intended a field to mean the formal conditions that make the appearance of meaning possible. One is able to quickly discern the gains of locating knowledge in the field of its historical practice, in that which grants it an official voice, and to discern the political context of power relations in which this voice situates itself. In the process, the notion of a field becomes primarily a notion of space, and Foucault's dominant concern is with the element of space in which language and thought can and do occur. However, Said, in conceiving Orientalist studies the way he did as a "power-in-space," in Gayatri Chakravarty Spivak's phrase (1985: 349), seized a peculiarly effective strategy to make the discipline visible as a monument in the Foucauldian sense—its symmetry of assumptions, metaphors, binary oppositions, even its physical solidity and power of interference. There is a certain ironic fit in the methodological apparatus of a field as applied to the narrative of colonization. Said seems to be gesturing toward the imperial aggrandizement of space—both the outer geographical space of the colonized country and the inner psychic space of the people within the colony. The notion of a field also tends to create startling relationships of similitude and difference between those who are made visible and those who are made invisible. By no means is the diachronic framework denied or obscured; in fact, the Foucauldian field pays attention to the time frame internal to a field (of study).

To consolidate this view, in the first chapter of *Orientalism* Said disrupts the chronology of narrative by intertwining the public speeches of Lord Bulghur, Lord Kromer, and Henry Kissinger (a war criminal as we are now finding out)[23] in order to familiarize the reader with the range of consensus or one-voicedness that is produced and disseminated by the discursive field of Orientalist studies. In fact, the entire first section of the book outlines the scope and sets the stage for a detailed examination of Anglo-French Orientalist scholarship. He is not undertaking a metatext of colonialism, which would contain a model anterior to its historical concreteness. His commitment is to histories rather than to "a grand, enveloping notion of History," to the specificity of the several different colonial histories of the downtrodden. As a result, the corollary of the search for origins is the search for *the* historical model of production-relations and the transition from feudalism to capitalism. Foucault suggests a more modest claim that returns the historian to his role as archivist without the privilege of and the claims to a universal truth: "The historical sense . . . must only be the acuity of a view that distinguishes, distributes, disperses, allows free play to deviations and limits—a kind of view that dissociates, is capable of dissociating itself, and is capable of erasing the unity of that human being who is supposed to carry the view in a sovereign manner toward his past" (1975: 301). Said comments on the constitutive ambivalence toward history evident in Foucault's writings, an ambivalence that stems from a reaction against the diseased historiography of the West (1984: 4–5). The positive side of this ambivalence is a commitment to a new kind of history directed against identity and based on countermemory that parodies monumental history and opposes the theme of history as reminiscence/recognition.

As Said sees it, the antecedents of the opposition between Europe and its exotic *Other* extend back to Aeschylus' *The Persians*. However, his provisional beginning is at the point in European history when the assumptions about identity and *Otherness* are organized, systematized, and institutionalized into a discipline with its own methodological apparatus. His method of approaching the field of Oriental studies, for example, is to grant it the status of a semi-autonomous production of discourse. He problematizes this mode of production not by asking the false question of its "primordial origins" but by making more circumspect inquiries: What are the first emergences of this field? What is its history of institutionalization? What is its characteristic way of approaching its object of study? What relationship does this field posit between the object of its study and the investigator? What are its buried cognitive metaphors, resemblances, depths, and surfaces, in fine, its correspondences?

Said attempts to answer this set of questions thus: the economic, political, and military appetites of nineteenth-century Europe are typified by, rather than attributed to, the method employed by Napoleon and his army of men of letters in the subjugation of Egypt. He tells us how a team of scientists, geographers, historians, and archaeologists compiled, cataloged, and made available a knowledge that was deemed essential for invading and placing Egypt under the imperial gaze. This operation was generally civilizing at "home," and "orientalizing" in the colony. This close alliance and mutual interdependence between scholarly research on the one hand and military administration and state policy-making on the other was such that the scholars, in Said's words, became the "learned division" of the army. In Said's reading of the event, Napoleon's campaign is not the first eruption of desire on the body of the colonial text, but it does mark the systematic impulses in what now becomes discernible as the Orientalist project. Said points to other features in the project that will recur again and again—Egypt becomes a site of desire in the power struggle between France and England, a newly discovered arena for the recovery of national and personal glory. Yet Napoleon's conscious strategy only sought out what was latent in the memories of his adolescence, "the glories that were attached to Alexander's Orient generally and to Egypt in particular" (Said, 1979: 80). Thus, the discovery of Egypt is only a re-vision, an imaginative engagement with the myth of Alexander, Europe discovering the glorious chapter in its own past and laying the foundations for the psycho-social phenomena of Napoleonism.

What differentiates the originary moment (Alexander's Orient) from the retracing (Napoleon's campaign) are the sources of desire—Napoleon's reading of Marigny's historical account and Comte de Voleny's travelog, the summary he makes of these documents in his youthful manuscripts and his written reflections assessing the difficulties in Egypt's annexation, culminating in the monumental twenty-three volumes of the *Description de l' Egypte*. Not only is the campaign and its consequences textual, but in fact the sources of Napoleon's desire belong to "the realm of ideas and myths culled from texts, not empirical reality . . . he saw the Orient only as it had been encoded first by classical texts and then by Orientalist experts, whose vision, based on classical texts, seemed a useful substitute for any actual encounter with the real Orient" (ibid., 80). The value of this textual knowledge in its preceding and postdating the military campaign lies in the way it enabled the military project to acquire currency in cultural practices. Napoleon's preparations involved appeals protesting his benevolence in Arabic to the people, and even took the form of wooing the local Imams into interpreting القرآن (*Al-Qur'ān*) in favor of his invasion because "Napoleon tried everywhere to prove that he was fighting for Islam." What Victor Hugo perceived as Napoleon's tact consisted of a veneration for the language, the commissioning of translations, and a whole technique that Said describes as the "use of the scholars to manage his contacts with the natives" (ibid., 82). The close interdependence between power and knowledge gave impetus to the scientific project in Renan's works and the geopolitical project in Lessep's Suez Canal.

The analogs between the power/knowledge formation in Napoleon's campaign and the power-in-knowledge of the Orientalists in Algeria, for example, repay examination. The scholarship of men such as Jacques Berque, the son of a حاكم (ruler) and *le devoir civilisateur* of the Orientalists in Algeria, consisted of the discovery of manuscripts and translations, the interpretation of religious texts, and the introduction of the printing press, all of which helped "to render [Algeria] . . . completely open, to make it completely accessible to European scrutiny." Not only did this scholarly work contribute to the administrative/military project of Empire building, but it also helped to reduce the native to the manageable proportions of a field of knowledge, just as "Egypt was to become a department of French learning" (1979: 83). My reasons for drawing attention to the relationship of similitude/difference between the Napoleonic project and the Orientalist one is to suggest the implications of Said's thesis—namely, that European political appropriation of the East was not a "sudden, dramatic afterthought 'but' a long and slow process of appropriation . . . transforming itself from being textual and contemplative into being administrative, economic and even military" (ibid., 210). Surely Brennan, whose essay is an invaluable achievement, must have glimpsed something of that dilemma. But this does not appear to be the case, even if he does present all the facts clearly and unambiguously. "The Illusion of a Future" therefore allows the reader to appreciate the immense labor that filled Said's life, but not the method that Said employed to construct *Orientalism*, which he meant as a stone thrown through the window of the West and which has become the model for the struggle to rewrite colonial history.

Brennan also falls short in cracking open the Saidian idea of acting counter to the past, and therefore in the present, for the benefit, let us hope, of a future— but the future is not a historical future, not even a utopian history; it is the infinite Now, the Nune that Plato already distinguished from every present: the Intensive or Untimely, not an instant but a *becoming*. Again, is this not what Foucault called the "Actual"? But how could the concept now be called the "actual" when Nietzsche called it the "inactual"? Because, for Foucault and for Said and also Brennan I presume, what matters is the difference between the present and the actual. The actual is not what we are but rather what we become, what we are in the process of becoming—that is to say, the *Other*, our *becoming-Other* (Deleuze and Guattari, 1977: 130–31).[24] The present, on the contrary, is what we are and, thereby, what already we are ceasing to be. We must therefore distinguish not only the share that belongs to the past and that which belongs to the present but, more profoundly, the share that belongs to the present and the actual (1972: 130–31). It is not that the actual is the utopian prefiguration of a future that is still part of our history. Rather, it is the now of our becoming. *Femmes d'Alger*, for example, is a painting of "indefinite description" where the real is not an already given object, but the point of a gathering cluster of descriptions opening onto the unknown. We need to find that point where the "real" and the imagination of other possibilities are linked to one another as when Proust says the true dreamer is the one who tries to go out and verify something.[25]

Contrary therefore to what Brennan thinks, it is precisely at this theoretical juncture that Said joins Foucault, who rejoins the materialist tradition at the point where he envisions power/knowledge as discernible only in their material, bodily, and institutional practices. Foucault's particular interest is in the material forms that are secreted around a discourse at the exact moment of its institutionalization. Thus, we are made aware of the process by which philology and anthropology acquire the power of self-perpetuation through the archive, the library, the society, and its modern avatar in area studies. Philology in its nineteenth-century manifestation invented a doctrine (unlocking the roots of esoteric languages) and an institutional site. For Said this institutional site, in Ernest Renan's case, consists of the sealed space of pedagogic practice—the classroom in which he instructed the initiate was reinforced by the sealed space of the library and the archive. Language as it circulates in these institutional sites is obsessed by its origins but never questions the privilege of its statement. Said maintains that similar impulses were operative in nineteenth-century anthropology. The discursive hierarchy in de Sacy's writings, for example, posits the relation between the Orientalist and the Oriental as one in which the former writes, whereas the latter is written about. Anthropology is essentialist in its founding presuppositions, for it reduces every discrete act of the Oriental's behavior under study to a predictable, preexisting Orientalist essence. Religious-ethnic categories are the basic unit of analysis, and only secondarily is the social and economic category employed. The arbitrariness of the premises of anthropology in the school of Silvestre de Sacy has been sardonically summarized by Claude Alvarez: the study of the White man is sociology; all the rest is anthropology.

The effectiveness of colonial discourse lies in its ability to veil its "lowly" origins, to make invisible its institutions, and to deflect attention from its material existence. To combat this tendency, Said emphasises the role of nondiscursive elements in constituting a discourse. He speaks of individual texts as utterances in order to call attention to "their status as events, and also their density as things—that is, their duration, and paradoxically, their monumentality, their characters as monuments" (1975: 290). Foucault, however, defines the materiality specific to discourse as follows: "[T]he rule of materiality that statements obey is therefore of the order of the institution rather than of the spatio-temporal localization, it defines the possibilities of re-inscription and transcription—the schemata of use constitutes a field of stabilization" (quoted in *Beginnings*, 1975: 291). This is his original contribution to the materialist conception of discourse. It enables Said to improvise a convincing argument about the growth of institutional sites that accommodated the Orientalists; systematized their endeavour; dictated the schemata of use, prescribed the first law of what can be said; and installed a mode of production that efficiently printed, translated, researched, and funded, until in time it acquired the habit of self-legislation and what Said calls the "habit of infinite self-reference." In the deliberate, patient, overwhelmingly elaborated texture of his work, Said is Foucault's exact opposite.

Said of necessity stands outside, as Brennan amply demonstrates, the philosophical tradition, which Foucault can simultaneously excoriate and embrace with ease. He cannot assume the authorial space of Foucault nor speak from his vantage point. This obvious truth dissolves the question of Foucault's influence on Said. The acknowledgment of this truth in a spirit of freedom enables the detachment with which Said can tell us about the "drama" of Foucault's work, a drama in which the latter "is always coming to terms with language as both constricting horizon and the energizing atmosphere within and by which all human activity must be understood. . . . Foucault . . . has been trying to overcome this tyranny by laying bare its working" (1975: 284). The tyranny of textuality is not binding but a strategic technique of estrangement. For if the Third World subject has been constructed as a semiotic field, and the colonizing impulse works in and through language, then we are not confronted by the tyranny of the already-happened of historical events, but instead we are faced with the possibilities of reinterpretation, revision, and change. In addition, the materiality of a text provides another kind of insertion/intervention by the Third World scholar. In *The World, the Text, and the Critic*, Said provides his own definition of textuality: "A text is a being in the world and has ways of existence that are always enmeshed in circumstance, time, place and society; in short, they are in the world, and hence are worldly" (1983: 165). The upshot is that the materiality of a text is liberating precisely because it is conditioned by usage, capable of being appropriated, and contains a discursive space in which each reader and writer can assume the subject functions.

Said's debt to Foucault therefore lies in learning a way of looking at language that discloses how it permits, legislates, and perpetuates discriminations of the Other and the Same. "This idea of differences" Said says, "can be theoretically extended to include differences among societies" (1975: 300). By contrast, Spivak has taken a somewhat more aggressive position—namely, that Foucault's study of the marginalized *is not* informed by the aggrandizement of space through imperialism, from which she concludes that Foucault's case studies of mental illness, clinical practice, the prison, sexuality, and the rise of the human sciences are "screen-allegories that foreclose a reading of the broader narratives of imperialism" (1999: 78). Such a serious omission has the "effect of consolidating the ideology of imperialism" and the illusion that analysis of any space in the West can be self-contained. Said is not alone in defining his position against and in relation to Foucault. The disruptive power of his rewriting the nineteenth-century *épistème* in *Orientalism* lies in the way he is able to read off the assumptions of its originating disciplines (philology, anthropology, Darwinism, the romantic cult of subjectivity, the beholding eye) and implicate them in the project of naturalizing imperialist power. As a result, he continues to be misunderstood as proscribing a will to power in all Orientalist texts when he only meant to suggest the suspicion of a relationship. In the course of his narrative, Said pauses to appreciate the humanist tradition within Orientalism in the persons of Raymond Schwab, Louis Massignon, Eric Auerbach, and Leo Spitzer. Yet the consequence of *Orientalism* has been to lay fissures of suspicion along the entire length of nineteenth-century discourses. The book's power to rupture, by posing what Terry

Eagleton calls the "genuinely theoretical question . . . (which) is always violently estranging, a perhaps impossible attempt to raise to self-reflexivity the very enabling conditions of a range of routinized practices" (1990: 89) can be gauged in the following paragraph:

> *Orientalism* is important because it addresses issues which are (or ought to be) central to the self-conception of scholars who are professionally social-ized in and work in one culture but who devote themselves to the study of another culture. . . . The essential issue he grapples with—and for which he ought to be read, whether all his arguments succeed or not—is the problem of what might be called the affiliations of knowledge. . . . Now, in the final analysis, even an ardent proponent of Said's critical approach would do well to decide where it must all end. . . . One can only go on protesting against the tyranny of the document or of language itself for so long; then one either has to reach some sort of agreement with oneself and get on with the scholarly work at hand, or else one must face up to the fact of ultimate inexpressibility and depart from the scene of the struggle—into silence or into some other walk of life (Kapp, 1987: 481—84).

The sense of paralysis evident in the above passage is specific to Western schol-arship that feels besieged by Said's potent question: How is an *épistème* of world view conveyed by certain relations of power, and what is the political imperative behind it? It is for the apologists of neocolonialism and the researchers advancing under its protection (in order to refine what Spivak calls the methods of "efficient information retrieval") to refuse the power/knowledge equation (1981: 386).

What Spivak ignores, however, is that the continual play between power and knowledge can only cease when the Third World scholar captures the institu-tional sites that churn out information about it. Until the Third World becomes self-determining both in its political institutions and in the institutions of civil society, Said's question is a necessary warning and a political imperative. There-fore he cautions against the tendency to extrapolate a method from Foucault's writings that can serve as a "pass key" to unlock texts (Spivak, 1975: 284). If Foucault's textual practice has any ideological core, it lies in his conception of the social function of the intellectual, which necessitates a dedication to uncovering the categories of *Otherness* that the West represses, outlaws, and commits to the margins. Said seems to be hinting that the definitive Marxist critique of Foucault's work has yet to be made. As a preliminary, however, it is no pretence to note that Said stands *outside* the culture wars and perceives, for his purpose, not an irrecon-cilable difference between Marxism and Foucault, but a broad consensus:

> I do not think Foucault and Deleuze are unjustified in seeing their philos-ophy of decenterment as revolutionary, at least in its reliance upon an

intellectual who views his role within his discipline and its institutional supports as an adversary one. The intellectual makes it his task to controvert the dynastic role thrust upon him by history or habit. . . . Here Foucault and Deleuze rejoin the adversary epistemological current found in Vico, in Marx and Engels, in Lukacs, in Fanon (1975: 284).

This is the role of the intellectual in opposition as embodied by Fanon, who writes: "Colonialism is not a thinking machine, nor a body endowed with reasoning faculties. It is violence in its natural state, and it will only yield when confronted with greater violence" (1964: 37). The statement occurs at the beginning of a lengthy meditation on the role of the intellectual in the process of decolonization. Fanon is concerned both with the reactionary consequences of the intellectual training of the colonialist bourgeoisie and the dilemma of the native intellectual. His prescription of deeds (not words) obviously refers to what he calls "violence in action," but his meaning can also be extended to, and be coterminous with, Foucault's idea of rupture by theoretical activism. "If I have so often cited Fanon," Said adds, "it is because more dramatically and decisively than any one, I believe, he expresses the immense cultural shift from the terrain of nationalist independence to the theoretical domain of liberation" (1993: 268). This shift entails a transformation of national into social and political consciousness, transcending the nation in its compass, and aiming at some kind of universalist humanism.

On a rare occasion, Said, in discussing the role الإنتفاضة (Intifada) should play in the liberation of Palestine, reminds us of Fanon,

[W]e should present the *Intifadha* as an alternative, an emergent formation, by which on the simplest level Palestinians under occupation have decided to declare their independence from the occupation by providing different, not so much models, but different forms for their lives which they themselves administer, develop and have in fact created. . . . It's a cultural movement which says that we are not going to cooperate, we can't any longer live under the occupation, and therefore we must provide for ourselves. . . . So what has happened is that now with the expropriation of land, with a domination of the network of settlements defended by the Israeli Army, there is the possibility for the Palestinians to provide an agricultural alternative to that one. That is to say, the use . . . of private gardens and houses and the creation of a food delivery service through the collectivization of bakeries . . . places on the West Bank . . . have become in effect liberated zones (Wicke and Sprinker ,1992: 237–38).

Several possibilities are opened up here by Said's alignment with Fanon's idea of liberation versus independence and raiding of the adversarial traditions of the

West. Foremost among them is the strategic positioning of the Third World intellectual who is able to maintain a perceptual distance vis-à-vis the official discourse, which is located far enough away for him or her to see its rupture and near enough to imagine another *épistème*. The maintenance of this perceptual distance explains the dichotomy between Foucault's antihumanism and Said's chosen label of a humanist. Many of us have felt disappointed in Said's allegiance to the nomenclature of humanism, because in the contentious scenario he draws, the humanist stance can only be read as weak-kneed liberalism. It is true that elsewhere Said has commented on the anomalies of choosing the humanist label "a description for which I have contradictory feelings of affection and revulsion" (*Reflections on Exile*, 2000: 123). The problem here involves much more than Said's political position; it has to do with the range of perceptual distance that the critic of colonialism accommodates himself or herself in, with regard to his or her situation in history and the mutations of his or her culture. Thus Said's beleaguered position as an academic fighting for the human rights of his fellow Palestinians from within the privileged world of the American academy makes the luxury of Foucault's antihumanism impossible.

This drive to merge the separate elements of humanism and dissidence on the one hand and aesthetics and resistance on the other has its attractions, but then the question arises: What would it mean for Said's thesis to again become experimental? Do human meanings remain as deliquescent as ever? Can we at all afford to rescue the question of subjectivity from predefined positions? The answer to this set of questions may be found in Sara Suleri's celebrated essay, "The Secret Sharers" (1993), which attempts the impossible. She reminds us of Nietzsche who links together the "lightness" of knowing and its "untimeliness," to give "body" and "space" to the arts and by doing so invents new effects and new precepts, new ways of experimenting and seeing: "One has to be very light to drive one's will to knowledge into such a distance and, as it were, beyond one's time, to create for oneself eyes to survey millennia and, moreover, clear skies in these eyes" (Nietzsche, 1974: 343). This is precisely what the intellectual generosity of *Culture and Imperialism* does. The book is perhaps best characterized by its desire to take everything into its orbit with both lucidity and compassion. The result is at its best dazzling and at its worst dizzying: in a multilayered narrative, Said moves with grace through a compendium of cultural readings. Any reader prepared to reflect on the urgency of erudition that impels his or her drive to *reinvent* theory will be bound to recognize the analytic skill with which Said represents the world to the text and to the critic. "One of the most redundant questions that could—and will—be asked of this project," Suleri perceptively notes,

> concerns what it may add to, or subtract from, Said's *Orientalism*. That the two are intellectually related but structurally completely autonomous works may be ignored. Whereas *Orientalism* attempted to reconstruct the

plot through which the "Orient" was made into a textual object, *Culture and Imperialism* concerns the diverse complicities that dictate the mutual histories of Orient and Occident. The sequel, in other words, belies easy misconceptions of *Orientalism*, although few contemporary critics have seemed prepared to acknowledge that the very flaws of *Culture and Imperialism* make it an exemplary articulation of developments that must occur in cultural criticism (1993: 31).

On a practical level, Suleri goes on to argue, the introductory chapter proposes a much-needed reconsideration of the discipline known as "comparative literature." As previously secure distinctions between nations and national literatures unravel in an ethnically torn world, teachers of obsolete chronologies have no recourse but to turn to a broader reading of the problem of culture. While her reading belongs to the immediacy with which she brings out the irreducible tension between center and margin, Suleri can also be read not only for her recondite and deep knowledge but also for the minute scrupulosity of its exactness, its wit.

The radical challenge to her reading of Said lies not in "thinking" but in "looking." It is a maxim akin to Wittgenstein's cry: "Don't think, look!" Today we need to stop "thinking" so as to start again to *see* what we cannot yet describe since we think too much. We need an art of description, of what is happening to us (Arabs and Muslims) particularly in the aftermath of 9/11. It is in this sense that Said's argument differs from standard models of cultural studies in his acute awareness of the interplay—or, more grimly, the incessant give and take—between imperialism and culture. To cite Conrad, an author who has provided Said with his most abiding and obsessive metaphors, Said demonstrates how the will to empire and the accident of culture are invariably "secret sharers" of each other. In *Heart of Darkness*, Marlow's narrative method is famously described as a technique that allows for no heart of meaning at all: "[T]o him, the meaning of an episode was not inside like a kernel but outside, enveloping the tale which brought it out only as a glow brings out a haze" (Conrad, 1993: 32). A similar claim could be made for Said in *Culture and Imperialism*. He does not exactly propose a thesis and then proceed to prove it. Rather, the narrative embodies its argument so that it becomes impossible to determine where theory ends and exemplification begins. As a consequence, the reader is offered an intensely engaged and richly engaging act of reading, in which there are neither lines of national demarcation nor the possibility of a no-man's-land. This could not be done without an acute sense of historicity: in a certain context, history is all, and the pursuit of culture is by no means an alternative space to the symbolic and actual fact of colonial practice (Suleri, 1993).[26] Said eliminates the segregation between *inside* and *outside* by turning to the canon of British and/or French fiction and demonstrating how completely invaded it is by the functions of imperialism. Such a reading is predicated upon a very obvious issue: in order to study imperialism, one need not simply turn to literary texts that are overtly concerned with questions of empire and its relation to postcolonialism. For every Jane Austen there is a C. L. R. James; for every Rudyard Kipling there is a Salman Rushdie; for every Joseph Conrad there is a Tayeb Salih; for every Albert Camus there is a Malek Alloula.

Having established, in the first half of the book, that domination is about subjugation as much as about profit, Said goes on, in the second half, to address himself to the implications of this insightful question: How was the tradition of textual "Englishness" and/or "Frenchness" formed and upheld by the condition of empire? And such is the *sort* of implicit question that belongs to his twofold response. First, Said articulates the urgency and novelty with which *Culture and Imperialism* poses questions to the study of postcolonialism. "Theoretically we are only at the stage of trying to inventory the *interpellation* of culture by empire . . . as the study of culture extends into the mass media, popular culture, micropolitics . . . the focus on modes of power and hegemony grows sharper" (1993: 81). The list of cultural interplays, in other words, has yet to be compiled. Second, Said offers an interpretive method that he decidedly calls "*contrapuntal* reading," which examines the subtexts that compel imperial narratives. These tales, he suggests, move according to plots that need oceans of imperialism upon which to float their tentative islands of equanimity or outrage. Each of Said's four chapters is divided into textual and interpretive sections, with juxtapositions as diverse as Verdi's *Aida* with Kipling's *Kim*, arriving finally at Camus and modernism. As Suleri has perceptively demonstrated, the texts are hardly unread territory, but they have certainly never been read in this order, or in quite this way. It is true that Said's references to secondary materials are often too hasty and perhaps indiscriminately admiring, but his governing question retains its power: How can we study such literatures beyond the vantage point of "postcolonial testimony"? "The emergence of formerly colonial subjects as interpreters of imperialism and its great cultural works has given imperialism a perceptible, not to say obtrusive identity as a subject for study and vigorous revision. But how can that particular kind of post-imperial testimony and study . . . be brought into active contact with current theoretical concerns?" (1993: 147). In a field dominated by identity politics or turgid abstractions, Said offers a refreshingly lucid alternative. His injunction, simply put, is "read by some other way of reading" as John Berger for instance would have it.

Given that so many works of literary and cultural criticism seem remarkably disinterested in detailed analysis, *Culture and Imperialism* demonstrates a welcome attentiveness to the primary texts themselves. While some of the readings—of *Kim* and Yeats, for example—are familiar material, others—*Aida*—are brilliantly reworked and interwoven. Thus we (as readers of imperial literature) are moved to gratitude by the eloquence with which Said recognizes the historical density of that superb, much-dismissed novel *Kim* and his ability to identify the peculiarities of Kipling's cultural location. His concluding sentences on *Kim* show him at his best and demonstrate how a work of criticism can rise to the power of the text it reads:

> Kipling's choice of the novel form and of his character Kim O'Hara to engage profoundly with an India that he loved but could not properly have—this is what we should keep resolutely as the book's central meaning. Then we can read *Kim* as a great document of its historical moment and, too, an aesthetic milestone along the way to midnight August 14–15, 1947, a moment whose children have done so much to revise our sense of the past's richness and its enduring problems (1993: 151).

Such a passage links Kipling with Rushdie in a gesture of cultural compassion that raises questions rather than pretending to provide answers. *Culture and Imperialism* abounds in such productive links; they defamiliarize even the most familiar of novels and writers. Said's attention to *A Passage to India*, for example, is quickened by his parallel reading of Edward Thompson's important but little-known work *The Other Side of the Medal*. He juxtaposes texts that are both about and vexed by the problem of cultural misrepresentation, but his intention is never to pass literal judgments on the political sagacity of the authors. Instead, Said studies their blindness along with their insight, constructing in the process "hybrid cultural work." He does not stop to linger over the casual aphorism, such as "No more than Forster could Thompson grasp that—as Fanon argued—the empire never gives anything away out of goodwill" (Said, 1993: 211). While such isolated points of analysis may be left undeveloped, however, the sequence of juxtapositions builds a coherence that gives unusual power, especially to the second and third chapters, arguably the book's strongest sections (Suleri, 1993).

Said does not confine himself to canonical texts of imperial literature. He is equally engaged in readings of resistance cultures and postimperial writers and is in continuous dialogue with Frantz Fanon as a figure in postcolonial discourse both as a theorist and as an icon. He serves as the conduit for Said's reading of colonialism. "When Fanon wrote his books, he intended to talk about the experience of colonialism as seen by a Frenchman, from within a French space hitherto inviolable and now invaded and re-examined critically by a dissenting native" (1993: 244). As can be seen in this passage, too much is addressed with an alacrity that is always elegant but is nonetheless urgent. The impetus of the concluding chapter occasionally appears to be a desire to say everything, name all the names that must be named, and range through imperialism, revolution, and postcolonial nationalism. Such a catalog is eminently worthy of genealogical interpretation, but its encapsulation into a single chapter tends to make history a trifle cluttered. Perhaps that is exactly as it should be. What is most remarkable about the later sections of *Culture and Imperialism* is the uncanny democracy Said accords to every subject and every text that rises to the surface of his capacious mind.[27]

The subtlety with which Said reads—in Eqbal Ahmad's phrase—the "pathologies of power" that continue to govern the process of imperialism is itself a subject worthy of study. Said's relation to such critical precursors as Eric Auerbach and Raymond Williams is yet another instance of his engagement in "hybrid cultural work" and underscores the intellectual confidence in his use of the pronoun *we*. In an academic milieu that appears unnecessarily reluctant to speak for collectivities, Said constructs a diverse and dynamic community of texts and writers. His work suggests that the globe rather than the nation can indeed be a fit cultural habitation. "We must expand," he enjoins, "the horizons against which the question of *how* and *what* to read and write are both posed and answered. To paraphrase a remark made by Eric Auerbach . . . our philological home is the world, and not the nation or even the individual writer" (1993: xx). Since our historical moment allows for neither nation nor ethnicity to supply unproblematic identifications of what it means to conceive of community, it is indeed moving to follow the cartography through which Said can locate an "us" that no longer needs a "them." Instead, *Culture and Imperialism* maps out a possible idiom of "us" as a cultural amalgam, one illustrated by the breadth and variety of Said's points of reference.

Few of his readers may share Said's insistence on such an irreversible improvement in the intellectual texture of our times. Most, however, will take sustenance from the implicit burden of *Culture and Imperialism*, in which the voyage in is only another way of articulating the difficult similarity between it and a voyage out. As Lord Jim to the cultural enterprise that much of the academy must now address, Said—to paraphrase Stein's judgment of Jim—voyages in to describe with bravery how that which is very bad is also very good (Suleri, 1993).

III

"It seems," Hannah Arendt once wrote, "as if certain people are so exposed in their own lives (and only their lives, not as persons!), that they become, as it were, junction points and concrete objectifications of *life*" (1992: 11).[28] Caught up by this passion in which life and thought are one and the same, Said's varied yet profoundly coherent intellectual journey continues to place life—in and of itself, and as a concept to be elucidated—at the center. Like Arendt's, Said's personal and political experiences lead to his adjusting his attention as well as his criticism to focus on the modern world, starting with an appropriation of a fundamental ontology that is centered on the "essence of man." In the process, his experiences lead him also to catch glimpses of the beginnings of political actions that are vehicles for a "*who*."[29] Thinking and willing lead him to meditations that are original and profound, meditations that dismantle theory just as they do politics and/or music, and they go on to sketch out a new way of looking at freedom, a way that is specifically Saidian. They also propose a way of articulating multilayered narration (story/history), a way that differs, in its originality, from the formalist theory of narrativity. What remains for us will be the duty to care for the Saidian way of telling and seeing, a way and/or a mind that is because it begins anew in the *plurality* of others and in that condition alone can act as a living thought that surpasses all other activity.

In the end, does not every major cultural critic lay out a new field of immanence, introduce a new substance of being, and draw up a new image of thought, so that there could not be two great critics on the same plane? It is true that we cannot imagine a great critic of whom it could not be said that he or she has changed what it means to think; he or she has "thought differently" as Foucault put it? When we find several theories in the same author, is it not because the theories have changed plane and once more found a new image? We ought to remember Maine de Biran's complaint when he was near death: "I feel a little too old to start the construction again."[30] However, those who do not renew the image of thought are not real thinkers but functionaries who, enjoying a ready-made thought, are not even conscious of the problem and are unaware even of the efforts of those they claim to take as their models. But how, then, can we proceed in theory if there are all these layers that sometimes knit together and sometimes do not?

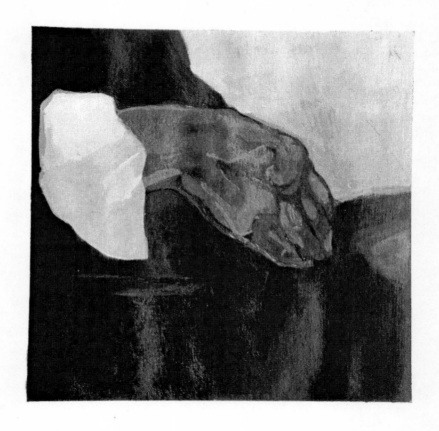

Ahmad Izmer, *Anatomy of Labor: Pen, Piano, and Palestine,* Acrylic on Paper, 31 x 40 cm. © 2002.

CHAPTER THREE

My Homeland, the Text

I am not solely a citizen of Palestine, though I am proud of this affiliation
and ready to sacrifice my life in defending the radiance of the Palestinian
fact, but I also want to take up the history of my people and their struggle
from an aesthetic angle that differs from the prevalent and repeatable
meanings readily available from an unmediated political reading.
　　　　　　　—Mahmoud Darwish, *Memory for Forgetfulness*, 73.

"Memory says: Want to do right? Don't count on me." So writes Adrienne Rich
in a poem from her book *An Atlas of the Difficult World: Poems 1988–1991*, opening
an unpunctuated sequence of horrors: Ireland, Rwanda, Kosova, Palestine:

> I am accused of child death　　of drinking
> 　　　　　　　　　　　　　　blood . . .
> there is spit on my sleeve　　there are phone-
> 　　　　　　　　　　　　calls in the night . . .
> I am standing here in your poem unsatisfied /
> 　　　　lifting my smoky mirror (1991: 43).

Memory's smoky mirror, like the witch's crystal, or the burning glass of the
Aztec god who demands human sacrifice, has become the prime instrument
turned on history by several of the most influential contemporary writers. In its
shadowed and unreliable depths Roland Barthes, James Agee, and Malek Alloula
have searched out their material, reflections of ourselves; and from *After the Last
Sky* to "Living by the Clock," Said, too, has been scurrying for glimpses of troubled
histories.[1] The essays frame a large question about exile and memory, asking to
what extent it is possible for individuals to live with the memory of enormous

107

suffering and how it is possible for an entire community, at the same time, to forget it so quickly. His more specific themes are displacement and homelessness, as experienced by a number of characters—some real and some imagined, some Palestinian and some not—who are forced to leave their country of birth and who find it almost (or in some cases entirely) unbearable to settle elsewhere. Said's tact—in choosing when to record, and when to invent, and in finding a suitable voice (neither too timid nor too intrusive) in which to register his characters' pain—informs not just *After the Last Sky* but also "Palestine, Then and Now," "Between Worlds," and "The Mind of Winter."[2]

Said has distinguished himself by his resistance to pieties; there is a quiet dourness and cussedness in his handling of the material; he pits himself against any kind of received wisdom, including the prevailing feel-good tendency of some Arab Palestinian writing.[3] His ironies work at everyone's expense: no one, Palestinian, Israeli, American, Arab is spared. Questions of national place, of roots, of where one belongs, depend on psychic identifications: where hostility and contempt are projected, where fear springs. Conversely, affinities are elected where sympathy rises, where love happens. Narrative, like a ventriloquist, can dissolve hatreds by deepening understanding: *The Persians*, in which Aeschylus dramatizes the terrible grief of the enemy Xerxes's mother, represents an early instance of this potential. In pursuit of this possibility, Said's works initiate the outsider into what exile means, on a daily basis, for Said himself and many of his people scattered throughout the world. Even so, it remains important, I think, to raise the following set of questions: What is this not being-at-home (*ne pas être-chez-soi*) in language? Does this "disorder of identity" favor or inhibit an amnesia? Does it heighten the desire of memory, or does it drive the genealogical fantasy to despair? Does it suppress, repress, or liberate? It is all of these at the same time, no doubt, and that would be another version, the other side of the contradiction that set us in motion and has us running to the point of losing our breath or our minds.

Another series of questions will need to consider the relationship between photography and writing and whether they convey the dialectic of exile and its overcoming, a double relation of estrangement and reunification. Where does the exile go "after the last sky" has clouded over, after Beirut, Cairo, Amman, the West Bank have failed to provide a home? The ambivalence expressed in this question is also inscribed in the delicate, intricate, and precarious relations of text and image (the *inside*) and (the *outside*), at it were, of the essays. What is particularly interesting here is the interplay between the intensely subjective and the overwhelmingly objective, between the emotional, profoundly "gut" feeling and the portentously historical judgement, in thinking about the loss of home, which can appear in so many different guises: in the choices the author makes—what he chooses to tell and what he elects to withhold, in his mode of address to the reader, in his willingness to allow for the fact that readers come to a book with different expectations, different sensibilities, in his use of material from real life—how carefully he handles the delicate process by which he remembers experience (his own and other people) is transformed into fictional incident; and, of course, in his choice of tone, the establishment of an authorial voice the reader can recognize. The *essay form* plays a central role here insofar as it gives rise to an abstract way to narrate a story, this مسيره (plight) Said jealously calls "his" story, a story which would be solely his.

There is another clue to the way Said sees this existential and perpetual displacement: his prose. He does everything but button his lip; his sentences mimic the histories he is excavating. Indecipherable fragments are picked out of the mud in which they were buried and handed over to be pieced together, making the reader work to comprehend them. In the end, he is a baroque writer, for whom the interest swirls and flares on the mobile and sumptuous verbal surface of both *After the Last Sky* and his other autobiographical works.[4] Said is an elliptical encrypter: what is happening is not what you see, but what you cannot see, until you adjust your perception—Wittgenstein's duck/rabbit. He performs quasi-autistically as he draws the rabbit and makes the duck at the same time. His storytelling manner is flat, his sentences short and bare of ornament; the rhetorical finesse exists entirely in the mimicry of voices he uses to narrate the experience of exile. How this reflects—and indeed extends—Said's inquiry into the history of unbelonging can be seen in the effect of paralysis that the flatness creates. History itself gives its evidence grudgingly, like a damaged child in a case study whose rare and enigmatic utterances must be carefully collected, examined, and pressed to yield meaning, which often enough they stubbornly refuse. The lacunae between them open, but meanings hide. As a result, the essays' population of exiles and immigrants, so many of the undone, appear in the cracks that fissure the clouded mirror Edward Said holds up stubbornly willing memory to articulate something we can perhaps count on, in spite of everything to the contrary.

From this splitting of rejection and a desire to belong emerges the question: How should one write about the "I" in "Between Worlds," "The Mind of Winter," or *After the Last Sky*—a book that, despite its unemphatic method and private grace, aspires to the force of a national epic, akin to the works by Mahmoud Darwish or Hoda Barakat,[5] offering a people their own heritage freshly caught on paper and raised to the heights of poetry? The author and the essays, some of them told with photographs, are hard to place, both for the writer himself and for his readers generally. They do not quite fit any of the fixed categories. They represent therefore to some degree the unclassifiable, the *sui generis*. "The writer acknowledges that he himself is the 'cracked lens,'" W. J. T. Mitchell comments, "unable to see, quite literally, the native country he longs for except in fragmentary glimpses provided by others" (1989: 12). The discussion of such a small body of narratives provides biographical information but barely reveals the linkages between the writer and his life.

I

Writing of exile, Edward Said observes:

The poignancy of resettlement stands out like bold script imposed on faint pencil traces. The fit between body and new setting is not good. The angles are wrong. Lines supposed to decorate a wall instead form an imperfectly assembled box in which we have been put. . . . This child is held out, and yet also held in. Men and women re-express the unattractiveness around them: [They] . . . seem unsettled, poised for departure. Now what? Now where? All at once it is our transience and impermanence that our visibility expresses, for we can be seen as figures forced to push on to another house, village, or region. Just as we once were taken from one "habitat" to a new one, we can be moved again.

Exile is a series of portraits without names, without contexts. Images that are largely unexplained, nameless, mute (*After the Last Sly*, 1986: 12).

Living in between, on the borderline, the anxiety to be elsewhere, itself a source of continual internal debate, is what keeps Said looking forward by always looking back. He hangs there, frozen in time, denied motion, suspended above his وطن (homeland).

Exile is a deceptive subject that paradoxically only achieves intensity if allowed to expand. A measure of luxuriating—or again, a stubborn refusal to lux-uriate—is part of it. Otherwise, one is left only with the bare circumstantial bones of what is apt to appear a circumstantial subject: who, where, what for, how long, how unhappy, how ended? It may even be argued that it is very often not a subject at all but just a filter through which experience is transmuted, something nearly as previous and unget-roundable and translucent as age or mood. It is no sort of kingdom but rather seems to cede territory as one looks at it. Classic Chinese poetry is probably the expression of exile par excellence, but what much of it actually is is another matter: the lamentations of servants (state officials) quite routinely sent away to distant postings as part of their work. Not that this invalidates the expression of feeling. Otherwise, exile would be best represented in a footnote, no more. But to get closer to Said's exile, to hear its complications and to understand its language, one must go back to the *trace*: there is a sense—from the Chinese, from Ovid, from Dante—that exile is at least in part a condition of the imagination, and that is the province of literature. The ultimate irony of exile, Said wants us to believe, is to long for the earlier exile he has been forced to leave, to remember forever the baffling, sudden beauty of that moment when, if only for an instant, the exile had caught himself longing for a home he or she never knew he or she loved.

If, for Salman Rushdie, the novel is the arena where he goes to explore the highest and lowest of humankind, for Edward Said, that arena is undoubtedly the essay, which is able to say something true about exile. To a considerable extent one of the central points made by the Saidian essay is that it, like its author, resists pigeonholing; they both defy classification according to any of the clear-cut boundaries that shape modern academic discourse. As a writer, Said inhabits a complicated, multiple world. An exile who is attached by all his roots to an Arab people and culture, Said has selected the essay form, a swift and well-aimed strike (almost recalling Gramsci and the "virtues" of guerilla warfare), to express the pain of exile. In the essay, the practice of writing is transformed, perverted by an "amoebalike" versatility often held together by little more than the author's voice.

Primarily an urban genre, the essay form allows the author to use himself as a starting point for digressions on the mundaneness of everyday life, while dialoging with an educated, heterogeneous readership. Ironically, the most modern characteristic of Montaigne's essays—their patchwork of quotations—was also its only concession to tradition and authority. The Saidian essay, however, points to the personal; it is distinguished by a fragmentary, aphoristic critical *écriture*, what Barthes aptly called "reflexive text." The displacement of the structural analysis of narrative by the readerly/writerly distinction appears to have also precipitated an internal shift. Whereas the move from Palestine to America may document Said's disaffection with the Occident, the move from genre to antigenre (the essay) engages in cracking open the boundaries of language. A case in point is *After the Last Sky*, which speaks to several different audiences. If some readers are distressed by his insistence on the worldly embroilments of literature, others are upset by his kindness to his foes. Still others are moved by his eloquence and sheer honesty as in the allusion about his debt to his predecessors as well as to his peers. The essay "becomes," Said observes, "an act of cultural, even civilizational, survival of the highest importance" (1985: 6). And as we read on, even as we take á propos with its diverse approach, we are shaken by its secret intimacy, its private risk, its boldness. This writing practice goes far beyond the critic positing himself as judge and jury, as canon maker. It asks ideological, linguistic, ethical questions while declaring itself susceptible; it reveals the restlessness of moving around, the constant breaking up of boundaries, both textual and territorial.

The exclusive concentration on what Barthes terms "vertiginous displacements" from literature to theory and politics reinforces Said's "oppositional" attitude as critic. And if there is an underlying unity in his essays, it is to bring together in one movement, in a single text, modes of discourse that have hitherto been kept on the margins—those of the restless Third World intellectual and those of the Palestinian people, who are constantly in search of an equilibrium on the *outside*. The lawlessness that marks some of the essays resembles the victims that Said writes about: both "orphans" and "aliens" at "home" and elsewhere. The result is a double text that constructs a home, a فلسطين (Palestine), and a narrative. As a practice of writing, the essay is generated from fragments outside established classifications that refuse a fixed center or totalizing scheme. Its composition consists of a heterogenous series "hinged" together by stubbornness, subversion, and containment. In the middle of these crowds of mapped-out solitudes, their myths, fantasies, and experiences, emerges once again the essay. Aimed primarily at a circle of readers in London and New York, as well as in القدس (Jerusalem), the Saidian essay is meant to harness our understanding of an exiled critic who tries to come to grips with reality. But the inward turn of *After the Last Sky*—itself full of stories, even if they are often brief, submerged, and sometimes only implied—not only marks a modulation in register but it also repeats and renews the essay's possibilities as they have been carefully collected, treasured, and cared for, just as the author cares for what he calls "Palestinian traditions" (1986: 23–30). Said alludes in a moving passage to Auerbach writing *Mimesis* in wartime exile in Istanbul, cut off from learned Western libraries, a deprivation that actually enabled the writing of such a bold, vast, composed essay.

It is all the more ironic that Said should attribute Auerbach's *Mimesis* "to the very fact of Oriental, non-Occidental exile and homelessness" (1985: 8). For one could just as easily argue that Said's notion that "reality is an event, a text" is born out of the ruin of another displacement, from the Orient to the Occident this time. But while Said is a victim of a modern exilic condition, Auerbach merely lived in exile to construct a great book: he did not see the recording of exile as the occasion for producing his text. The juxtaposition of the two writers is significant in that Auerbach, the cultivated Western intelligence sitting out the war in the Orient (Istanbul), separated from the scholarly environment, was able to write a great work on literature by reading only the texts, while Said, the Oriental, the Palestinian intellectual, whose locus of activity is the West, finds it more and more difficult to maintain a cultural and political position "outside" the Occident from which, in security, he continues to operate. Moreover, Auerbach's exile is different from Said's, just as Said's commitment to resistance is different from the absence of such commitment in Auerbach's exile. *Mimesis* grew out of a dislocated exilic existence, and while one might want to read it with this condition in mind, most interpreters locate its context with humanity at large, as transcending national boundaries. Said's text is prompted by estrangement, not just exile. This dimension of estrangement is absent from Auerbach's book. Grounded in the analysis (mainly systematic) of passages selected from texts in some nine different languages, ranging from Homer and the Old Testament to Virginia Wolf, *Mimesis* assumes throughout that reality has an objective existence, is open to perception and needs no apologetic inverted commas. Reality can be and is endearingly represented by writers whose work bears the imprint not only of their own individuality but of a particular historical context, a social and cultural milieu. Auerbach's narrative remains, for many readers, one of the great critical achievements of the twentieth century: a work marked not only by its scholarship, breadth of sympathy, and imaginative range, but also by its author's ability to validate his generalizations through scrupulous attentiveness to the smallest details of a text.[6]

Although Said's غربة (exile and estrangement) differs from Auerbach's insofar as it is fraught with an ideology of difference and resistance, it is nevertheless disseminated by the same means—the "essay," which Said regards as itself essential. Criticism, he believes, should be "constitutively opposed to the production of massive, hermetic systems." This being so, "then it must follow that the essay—a comparatively short, investigative, radically skeptical form—is the principal way in which to write criticism" (1983: 26). Suffice it to remark here that the Saidian essay is something of a blend of German and French philosophy. It exemplifies an almost Eurocentric bias; addresses significant questions such as the world forms (the novel), objects (the text), praxis (criticism); draws out clearly the implications and findings; and engages the attention of its readers through a concise format. And while in the German tradition the philosopher is a thinker, in the French tradition the philosopher is an essayist. Hence, André Glucksmann notes that

> the style of the essayist . . . is not to have set rules. . . . Most human science texts are methodology texts, canons of sorts that often take an entire book to explain how to write good books. The essay does precisely the opposite: the first step is to write and to think; only after that do questions of method and formulas come up. So I think of my books as essays and in fact would have them be relatives, distant cousins, the bastard children even, of Montaigne's *Essais* (1985: 144).

Said's role as essayist-critic, like Glucksmann's as essayist-thinker, does not respond to the traditional categories of analysis. His essays on exile show that his skills of composition and expression are indivisible, that they provide him with a technical resource of wide range, power, and intensity, which he uses to write about his predicament and that of his people.

After the Last Sky, Said's most profound and moving essay on the "*figure* of the exile," as he calls it, deals with an ardent and intensely lyrical episode in the author's life. The essay can be viewed as separate or apart from the rest of his *oeuvre*, for it offers a personal evocation of "Palestinian Lives" (his included) as well as an imaginary literary family (made up of the likes of Joyce, Adorno, Auerbach, Iqbal Ahmad, Faiz Ahmad Faiz, and other exiles) and of his own position among them. In writing about Said the exile, I confront the painful honesty of the essay. Said admits the faults and mistakes of other Arabs and of the Palestinians as well; he accepts too that not all Palestinian suffering has been inflicted by the Israelis. "Victims of the destruction of our society, dispossessed ever since, regularly the target of genocidal intentions, we are," Said writes, "expected meekly not to resist; in addition, we are lectured on the need to renounce violence, to stop insisting on designating our own representatives, to give up our wish to have an independent state of our own, to respond to American demands for peace" (*After the Last Sky*, 1986: 56). A viewpoint with which even his foes sympathize.

Palestinians have for too long been the object of studies by non-Palestinians, particularly in the West. All but a handful of scholars and writers have in their "objective" accounts dehumanized their Palestinian subjects. By Said's own admission, the essay is not an "objective" study; it is, rather, a work the value of which lies in its ability to provide the reader not with a definitive history but with a penetrating assertion by a Palestinian of his people's sovereignty over their own history. In many ways a more fruitful point of comparison might be with Seamus Deane's novel/memoir *Reading in the Dark*.[7] The two books share the same sobriety, the same reasonableness of tone; both are about the ways in which lives—whole generations of lives—can be paralyzed by the memory of suffering and injustice; and both are committed to the notion that novelistic shape can be given to remembered experience (patterns observed, narratives traced, symmetries teased out) without falsifying it. My view is that *Reading in the Dark* falters whenever it tries to become too novelistic: that somewhere deep beneath its immaculate surface contend two competing narrative forms—the family history and the fictional "plot"—which the book itself is not supple enough to reconcile. *After the Last Sky* is a more nearly perfect work because it is more formally radical. It is, in fact, an unclassifiable book, not least because the text itself stands in complex relationship to a series of photographs, appearing on almost every page: pictures of faces, household objects, buildings, notices, family groups, the pages of a diary, landscapes, cityscapes, old postcards. These photographs are never captioned. They offer themselves up to the reader placidly, mute but eloquent, bolstering the sense of documentary reality but also reminding us that even in a book that is crammed full of carefully chosen, carefully organized words, there should also be a place for wordlessness.

Reminiscent of Fawaz Turki's *The Disinherited*, *After the Last Sky* is as much an essay of self-exploration as of national examination and exposition. It is the attempt of an exile—perhaps the most articulate exile—to come to terms with the Palestinian historical experience. Nearly forty years after the النكبه (1967 Defeat), Said, an American citizen, yet no less a Palestinian, offers his readers the opportunity to travel with him through his own recollections to explore the political, economic, social, and cultural aspects of modern Palestinian identity. He uses a smaller canvas this time. In writing the essay, Said says, "I found myself switching pronouns from 'we' to 'you' to 'they' to designate the Palestinians" (1986: 6). In doing so, he brings together some of the many dimensions of this exilic experience.

Though I live and write in New York, at a great distance from the Middle East, I have never been far away from the Arab world in which I was born and grew up. In 1948 my entire family became refugees from Palestine. We lived variously in Egypt (where I spent my youth), Lebanon, Jordan, and the United States. Whether I wanted it or not the fate of the exiled and dispossessed Palestinian people has been my fate too, although my circumstances have been very fortunate in comparison with those who are still stateless and under military occupation (*The Politics of Dispossession*, 1996: xxv–vi).

Distance has, however, given people like Said a perspective by which to see and judge matters that might be imperceptible or difficult to assess by those who live in the middle of rapidly unfolding events and competing narratives. The book contains four chapters; however, the prose flows naturally from one topic to the next, and the material is not divided according to a rigid formula. The first chapter, "States," examines Palestinian fragmented identity. "Interiors" looks at some of the differences between Palestinians "at home," who continue to reside in historical Palestine, and those who live abroad.

The essay discusses the crucial role of women in the resistance movement and includes a rare glimpse of how Palestinians interact in the oppressor's world. "Emergence" charts the Palestinians' development from a largely agricultural people who did not engage in written self-description or analysis to a self-conscious, politically sophisticated, and articulate people with a host of gifted intellectuals. "Past and Future" ties the essay's many threads together. The postscript is a lament for what Beirut symbolized and what it has become, a lesson in power politics, in the strong devouring the weak. Although much of what Said recounts is peculiar to the Palestinian experience, many of the problems and concerns he sees among Palestinians have parallels in other parts of the Middle East. Regimes throughout the area have developed expertise in—if nothing else—the repression and control of their own people. A defenseless subservience has become an official way of life in the Arab world, with no moral or political principles to rectify it.[8]

After the Last Sky belongs to a genre insofar as it raises certain questions about marginality, boundary, minority, space, theories of narrative knowledge—textuality, discourse, enunciation, the unconscious as language, to name only a few strategies—in order to evoke the ambivalent margin of space and its in between. The essay asks those questions through a form of critical dialogue with other "texts," texts in the form of photo essays. What is clear at the outset is that the author's sensibility—marked almost at birth by the solitary wanderings of a country boy through an ominous nowhere—has spontaneously generated a style of delightful specificity, of out-of-time progression, and elusive narrative drives that comprise a vivid and incisive prose realization of the displaced *mentalité*. As unique as the subject is the voice that originates in a wounded consciousness that is pitched somewhere between amnesia and memory and that situates the fiction it narrates midway between parable and history.

> Memory: the summer of 1942—I was six—we rented a house in Ramallah. My father, I recall, was ill with high blood pressure and recovering from a nervous breakdown. I remember him as withdrawn and constantly smoking. My mother took me to a variety show at the local Friends school. During the second half I left the hall to go to the toilet, but for reasons I could not (and still do not) grasp, the boy-scout usher would not let me back in. I recall with ever-renewed poignancy the sudden sense of distance I experienced from what was familiar and pleasant—my mother, friends, the show; all at once the rift introduced into the cosy life I led taught me the meaning of separation, of solitude, and of anguished boredom (1986: 48).

The gist of this passage lies in its rhythmically subtle meditation: flowing between memories, distilled and recreated voices and scenes fade in and out in a kind of dream or film sequence, evocative of the history of Said's childhood, his reflections on his own trajectory through the "disorderly sequence of time." Through it all runs the self-questioning of Said the exile. Montage, indeed: text and photo essays illustrate one another. Together, they give a sense and sampling of what the reality is, while offering insight into the subjects' and objects' interiors. They also form the story, the story of a people seeking to speak, to act, to be. The photo essays speak volumes: they shoot their way through the oppressor's omnipresence. They bring out aspects and subtleties not apparent in the narrative placed next to them.

The photo essay of the four boys smiling at the intruder while setting a bird free is the one around which the rest are built. It is the most powerful photo in the group and clearly defines what the story is about. The picture could convey the message of the essay even if it had to stand alone, as it does on the book cover. Other photos represent the Palestinians as women, children, businessmen, teachers, farmers, poets, shepherds, and auto mechanics. "The idea of the book, then," W. J. T. Mitchell remarks, "is ultimately to help bring the Palestinians into existence for themselves as much as for others; it is that most ambitious of books, a nation-making text" (1989: 12). Both narrative and photo essay are therefore meant to nourish and enlarge our sympathy and our imagination exactly the way that social understanding requires. They allow vignettes or anecdotes of Palestinian life, as Said remembers it from childhood, to emerge out of and disappear back into general reflections upon the Palestinian مسيره (plight). For Said, the ultimate offense that has been committed against him is that, pushed into the margin of textuality and history, he has been remade negatively, in the general imagination, or always by reference to something he is not. Even the term *polemicist*, which power politics has forced upon him, defines him in terms of how he answers back to those who have what he does not—namely, a homeland. The stories, memories, scraps of history and poetry, perceptions, and aphorisms that Said assembles are intended to fill this void, to describe him in himself or as he is. He struggles to find a way of talking that can express what is fragmented in Palestinian society. The whole narrative conveys the effort to express a sense of loss, invasion, and rupture, both in a writer and in a people from whom he in the United States is himself separated by time and distance.[9] The odds against finding a way of "telling" are great. The endless betrayals and somersaults of *realpolitik* alliances, the labyrinthine treacheries of the Middle East, confuse even the most well intentioned. And there is always someone, not necessarily in bad faith but nevertheless willing, to inflict injustice upon "Said *pluriel*," in Abdelkebir Khatibi's phrase. Like Nabokov, Said reveals a tenderness for whatever is neglected.

Commenting on the chiasmatic intersections of the narrative and its relation with the people, he writes, "It is a personal rendering of the Palestinians as displaced community—acting, acted upon, proud, [and] tender" (*After the Last Sky*, 1986: 6). Not that he collects the items (plates, old pictures, tiny Palestinian flags, replicas of the past, signs of hospitality and offering, displays of affection and of objects) individually. These objects appear in the narrative, but only as they are seen and only in their identity as objects without memory. Yet they clarify what is most outrageous about memory—its absolute betrayal. As Gilles Deleuze would say, the piano, the photo, and the bathtub in the garden are souvenir images that crystalize time from another epoch, from what has already taken place, and that exist still in a state of ruin. It is the case with almost all images of Palestine. They appear in the narrative but do not say who they are; they carry within themselves complete, real autobiography, a mixture of the imaginary and the fictitious. Said defends such objects generally, presents their apologies, would like to save them from the depredations he knows they cannot escape. One feels Said himself would like to be remembered as a fragment of that tradition—"emergent," restless, staunch: an apposite presence, unforgettable, gentle and large—yet nothing like a monument.

After the Last Sky tries to elaborate a theory of this tenderness. There is an "obvious" sense to the image, Said suggests, which includes both its literal and its symbolic meanings. Then there is a third, devious, elusive meaning, a semantic meaning, which Roland Barthes calls "obtuse," accepting the pejorative overtone as part (but only part) of the implication. The "obtuse," Said notes, is a scar on the "obvious" meaning, and, needless to say, it is much more interesting. The strategy here is similar to the one Barthes adopts in *Camera Lucida*, where the *stadium* of a photograph (what it sets out to show, what a competent reading would find) is distinguished from its *punctum* (its point or edge), what moves about it, "bruises [him]" (1981: 21). In both cases, Said, like Barthes, wants to shift from an old arguing practice of his—what Barthes once called "*banalité corrigée*," the orthodoxy uncovered or invented and then attacked—into a more conciliatory stance. There will be what one is supposed to see (and does see), and there will be a *supplement*, an extravagance, which will cheer us up, saving us from the dreariness of doing what is expected of us. It strikes me not as "obtuse" but as generous to try so hard to be understood and yet to meet with rejection and exclusion. In any event, Said's theory does not do justice to his own tenderness, which is less edgy and more agile than these laborious distinctions might suggest. The narrative reflects, comments, argues, and uses autobiography and critique to engage the reader with facets of the experience of a dislocated artist rather than with some vision of totality. Said is constantly crossing another territory, forever making a new, precarious space *in* and *out* of contexture. He repeats and re-creates the manners and décors of an ever-receding but continually reimaged place, a past, the actuality of a home, a فلسطين (Palestine). For every major battle there are a thousand "tiny offenses against scattered truths" (Said, 1985: 81). To combat them requires constant attention, alertness, and focus—Said's transposed version, perhaps, of absence, displacement, and resistance.

The focus on temporality resists the equivalence that the linear narrative proposes and provides instead a perspective on the forms of representation that signify a people, a dislocated nation, or national culture. What is displayed in this displacement and repetition of terms is the Palestinian people's predicament, shown as a measure of liminality. It, however, requires no lesser vigilance to break down the boundaries or to transcend the obdurate assertiveness numbing the observer, the fetishizing of military postures, and the self-deceptions of the marginalized. Self-assertion and an insistence on continuing a historically anchored identity can easily appear, to the bored or hostile, as just so many proofs of a cause defeated—the pathetic, irritating repetitions of the Baraks and mini-Baraks, the Netanyahus and mini-Netanyahus, the Sharons and mini-Sharons, the Arafats and mini-Arafats, who simply will not accept that the odds have become too great, that the times have changed, that everyone should just coexist with one's neighbors—even though, as it seemed, the future held brighter times, thanks to الإنتفاظه (Uprising) (surely one of the greatest anticolonial uprisings in modern history), which changed the perception of the outside world toward a people whose sole raison d'être has been to reclaim their place in a world that continues to shrink day by day. It is not difficult to grasp Said's own bafflement and the unrelenting hostility directed to "We-You-They," as he put it. He is a rationalist, in the last analysis, for whom the following question has no easy answer: "Despite our subordinate status, our widely scattered exile, our reduced circumstances, our extraordinary military weakness relative to Israel (and the other Arabs), how is it that we appear so overwhelmingly threatening to everyone?" (*After the Last Sky*, 1986: 110). To reread this is like scenting a Madeleine of the drama and struggle that once was.

In approaching the question of the identity or self-identity of Said's narrative, we might have recourse to a distinction made by Maurice Blanchot, taken up again in an essay by Jacques Derrida, which has to do precisely with the question of identity and with the relationship between identity and placing. Said has this to say about the subject of Palestinian identity:

> Identity—who we are, where we come from, what we are—is difficult to maintain in exile. Most other people take their identity for granted. Not the Palestinian, who is required to show proofs of identity more or less constantly. It is not only that we are regarded as terrorists, but that our existence as native Arab inhabitants of Palestine, with primordial rights there (and not elsewhere), is either denied or challenged. And there is more. Such as it is, our existence is linked negatively to encomiums about Israel's democracy, achievements, excitement; in much Western rhetoric we have slipped into the place occupied by Nazis and anti-Semites; collectively, we can aspire to little except political anonymity and resettlement; we are known for no actual achievement, no characteristic worthy of esteem, except the effrontery of disrupting Middle East peace. . . . We have known no Einsteins, no Chagall, no Freud or Rubinstein to protect us with the world's compassion. We are "other," and opposite, a flaw in the geometry of resettlement and exodus (*After the Last Sky*, 1986: 16–17).

In "Living On," Derrida distinguishes the "narrative voice" from the "narratorial voice," which in *After the Last Sky* would be that of Said the (nostalgic) subject, the "voice of a subject recounting something, remembering an event or a historical sequence, knowing who he is, where he is, and what he is talking about." The "narrative voice," by contrast, is "a . . . voice that utters the work from the placeless place" (1979: 101). The narratorial voice can be located and identified—it confers on the work a بطاقة هوية (an identity card), in Mahmoud Darwish's formula. But Said's narrative voice has no fixed place; it is both nowhere and everywhere at once. He explains:

> For where no straight line leads from home to birthplace to school to maturity, all events are accidents, all progress is a digression, all residence is exile. We linger in nondescript places, neither here nor there; we peer through windows without glass, ride conveyances without movement or power. Resourcefulness and receptivity are the attitudes that serve best (Ibid., 26).

This is Said's estranged voice at its best. It is "ghostlike," a specter that haunts the narratorial text and, itself without center, placing, or closure, disrupts and dislocates the work, not permitting it to exist as finally completed or closed.

This ghostlike atopicality and hypertopicality of something that resists definitive placing or closure may remind us of the victims who have been denied the most basic human rights. The photograph by Jean Mohr on the cover of *Blaming the Victims* is, in Said's terms, the "non-narrative," which is in turn integral to the story. Said uses the words *narrative, text, event* almost forty times in a single essay.[10] This might have been too much even in the present state of litcritspeak, and even in an essay on, say, narrative. On this occasion, however, he is writing not about literary texts but about the Palestinian troubles: an affecting topic, on which he writes with a generosity of vision that deserves the respect even of those whose loyalties are opposed to his. The word *text* is used most often, perhaps, in the phrase *Palestinian lives*, variously meaning or implying *history, story, predicament, side of the question, perspective, version of events,* and occasionally nothing at all, or what is aptly called in linguistics: "an absence that signifies." There is an accompanying vocabulary of story, tale, romance, but *text* is the main word, and it acquires an increasingly significant orchestration as the dialectic of belonging and its opposite, unbelonging, progresses. Said's heartfelt *account* of the Palestinian question reflects his political sentiment toward a nation that is *organically* dislocated but not out of context. This blend makes him, in addition to being an academic practitioner of literary criticism, a passionate and informed commentator on public events. The combination is honorable, potentially vitalizing in both directions, and, regrettably, rare.

Both *After the Last Sky* and *Blaming the Victims* undramatize, the better to allow us to approach the Palestinians with at least some hint of the ordinariness we need to sense before we can feel the extraordinariness of their situation. Where Said in the narrative evokes a world and a social order irrevocably past, Jean Mohr in the photo essay catches the prosaic actualities of a society that may be fractured but is not incoherent: workers sit tired and drawn at the end of the day in a Nablus soap factory. Having their claims excluded from a debate in which their oppressors often discuss their lives and culture contemptuously and without risk of rebuttal is for the Palestinians like peeping into the world from a knothole in a fence. They glance sidelong at the intruding camera and make the viewer feel intrusive—but intrusive on something real, rather than something created merely to infiltrate. Many of the photographs capture a moment of action in a remarkably unforced way. These portraits draw no attention to the art of the photographer. They do not dramatize the transforming power of the lens, but neither do they appeal to a documentary realism. They are not "picturesque." It seems entirely appropriate that *After the Last Sky* should end with the Swiss photographer himself shot in mime by two small children mimicking and mocking his surveillance. The energy and clarity here stimulate the reader-critic to question reflection.

The importance of *After the Last Sky* as his most personal work is captured with consummate skill by Arif Dirlik in the following passage, which I must quote at length:

> *After the Last Sky* is in a fundamental sense a skillful work of propaganda (in a positive sense of that term), if not just a work of propaganda. It was written for Western readers, to impart to them a sense of Palestinian life in all its

variety in order to humanize Palestinians against their de-humanization in a hostile environment. It is also a deeply "place-based" work, thanks largely to Jean Mohr's photography which seeks successfully to capture Palestinian life in its concrete everydayness. Said, who at the time of writing had been away from Palestine for almost four decades, in his commentary reflects on these photographs which recall for him memories of Palestine, but also serve as reminders both of the varieties of Palestinian life, and his own distance from the immediacy of Palestine.

He continues:

If . . . [Said] essentializes being Palestinian against his recognition through-out the text of the diversity of Palestinian life in Israel/ Palestine and in exile, it is only partially out of nostalgia; for without the self-identification he reads into the photographs, the work would have lost much of its prop-aganda value. These considerations may not make the writing any the less essentialist (in a way that contrasts with the place-based diversity implied by the photographs), and Said's self-identification any the less real, but they suggest a need for reading the text in more complex ways, with due attention to its politics, the distance between the author and the text, and the ambivalence that peeks through its homogenizing nationalism. Said's self-identification as a Palestinian in this text is an imagined if not a willed self-identification; or, as he puts it, a "metaphorical" one.

Then Dirlik quotes Said as saying:

A significant segment of Arab Palestinian history has been made up of peasant farming and agricultural life. . . . Pastoral and rural forms of exis-tence dominate in our society. The chances are today that one out of every two Palestinians you meet is descended from farmers or shepherds, and has deep roots in a land descended from farmers or shepherds. It is therefore very tempting to think of this life as essentially timeless and anonymously collective. I am perhaps an extreme case of an urban Palestinian whose rela-tionship to the land is basically metaphorical, I view the Palestinian commu-nity at a very great remove (2001: 14–15).

Dirlik explores the filiation between the essay and the photographs on the one hand and Said's cosmopolitanism and pastoral nostalgia on the other. Like some other small or "faraway" country in our past, Palestine is one of those which—to its glory and its misery—has produced more history than it can consume locally.

However, Dirlik falls short in reading the photographs as signs of impotence and/or castration. Like Barthes's Spectator in *Camera Lucida*, the reader must view the photographs "not only as a question (a theme) but as a wound." And yet, unlike Barthes, who thought "never to reduce [him]self-as-subject, confronting certain photographs, to the disincarnate, disaffected *socius* which science is concerned with," Said recognizes in his own vision the influence of a *socius*, neither disincarnate nor disaffected but historically branded (1981: 74). This stamped history is consolidated by the narrative.

> [The] . . . photograph of a small but clearly formed human group surrounded by a dense layered reality expresses very well what we experience during that detachment from an ideologically saturated world. This image of four people seen at a distance near Ramallah, in the middle of and yet separated from thick foliage, stairs, several tiers of terraces and houses, a lone electricity pole off to the right, is for me a private, crystallized, almost Proustian evocation of Palestine (*After the Last Sky*, 1986: 47).

The nonnarrative or the photo essay, then, offers the reader both the possibility of ghosts and the denial of them. But there is also in the narrative a textual ghost that inhabits and dislocates the identity conferred by Said's narratorial order and its preoccupation with linearity, propriety, and proper place. All we have is a Saidian text, but inscribed within it is a مسيرہ (the plight) of many misplaced voices. Derrida speaks of the "linear norm" and the "form of the narrative" in "Living On," of the undoing of the linear that takes place in the margins and "between the lines." Said's narrative, with its own emphasis on marginal subjects, itself provokes a double reading in which reality locates itself under a single narratorial voice. To paraphrase Derrida, the order and identity of the narrative, and that which is in the margins or between the lines becomes part of the text's own subversive dislocation of identity. Both logic and the logic of identity are founded, for Said, on the opposition of *inside* and *outside*, which inaugurates all binary oppositions—where each of the terms is simply external to the other. The expulsion of one involves a domination or mastery, like naming itself, which Nietzsche (speaking of the opposition of "good" and "evil") links to a taking of possession or appropriation. But, once expelled, the "outside" functions as a ghost: the identical is haunted, as Michel Foucault says of the table or grid, by what it excludes. The principal Saidian narrative and nonnarrative tell of the usurpation of a history, a home, a text.

Tactfully, Said realizes the importance of the facts, and indeed, *After the Last Sky* can be seen as a marker not just of the state of pre-Intifada writing, but of the point at which the essay itself seems to have arrived in the closing decades of the twentieth century. The slow death of the imagination, the palpable erosion of faith in stories as a way of explaining the world, might be epitomized by this writer with his rigorous preference for fact over invention. Our awareness is heightened at almost any given moment while reading the essay. That we are reading truth rather than fiction chimes with the Saidian thesis about memory, his insistence that remembered fact is indelible. And whereas others may stress that memory is unreliable, and that even under normal conditions a slow degradation is at work, an obfuscation of outlines, a, so-to-speak, physiological oblivion, which few memories resist, Said shows us that there are some things that can never be forgotten and then goes further, arguing that they can never be fictionalized, either. Indeed, it even implies that these two processes might amount to the same thing and that a writer's desire to weave a web of invention around the sufferings of his real life models is as distorting as the collective amnesia Said continues to identify among his colonizers—the mental impoverishment and lack of memory that mark Zionism and the efficiency with which they continue to clean everything up—which by the end of the essay are beginning to affect the reader's head and nerves.

What is at work, at least in some uses of the power of remembering, may be seen from a close look at *After the Last Sky*, Said's evocation, and his showcase of displaced Palestinian voices and his own position among them: "A part of something is for the foreseeable future going to be better than all of it. Fragments over wholes. Restless nomadic activity over the settlements of held territory. Criticism over resignation. The Palestinian as self-consciousness in a barren plain of investments and consumer appetites. The heroism of anger over the begging bowl, limited independence over the status of clients. Attention, alertness, focus. To do as others do, but somehow to stand apart. To tell your story in pieces, *as it is*" (*After the Last Sky*, 1986: 150). An essay about being deprived of a home, the book is structured, as are all his books and articles on Palestine, in brief, clear-cut episodes. It crams into a short space a large number of diverse lives and does so by cherishing each encounter with uprooted Palestinians *inside* and *outside* as if it were a short story, shaping it, giving it a turn or a twist, as evidenced in the story about, among others, the former mayor of Jerusalem and his wife, in exile in Jordan. Behind them, a photographic mural of the Mosque of Omar in Jerusalem occupies the entire wall of their living room. "The collaboration of image and text here," W. J. T. Mitchell writes, "is not simply one of the exile whose memories and mementoes, the tokens of personal and national identity, may 'seem . . . like encumbrances.' The mural seems to tell us that the former mayor and his wife *cherish* these encumbrances, but their faces do not suggest that this in any way reduces their weight" (1989: 11). Nobody reading *After the Last Sky* could mistake it for an attempt to give a comprehensive or balanced view of its characters. In fact, Said is discarding some of the storyteller's traditional concerns and bringing to his work the technique of a novelist. The four chapters—miniaturelike in their composition—are reminiscences of the old country that read like fiction. He leaves out explanations of how he got from one place (Jerusalem) to another

(Beirut). The voice the reader hears is elliptical, pungent; and the eye is that of someone clearly drawn to the unexpected, the contradictory, the sharp-edged. There is autobiography but no personal confession. There is also reportage, history, *and* storytelling.

After the Last Sky slides from fact into fiction. Consequently, the form that Said has chosen for this *travail à deux* between his words and Jean Mohr's photographs does not "tell a consecutive story"; its form is "unconventional, hybrid and fragmentary" and is "quite consciously designed" as an "alternative mode of expression to the one usually encountered in the media, in the works of social sciences, in popular fiction." The result is that everything in it is alive insofar as "no clear and simple narrative is adequate to the complexity of our experience" (*After the Last Sky* 1986: 6). The photo essay therefore becomes a work not about exile but about migration: objects migrate, people migrate; archaeology and origin begin to shift uneasily as strange ideas about man's ancestry are floated. The essay itself circles back to its accumulated sources, the form of the author's notebooks, from which extracts are pillaged, juxtaposed, rearranged in the manner of a collage or a long modernist poem. It will not and cannot settle its materials, mainly because it is the most jewelled of Said's works on *his* Palestine. The paragraphs are tiny. The sentences are short, clenched, and lapidary. There are words and phrases in Arabic and arcane pieces of information as well as pictures of Palestinians as they go about their daily chores. "The relation of photographs and writing," Mitchell continues, "is consistently governed by the dialectic of *exile* and its overcoming, a double relation of estrangement and reunification" (1989: 11). Oh, memory so fresh, so not! Oh, memory so reliable, so not!

Without being overingenious it seems possible to say that this brave and subtle essay is a declaration of resistance, which, in the end, leaves us with the serious question of whether there is indeed a way out of the impasse insofar as Palestine is seen as the supreme paradigm both of colonial exploitation and of Palestinian-Israeli relations, what Said, quoting Nadine Gordimer, called the "last great colonial extravaganza" (1994: 23). I can think of no other way that so well illustrates the ambiguous predicament of a people. Said has done them some service in reviving their predicament in talks, essays, interviews, statements, memoirs, reflections, photographs, and reports covering fifty years of dispossession. In doing so, he offers us plenty of details, too, but also another model for writing as an exile, not as the creature of the condescending Israeli imagination, nor as the writer who is also a Palestinian but as the writer who remembers every determining fact about his people and incorporates them into his writing. He does not forget that he is an exile because he cannot, any more than he can forget he is an Arab or a leftist or a former member of the PNC or getting old. But his remembering is a complex affair, a whole art. Or, to put this another way, the delight and satisfaction is not so much in the excavation of forgotten lives itself but in recognizing memory when it surfaces, when it is alive, not so much in the original work site as in all the echoes, shades, turns, and pivots that the reader must decode.

II

In the reflective but elusive "Palestine, Then and Now," Said attempts to write the narrative that is his life. In doing so, he enters into his world of the transient, the immigrant, the person without a real home. The alternative to exile, he suggests, is not the one provided by biology but by affiliation between communities made of people, institutions, associations, and constituencies whose social existence is represented by the warmth of the human spirit. "Childless couples," he writes,

> orphaned children, aborted childbirths, and unregrettably celibate men and women populate the world of high modernism with remarkable insistence, all of them suggesting the difficulties of filiation. But no less important in my opinion is the second part of the pattern, which is immediately consequent upon the first, the pressure to produce new and different ways of conceiving human relationships. For if biological reproduction is either too difficult or too unpleasant, is there some other way by which men and women can create social bonds between each other that would substitute for those ties that connect members of the same family across generations? (1985: 17).

"Palestine, Then and Now" engages head on with the question Said poses. The practical focus on this journey provides an occasion for glimpses both into his mind and into the kind of reality it represents. The essay shows the plight of a transplanted family in search of its roots. This is made all the more clear in the narrator's vision of distant times that he brings to bear on imagined individuals and families caught in the fantasy of home. Said's imagination has always centered less on Cairo where he grew up and went to school than on القدس (Jerusalem), where he was born and spent the early part of his childhood. In this essay the latter place takes on a vividness at once welcoming and hallucinatory, but the welcoming is emphatically that of the not-at-home. The result is a confluence between the specific and the abstract, as particular events mark general movements in a voice that clings with obsession to the relics of memory, a memory exemplified in the author's presentation of the joys and sorrows of a family reunion with the *trace*:

> In Miari's car my family and I were driven up to Jerusalem, that extraordinary city, in the quickly darkening twilight. When we arrived a brilliant star-dotted sky swept by cold winds vaulted the city's heights, and as we crossed the handsome stone threshold of the American Colony Hotel, I was already conscious of trying to stem the torrent of memories, expectations, and disoriented impressions that assaulted me (Said, 1992: 48).

The last sentence stands as a necessary warning, for although "Palestine, Then and Now" obviously draws on Said's past and present life, it is very much a travelogue essay. However, the contradictions do not lend a kind of *People* magazine piquancy to his discussion of journeying with the family. There are things the reader must understand about Said to reach a full appreciation of the essay, because its language and form are shaped by his political dilemma. The procedure in the search for the sensation initially overwhelms any response to what he has produced, because his situation is so precarious: a Christian Palestinian who sees himself as an Arab and writes in English. Even the most well intentioned would have great difficulty simply absorbing the sequence of Said's identity; one cannot take in so much paradox. In describing the complexities of his identity, one could use the expression for the infinite regress of a reflection within a reflection or an escutcheon within an escutcheon, a nest of boxes pleasure.[11]

What I want to explore here is the celebration of memory: How does Said walk toward a place of endless thoughts and feelings, with each voyage leading to another? Is Said's country (an imaginary homeland, perhaps!) a place where he sees only the *invisible*? Memory, which summons forth only old perceptions, is obviously not enough to get away from lived perceptions; neither is an involuntary memory that adds reminiscence as the agent of preservation of the present. Forgetting is not the opposite of memory. Paul Ricoeur distinguishes between what he calls "definitive forgetting"—forgetting by wiping out all *traces*, in the brain, in moments—and the "return of certain memories," which shows us that we forget less than we think. Suddenly one can regain whole chunks of childhood memories. "So I see," Ricoeur adds,

> the question of forgetting as a kind of contest between the forgetting by disappearance and the forgetting of what has been stockpiled. It is what Bergson aptly called the "survival of images." In the end, there is a forgetting of survival juxtaposed to the forgetting by disappearance. In the case of memory, however, we can talk about a duty of forgetting because it can be targeted: one can recall this or that, but one cannot target forgetting, it is a state. There is forgetting that happens involuntarily and which requires us to tell or recount. We do not recall everything because we cannot: telling is selective, there is an interstitial forgetting. And there is perhaps a forgetting that is beneficial, which is the greatest reward of reconciled memory. It is what I would call "carefree": a rare and precious state of mind, linked to beatitudes (2000: 47).

Memory plays a small part in art (even and especially in Said). It is true that every work of art is a *monument*, but here the monument is not something commemorating a past; it is a block of present sensations that owe their preservation only to themselves. In doing so, they provide the event with the energy that celebrates art.

The monument's action is not memory but remembering or what Ricoeur terms "trop de mémoire ici, là trop d'oubli." Said writes not with childhood memories but through blocks of childhood that are the becoming-child of the present. It is not memory that is needed but a complex material that is found not in memory but in words, sounds, smells, and feelings. In the process, the triumph of despair and death is not where Said leaves the story. Instead, the final remark in the essay turns away from the melancholy of the traveler and is followed by disappointment and disillusionment. Thus, in his acute reading of Palestine, the passing reference points become the critical basis for the representation of the intimacy and grace of the place as he knew it in the 1940s. To disclose such intimacy of place, Said reminds us, we must remember the past that shaped us as well as reflect on the present that is, to some extent, being shaped by us. The essay has already drawn much criticism. Said informs David Barsamian that when he reported in *Harper's Magazine* on his visit to Palestine/Israel—"to the sites of personal catastrophe for me"—both the magazine and the author received many "angry, appalling letters. . . . One person who claimed to be a psychiatrist, for example, prescribed a psychiatric hospital for me. Others accused me of lying. . . . I found that very disheartening." This posture of militant intolerance is not confined to letter writers.[12]

"Palestine, Then and Now" may seem like a very lonely artifact, the first essay Said wrote following a visit to his homeland after forty years of separation. But in fact, it is through a haunting glimpse into yesteryear that he hopes to find a niche in the Israeli narrative. He set himself the task of carving out a space for himself and for his family—to write an essay, as he says, that would serve as his identity card. And it had to embrace the paradox of who (he) they (is) are: if his son and daughter are American Palestinian, the reverse is true for Said: he is Palestinian American, but with a nagging sense of how fragile that identity is. In the essay, as in real life, his family has drifted from Palestine to Lebanon, from Jordan to Egypt to America:

> I had come to the United States as a schoolboy in 1951, but in the years that followed I would remain close to the Arab world, becoming actively involved in the struggle for Palestinian rights. Most of my extended family, all of whom left Palestine in early 1948, had found refuge in Beirut, Amman, and Cairo, and I had visited them many times. Now I was returning with my own family (1992: 47).

But Palestinians they are, not only because the surrounding Israelis ensure it but also because of the grief of dispossession that is never far from everyday reality: "[E]ven those many of us whose passports and safe jobs made it feasible to return needed a long time to make the trip, cross the barrier, and confront the difficult reality" (ibid., 52). The harsh every day life Said describes reminds the reader of the Palestinian song:

Taxi, taxi, take me for free—
Had not the Welfare saved one in three
They'd all be dead, the refugees.
Taxi, taxi, take me for free.

"Palestine, Then and Now," moreover, is the story of a Christian family whose religion is of central importance in their lives. "The Church of the Holy Sepulcher," Said writes, "that center of centers, was exactly as I recalled it—a run down place. . . . I remembered being carried around here on my father's shoulders, wondering: Who were those bearded foreigners? Could this be the acute sight of Christ's last hours? Both Najla and Wadie seemed perplexed" (1992: 48). The Saids' Anglicanism sets them apart from their oppressors, the Jews, their more numerous Muslim neighbors, and an entire outlying Arab world, one that would refuse Said's father the right to be buried in Lebanon. Said speaks movingly about the death of his father in 1971 in Beirut. One episode in particular still haunts him to this day. It is sadly and eloquently narrated in *Out of Place*:

> In early 1971 when he was near death he told us that he wished to be buried in Dhour, but that was never possible, since no resident was willing to sell us land for a little plot on which to grant his wish. Even after his years of devotion to it, his many material contributions to its communal life, his love for its people and locale, he was still considered too much of a stranger in death to be allowed in. The idealized pastoral existence we thought we were enjoying had no real status in the town's collective memory (1999: 269).

Exclusion notwithstanding, the underlying form of Said's experience of displacement is assimilation—since he remains an Arab, very much part of the culture—inflected by rejection, drift, errantry, and uncertainty.

Arab Muslims are as inescapable as the Israeli Jews, surrounding the Saids with a volatile intimacy that embraces every shade of relationship, from love that leads to murderous hatred.[13] Said's relationship with Jewish Israel and/or Muslim Lebanon is by no means purely negative. He shares the interests and knowledge expected of a Jewish intellectual; it is surprising and affecting to discover that Said finds Adorno, Trilling, Spitzer, and other Jewish intellectuals haunting, strangely attractive, and compelling. He once commented, "Sometimes I have the strange feeling I'm the only Palestinian in New York, a Jewish city *par excellence*."[14] His voice is indeed that of Palestine—combative, urgent, and coruscating in its attacks both on the cruelties that have been inflicted on his people by the Jewish State and on the Western policies and double standards that have underpinned more than fifty years of Israeli domination.

Until the mask of benign, relatively painless Israeli occupation of the West Bank and Gaza was stripped away by the sustained revolt led by an unarmed population after thirty-five years of alien military rule, to argue the Palestinian cause, even in ultraliberal circles, was dismissed as anti-Semitic. It is here, in such acts, that, as Paul would have put it, there effectively are no longer Jews and Palestinians, full members of the polity and *homines sacri*. One should be unabashedly Platonic: this "No!" designates the miraculous moment in which eternal Justice momentarily appears in the sphere of empirical reality. An awareness of moments like this is the best antidote to the anti-Semitic temptation often pointedly hurled at critics of Israeli politics. And Said's sense of history is too scrupulous to allow him simply to discard the history and fears of Israeli Jews. He recognizes that Israel's exemption from the normal criteria by which nations are measured owes everything to the Holocaust. But he does not see why this unique legacy of horror should be exploited to inhibit the political rights "of a people who are absolutely dissociable from what has been an entirely European complicity." The question to be asked, he writes,

> is how long can the history of anti-Semitism and the Holocaust be used as a fence to exempt Israel from arguments and sanctions against it for its behavior toward the Palestinians, arguments and sanctions that were used against other repressive governments, such as that of South Africa? How long are we going to deny that the cries of the people of Gaza . . . are directly connected to the policies of the Israeli government and not to the cries of the victims of Nazism? (*The Politics of Dispossession*, 1994: 34).

The double standards and special favors insisted upon by Israel and its supporters are not confined to Israel's actions in the Occupied Territories. Said sees Israel, like the old South Africa, as inherently racist. In its public, juridical, and international practice, it is the state of the Jewish people, not a sovereign independent state of citizenry regardless of confession. The Law of Return and the Nationality Laws are explicitly discriminatory: a Jew from anywhere in the world is entitled to immigrate to Israel and to acquire citizenship. No Palestinian has any such right, however long his or her family may have resided in Palestine. "Just imagine," Said intones, "what would happen if America were to be declared the state only of WASPs" ("Which Country?" 1996: 14). If Said could pass one law, it would certainly be one that gives the Palestinian people the right to return. Said's voice may be a lonely one, crying in the Manhattan wilderness, but his view of exile makes more sense if one is aware of his political position: that he is an Arab living and writing from *within* the safety of the West, entitled to precisely the same rights as any other citizen.

Said chose to write "Palestine, Then and Now" in the form of an essay, with a handful of tales, anecdotes, diary entries, and silent monologues, all patterned in the arabesque's timeless circle. This makes it all the more difficult to convey a sense of belonging and absolutely impossible to discern its twists and turns. To begin with, it unfolds, arabesquelike, as a *narrative* and by *narrators,* too. The two modes are spliced together like scenes from two completely different films. Both are crammed with incident and peopled by a bewildering cast of characters. The *narrative* portions give the history of the Saids, whose home was in the quiet neighborhood of Talbiya, an elegant quarter where well-to-do Arab families earlier in the twentieth century built houses with thick stone walls, now covered with flowering vines of bougainvillaea; they elaborate a tale of Said's life as part of a distraught community who used to be rooted in their old habits and ways of life. The poignancy of Said showing his children the home in which he was born is deepened by the fact that Christian Zionists now occupy it. He is skilled at evoking reflections that link the personal and political in a vigorous voice committed to its people, their struggle and a single standard of human rights and justice. The *narrative* is set in the present, as Said scrambles to forge an identity as a visitor to his homeland and/or writer. The action shifts from the "road to Jerusalem" to "into the old city" to a "search for family landmarks" to "driving north" to the "Palestinians inside" to "descending into Gaza" and finally "toward the future."

> Gaza is surrounded by an electrified wire fence on three sides; imprisoned like animals, Gazans are unable to move, unable to work, unable to sell their vegetables or fruit, unable to go to school. They are exposed from the air to Israeli planes and helicopters and are gunned down like turkeys on the ground by tanks and machine guns. Impoverished and starved, Gaza is a human nightmare ("What Israel Has Done," 2002: 3).

By telling the story in this way, by cutting the narrated figure itself from the whole in order to see only the personal, Said evades perhaps a certain complication of the narrative structure, which is announced in the exercise of writing. The primal scene (not in a Freudian sense) is thus performed, we are told not by the narrator alone but by both the *narrated narrator* of the narration and the narrative sequence.

The narrative fragments present a folkloric, fictionalized history of the world of Said's people, the Palestinians. This beleaguered, tight-knit community of men, women, and children, farmers and artisans, priests and warriors, teachers and students, grocers and shoemakers offers and courtships, failed and successful, hunger and resistance, local legend and Christian/Muslim piety. The cadences are sometimes mythical but are more often the apparently casual meanderings of a tale told by the fireside. There is, however, nothing casual about it at all. Each particular offshoot of telling has its own rich and complex history. "There were times when I didn't feel like an outsider," Said observes "but rather like a partner, one of the 'we'" (1992: 49). The tale is dauntingly dense, as each chatty anecdote twists into complications that defy paraphrase. A single example, which spills into both the narrative and narrator's modes, that of the "new Baptist church," which incidentally, has an unbecoming honeycomb-like facade, and, as a friendly American voice told me over the phone, my grandfather's tomb had been moved from the old church to a nearby cemetery. "We did it very well," he assured me, with Israeli health inspectors to ratify the proceedings, and then added, as if apologetically, "All we found inside were some old bones and a Bible!" I prevented myself from asking what else he had expected after seventy years (ibid., 52).

This is only the beginning of Said's role in the narrative. The seemingly distant memory becomes central to Said the narrator, as he tries to untangle his own history. Rediscovering the remains of his maternal grandfather's grave as the result of a phone call locates that first moment in time and space. Certain distinctions that were added at the moment when the "story" is presented merely lead to "some old bones and a Bible!" At first reading, we may distinguish a drama, its narration, and the conditions of that narration. Then the drama becomes the recounted action, the (narrated) *history* that forms the "essay's" proper object. The narration, in fact, heightens the drama of finding a place for oneself to such an extent that without it no *mise-en-scène* would be possible. Locating the tomb may or may not hold the answer to Said's "grey Victorian Anglican" past (ibid.). Said is at his best when he is writing about some aspect of life or politics that reflects his interior self: he contains a multitude of worlds, and those worlds are his true subject of inquiry.

This Byzantine complexity of plot, this intermingling of historical fact and idiosyncratic fantasy, memory and remembering, is characteristic of the entire essay. The bewildering twists and turns of the story are often illuminated by the recurrence of some small measure of hope that things are somehow improving; that some people are at peace, at least with themselves. The example of Abdel Shafi is a case in point.

Abdel Shafi immediately communicated the sense of calm decency that has elevated him to universal admiration in Gaza and throughout the Palestinian world in part because, unlike, say Arafat, he is not principally a political man. Speaking to him and his wife, I suddenly felt the whole fragmented picture of Palestinian society making some sense, because in people like the Shafis and Raji and so many others that I met during that fateful trip to Gaza, the idea of an actual society that bound us all together somehow *did* survive the ravages of our history, its tragic mistakes, and the destructive course of Israel's policies (Ibid., 54).

This is useful in a story in which every incident, however minute, however seemingly random, is interlocked with everything else: from domination to rejection, from exclusion to xenophobia. In the *narrative* sections, the storyteller's insouciant air of leisure allows some wonderful effects such as the encounter over a laden table with the celebrated Palestinian author Emile Habibi. One of Said's uncles, Munir, inherited the "wrinkle of the wind," to use a phrase from Anton Shammas, that led him to travel outside of Palestine. Said's mother, however, never ceases to be there, to be with him during the journey. A page later the reader is given the full story: "My mother's family was originally from Safad, north of Lake Tiberias, and then moved to Nazareth. . . . Until her dying day, my father's sister, Nabiha, referred to her closest friend as 'Mrs. Marmura,' who in turn always referred to "Mrs. Said," and this after more than fifty years of friendship! I was heading north in search of this past" (ibid.). The Saids's troubled wanderings (Jerusalem, Cairo, Beirut,) and troubles are often dictated by the actual brutal history of the region; alien conquerors come and go, to be fought by almost equally displaced Muslim rebels. But the Said clan also shares a spiritual and mythical history, a search for redemption symbolized in the journey back to the Holy Land.

This fragmented history, seamless and artfully artless, is undercut by chunks of the narrator's portions: jagged, postmodern interjections by a host of alienated and self-conscious voices. Said the narrator is much given to Brechtian slaps, ending a long journey (forty years in all) in search of an identity by deciding ultimately not to go inside the home of his birth. Only a short walk separates him physically from it, but the distance is greater when he revisits it in the rush of sudden memories. The years seem to have borne testimony to the condition of exile, an exile with enough light for him to make sense of his comings and goings.

Said's memory is so acute that time has stood still for him. The refusal to go in to visit the old family home and face up to the present strips the narrator of his romantic, almost idyllic, past; for only through memory/imagination could he enter that home and confront the past and the memories of a love for the place that was once his. The visit to the house stands as a kind of ritual, a purging of the past, it represents the last physical hope of ever returning to the land that was Palestine and is now Israel. The contrast between the unbearable shame of the narrator and the apparent indifference of the onlooker is telling: the narrator alone sees himself outside. And in looking at himself outside the house of his parents he is alone. Here, only Said feels that dispossession has inflicted an unforgiving affront on him. It is a slap in the face, one of those eradicable jests, a mockery hitting home, at the very spot that was not to be touched.

It is true that the narrator's sections do not work as well as the narrative. At best, they seem flat in comparison to the hallucinatory intensity of a haunting tale. In these sections, the flights of poetic language can seem strained almost to the point of insincere *bathos*: Said tries to fuse the two modes by weaving themes and images from the narrative portion into the narrator's present. But it feels forced. The two types of writing are so discordant that the reader begins to suspect that two separate pieces of narrative have been shuffled together like a deck of cards. It is difficult to understand the pressures bearing on Said, who shows an acute awareness of the past as well as of the present, inside and outside of the essay. The narrative sections, bitter as they are in parts, are simply too safely alien to modern Israel, too cosily Arabesque, to be allowed to stand alone for a writer who wants to reclaim his identity card. But the narrator's portions are urgently needed if Said is going to block Israeli readers from imposing yet another simplified and unwanted image on him. The quaint charm of the narrative sections alone would allow Said's intended readers—Israelis and Arabs alike—to see him as a literary curiosity, an insider/outsider reporting on a visit to his country of birth as well as theirs. And it is not Said's intention to flatter Israeli readers. "Palestine, Then and Now" never reflects the kind of corrosive hatred you might expect from scenes of Palestinians being surveilled, imprisoned in appalling conditions, or simply driven away by the hundreds from their homes, but it gives no quarter either. Israeli Jews are shown at times behaving very badly indeed, sometimes with simple physical brutality, sometimes in delicately nuanced emotional ways. "What immediately struck me about Muhammed," Said notes, "was how easily, unaffectedly, he spoke with the uniformed personnel, all of whom were Israeli Jews. I had assumed that there would be a manifest uneasiness or even fear, as between members of subaltern and dominant groups. I was already learning the reality of things" (ibid., 48). Here Said plays the witness; he tells us about all the signs of a very singular concern: what the Israelis offer in public is first filtered, selected, and actively delimited. Still, he is not content with his status as an outsider even though "there were times," he notes, "I didn't feel an outsider—which in many ways I was—but rather like a partner, one of the 'we' in the problems and hopes encountered by people in daily life" (ibid., 53). The phrasing strikes echoes across the different comings and goings of life, the goings-on, as the several stories and characters twist through time and place, until Said brings the various themes together in a carefully poised, tender, and melancholy coda.

The الإنتفاضة (Uprising) and its victims (among whom Said counts the survivors: this is an essay in which no one escapes damage) occupy the foreground, but it is Palestine as the dream of the Promised Land that provides the essay's tragic core. Because Palestine, the sense of home, cannot exist except as yearning. However clearly it appears on the atlas, it eludes the colonizer and the refugee alike in the restless involutions of the mind's desires. Much of the essay is a meditation on the predicament of the Palestinian people under Israeli occupation in general and on the Palestinians' unfailing generosity and gentleness in the Occupied Territories in particular. The most important alternate narrators, after the persona of Said himself, are the people Said meets with on the way: the Khalidis, the Abbouds, the Raji, the Shafis, Um Mohammed, George Giacaman, Mohammed Miari, and the list goes on. In this sense, the "narrator is not effaced," Derrida observes, "as the 'general narrator,' or rather, in effacing himself within the homogeneous generality, he puts himself forward as a very singular [voice] . . . within the narrated narration" (1978: 433). Said's meditations on encounters, life, death, burial, memory, and the madness that inhabit the region and its languages, exile and the threshold, are so many signs addressed to this question of *place* and *trace*, inviting its subjects to recognize that Said is first of all a guest in the Derridean sense of the word. When we enter an unknown place, he tells us, the emotion experienced is almost always that of an indefinable anxiety. There then begins the slow work of taming the unknown, and gradually the unease fades away. A new familiarity succeeds the fear provoked in us by the irruption of the "wholly Other." If the body's most archaic instinctual reactions are caught up in an encounter with what it does not immediately recognize in the real, how could thought really claim to apprehend the Other, the wholly Other, without astonishment? A question that has no easy answer.

I cannot begin to unravel all the complexities of the phrase: "I think I needed the chance metaphorically to bury the dead, and, what with the large number of funerary associations for me, what had been Palestine was indeed a mournful place" (1992: 55). It suggests two things: First, the density of allusion and irony that readers other than Palestinians are unlikely to catch in "Palestine, Then and Now." Second, Said needed to make his narrators and their splintered voices his own. In doing so, he continues to enliven the story, even if it is pursued out of simple curiosity, just to see for himself. For Said decided to make the trip to the Holy Land only after he "had received a shocking medical diagnosis: I was suffering from a chronically insidious blood disease. This news," he writes, "had convinced me for the first time of a mortality I had ignored, and which I now needed to come to terms with" (ibid., 47). The reader does not have to torture that theme of filiation out of the essay's nuances for the writer forces him or her to face it. The voice of those nameless refugees, whose tangled history was outlined earlier, contributes another ironic allusion to the mutilated past that Said wishes to unearth. He is so concerned that a reader might miss the reference that he includes a photo. I am not saying that "Palestine, Then and Now" is not worth reading simply as an essay, without a scrap of information about the literary and political contexts in which Said writes. It is a wonderful, if flawed, piece of travel writing. And I am not claiming that an awareness of the dense web of cross-reference elevates the narrator's sections to great literature. (The narrative portions need no such assistance. They stand splendidly on their own.) But the narrator's passages do seem to me of much greater literary and intellectual interest. Because it has to be said, at the risk of melodrama, that if "Palestine, Then and Now" constitutes Said's Arab identity card, it effaces his Palestinian one: "I would find it hard to live there," he remarks. "I think exile seems to me a more liberated state, but, I have to admit, I am privileged and can afford to experience the pleasures, rather than the burdens, of exile. [Or, of an utopia of liberty]" (ibid., 55). As a matter of fact, Said's work is rooted in the experience of displacement, where it implies a temporary distance, a notion that does not seem allied to any country in particular. "Which country?" he once asked.

> I've never felt that I belonged exclusively to one country, nor have I been able to identify "patriotically" with any other than losing causes. Patriotism is best thought of as an obscure dead language, learned prehistorically but almost forgotten and almost unused since. Nearly everything normally associated with it—wars, rituals of nationalistic loyalty, sentimentalized (or invented) traditions, parades, flags, etc.—) is quite dreadful and full of appalling claims of superiority and pre-eminence. But perhaps those are the results of applied patriotism. Is theoretical patriotism really that much better? Thinking affectionately about home is all I'll go along with.[15]

And if a writer is going to suffer at least the psychological violence of homelessness, surely he or she is entitled to play for higher stakes than a charming fantasy about the pious, pastoral, communal life they have lost through their education and avocation.

The narrative sections alone might have made a more perfect essay but one that would avoid the set of questions Said most wanted to explore: "'[J]ust a minute, please,' said the young immigration officer, taking my American passport with her to a nearby office, leaving the three others on her desk. Would they send us back? Would they grill us—me especially—and go through our bags? Or—this was my private nightmare—would they march me off to prison?" The colonizer's answer is: "'Okay,' she said. 'You can go on now'" (1992: 48). The Jew is *there*. She may be ruthless just like any other occupier, but she is tolerant enough to allow another, no less native, to be also *there*, at least to visit. Said stubbornly uses a structure that insists on *his* right to be there, inside Palestine and as Palestinian as anyone, as complex and as disturbing as any other exile. In the end, he insists on his right to be the subject of his own narrative. Like any displaced Palestinian's, Said's life narrative is split.

Said's personal ideals remain centered in America, but his experience is set in the homeland (Palestine), or what remains of it, for Said does not hide the feeling that it has been completely disfigured. Since 1967 Israel has occupied the West Bank and Gaza, destroyed the Palestinian economy, planted illegal settlements, tortured, killed, maimed, demolished houses, expropriated land, all with scarcely a peep from the majority of American Zionists. In addition, Israel has bombed civilian refugee camps, hospitals, schools, orphanages in Lebanon and has behaved like an international gangster, supported of course by the United States. The massacre that took place in the Jenine camp is a grim reminder of the reality on the terrain. The Jenine camp is a refugee camp, some two kilometers long, ravaged for days and nights on end by tanks and exposed to a downpour of missiles—over

400, by all accounts—fired from helicopters. Many hundreds died. Inhabitants were buried in the debris of their houses, which had been leveled by bulldozers. Thousands of injured were deprived of help. Mothers gave birth to dead babies at checkpoints. In the streets roaming children were caught in tank fire. And how many Israelis soldiers were crushed by their ordeal? Not only did they have to kill civilians, but they also had to hide the dead from the eyes of the international community and the press. How many died in Jenine is still unknown.[16] An occupying army that commits such acts has lost every claim to legitimacy. Such an army is no longer anything but a brutal force of humiliation. Colonial history has proven on numerous occasions that this is not the way to win a war.

Much more significant in the long run is the Israeli occupier who continues to block the Palestinian future. This is a war of agoraphobia, the authority of the narrative, not the political authority for which Sharon or Bush might hope, for a time, to instill respect by way of tanks and bombs, but the authority of that which is narrated, the resistance of a story that digs in its heels. There is a remarkable story by Kafka, *In the Penal Colony*, about a crazed official who shows off a fantastically detailed torture machine whose purpose is to write all over the body of the victim, using a complex apparatus of needles to inscribe the captive's body with minute letters that ultimately cause the prisoner to bleed to death. This what Sharon and his brigades of willing executioners are doing to the Palestinians, with only the most limited and most symbolic of opposition. But Sharon is blind to the truth, for he well knows that one can be a people without land or a state, but one cannot long remain a people without a narrative. Toward the end of "Palestine, Then and Now," the narrator's voice moves on to reveal the intricate intimacies and unbridgeable distances between such narratives and/or peoples "locked together without much real sympathy, but locked together they are" (1992: 55). In spite of that stubbornness or because of it, Said's hybrid world refuses to be bound in any way possible even though he, at times, allows himself to be pulled now in one direction, now in another. Yet one senses that he remains, really, a writer who insists on cultural hybridity as evidenced in his recollection of Cairo in the 1940s: "Malleable did the city seem, so open to expatriate colonies existing in separate structures at its heart that there was a Belgian, an Italian, a Jewish, a Greek, an American, and a Syrian Cairo, lesser spheres all of them, each dependent on all the others" (*Reflection on Exile*, 2000: 20). Proud of his past while striving to shatter old stereotypes, Said looks for recognition of his heritage among other cultural cross-currents. Hospitality, or the lack of it, proximity, enclave, hate, foreignness make the essay look like a spirit of solitude; its language remains, however, crowded, poetic, jammed at times with intricate landscapes, actual or psychological. What the reader retains from it is a narrative voice that has the quality, beyond style and personality, of a real presence.

Ever since 1992, when he journeyed back to Palestine with his family, Said's visits have been more frequent. However, his summer 1996 visit made him realize that he is no longer welcome there. "Feisal Husseini was expecting us at his Ramallah office," he writes in "In Arafat's Palestine," "we headed north again with some apprehension. I had no idea what our reception would be like. I sometimes suspected (though I was usually able to banish the thought from my consciousness) that Arafat, or one of his over-zealous security people, might mean me some physical harm, or that they would try to detain me in some fashion" (1996: 13). The essay is a countertext that runs the risk of slippage from the oppositional to the surreptitiously collusive position he has embraced since the signing of Oslo I and Oslo II. The narrative of his visit to Palestine, following an invitation from his son, Wadie, who worked as a volunteer in Ramallah at an NGO called the Democracy and Workers' Rights Center (DWRC), is split between a feeling of belonging and another of rejection. At its heart lies the unresolved conflict between the colonial master and the native, which the mystery at the center of its plot both reveals and conceals. The essay's language therefore establishes a dynamic between the unspoken and the "spoken for"—on the one hand the silenced colonial subject rendered inadmissible to discourse, on the other that discourse itself that keeps telling the story again and again on its own terms. Here is how Said puts it: "The regular confrontation of a sullen, almost impersonal authority directed at one's personal freedom, in which one can only acquiesce without complaint— this was the reality that prevailed throughout the Middle East from my father's generation under Ottoman and British rule to mine under Israeli and undemocratic Arab rule. Now my son was experiencing it. Each generation seemed to hand it on to the next" (ibid., 12). Pain runs deep in the family's history, a history marred by expulsion, displacement, and dispossession. Perhaps even more hurtful is the rejection and denial of authorship to a place that was once home.

"In Arafat's Palestine" as a text cannot unbind all its historical ties to Palestine. Conversely, its ability to retrace the unseen and the unsaid of an oppressed people renders it peculiarly well-adapted to articulating the untold stories of oppression. The emphasis on the "unspeakable" is great both in the intensive sense of nameless horrors perpetrated by the Israeli army, and in the play of the narrative structure itself, with its many folds, stories within stories, secret confessions, and general difficulty in getting the story told at all. One of the oddest encounters between colonizer and colonized, as provided by Said, runs as follows:

> Wadie only spoke to [Israeli soldiers] if they addressed him; and invariably he did so in English. "What should I say?" I asked him. "Don't say anything until they speak to you. Don't even show your passport until they ask," he answered. I let him be the guide in this, except for the one time that a soldier appeared on my side of the car. "Passport," he asked, "Where are you from?" to which I almost replied "from here" but prudently settled for "New York" instead. "OK," he said noncommittally, and nodded us through. (Ibid., 10)

As a result, the Said *story* does get through, but in a muffled form, with a distorted lens accompanied by a kind of despair about any direct use of language. The essay is a passionate, seductive, and obdurate celebration of the plight of the Palestinians under Arafat. Its form is semiautobiographical, and in the tales of family pride and tribal loyalty, there is a good deal of sentimentality and nostalgia, offset by moments of empathy with the Israeli army. Its primary concerns are the fatal flaws of the PLO's bargain with Israel as well as the banality of working-class deprivation among poor Palestinians, depicted with an energy that is more visceral than intellectual. Perhaps this gutsy defence was Said's only tolerable option, a last-stand testimony, written in the summer of 1996, six months before the Israeli semi-withdrawal from Hebron (Said 1996: 54–62).

Said's language of passion captures the siege mentality that dominates the area. A string of endearing portraits of family and friends forms a fragile archipelago of insular and innocent lives overwhelmed by the rising tide of Jewish and Arab fundamentalisms. At times, one senses that Said has his back to the wall in summoning up a family history, nowhere more battered and engaging than in the evocation of the father, whose dislike for Jerusalem had a disarming combination of panache and pathos.

> My father spent his life trying to escape these objects, "Jerusalem" chief among them—the actual place as much as its reproduced and manufactured self. Born in Jerusalem, as were his parents, grandparents, and all his family back in time to a distant vanishing point, he was a child of the Old City who traded with tourists in bits of the true cross and crowns of thorn. Yet he hated the place; for him, he often said, it meant death. Little of it remained with him except a fragmentary story or two, an odd coin or medal, one photograph of his father on horseback, and two small rugs (*After the Last Sky*, 1986: 14).

Said, too, voices the same discomfort with the City of Jerusalem:

> As the Holy Land's nerve centre, and the likeliest source of future unrest, Jerusalem has never been especially attractive to me, although I was born there. There is something unyielding about the place that encourages intolerance; all sorts of absolute religious and cultural claims emanate from the city, most of them involving the denial or downgrading of the others (Ibid., 10).

The sting in the tale here is a studied and cutting reversal of the terms *born* and *intolerance*, as Said presents an exile's view of the reality at hand. And yet these heady family memories form a clear, and, most might say, dangerous anachronism when seen alongside the bloody actuality of occupation. They establish, too, the America-Palestine axis that gives the essay its backbone and the conflict its cutting colonial edge. Said's own view as to his son's future is incisive:

> After three-quarters of a year there Wadie now feels that he too is not moving forward. The daily tensions and uncertainties have accumulated; frustration turns into neck and head pains, insomnia, weight loss. My wife and I think it is time for him to leave, and he is coming round to that view. "But," he told me on our way to the airport, "I will always come back" ("In Arafat's Palestine," 1996: 14).

The road to freedom for those Palestinians living in Gaza and the West Bank seems clear. *They* are the ones who must bring about the changes for the better. In the short term, no part of the struggle on the terrain is available for Said. He must continue to live in exile while articulating the testimony of lived suffering. His sense of belonging, his pride in Palestine's heroism, and his pain at its defeats are felt from a distance. And ultimately, "In Arafat's Palestine" stands as a valediction, a leave-taking that is both private and public. Thus, Said, even though divided between his sense of loyalty to both his native Palestine and his adopted home (America), is still attempting to hold the line against a supposed "end of history," which alternates with an apparently irremediable loss of a homeland.

III

If the dominant perspective of *After the Last Sky* and "Palestine, Then and Now" is the displacement of "Said *pluriel*," in "The Mind of Winter," Said extends his reflections on life in exile to another displaced minority group. Exiles such as Joyce, Beckett, Pound, Simone Weil, and many other writers become part of another family; they are his literary forebears. Magisterially, he charts the progress and indeed the lived texture of their estrangement. Let me suggest that a writer such as Said has access to a second tradition, quite apart from his own racial history: the culture and political history of the phenomenon of displacement. He can therefore quite legitimately claim as his ancestors the Anglos, the Irish, and even the Jews. The literary past to which he belongs is a multicultural past, the history of immigrant America. José Marti and C. L. R. James are as much his literary forebears as Nabokov and Adorno. Said is quick to stress the importance of both intellectual mobility and counterhabitation: to live as migrants do in habitually uninhabited but nevertheless public places. It is what he calls the "spirit's nomadic wanderings." "When I say 'exile' I do not mean something sad or deprived. On the contrary, belonging, as it were, to both sides of the imperial divide enables you to understand them more easily" (1993: xxvii). He at his best identifies and then draws conclusions from firsthand exilic experience in the United States, a country built of multiple diasporas. His sharp-eyed and demystifying account of the issue of other displacements in a nation of immigrants is trenchant. America, he writes, has created great literature out of the phenomenon of cultural transplantation and the ways in which people cope with a life in a new world.

It may be that, by discovering what he has in common with those who preceded him, he can begin to reflect on his own predicament. And he does. He stresses that this is only one of many possible wanderings, for he thinks that we are inescapably nomadic at a time when the essay is the international way of writing back to a decentered center. Said finds pleasure in paying handsome tribute to exiles such as Auerbach, Conrad, Joyce; cross-pollination is everywhere. And it is perhaps one of the more pleasant freedoms of the literary migrant to be able to choose his ascendants. Said's, selected half consciously, half-not, include Nabokov, Weil, Steiner, Faiz, a polyglot family tree against which he measures himself and to which he would be honored to belong. He reminds one of that beautiful image in Saul Bellow's novel *The Dean's December*. The central character, Corde, hears a dog barking wildly somewhere. He imagines that the barking is the dog's protest against the limits of dog experience: "For God's sake," the dog is saying, "open the universe a little more!" (1982: 143). Bellow is not just talking about dogs, and the dog's anger, frustration, and desire to break down the boundaries are also Said's as well as our own. "For God's sake, open the universe a little more!" It is (and is not only) as a Palestinian that Said movingly accepts "our wanderings," pleading for the "open secular element, and not the symmetry of redemption" (*After the Last Sky*, 1986: 76). A request with which even his enemies agree.

Unlike *After the Last Sky* or "Palestine, Then and Now," "The Mind of Winter" confronts yet another predicament, that of the imaginary literary community. Making distinctions between exiles in the West and those in the East, Said offers a geopolitical contrast between those from the First World and those from the Third World. He finally settles for that other severed writer, Joseph Conrad. I have often wondered about Said's attachment to Conrad. His first book was about him, and references to the Polish exile abound in nearly all his works. Conrad was an exile who, like Said, crossed the boundaries of culture and mastered another's language. Said does not mention this affiliation but speaks of an intellectual debt to Conrad: "I felt, first coming across Conrad when I was a teenager, that in a certain sense I was reading, not so much my own story, but a story written out of bits of my life and put together in a haunting and fantastically obsessive way. He has a particular kind of vision which increases in intensity every time I read him, so that now it's almost unbearable for me to read him" (1987: 76). "The Mind of Winter" inhabits the discrepancy between a specific condition of a Palestinian exile and a more general twentieth-century range of options. In the first part we see him shivering without a "home" in winter, sustained only by the thought that back home (Palestine) the self is being reconstructed out of the refractions and discontinuities.

"The Mind of Winter" is nothing if not structured. With its "title apparatus," as Gérard Genette understands the term, it is an example of subversion. I would argue that the fourth section forms a *supplement*, in which the question of sign is both a philosophical and a linguistic matter: hence the necessity of a doubly ambiguous analysis, that is, an analysis on the one hand of linguistics operating within metaphysics and on the other of metaphysics inserted into linguistics. It is on the basis of this double *problématique* that Said proposes to look for new frontiers, new borders, new margins. As Derrida observes, the *supplement* is meant to harbor "within itself two significations whose cohabitation is as strange as it is necessary, it . . . adds itself, it is a surplus, a plenitude enriching another plenitude, the *fullest measure* of presence. It cumulates and accumulates presence" (1979: 144–45). For Said, the *"supplement"* is that "extra section," that gives rise to yet another page in history. The fourth section represents the next page, where the placement of the Palestinian plight within reality begins. The idea of the *supplement* becomes a joyride into the great unconscious of representation in an orgy of dissemination or the uninhabited scattering of meanings. What Derrida sardonically calls the "police forces of language" are juxtaposed to the main text. In Said's case, the *supplement* in *After the Last Sky* is conveyed through photo essays. In "Palestine, Then and Now," it is disclosed through a multitude of voices and that includes the author's. In "The Mind of Winter," each page contains two columns: one of prose, the other of prose and illustration. The latter column stands as a footnote insofar as it relates to matters raised on the page in question. Said's side notes float free and can be read at whatever point the reader wishes. Or can they? It is indeed at this point that reading "The Mind of Winter" becomes an oddly random experience, for, apart from the insets, there is the larger question of how to read the main column of print. It is a commentary on or exposition of the predicament of the exile as artist. And if the two columns resonate against each other, they are also two sounding bells with but a single clapper, the ricocheting reader. The essay imposes a certain vagrancy on the eyes and attention of we who read it so as to break us of our nasty linear habits. And if knowing in which order to read it is already a problem, making sense of it is a still more intractable one. It helps to have read something of Steiner and Darwish first, because they convey the same feeling of estrangement that Said wishes to convey. Hence his inclusion of what they have written on exile, for, by making them part of his text, he hopes to nurture his narrative on homelessness. For Said, writers do not own what they write. As a result, "The Mind of Winter," a movingly clever text, is as much ours as his, since what we get out of it may not be at all what he put into it. It performs the language as the spacing out of differentiation in a process that can have no single, undifferentiated origin. That would not have been Said's intention, of course.

In retrospect, one could argue that the optimistic mobility, the intellectual liveliness, and the logic of daring were more apposite images than the artist intended. "[I]t is no exaggeration to say that liberation as an intellectual mission, born in the resistance and opposition to the confinements and ravages of imperialism, has now shifted from the settled, established, and domesticated dynamics of culture to its unhoused, decentered, and exilic energies, energies whose incarnation today is the migrant, and whose consciousness is that of the intellectual and artist in exile, the political figure between domains, between forms, between homes, and between languages" (Said, 1993: 332). A similar notion of what Said intends occurs in *Mille plateaux*. It is what Gilles Deleuze and Félix Guattari aptly call "nomadologie," by which they mean precision, correctness, continuity, form—all these have the attributes of a nomadic practice whose power is not aggressive but transgressive.

Like *Out of Place*, of which I shall speak in the next chapter, "The Mind of Winter" seduced us with its brilliance at the time of its publication. There were those brief cumulatively hard-hitting paragraphs, and the irreverent, punchy writing style, honed in underground journalism. Even the arrangement of some of the essays (choice of quotations outlined in black breaking up pages at random) seemed novel. What makes these autobiographical works so germane to an understanding of the "Said phenomenon," though, is the multifacetedness of its author. Here is an academic trained in the arts of rhetoric and polemic, with an armory of literary and historical references, who is also explicitly oppositional. Of course, the author of an earlier exilic classic, *Minima Moralia*, had also combined formal academic training with a tumultuous private life. But Theodor Adorno siphoned his more extreme autobiographical references into his essays. Said, by contrast, drew richly and in depth on his exilic experiences. The use of the visual faculty to restore the nonsequential energy of lived historical memory and subjectivity as fundamental components of representation is alluded to by Said toward the end of "Opponents, Audiences, Constituencies, and Community," (1982) where he makes clear the aim of alternative photomontage: to tell other stories, to have "permission to narrate," as he put it (1984: 13). His use of the photo essay is to expose what has been repressed or framed in a context of confrontational hostility. In doing so, he reminds one of Barthes's "third meaning," that informational level that gathers together everything that can be learned from the setting. "This level," Barthes writes, "is that of communication" (1977: 52). By all his autobiographical works, Said recovers a history hitherto either misrepresented or rendered invisible. In having attempted such a recovery of buried lives, he hopes to alert us to the next phase, which is concerned with an ongoing political and social praxis. For without that, we are bound to sink again; the recovery would stop us from undoing what has been done. There would be no use in rearranging words into prodigal rhetoric.

Said's autobiographical detail a growing pain at having to "see ethnicity" after a life he characterizes as having been lived entirely on merit. Understanding the work of transplanted writers as a means of contributing meaning and values that are necessary and useful to people (readers) is thus vital to comprehending his plight. It was an easy thing, to be sure, even during the high noon of the bull market, to scoff at the dot coms, the hedge funds, the Silicon Valley millionaires, the day traders, and all the other ephemera of prosperity. But beneath all the prodigious bubbling, counsel to the wise, Said stands as a human icon as solid and reliable as Adorno or C. L. R. James, insofar as he is also a complex being, not easily understood by the earthbound and the pessimistic. His power is not a matter of simple force; nor does our faith in him resemble the native patriotism of the early انتفاضة (Uprising). Said, the public and private man, correctly and incorrectly understood, is a relationship, a thing of nuance and complexity, of irony and evasiveness. We are at once skeptical about him and more than ever ravenous consumers of his works. Writers like him are interactive beings who earn our loyalty through endless repetition and constant adjustment. A particular sensibility, not a cumulative argument, links together the essays I have been discussing; a perspective that combines erudition, ardor, and heterodox opinion. Said is after a different quarry from perspective, color, structure, tone. He is more a cerebral writer perhaps than a sensuous one. His sharp interrogative approach introduces an awkwardness into our relationship with his people. But that is a virtue. It is one of the ironies of postmodernism that these essays, so daring and jolting to his contemporaries, should have taken on a fully rounded existence in the first decade of the third millennium as testimony to displacement. They, with their sharp questions and peremptory demands, paint life in all its grand fun, unease, and pain.

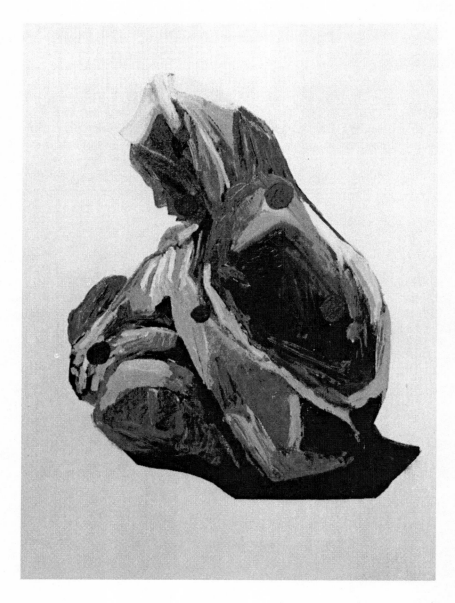

Ahmad Izmer, *Kharbaga; Or, Where D o We Go from Here?*, Acriylic & Clay, 26 x 34 cm.
© 2002.

CHAPTER FOUR

THE SITE OF MEMORY

A woman wailed
          and sang keens
                    the glutton element
flamed and consumed
          the dead of both sides.
                    Their great days were gone.
Warriors scattered
          to homes and forts
                    fewer now, feeling
the loss of friends.
          No ring-whorled prow
                    could up then
and away on the sea.
          Wind and water
                    raged with storms
wave and shingle
          were shackled in ice
                    until another year
appeared in the yard
          as it does to this day
                    the seasons constant
the wonder of light
          coming over us.
                    Winter was gone
earth's lap grew lovely
          the longing woke
                    for a voyage home.
                —Seamus Heaney, *The Spirit Level*, 97.

Edward Said grew up in times that had all the more influence on him because they were conservative, and he was not. He remained constantly open—almost to a fault, given the confusion of mind it was capable of producing in him—to what was being thought or written and what was happening privately and publicly around him. He who preferred to write about his childhood in Jerusalem and Cairo in our own day and age is duty bound to make less of his idiosyncracies—the three-piece suits, the pipe, the field sports, the riding lessons, and the occasional amours—so fatuously overdone in the past, and more of how his relation to the social, aesthetic, and political ideas that came and went in the Middle East in the 1940s and 50s. It suited him well as a rebel to mediate between the two environments known to him: at home and outside of it—the one rough but in its way supportive, the other civilized, mind-sharpening but also callous. And as with dissonant milieux, so it was with individuals: here, too, Said, when he writes, portrays himself as brokering an armistice between parties who could never in reality agree. If having been born astride two worlds was the unmaking of him as a child, it was the making of him as a writer and as someone who, when the moment came, threw in his lot politically, and instinctively one can but add, with the democratic Left. The lifelong *rêve du bon*, which has kept him writing year in year out, and which he feared he could not give up on without lapsing into wordless depression, may look flimsy, escapist even, when set against the social and political facts it could do little to mitigate. But, dreamer or not, today he is *in place* among the other truly important intellects of our century.

This chapter limits itself to Said's "oppressed memories": the quickness to indignation in *Out of Place* has its roots in a visceral early experience of knowing the oppressor (father, teacher, colonizer) too well. In the process, I shall draw on St. Augustine to prevent "mixture and the confusion of kinds." This way of reading Said serves "to keep things apart or in their place" (1998: 143). In section 2, I discuss what Pierre Nora calls "milieux" and "lieux de mémoire" in Said (1989: 7–25). In Jerusalem, Cairo, Alexandria, Dhour, as vanishing environments of memory and/or locations of identity that are either textual, monumental, emotional, or topographic, the past survives as a fetish of itself. *(Mi)lieux de mémoire* are therefore cultic phenomena, objects of pilgrimage and veneration, the jealously guarded ruins of cultural ensembles possessed by a need to stop time or, better yet, to launch a voyage of return to the past. Said does not forget this "memory world," to use Péguy's expression. He has his heart set on such a vanishing world, a world of olfactory memory, memory of childhood places, of the body, of childhood gestures, of pleasures. Memory nourishes the heart, and grief abates. What interests him is the *invisible*: his place of birth, Jerusalem; of childhood, Cairo; of holiday, Dhour; of nostalgia, Alexandria, are clearly, in this sense, *lieux* and *milieux de mémoire*. To choose a place, to move about freely is the right that our world, more and more, denies to Said *pluriel*. What is therefore the significance today, for Said and us, of this displacement that consists so often of no longer having a place? How real is the sorrow and/or loss of home? Can the past be recuperated from so much power arrayed against it? Can identity identify with itself? Said's works enact the paradox of dispossession as it takes possession of its place in the world, fragile yet strong enough to survive any mutilation.

I

In his essay on laughter, Bergson argues that comedy is chastening, not charitable. Laughter is defined by a certain absence of sympathy, a distancing and disinterestedness. A world that contained only pure intelligences would probably still include laughter; a world made up of pure emotionalists probably would not. Bergson appears to have been universalizing from the example of Molière, and in so doing produces a description of comedy that is mightily contradicted at almost every station of literature (1998: 34–41). For literature's greatest category might be precisely one of systematic comedy: in particular, that paradoxical shuffle of condescension and affiliation we are made to feel by Bottom the weaver or Don Quixote or Uncle Toby or Zeno or Pin. Such characters have busy souls. They are congested by an aspiration that outstrips their insight. They claim to know themselves, as Said does in his memoir, but their selves, like Said's, are too dispersed to be known. It is we who know them, because we know at least something about them: that they are self-ignorant. They are rich cavities, into which we pour a kindly offering. If we are the only ones who can provide the knowledge they lack about themselves, then we ourselves have become what they lack, have become a part of them.

Said, both as narrator and as character in *Out of Place*, belongs to this company. Along with language, what else is at the core of his memory? Where does geography—especially in the displaced form of departures, arrivals, farewells, exile, nostalgia, homesickness, belonging, and travel itself—fit in? How do we get from the lone, fragile child to the consummate public intellectual? Is the canvas he paints the necessary outcome, the "truth," of Said the heroic dissenting child? To put it in Hegel's terms: How does the ethically impeccable "noble consciousness" imperceptibly pass into the servile "base consciousness"? Of course, for a "postmodern" Third World reader immersed in New Age ideology, there is no tension: Said is simply following his destiny and deserves praise for reclaiming a transcultural and often painful upbringing, the "experience of multiplicity, its torments and confusions, but also its liberations and possibilities. To read him is to come to know his family and his younger self as closely as we know characters in literature, and to be shown, intimately and unforgettably, what it has meant in the last half century to be a Palestinian."[2] The memoir tells, sometimes quite movingly, of the author's passage from the hothouse home life he was subjected to into a larger, non-Arab world wherein he finds himself reduced all too often to a mere stereotype.

The memoir restricts Said himself to what Michael Holroyd calls "a good walk-on part," assigning the leading roles to friends and family. Avowedly happier with the lives of others than with his own, Said remains as close as circumstances permit to the condition of the invisible watcher. *Out of Place* had formerly provided an "exit from myself," he observes. "These details are important as a way of explaining to myself and to my reader how the time of the memoir is intimately tied to the time, phases, ups and downs, variations in my illness" (1999: 11). The narrative shows Said stepping from his own life into those of other people where there seemed to be so much more going on. He suggests that in the first instance conveying the story to the reader was a crucial part of his larger mission as a witness to a period long gone. Second, perhaps more important, he reminds us, so he maintains, of St. Augustine, who observes: "When I am recollecting and telling my story I am looking at its image in present time" (*Confessions*, 1998: 67), and Said often rather delicately directs our attention to his memorabilia (photographs, anecdotes, pen, paper, manuscript). All this is happening, we are to believe, as he writes. He will suddenly say of some object like the batch of films he recovered six months after his mother died, each one carefully encased in the white and blue boxes, left over from the past, "I touch them with my fingers"— they are there on his desk or at the bottom of one of his nondescript cardboard boxes, provoking his curiosity every now and then as to which portion of his life is preserved in them as they slowly sink into oblivion and final disuse; he remarks their present in thinking of their past. One's angle of vision on the past varies along with the passage of time, always in the present and always giving the past a different appearance or history.

"All families invent their parents and children," Said states,

> give each of them a story, character, fate and even a language. There was always something wrong with how I was invented and meant to fit in with the world of my parents and four sisters. Whether this was because I constantly misread my part or because of some deep flaw in my being I could not tell for most of my early life. Sometimes I was intransigent, and proud of it. At other times I seemed to myself to be nearly devoid of character, timid, uncertain, without will. Yet the overriding sensation I had was of never being quite right (Ibid., 1999, 3).

A Conradian scholar, Said is also, like the subject of *The Nigger of Narcissus*, a sick man who is nevertheless determined to live until he dies. One thing to be said about *Out of Place* is that it is a heroic instance of writing against death. Reminiscent of Proust's great novel-cycle because of its own recapturing of lost time, and of Balzac, for the clarity of its social and historical perceptions, the narrative repeatedly explores the negative effects of exile, division, and estrangement, shifting focus from Cairo to Beirut, with Jerusalem in the middle, moving with provocative ease between collective and individual consciousness. As its beginnings show, it is keenly aware of the inventions, blurrings, and imaginative figments that go to make up our sense of ourselves and our kin. It knows everything there is to know about displacement, about rootings and uprootings, about feeling wrong in the world, and it absorbs the reader precisely because such out-of-place experiences lie at or near the heart of what it is to be alive in our jumbled, chaotic times.

The creative wholeness that connects Said's early emotional experiences with the political form of adult imagination makes it clear that a chronic and consuming need to be "located" (to use his word) in a known, possessed *place* encourages the writer to underanalyze his politics and to simplify his way to ambiguity. This is not a sly way of saying that Palestinian nationalism is a neurosis and that Said's fear of dislocation could be resolved more effectively by visiting a therapist than by writing about the oppressed and the silenced. It is, however, to respect the honesty of his acute observation that he remains faithful to much received thinking about Palestine, because the brokenness of the Palestinian past, as understood through a quasinationalist perspective, matches his sense of self, "its fragmentations extended into mine," he maintains (ibid., 189). There is a duality to *place*. By this, Said means that a place that develops in time both happened and happens to *us* but also that, because the imagination mediates such happenings, Jerusalem and/or Cairo is inseparable for him from another familially significant site, hundreds of miles away, where the extended members of his family spent their summer holiday. Said writes movingly about Dhour el Shweir as "fragile and transitory" (ibid., 209). He makes us freshly aware of how *this* place composed of lives in a state of process occupies a transitional zone not just between town and country but between the young vitality of new families shouting and calling far into the summer night and the quiet of streets with mature gardens from which children have departed. For him, the temporality of Dour el Shweir is most to be valued, however, because it is open to space-time border crossings. But even there, Said cannot write of "permanence" without qualifying it as "illusory." It is as though, by thinking about dislocation in time as well as in place, he has translated unhappiness at exile into anxiety about a forbidden place, well beyond the academic example of Plato and the poets driven riven out of the city.

In principle, a memoir is the most intimately particular of all forms of writing, philosophy the most abstract and impersonal. They might be oil and water. But it was Augustine and Rousseau who gave us the personal and sexual confession and Descartes who offfered the first "history of my mind" (2000: 31). In modern times, Nietzsche and Russell, Sartre and Barber, all left records of themselves more memorable than anything else written about them. Said, too, entered the list with a work he invites us to read as the flip side of life. For *Out of Place* illustrates a line in a poem by Philip Larkin: "They fuck you up, your mum and dad" (1991: 211). It is a candid and searing examination of parental effect, told with a

mixture of love, perplexity, and resentment. It is also a story of cultural displacement and historical crisis, but, overwhelmingly, private life dominates public
events. The Said family members are Palestinian by origin, largely resident in
Cairo, and possessors of American passports—except the mother, who is in consequence like a soul in limbo, forced to wait for a passage across the Styx. They
are Christian Arabs, who alternate between speaking Arabic and English; they
are wealthy amid the poverty of the Levant. They have a foothold in several cultures and an abiding home in none. And all around, their world is in turmoil.
Yet, given all this rootlessness, the directing force of Said's growing up in Cairo
is intimate and familial, governed by the personalities of his parents, who had
many houses, having been, originally, a family of substance. Here their history,
both as it really was and as it was sometimes falsely represented, is told at some
length. Said, a lover of documented fact, does his family proud in a literary sense
in that it vividly steps from the page. Both father and mother loom largest in the
recollected narrative, prompted, as Said poignantly states, by the diagnosis of the
incurable illness that has afflicted him for the past seven years and that he likens
to the "sword of Damocles" (Ibid., 215). Said's most intimately personal book,
and a conscious effort at a more literary form, the memoir, covers Said's life until
the early 1960s and forms a record of a lost world. Its spur was personal grief.
"My mother was dying [of cancer] at the time and I thought, there's an end to a
special part of my life" (ibid., 195). And in order to accede to the daylight of the
public space of the narrative, in the muffled resistance of a life on the edge, it
also happens that another space becomes the ultimate recourse for tricking time
and thereby defying death.

Like the narrator's mother in Proust's *À la recherche,* who leaves the love bits
out in case her cosseted boy is not yet ready for them, Hilda Said had a "fabulous
capacity for letting you trust and believe in her, even though you knew that a
moment later she could either turn on you with incomprehensible anger and
scorn or draw you in with her radiant charm. 'Come and sit next to me, Edward,'
she would say, thereby letting you in her confidence, and allowing you an amazing
sense of assurance" (ibid., 60). The attractive portrayal of Hilda as energy itself is
the record of a muddled life lived with estimable generosity and resilience. You do
not have to read every word of *Out of Place* to form high opinion of the person
who went through it ceaselessly probing, judging, and captivating her *enfant terrible,* a *lustus naturae,* who grew up to be the Arab world's paragon. At times,
though, one wonders whether the portrait of Hilda (so sedative is the effect of
her voice on her jumpy Edward) has turned not so much on memory, but rather
on the bilateral relationship between mother and son, "a constellation only she
could see as a whole" (ibid.). This constellation so dominates the narrative that at
times it rather resembles a double bed of which only one side has been slept in.
The varieties of her vicariousness make Edward full of comedy and mischief.
Though his representation of her is often tender, it is rarely needy; it is never in

doubt that it is this teenaged boy, the only son, who has the greater power—the power to excite, to disappoint, and to impress his mother. She remains devoted to her son. He explains:

> By the time I was fully conscious of speaking English fluently, if not always correctly, I regularly referred to myself not as "me" but as "you." "Mummy doesn't love you, naughty boy," she would say, and I respond, in half-plaintive echoing, half-defiant assertion, "Mummy doesn't love you, but Auntie Melia loves you. . . ." "No she doesn't," my mother persisted. "All right. Saleh [Auntie Melia's Sudanese driver] loves you," I would conclude, rescuing something from the enveloping gloom (Ibid., 4–5).

In one sense, then, Edward outgrew his mother before he himself grew up; and if this is the case, then he had outgrown his mother early on, because his mother's emotional need of him had always been more acute than his of his mother. This outgrowing of his mother naturally produces at times a stiff loneliness, as when he writes to one of his sisters that his mother's devotion to him makes him feel both loved and sad. At other times, that loneliness—or perhaps "aloneness" is the better word—erupts into a slightly grotesque hypertrophy of authority, in which the teenager feels impelled to instruct his mother.

Hilda Said, whom Edward worshiped, is an extraordinary mixture of naivety and sophistication. She smothers her only son with attention and concern, but her ambivalence has him in a constant state of uncertainty. At one moment she is all admiration and affection; at another, she is cold and dismissive. He is forever in pursuit of her approval. "As I look back over the years," he writes with gripping affection,

> I can see the real anxiety induced in me by my mother's withdrawal, where the need to reconnect with her was kept alive paradoxically by the obstacles she placed before me. She had become a taskmaster whose injunctions I had to fulfill. Yet the emptiness into which I fell during and after my errands when she gave little warmth or thanks genuinely bewildered me. The intelligence of our relationship was temporarily gone, in Dhour replaced by the series of drills set for me to keep me out of everyone's way (Ibid., 156).

In later life, she tells him: "My children have all been a disappointment." He is devastated and reflects with the wisdom of adult vision that her overwhelming effect has had disabling consequences on his relationships with other women. But she is also his mentor and support. Brilliant and manipulative, Hilda set her children at odds, always keeping Edward and his sisters "off-balance." Neurotically difficult to please, Hilda always gave the impression that "she had judged you and found you wanting," yet she instilled in Edward the love of literature and music on which he built his career (ibid., 211).

Edward's relationship with his father, though a more intimidating one, is still a matter of subdued will. Wadie is seen to be both funny and pathetic in his desire that his son should not follow his own downward path. He—who called himself "William" to emphasize his adopted identity—is a powerful but silent presence in the narrative. Tall, taciturn, overbearing, and uncommunicative, "a devastating combination of power and authority, rationalistic discipline and repressed emotions," Wadie is portrayed as a laconic man whose Victorian strictness instilled in Edward "a deep sense of generalized fear which I have spent most of my life trying to overcome" (ibid., 71). He never told his son more than "10 or 11 things about his past" (ibid., 82). As a result, Edward reveals himself as agonized, introspective, and to a considerable degree self-regarding—an uneasy person sprung from an uneasy background.

Generous, combustible, nobly hysterical, facetious when he would like to be solemn, stoical in resolve but crumbling in practice, free in spirit but actually confined to the train of his destiny by the nature of his ticket, Wadie is in fact an affecting father, with a kind of anxious serenity. *Out of Place*, a moving book, shows that he was less naive, much less unlettered, and more worldly than his son; but the two men share an ungoverned generosity and are, at the same time, stalked by an ungoverned anxiety. Dad is an overflowing spirit, breathing the germs of vicarious aspiration over his clever and dutiful son. There is often a hope, however unwitting, that the son may not resemble the father, who grounds his own dreams in his liberated and intelligent Edward. In some respects Wadie Said must have been an ideal father: he existed to be outgrown and knew it; and yet his support for his five children was absolute and could never be outgrown, or even rivaled. His love was greater than his authority: thus he was never paternally ex officio, but always instead a kind of civilian in fatherhood, an amateur at paternity. What is delightful about the father who lives in these pages is that unlike most ambitious parents, he does not squeeze his son for guilt. Quite the opposite. He does not envy his son his experiences, or reproach him for them, but instead identifies with them so strongly that he shares them, takes them over. It is as if Dad, in dispensing advice so freely and confidently, has already lived, in a previous incarnation, the experiences he so longs to hear about; his son is his avatar. It is here that Said combines analysis with reverence for his domineering but loving father in vivid, evocative prose:

> In June of 1957, when I graduated from Princeton, it culminated in my father's insisting on taking me to a brace and corset maker in New York in order to buy me a harness to wear underneath my shirt. What distresses me about the experience is that at age twenty-one I uncomplainingly let my father feel entitled to truss me up like a naughty child whose bad posture

symbolized some objectionable character trait that required scientific punishment. The clerk who sold us the truss remained expressionless as my father amiably declared, "See, it works perfectly. You'll have no problems" (Ibid., 64).

And, of course, Dad *has* really lived these experiences, because he has imagined them so many times. There is a nobility in this attitude, a mental triumph. Dad has a tendency to overcome difficulties, because his fantasy is an army, running on a thousand legs.

As a result, the son who was rather mediocre at school seems at first unrelated to his emotionally ragged father. He tends to hoard himself, whereas Dad is more generous with himself. While Wadie is amiably generous to all, Edward can be royally haughty. While Dad is uncertain, burying his human fragility in a muff of warm advice, the son seems for his years adamantine, extraordinarily confident, and penetrating. While the father is lavish with verbal banalities, the son's responses are defined by the thrift of their omissions. One has a sense of a young man reserving the essential self for his work and sharing only his dilutions with his family. Edward does eventually reveal himself in time, and the reader is able to discern an anxiety and pride that seem reminiscent of his father's. "I only realized years later, when I had gone my own way: that there was more to 'Edward' than the delinquent yet compliant son, submitting to his father's Victorian design" (ibid., 79). While his father has labored all his life for his small supplement of liberty, in America, young Edward already has an incipient aristocratic liberty of mind. The difference derives in part from the fact that the son, unlike the father, is able to feel free with so little freedom. The passing respect of a *suffragi* (butler) suffices, because such gestures are essential to Edward's sense of life but not to his sense of self. Dad's political metabolism is, by comparison, inefficient; his sense of freedom is too clumsy and ponderous to be nourishing. Edward's wants are superbly narrow. He desires to be respectfully left alone so that he can concentrate his self-originated freedom and convert it into writing. "I wanted to get beyond the various cages in which I found myself placed, and which made me feel so dissatisfied, and even distasteful to myself" (ibid., 31). His family, and especially his abundant mother, provokes his warmth. In time, he learned to perform, to act a part. Again, one has the impression of the true self, a writing self, waiting in the wings.

Whether as an embattled boy in the English and American schools of Cairo or as a university professor at Columbia, Said has *chosen* to remain the misunderstood stranger. He describes a bourgeois rearing few will envy—the burden of expectation onerous, the criticisms picayune and mean-spirited, the surveillance constant and sometimes plain crazy. He recounts a scene in which his parents rage at their pubescent son for failing to have semen stains in his pajama pants. He must be abusing himself, they reason. (Can Wadie really have commanded, in

English, Arabic, or any other language, "Have a wet dream!" as the author claims?) In trying to find an answer to the question posed here, one comes away with a dizzying sense of contradiction. On the one hand, "My father never spoke of making love," Said writes, "and certainly not of fucking," and on the other, his mother gets impregnated because she, with the help of her husband, "wrote a letter to Jesus and he sent us a baby!" (ibid., 71). The world of young Said, who tells us that these family depictions are the outcome of a psychoanalysis, is bizarre and disturbed, to say the least. While writing his impressions down may have been therapeutic, they are too drawn-out and display an unironical self-involvement.

The bonds in Arab families usually extend far beyond parents and siblings. Said convinces us that he regarded his aunt's house as "home" even if it was not his actual domicile. The nostalgia for it persisted. As time went by, the life with his extended Jerusalem family acquired a languid, almost dreamlike aspect for him, in contrast to the more tightly organized and disciplined life with his sisters, who are a shadowy presence in the memoir. Edward was the central figure; that is made clear. During a summer vacation in Dhour el Shweir, in retreat from Victoria College (Cairo) where he had done less than brilliantly in his first year of school, Said found himself talking to Zeine Zeine, professor of history at the American University of Beirut. As he explains, he sensed, at the time, a power in the encounter. Now it strikes him with the force of a delayed remembering: "A gifted storyteller, Professor Zeine went with me on my first museum visit, to Cairo's Wax Museum, where in the funerally still, empty rooms framed by elaborate wax scenes from modern Egyptian history, Zeine would speak grippingly about Muhammad Ali, Bonaparte, Ismail Pasha, the Orabi rebellion, and the Denshawi incident" (ibid., 166). Another no less important person in Said's life as a child is his Jerusalem aunt Nabiha, his father's sister. She is an emblem of all the realities abstracted from the Jerusalem-Cairo-Beirut axis. She stands for the sufferings of ordinary folk—not least because, according to Said, she was the first person to give shelter to the many displaced Palestinians who flocked into Cairo after 1948. Reading about her, the narrative allows us to identify the grounds of المنفى (exile and estrangement), where the complexity of collective history meets, and is partly defeated by, her investment in a psychology of belonging. Said's engagement with Palestine, as he describes it, drew on deep emotional roots, particularly his affection for his aunt. "Whatever political ideas she may have had were hardly ever uttered in my presence: they did not seem necessary at the time. What was the central importance was the raw, almost brutal core of Palestinian suffering, which she made it her business to address every morning, noon and night" (ibid., 154). Later, Said would observe that it was both the annexation of Palestine by Israel in 1948 and the sheer scale of the Arab defeat in 1967, with the new wave of refugees it unleashed, that reconnected him with his younger self.

Augustine, patron saint of confession, also writes about its paradoxes. "I can be far from glad remembering myself to have been glad, and far from sad when I recall my past sadness" (*Confessions*, 1998: 211). Said's account of his family home environment emphasizes its constant moody temper and its joyless eccentricities, but he recounts them with suave good humor as if they had by now become enjoyable and even funny.

> He had arranged his days so that they were a harmonious succession of little joys, and the absence of the least of these joys threatened the whole edifice. . . . [A] thousand quiet pleasures which were waiting for him at every turning of life, which he had foreseen and looked forward to, were as necessary to him as the air he breathed, and it was thanks to them that he was incapable of feeling any real suffering.[3]

Or, the "annals of anonymity," in Paul Valery's formula, link a way of operating to a way of living. *Out of Place*, too, rejoices quietly and continually in the painful practice of everyday life and the idiosyncrasies of the family. It impresses its family portraits upon us as well as teaching us a good deal about bourgeois behavior, which creeps into the narrative through the servants' entrance. The note is perfectly struck in the descriptions of the *other* Arabs, the underclass of Egyptian Muslims (the Salihs, the Azizes, the Ahmads) who are made to clean, wait on, drive, baby-sit, and serve the Saids. Kitchen maids, house maids, chauffeurs, gardeners, hurrying messengers, and other unlettered characters are not allowed to represent themselves or tell their stories. In fact, they are scarcely perceived as having stories, which are not so much refused as ruled out by the author. It is in keeping with Said's carefully controlled tone that he makes as little as possible of their presence, except, that is, as subalterns *operating from below*. His ability to discern and identify the hidden political agendas and contexts in the canons of Western culture—from the invisible colonial plantations that guarantee the domestic tranquility and harmony of Mansfield Park to the hundreds of Egyptian lives sacrificed before the imperial spectacle marked by the composition of *Aida* (the opening of the Suez Canal)—falters when it comes to servant figures, acting as doubles, who, it seems, played a major role in the making of their masters (the Saids in this case). They come across as unimaginable pieces of history. If the East was used by Europeans who carved careers out of transmitting, interpreting, and debating representations of the native *Other*, it is also used by Said who, in placing the subaltern in the margins of his narrative, exults in the role of the dominant master. *Out of Place* provides a fierce instance:

> As my day began at seven-thirty, what I witnessed was invariably stamped with night's end and day's beginning—the black-suited *ghaffeers*, or evening

watchmen, slowly divesting themselves of blankets and heavy coats, sleepy-eyed *suffragis* shuffling off to market for bread and milk, drivers getting the family car ready. There were rarely any other grown-ups about at that hour (1999: 37).[4]

An instance like this one strikes the reader as a portrait of the native servant as a resourceful Sam Weller or a solid Nelly Dean even if Said gets a good deal of quiet, sometimes slightly pained, fun out of it.

Holding and discovering secrets, the servants by their disclosures are often the means of the plot. The relation the reader perceives between them and those they serve is dense with complexity and sophistication. Their presence creates space in which the narrative is at liberty to move beyond itself: they provide another way of seeing the motivation and action of the dominant class represented here by Wadie Said (Anglo-Protestant business male). The dust jacket of the American edition of *Out of Place* blithely exhibits the order of things: the poorly dressed faithful figure wearing a طربوش (Tarboosh) standing alone in front of the main branch of the Cairo Standard Stationery Company on Malika Street (Cairo) embodies silent gestures toward the overpowering Wadie Said (in a bow tie in the doorway) who is seen to relish his narrative mission of bringing knowledge and order to the Arab world. It is the subaltern's resilience that defines his or her literary representation. He or she is often the interface between the reader and the text's scheme of values, which is regularly undercut by the subaltern's canny presence, still winking at the reader.

The strong heritage of servants means that their presence challenges the narrative's pretensions to realistic truth. The servant's disobedience, or conversely fidelity, becomes a means of breaking free from the ground rules of realism. Freedom within service is marked in his or her language. Full of proverbs (the proverbial servant is as old as Miranda or Sancho or older) and malapropisms, quotations, and garrulous eccentricities, the language of the servant can express a refusal to follow directions issued from above. More telling still are the assumptions that underlie the servant's language. "Everyone lives life in a given language," Said observes. "Everyone's experiences therefore are had, absorbed, and recalled in that language" (ibid., xiii). Here, Said knows that it is not his vocation to speak for the domestic minor and the marginal, even if at times he seems sympathetic to their condition as an underclass.

The families close to us all had their own staff of drivers, gardeners, maids, washerwomen, and an ironing man, some of whom were familiar to all. "Our" Ahmed, the Dirliks' Hassan, the Fahoum's Mohammed, were almost talismanic in their presence; they turned up in our conversations as staples of our quotidian diet, like the garden or the house, and it felt as if they were our possessions, much like old family retainers in Tolstoy. . . . I felt that I was like the servants in the controlled energy that had no license to appear during the many hours of service, but talking to them gave me a sense of freedom and release—illusory, of course—that made me happy for the time spent in such encounters (Ibid., 197).

Said sees himself fulfilling the task of writing a memoir (which he conceived as a testimony to his children) from a position of cultural ascendancy and seems untroubled that his handling of the *other* narrative, that of the faithful servant, might in itself dwindle into the marginalized utterance of a lost cause. And while Said celebrates the "placelessness" of place (New York comes to mind), he associates "place" "locale" with cosmopolitanism. He in fact speaks

> of them with a hint of contempt, as in his condescending reference to Youngstown, Ohio, in his conversation with Salman Rushdie, as "a town I don't know, but you can imagine what it is like" (Said, 1994b: 115). According to Said, Youngstown, Ohio, is a recipient of Palestinian immigrants, and he is concerned mainly with their plight. But Youngstown, Ohio, in the American "rust belt," is also an old working class city in decline with the decline in steel industries, and the globalization of the U.S. economy; its non-Arab inhabitants, too, may be deserving of empathy and solidarity (Dirlik, 2001: 21).

Said's attitude toward the native Egyptian Arab working class heroes, the local poor workers or the new Palestinian immigrant to Youngstown, Ohio, chimes with what Slavoj Žižek has aptly called the "interpassive socialism" of the Western academic Left. These leftists are not interested in activity—merely in "authentic" experience. They allow themselves to pursue their well-paid academic careers in the West, while using the idealized Other (servant in this case, in other instances, it could be Cuba or Nicaragua) as the stuff of their ideological dreams: they dream through the Other but turn their backs on it if it disturbs their complacency to abandon socialism and opt for liberal capitalism.[5]

If Said were only his stories of an edifying Western bourgeois liberalism, of the sort Žižek describes, then we could safely abandon him to a museum case, but he is of course a creation of a time and a place. And in his time and in his place he was as enmeshed within family life as any of us. The conception of *Out of Place* arises, too, out of a compelling personal situation. Diagnosed with leukemia and struggling with side effects of the treatment, Said decided to write the memoir as therapy and as an introspective journey into the past. It is the private view of a public man. The impression that endures is that of a restless spiritual energy ceaselessly grappling with the contradictions, complexities, and injustices of the world from the privileged minority perspective he inherited from his wealthy but dislocated family. The circumstances in which the book was written, in periods of remission or between bouts of chemotherapy, add to its testamentary force. "Despite the travail of disease and restrictions imposed on me by my having left the places of my youth, I can say with Coleridge: 'Nor in this bower, / This little lime-tree bower, have I not mark'd / Much that has soothed me'" (Ibid., 11). The memoir is not an apologia hastily assembled to counter Zionist polemics. It is a powerful and, at the most fundamental level, a thoroughly convincing statement from a man who has helped to illuminate our crisis-ridden world.

The greatest modern autobiographers rejoice in the difficult awareness that, while one is inevitably the protagonist of one's own story, adjacent lives are just as real and just as sovereign in their interest. Out of such awareness spring the humor and irony that are fundamental to great autobiography. In a book such as Nabokov's *Speak, Memory* the reader is made to experience the independent reality of those who have peopled the author's life; they are not just there to get their comeuppance. Reading *Out of Place*, one wishes in vain for such emphatic discoveries. Instead, a tone of peremptory self-justification prevails, which sometimes degenerates into chilling detachment (a quality, to be fair, that the author recognizes in himself). One revealing passage, near the end of the book, tells of a terrible collision Said had with a motorcyclist while traveling in Switzerland. The man on the bike was killed, and Said was injured and transported to a hospital. In the three remaining pages of the book, he has, astonishingly, not another word to say about the dead man. But after such a terrible experience, regardless of who was at fault, does not one have (as any of the great autobiographers would know, as the Conrad scholar ought to know) a secret sharer?

Most modern autobiographers seem to think of themselves as outsiders, drifters, solitaries, especially if they were writers before they turned to self-revelation. And Said is no exception. Certainly this book is *written*. For all the evidence that the atmosphere of his home was saturated with unhappiness, the narrative that describes it sounds reasonably contented. Home was material for a text that tries as hard as possible to be a set of "biographemes," in Roland Barthes's formula. The calm, though, belongs to the writer at his desk, remembering pain with a pleasure not immodestly insisted on and enhanced by a liberal use of legitimate real voices. At its center, *Out of Place* turns out to be a stirring coming-of-age story, detailing the writer's journey from youngster to university student to fully fledged artist and critic. Inventive in its style and technique, Said's narrative paints a moving portrait of its hero's quest to create his own character, language, life, and art, "to forge in the smithy of . . . [his] soul the uncreated conscience of . . . [his] race" (Joyce, 1991: 23).

II

The power Said recognizes in a place (Jerusalem, Cairo, Dhour, Alexandria), the power of certain tradition-soaked places to secure and bestow identity, is one that Pierre Nora discusses in his essay "Between Memory and History: *Les Lieux de Memoire*." He distinguishes between "history" and what he calls "places" of memory (1989: 7–25). The distinction Nora draws between *milieux* and *lieux de mémoire* rests on his conviction that history has so nearly triumphed over memory, that remembrance can survive only as a sort of fetishism. By history, Nora intends something closer to historiography, something like what Hans Georg Gadamer called "historicism"—the systematic knowledge of the past that succeeds a "traditionalist" recuperation of the past. History, for Gadamer and his followers, disenchants the past. It preserves the past as one or another representation of itself. It regards the past as an object of labor, as a complex fiction susceptible to endless reinterpretations, as something we rework but, crucially, something incapable of making any meaningful claims on us. Memory, by contrast, is effortless but demanding. It defines who we are. It delineates an environment in which we live and move and have our being. *Lieux de mémoire* are not, therefore, static. Curiously then, it is precisely at the moment that we become aware of our environments of memory, precisely at the moment that we pause to contemplate the past expanding the present, as the past ceases to be an environment and becomes an object or, more properly, an invitation to an inquiry into a subject, that memory almost immediately reappears as History. And this, Nora suggests, is our moment when memory survives the traditionalist moment and becomes a trace of itself, as a precious residue, a lingering scent haunting certain, prized, *lieux de mémoire*. They are places where an identity-preserving, identity-enchanting, and identity-transforming aura lingers or is made to appear (Baucom, 1999). They are, for Said, the places in which he can locate and secure his identity. These *lieux de mémoire* may be either natural or man made, either people or landscapes. The implicit argument of each of these places and/or people is that they determine Said's hybrid identity.

There is always a sense of shrewd organization in Said's performance, an organization that completely eschews scholarly effects but relies instead on precise verbal articulation, clarity of interpretation, and mastery and control of subject, including the most esoteric ones. "Homage to a Belly-Dancer" and "In Memory of Tahia" are both good examples of what I mean. The essays pay handsome tribute to a female artist—namely, Tahia Carioca, the renowned Egyptian belly dancer. Said paints her portrait with a meticulous brush. A left-wing radical, an actress-activist and political militant, and, like Umm Kalthoum, the remarkable symbol of a national culture, she stood unique throughout her career. He expounds:

> Her career lasted 60 years, from her first days as a dancer at Badia's Opera Square Casino in the early Thirties, through the rule of King Farouk, of Gamal Abdel Nasser, Anwar al Sadat and Hosni Mubarak. Each of them, except, I think, Mubarak, imprisoned her at least once for various, mostly political offences. She also acted in hundreds of films and dozens of plays,

took part in demonstrations, was a voluble, not to say aggressive member of the actors' syndicate, and in her last years had become a pious (though outspoken) Muslim known to all her friends and admirers as "al-Hagga" ("In Memory of Tahia," 1999: 25).

It is, I think, some sort of testimony to the stubborn durability of the Saidian prose that fascinating aspects of it emerge in eccentric works like "Homage" and "In Memory," which are profoundly moving accounts of the plight of a displaced female artist in the Arab world today, seen not exclusively as the result of oppression and injustice but also as the extension of problems endemic to Arab society.

Tahia's life and death—despite the proliferating videos, the retrospectives of her films, the memorial occasions when she will be eulogized—symbolize the enormous amount of life in that part of the world that goes unrecorded and unpreserved. None of the Arab countries I know has proper state archives, public record offices, or official libraries any more than any of them has a decent regard for their monuments or antiquities, the history of their cities or individual works of architecture—mosques, palaces, schools, universities, museums. What we have instead is a sprawling, teeming history off the page, out of sight and hearing, beyond reach, largely unrecoverable. "Our history is mostly written by foreigners—visiting scholars, intelligence agents—," Said goes on to say, "while we rely on personal and disorganized collective memory, gossip almost, and the embrace of a family or knowable community to carry us forward in time" (ibid., 24). Said in writing about a cultural monument like Tahia, interweaves a number of strands, all of them connected to the main protagonist and illustrative in quite inventive ways of his central idea, recovering the life of an artist, in spite of other competing Arab narratives.

In the following excerpt, he describes the Cairo where he set out to write about the official history of this unique Egyptian dancer and actress. To best convey appreciation of his bare, involuted prose I quote him at length.

[T]here is a paradox in a city at once a great metropolitan center, a great alternative site (1) to the powerful contained interests of the metropolitan West in the Orient and (2) to Alexandria, the Levantine city par excellence; and yet, most impressively, Cairo is a city that doesn't force upon you some sort of already-existing totality. In other words, there's a certain relaxation in the idea of Cairo—at least the way I've gradually grasped it—which makes it possible for all manner of identities to exist unhurriedly within this whole. The idea is an indistinct one but you can actually experience it. All kinds of histories, narratives, and presences intersect, coexist in what I suggest is a "natural" way. For me that defines the pleasurably urban—not Paris, the vigorously planned city as an Imperial Center, nor London, with its carefully displayed monumentality, but rather a city providing a relaxed interchange between various incomplete, partially destroyed histories that still exist and partially do not, competed over, contested, but somehow existing in this rather, in my view, fascinating way. Cairo has come to symbolize for me, therefore, a much more attractive form of the way in which we can look at history, not necessarily to look at it as something neatly manageable by categories or by the inclusiveness of systems and totalizing processes, but rather through the inventory that can be reconstructed (1992: 223–24).

Said's archival method of excavating history and culture brings the reader up short with a gesture or a sequence that rends the veil of sentimentality. Most of the participants (the Lebanese woman who compiled a list of eighty or ninety of Tahia's films and just gave them to him, the librarian and the belly dancer herself) are committed people even if they perform the required volte-face with conviction. Said's own work is much more self-consciously avant-garde. His narrative style in "Homage" and "In Memory" is understated, although his realization of the story greatly amplifies and elaborates the narrative. Odd bits of comedy and despair jostle each other. What makes the essays a pleasure to read is their *contrapuntal* unexpectedness, their hypnotic rhythm, their eccentricity, their almost tangential connection to Cairo itself. It is as if this work of narrative mastery, by turns witty and unutterably sad, has established a new nondiscursive medium for Cairo, which in one of its trajectories has gone beyond the dominant and insurrectionary aspect of Arab life.

Cairo has always been at the center of Said's life. "Cairo Recalled" (a kaleidoscope of the years of his childhood and adolescence in Palestine and Egypt just before the time when he left to come to America) is a testimony to the world of that gray zone in one's life, what Hélène Cixous terms "frail roots" (Cixous and Gruber, 1997: 261). The paradox of living on a borderline, in between, puts Said in a double bind. "Said is American" is a lie or a legal fiction; and yet for him, to say, "I am not American," is a breach of courtesy and shows a lack of gratitude due to hospitality, the stormy, intermittent hospitality of the state and of the nation in the first instance but also infinite hospitality of the language, the medium he uses to write back to the West. Not only in "Cairo Recalled" but in "Cairo and Alexandria," as well, the themes of memory and forgetfulness are staged conjuncturally: Said the cultural critic conceives of his childhood, which is indivisible from adolescence and adulthood, from a remembrance perspective. Just as the sliding of signifiers cannot go on forever, the power to remember, no matter how great, is strictly limited. I excerpt from "Cairo Recalled": "'Since Cairo,' I have often said to my mother, 'since Cairo' being for both of us the major demarcation in my life and, I believe, in hers. . . . Part of the city's hold over my memory was the clearness of its nearly incredible divisions" (1987: 20). "Cairo and Alexandria" goes on to open the field of inquiry into the subsumption of Said the child into Said the adult within an Eastern context.

Cairo is at least as historically rich in its own way as either Rome or Athens, but you never get the sense of history carefully preserved. Cairo doesn't present itself readily, and its finest spots and moments are either (it would seem) improvised, or surprising in the often spiteful juxtapositions of memory and actuality. . . . In Cairo you see evidence of many different narratives, identities, histories, most of them only partially there, many of them now either ragged or diminished ("Cairo and Alexandria," 1990: 6).

Said develops two ideas here. First, that memory is always imperfect. We do not use it in a disinterested way, but more often than not to protect ourselves from the past. It is therefore neither faithful nor worthy of confidence. We rearrange the past according to our own interest and in keeping with prevailing stereotypes. Each perspective, whether of space/time (the pathways or the years), carries a line of escape within itself. Each line of escape stretches toward the infinite of the world without memory. We know that the world is finite—it tends toward the finite—but memory has no end. It belongs to places not to people or to people of certain places. People come and go, and places remain. They are saturated with layers of meaning; they make the expansion of memory a fictitious imaginary. How many books have been read in this garden; how many steps walked beneath the leaves of spring, fall, winter, and summer; how many sunbeams, raindrops have fed the trees; how many tears, how many? The number is infinite, because there has never been and there will never be anyone, not even a computer, to count them—pure, uncountable, time.

Second, to express this feeling in a way that is not articulated by Said but that seems to epitomize his thinking, I would argue that exiles like him have the right to remember, while their oppressors have instead the obligation not to forget. Only in this way can the latter acknowledge the existence of their crimes; even if they do not expiate them they can at least begin to regret them. In this way too, exiles can find some kind of peace.

These observations and distinctions seem incontestable. I would simply like to add a few thoughts grouped around the terms of *memory* and *offense*, in an attempt to make explicit what Said only suggests. If our recollection of the past is not as faithful as we might wish, it is because our memory is not a separate mechanism, completely isolated, something that we could replace with the so-called memory of a computer, for instance. There is of course a sense in which I could say that I am (and I am no more than) whatever I represent at this specific moment, the perfect identity between me and myself, my body, and my brain, here and now. But in another, less commonplace sense, this coincidence between me and myself is a mere illusion. I am always much more than I seem, for I extend far beyond myself in both space and time. I am not simply me, here, because others are part of me, and I am made of my encounters and exchanges with them. And I am not simply me, now, for my past constitutes my identity. To reveal to me that this past is quite different from what I believed, or on the contrary to forbid me to put aside parts of it so as to live happily, challenges not just an isolated compartment of my being but my very identity. I cannot just allow such things to happen; to exercise control over them is thus in the very logic of things. Let me rephrase: one could argue that to preserve the past is not good in itself; it is only good as a function of a system of roles and actions. When I tell myself or others the story of my life, the narrative falls into a linear sequence: "And then . . . and then . . . and then . . ." This is the pattern I am familiar with from novels and autobiographies, and it is the one I naturally slip into. But when I am not in the process of telling it my life does not seem to be like that at all. Far from falling into a pattern, it remains dark and confused, without discernible shape and hardly amenable to words. This is what Paul Ricoeur shrewdly termed "*l'étrangeté de la mémoire.*"

From one point of view this is a state of weakness, even of anxiety, which writers need to escape from as quickly as possible. But from another angle it is the stories writers tell about themselves that make sense of their lives. They feel that as soon as they start to tell these stories they move toward rather than from themselves. Said writes about forgetfulness and about how memory becomes transmuted, how it corrupts or enhances its own contents. "You can't change the past" is a slogan he would not endorse. In his striking and capacious essay "Between Worlds," he writes:

> As the author of a book called *Beginnings: Intention and Method*, I found myself drawn to my early days as a boy in Jerusalem, Cairo and Dhour el Shweir, the Lebanese mountain village which I loathed but where for years my father took us to spend our summers. I found myself reliving the narrative quandaries of my early years, my sense of doubt and of being out of place, of always feeling myself standing in the wrong corner, in a place that seemed to be slipping away from me just as I tried to define or describe it (1998: 5).

Said's world is peopled by the vital dead. As we read him we glimpse history in the process of becoming myth.

Said recognizes, in short, that the temptation to deliver judgments based on personal conviction is strong. He makes a deliberate effort to avoid the often righteous tone of his ideological writing by displaying an expected tolerance of diverse peoples in a place of shifting elements and boundaries. His point is plain: we prize origins and returns over and above the time spent between returns, even though we spend most of our lives between returns. This state of "étant assis entre deux chaises" necessarily entails another kind of reasoning. At one time or another, the difference between the stranger who gets asked: "Who are you? Where do you come from?" and the *émigré*, who is not, quite, a stranger becomes all the more striking insofar as the people left behind demand a sacrifice when an *émigré* returns. As "Cairo and Alexandria" amply reminds us that the battle-cry is not about displacement in the ordinary sense, but about the predicaments of both exile and homecoming. More interestingly, behind narrated narration's self-assurance lies the belief that the uprooted does not know what is going on at home and does not know how his or her life would have turned out if he or she had stayed. The people who stay behind forget the ones who leave and fail to notice how they themselves change. Delusions quickly fill the space once filled by intimate knowledge. As the past is being recuperated and reshaped, Said hears many nostalgic family narratives of lost properties, eroded status, demolished great houses, vanished ways of living, of descent into insignificance and poverty.

In a surprisingly remarkable and unexpected passage, Said cannot, in effect, repress his nostalgia for the *place*; the words had already become, to him, something of the metaphor of "re-story-telling" that lies hidden in the predicaments of exile. In this light, a sentiment is turned into a kind of blundering, and this is his point: How much ignorance surrounds the exile?

> I was much more aware now of Cairo and Alexandria as historical, political, and cultural sites than I had been when I lived in Egypt: I had in the past experienced each of them as a stream of smells, sights, and sounds (Alexandria ruled by wind and sea, Cairo by river and desert). Since then Nasser and Sadat had come and gone, the results of the 1967 war and Camp David had been absorbed, and Egypt seemed to me to have fashioned a new regional profile out of its unimaginably long complex history. . . .
>
> When I left Cairo in 1960 it had a population of about three million; today metropolitan Cairo has over fourteen million inhabitants, and so the relative safety one feels in their midst is remarkable. Overcrowding is apparent everywhere, but as a visitor you also feel a sense of space and rest in ways that are theoretically impossible. Walking and loitering, for example, are both considerable pleasures
>
> I walked [the] . . . route with Mahfouz's most gifted disciple and younger friend, the novelist Gamal el-Ghitani. . . . Ghitani's theory about the various turns in the street is psychological: that rather than constructing an endlessly long street in a straight line, the architects broke it up to create a sense of what Ghitani calls *wa'ad bil wusul* (promises of arrival). Just when you think you're at the end, the street veers off sideways and then back in its original direction, deferring the distant trajectory and supplying you with momentary relief (Said, 2000: 337, 338, 342).

The delicacy and reserve, yet also the tense candor of this passage, which I had to quote at length, lies in the claim it makes: being of Palestinian origin often involves such narratives and a command over the minutiae of migration histories, one's own and others. Geographies, trajectories, itineraries, genealogies, and histories are argued over, refined, claimed, and denied to others who share the interest and the origin. To some like Said it all matters intensely, to others hardly at all, or only in limited situations.

Among the many concerns of "Cairo and Alexandria," the modes and nuances of representation might be said to be central—the way events and memories are given meanings and emphases by becoming inseparable from certain ways of telling. Said first investigates written records principally, the evidence left by the colonial master. The essay then goes on to examine the ways in which such records have been appropriated by different, sometimes conflicting histories—the postcolonial, on the one hand, and the nationalist, on the other. Said's engagement with the local people is conducted in such a way as to construct an alternative picture of the event and its key players. His aim, it appears, is not so much to write an exculpatory reassessment of the home and exile, or even to arrive at the "truth" about it, but to examine the ways in which it was transformed into a "metaphor" in mainstream historical accounts; how these accounts are limited by their representational procedures and ideological assumptions, and to enrich and complicate our understanding of the reality on the terrain by using oral evidence to qualify the canonical histories. My only complaint against this theoretically rigorous yet accessible narrative is that we are not given a full, or detailed, sense of the mainstream history of the *place* (Cairo and Alexandria) except the one Said remembers as if it existed for the purpose of colonial habits only. Thus, the postcolonial and nationalist histories are liable to remain abstractions that the text uses to construct and advance its own narrative, but seldom addresses directly.

A substantial part of the beginning of the essay is devoted to uncovering what the nonsensical-sounding place-name, Cairo/Alexandria, really means, enabling it to shed its negative resonance by allowing it the physical contours of a real place and culture. As Said tells us, the reality, like so many things, owed its existence to the cultural and economic intermingling peculiar to a landscape transformed by independence and nationalism. He, rightly, devotes as much energy to reconstructing the life of the community as he does to the visit itself. The following insight provides us with a meticulously detailed and, with hindsight, poignant account of everyday life. "While I was in Alex (as the city is often called) I learned that sewage and general waste are simply flooded into the sea off the city's best beaches. Even the Montazah beaches, once among the finest anywhere and now parceled out into small private lots, are littered with eggshells and orange peel; the odd plastic bottle rides the waves like a forlorn buoy, most certainly not making a site for bathing (Ibid., 343). Or, to put it differently, the introduction of technology into local conditions seems to have been mirrored, characteristically, by certain technical terms being received into the local language and taking on, in their corrupted form, a renewed psychological life. Such an account not only serves as a background: it also rescues perhaps Cairo but certainly not Alexandria from its existence as a "metaphor" in postcolonial discourse, and gives it an organic and evolving life which it has not possessed so far.

Much of what Said tells us about the city of Cairo and/or Alexandria and their changing culture has interesting parallels with what is happening, or has already happened, in other parts of the once colonized world—say, Algiers. His testimony is central insofar as it represents the local memory that has become a metaphor in postcolonial and nationalist discourses. Through the voices of the people he met with during his visit, Said briefly brings the time to life. But, after the euphoria of independence there was silence: ". . . not even a sparrow chirped in Alexandria the next morning" (Ibid., 344). The tensions and negotiations between one sort of history and another contribute to the unexpectedness of his aesthetic world, and also, in fundamental ways, constitute the subject-matter of the essay. The exile asks the implied unanswerable question again and again: Is he happier in his new life than he would have been if he had stayed put?

There is no doubt that in the composition of these contrasting scenes, the writer's intelligence is always at work, setting the accidents of an individual life in the cross-currents of a graphically delineated space and time. The picture that emerges, with considerable artistry, is of a private man unlike conventional images of the public man: solitary, somewhat abstracted and introspective, gradually more confident of his powers. The tone of the narrative with which he wound up his visit is grave to say the least. From a literary point of view, it could well have stopped there. We would then have had something close to a masterpiece of calm truncation, moving and tantalizing in equal measure, that Sartre has left us—journey to the age of reason, or passion, that leave us at their threshold. If this thought is not incongruous, it is because, rather than preparing the way for a portrait of the writer as visitor, the passage quoted above closes the door on further exploration of the self of this kind. A deeply felt, imaginative re-creation of the days Said spent in Cairo and Alexandria abruptly gives way to another kind of mood. We never glimpse the same inner landscape again.

With yet greater awareness of decolonization, Edward el-Kharrat, another leading Arab writer, born in Alexandria in 1926, claims the city was as Westerners like Cavafy and oddly enough Said have thought the heir not only to Western colonial glories but also to the ancient spiritual treasures of the age-old, long-protracted Pharaonic era. In his two novels *City of Saffron* (1989) and *Girls of Alexandria* (1993), al-Kharrat displays emotional and cultural bonds to his birthplace; Alexandria is "a blue-white marble city woven and rewoven by my heart."[6] His aim is not just to recover fictional territory but to express the repressed history of his region and culture. In doing so, he resists the incorporation of his تراث (heritage) into the culture of the West—as has happened over so many centuries in the process of Orientalism, which made, as Said amply demonstrates, the Arab world just so much exotic space for the Western imagination.

In such circumstances writing assumes its basic task of bearing witness, telling the truth, and subverting what the French resistance poet Pierre Seghers called the *"fausse parole,"* the lying word. "How Did They Kill My Grandmother?" Boris Slutsky's poem asks: "I'll tell you how they killed her."[7] El-Karrat and Said become such recording angels; it is a traditional role for the intellectual as a representative figure. Writerly brotherliness has been one of the finest humane resistances: the voice offered to combat the evils of colonialism, which necessary or otherwise, history imposed. The النكبة (1967 Defeat) left a changed map of the Middle East: politically, morally, artistically. Most writing since has been executed in its shadow. Generation after generation of writers returned to it as a subject, especially to the struggle for linguistic meaning with which the 1967 Defeat burdened a grotesque period in the history of the region. (This is much more typical than the daily emphasis on the randomness of suffering and of mere human endurance in Darwish's *Memory for Forgetfulness* and Hoda Barakat's *The Stone of Laughter*—and, even more arresting, the recurrent sense in them of standing up against all kinds of oppression, of Palestine by Israel, of the Orient by the West, of female by male, of the dark race by the White race.) All this is manifest too in Said's distinguished career. His conscious determination to place his narrative outside history—to explore identity, memory, exile—may strike some as disingenuous. Yet it is his boldness and his transcendence of boundaries that give us a sense of his full trajectory.

For most of his life, Said has lived in exile. Such turbulence is simply too much for a human life, which is too short to absorb all the shocks and changes. Ironically, he insists on the irreducible mystery of life, a mystery subject to no political or religious solution. And even though his bruised wariness is shared by other exiles, he maintains that exile has given him a detached, guarded skepticism—about notions of the collective, the nation, and language. Such detachment, according to Said, is a "privilege" as well as a burden; the exile experiences life as "multiple, complex," and full of illusions (1984: 48). Although it confers on him certain responsibilities of witness and engagement, it also puts him in touch with a larger truth of loss: life cannot be pushed back. Time is not a reversible process. "Between Worlds" takes us through Said's accomplishments; the burdens of history; the determining social effects of culture, love, dislocation, death, and betrayal; and the anxiety arising from the individual's responsibility for his own fate and name. "With an unexpectedly Arab family name connected to an improbably British first name—my mother very much admired the Prince of Wales—I was an uncomfortably anomalous student all through my early years" ("Between Worlds," 1998: 3). The essay is also rich in intimate observation: Said rummaging to find broken and discarded objects (a picture of his grandfather on horseback, a small rug, an old Jerusalemite expression, a fragmentary story, an odd coin or medal, one photograph of his mother), which he likes to restore and with which he likes to surround himself (to his family's patient dismay), or recounting the qualified pleasures of exile, including a knowledge that one's sleep will be disturbed only by nightmares, by dreams of being at "home" (in Palestine) and unable to get out, a nightmare common to many exiles, rather than by the midnight knock of the state police.

The impetuous ferocity of the Said *Story* is best captured by Said himself in the following excerpt, describing the feelings and thoughts of a Palestinian (غريب, a stranger, is the euphemism) longing to recapture a memory of *his* Palestine, a memory that is both voluntary and spontaneous, perceived through the language of the senses rather than the language of abstract thought. It is triggered by smell, touch, sound, and sight, while it remains invisible, and, like snap-shots from the past, it sneaks *in* and *out* of consciousness, acting like a hook whereby he maintains a tactile but unspoken knowledge of his personal history. Thus in a penultimate passage of "Between Worlds," Said breaks into a litany of reminiscences—his family, home, language:

> The day in early September 1951 when my mother and father deposited me at the gates of [Mount Hermon School] and then immediately left for the Middle East was probably the most miserable of my life. Not only was the atmosphere of the school rigid and explicitly moralistic, but I seemed to be the only boy there who was not a native-born American, who did not speak with the required accent, and had not grown up with baseball, basketball and football. For the first time ever I was deprived of the linguistic environment I had depended on as an alternative to the hostile attentions of Anglo-Saxons whose language was not mine, and who made no bones about my belonging to an inferior, or somehow disapproved, race (5).

The gist of this passage lies in Said's memory of home as he knew it, which has remained with him all his life; in struggling to forget, he manages in fact to recall. Put differently, anytime memory is suppressed, it gains power. While we consider memory at times to be a matter of choice, it is not so readily determinable, in that it is easy to feel that life leaves either too many or too few traces, scarcely ever the right amount: either fingerprints everywhere or total erasure. In such a mood, one's memory itself becomes a double agent, and we may be ready, like the hero of Orson Wells's *Mr. Arkadin*, to hire a private eye to explore our own past. And explore Said does. The ability not to forget, the remembering, makes his work on dislocation something of a *retour*, in Aimé Césaire's sense, to his native Palestine. This "return," in which the foldings of memory and identity converge, becomes concrete in a way that allows Said to reengage, across the mediating distance he has traveled, his own cultural memory and identity so as to mark out their aesthetic terrain. He, like Stephen Dedalus in *A Portrait of the*

Artist as a Young Man, leaves his native land and seems destined not to go back. Yet he stays bound to the inventory of its streets and its place names, as if in the Jewish covenant: "If I forget thee, O Jerusalem, let my right hand forget her cunning."[8] An idea sets him within a field of memory that precedes his اصالة (biographical authenticity, roots, basis): the idea of Palestine. Said explains:

> Palestine is central to the cultures of Islam, Christianity, and Judaism; Orient and Occident have turned it into a legend. There is no forgetting it, no way of overlooking it. . . . The sights, wares, and monuments of Palestine are the objects of commerce, war, pilgrimage, cults, the subjects of literature, art, song, fantasy. . . . When we cross from Palestine into other territories, even if we find ourselves decently in new places, the old ones loom behind us as tangible and unreal as reproduced memory ("Between Worlds," 1998: 3).

Palestine is much more than the land of lands; it is a metaphor of expedition for all of us who are seeking the sources of our identities. The history of the Palestinian peoples is encased in its mystery and its historical significance. While it has been coveted by all the colonial powers, it has been conquered by none. Similarly, or metaphorically, what matters for Said is that he, too, has not been vanquished. In spite of all that has happened to him and the scars he carries within himself as a result of dispossession, he has managed to survive with his memory intact. And there is the memory proper. Said has a tenderness for the memory of those he loves. They are the only ones who rejoiced when he was born, who may mourn his death. Memory of an ancient homeland where the suffering of the people is embedded in the depth of memory, affects the imagination—memory where the idiom is not the burden of defeat, but the value of constant struggle. And when the reader awakes, he or she may exclaim, along with Roland Barthes, *"c'est précisément parce que j'oublie que je lis"* (1978: 13). Thus, for Said, writing is an act of remembering, a faculty of "memory for forgetfulness," in Mahmoud Darwish's celebrated phrase, for retaining mental and physical impressions in, and for recalling them to, the mind. For the reader, the writer's act of remembering is transformed into a text, and his recollection becomes an act of memory, a remembrance *against* forgetfulness.

Memories originate in memory. We make sense of our lives through our senses—through what we see, taste, and smell. It is scarcely surprising that Said, in writing about exile, comes up with stories prompted by the memories and associations that Palestine evokes in him. Speaking of the *arch(écriture)*, in Genette's formula, of his memoir, he observes:

> It's a text that I think exists only in performance and not something I can easily describe. But it would certainly be an attempt to connect . . . the imaginary and fictional resonances. A lot is based on the following: in

much of my childhood there was in a certain sense, an unknowing too much, for all kinds of reasons that have to do with my schooling and my family, the restrictions, the sense of belonging and a little series of compartments that led me into the colonial avenues and finally brought me to this country. There was a constant narrowing from the English system into the Western cultural orbit. Part of what I am trying to do now is to go back and to open up the things that I didn't know then, to see if I can do that, since I can only do it through speculation and memory and imagination. . . . I want to try and do the Cairo-Jerusalem-Beirut axis, which is the one I grew up in, in a pre-political way in which all the political realities of the present nevertheless are somehow there in a figured or implicit form, held in suspension.[9]

Out of Place, like the rest of Said's writings, is meant to be a lesson in how stories should evolve—a reminder that well-wrought stories not only are rooted in memory but also are there, in a book, to be taken seriously. They need have no moral except for that which teaches one to view the world not as a place to dash around in and to moralize about by oneself the way the United States is doing today but as a place to be shared with others. Stories need not demand of us some higher calling to be a rebel against hidden pressures and manipulations and to be a doubter of systems, of power and its incantations. Memory is also meant to give the writer that is Said a chance to make sense of his life. And that is enough.

CHAPTER FIVE

THE WILL TO
AUTHORITY AND TRANSGRESSION

Everything, yet nothing, is a variation.
—Theodor Adorno, *The Philosophy of Modern Music*, 67.

Edward Said, like other descendants of those displaced by the violence of the twentieth century, came of age to find the world he expected to inherit rent apart, turned nearly unrecognizable. For some, to move forward has required that they allow the ruptured, destroyed world to recede. For others, like Said, it has been a matter of survival to reenter the past, searching its remains for the means to create a redemptive history. What this means is that the life he was born to, an inheritance rife with the contradictions of Middle-Eastern nationalism in the postcolonial era, is half a life. Trained in Cairo as an accomplished pianist and educated in the United States, he has performed and written opera as well as other music. It is the virtue of his writings that deal with classical music—comprising his 1991 Wellek Lectures, essays on opera productions, music festivals, recitals, and a homage to a belly dancer—that in them the reader is bracingly confronted with a genuinely innovative and adventurous style of investigating musical compositions. First, Said does not give the impression of having written them hurriedly, pouring out thousands of words with little sweat. Each of his sentences is crafted with a sense of actual experience, being articulated in deliberately chosen language. Reading him therefore requires considerable attention to nuance and tone, and although he writes within a recognizable Left tradition, there is no jargon.

Second, Said's argument about music is both daring and convincing. What makes this stance so apt is that Said is reacting resourcefully to a set of predicaments (or impasses) in modern critical thought. One of these, for the listener, is

the overperfection of the piano, which has resulted in boredom: boring interpretations on boring pianos. Not that the boredom of modern classical music
performance is confined to piano music; it is just that piano playing offers a particularly acute instance of a disease that has blighted large areas of the classical
music repertoire, with the exceptions perhaps of contemporary and early music,
where the stultifying effects of repetition have not as yet set in.[1] Criticism of
this sort has come mainly from theorists of the Left—from the likes of Carl
Dahlhaus, Alfred Brendel, Theodor Adorno, John Cage, and others—or from
composers (Brahms, Wagner), who have had good reason to be dissatisfied with
a system that places no more emphasis on the performance of music that is alive
than on the importance of maintaining a vast musical museum. Meanwhile,
except for the happy few (Glenn Gould comes to mind), the performers have
tended to keep quiet. As employees of the museum, they have had most at stake
and have understandably, if regrettably, felt themselves badly placed to undermine it.

Third, how can we honestly factor in Said's career as a Julliard-trained pianist
while at the same time taking into account the fact (something Said himself
never does) that his childhood was rather a privileged one, in class and gender
terms? Is it at all possible to read him without hearing, in the authorial voice, all
those signs of high bourgeois cultural sensibility, of a sense of truth, individuality,
freedom, humanity, suffering? What is it that Said finds appealing in Glenn Gould,
a musician who had phenomenal technical gifts, a perfect memory, a very high
intelligence, but in addition was self-conscious and self-observant to an extent
most other performers would scarcely be able to imagine? Said—always provocative, sometimes provoking—places the musical act under a scrutiny (his reading
of Beethoven is a case in point) that is at once profound and multidimensional.
His critique remains unparalleled in terms of the sheer multiplicity of vantage
points from which it probes its subject. Solidly rooted in Adorno, his thought is
often complex and complicated in expression. Shining *contrapuntal* clarity, his
strategies can never be pinned down because he derides any notion of mainstream, "definitive" performance. He is nothing if not an exploratory pianist.

Fourth, in everything he does, Said presents the established Western system
with a challenge that includes critical musical discourse. Therefore, the question
that comes to mind is: How can one investigate the career of Said the music
critic and/or performer as informed by his life, his intense musical education, and
his musical predispositions? These break down into two main themes: the way in
which music "transgresses" boundaries and the role of "silence, meaning and restlessness" within Said's reframing of the questions governing the ways in which
Western art music is received.

It is an interesting paradox that the United States, the home of hard-nosed
capitalism, has produced Steve Reich, Philip Glass, Robert Wilson, Peter Sellars,
Edward Said—all key players at the cutting edge of opera and classical music.

Said, of course, stands out among these as a Euro-centered postcolonial critic and musician whose motivation creates a sense of necessity. After all, he lives in the culture that is currently being imposed all over the world, in the name of freedom (but of course it is its own form of enslavement); a critique of that culture becomes imperative. And an alternative becomes urgent, because we can see the deadening results of the culture's influence played out around us.

In proposing to explore some of these matters, I find myself inevitably led to think about performance of music and of opera. Pianists (Glenn Gould) interpret every note with peculiar antics on stage, as do singers (Jessye Norman) and conductors (Daniel Barenboim). New opera productions such as those of Peter Sellars are radical enough interpretations—with new translations of surtitles, new settings, new contexts.[2] I will also deal with what Said has called "living by the clock." Ever since 1992, the year he was diagnosed with leukemia, Said has been candid about his coming to terms with his own mortality. The increasing rigors of his illness have forced him to contemplate several changes in his life, which he now realizes will be shorter and more difficult. Because he has had to face death, Said's engagement has become intensely personal. He explains:

> For me, sleep is death, as is any diminishment in awareness. . . . Sleeplessness for me is a cherished state, to be desired at almost any cost; there is nothing for me as invigorating as the early-morning shedding of the shadowy half-consciousness of a night's loss, reacquainting myself with what I might have lost completely a few hours earlier. I occasionally experience myself as a cluster of flowing currents. I prefer this to the idea of a solid self, the identity to which so many attach so much significance. These currents, like the themes of one's life, are borne along during the waking hours, and at their best they require no reconciling, no harmonizing. They may be not quite right, but at least they are always in motion, in time, in place, in the form of strange combinations moving about, not necessarily forward, against each other, contrapuntally yet without one central theme. A form of freedom, I'd like to think, even if I am far from being totally convinced that it is ("Living by the Clock," 1999: 11).

This record of a life and the ongoing course of a disease are one and the same, it could be said; the same but deliberately different.

I

Growing up in the cultural cross-currents of 1940s Cairo with its paradox-ridden world of privilege—enchanted places and pure creations of the colonial imagination, such as polo fields, cricket pitches, tea rooms, football fields, bowling greens, a racetrack—and outside of a punishing extracurricular schedule of many sports and piano lessons, Said could occasionally touch something of the vast city beyond, teeming with the possibilities of Eastern sensuality and wealth, both of which were conducted, so to speak, in European modes. Opera recitals, classical music concerts, tennis tournaments, various cultural programs sponsored either by the British or the French filled the social agenda, in addition to countless dances, cotillions, receptions, and balls, and to the extent that Said participated in or read about them, he apprehended a sort of Proustian world replicated in an Oriental city whose prevailing authority, the British sirdar, or high commissioner, outranked the ruling monarch ("Cairo and Alexandria," 1987: 32–33).

At home, Said owes his interest in music to his "mother's own wonderful musicality and love of the art. Over the years," he movingly writes, "she has always been interested in my playing, and we have shared many musical experiences together" (*Musical Elaborations*, 1991: xi). The underlying motifs for Said have been the emergence of another side to him buried for a long time beneath a surface of often expertly acquired and wielded musical characteristics belonging to the self that his mother tried to construct according to her design, the "*Edwaad*," as she would have it, and of which he speaks intermittently in his memoir.

> I am still haunted by the sound, at exactly the same time and place, of her voice calling me *Edwaad*, the word wafting through the dusk air at the Fish Garden's closing time, and me, undecided whether to answer or to remain in hiding for just a while longer, enjoying the pleasure of being called, being wanted, the non-Edward part of myself finding luxurious respite in not answering until the silence of my being became unendurable (*Out of Place*, 1999: 8).[3]

In "Living by the Clock," he describes in affecting detail how late in her life, although stricken by an unforgiving illness—her cancer symptoms already pronounced—,

> she arrived in London from Beirut on her way to the US to consult a specialist; I met her at the airport and brought her to Brown's Hotel for the one night she had to spend there. With barely two hours to get ready and have an early supper, she nevertheless gave an unhesitating "yes" to my suggestion that we see Vanessa Redgrave and Timothy Dalton as Anthony and Cleopatra at the Haymarket. It was an understated, unopulent production, and the long play transfixed her in a way that surprised me. After years of Lebanese war and Israeli invasion she had become distracted, often querulous, worried about her health and what she should do with herself. All of this, however, went into abeyance, as we watched and heard Shakespeare's lines ("Eternity was in our lips and eyes, / Bliss in our brows' bent") as if speaking to us in the accents of wartime Cairo, back in our

little cocoon, the two of us very quiet and concentrated, savoring the language and communion with each other—despite the disparity in our ages and the fact that we were mother and son—for the very last time ("Living by the Clock," 1999: 9–10).

But Said sees the last and best result of the Cairo traffic in Ignace Tiegerman, his music teacher and friend,

[He was] a tiny Polish-Jewish gnome of man who came to Cairo in 1933, attracted by the city's warmth and possibilities in contrast to what was coming in Europe. He was a great pianist and musician, a wunderkind student of Leschetizky and Ignaz Friedman, a lazy, wonderfully precious and bright-eyed bachelor with secret tastes and unknown pleasures, who ran a Conservatoire de Musique on the rue Champollion just behind the Cairo Museum.

No one played Chopin and Schumann with such grace and unparalleled rhetorical conviction as Tiegerman. He taught piano in Cairo, tying himself to the city's *haute societé*—teaching its daughters, playing for its salons, charming its gatherings—in order, I think, to free himself for the lazy indulgence of his own pursuits: conversation, good food, music, and unknown kinds (to me) of human relationships. I was his piano student at the outset and, many years later, his friend.

Ignace Tiegerman inspired inordinate devotion not just in those like Said who became close to him, but also in those who knew him only from his teaching, like one of his female students,

a stunningly fluent and accomplished young married woman, a mother of four who played with her head completely enclosed in the pious veil of a devout Muslim.

Neither Tiegerman nor I could understand this amphibious woman, who with a part of her body could dash through the *Appassionata* and with another venerated God by hiding her face. She never said a word in my presence, although I must have heard her play or met her at least a dozen times.

Said concludes:

Like Tiegerman, she was an untransplantable emanation of Cairo's genius; unlike him, her particular branch of the city's history has endured and even triumphed. For a brief moment then, the conjunction of ultra-European and ultra-Islamic Arab cultures brought forth a highlighted image that typified the Cairo of my early years ("Cairo Recalled," 1987: 32).[4]

Tiegerman caught people's imagination and continued to do so long after Said left Cairo. This is partly explained by the existential romance of his life, by his appearing to have sacrificed himself to his art: a process of self-destruction painfully visible in the photographs taken at various stages in his career—the androgynously beautiful, ecstatic figure of the young Tiegerman transformed by the end of his life into a human wreck, crouched over the piano like an old vulture.

Not that Tiegerman was the first or last great pianist to have lived an intense life. There was Toscanini, Gould, Horowitz, Pollini, a polyglot family of musicians against which Edward Said measures himself and to which he would be honored to belong. Said, like Tiegerman, also seems to have lived with the same intensity and refusal to compromise by going to the most extreme point and beyond it, destroying himself in the process.

> For years I seemed to be going over the same kind of thing in the work I did, but always through the writings of other people. It wasn't until the early fall of 1991 when an ugly medical diagnosis suddenly revealed to me the mortality I should have known about before that I found myself trying to make sense of my own life as its end seemed alarmingly nearer. A few months later, still trying to assimilate my new condition, I found myself composing a long explanatory letter to my mother, who had already been dead for almost two years, a letter that inaugurated a belated attempt to impose a narrative on a life that I had left more or less to itself, disorganized, scattered, uncentered. I had had a decent enough career in the university, I had written a fair amount. . . . I was a compulsive worker, I disliked and hardly ever took vacations, and I did what I did without worrying too much (if at all) about such matters as writer's block, depression or running dry ("Living by the Clock," 1998: 3).

It was this quality of compulsive worker that transformed the real Said from being simply a student of music into a professional pianist. Importance is an attribute that is almost never applicable to performing musicians. However great they may be, they have no importance. To understand why Said is an exception to the rule, we need to look at Said's other Cairo—the indigenous one.

Said's disorderly palimpsest Cairo was characterized by an endless stream of consciousness (the Egyptian cinema), a cohabitation of Islamic, Mediterranean, and Latin erotic forms. The latent promiscuity of this semi-underground Cairo also teemed with musicians, song writers, and performers, such as the exiled Farid Al-Atrach, the melancholic lute composer-interpreter; his sister Ismahan, the electric singer with a sparrow-like voice; Muhammed Abdel Wahab, the aesthete composer with an attitude; Tahia Carioca, the enchanting belly dancer extraordinaire and *femme fatale*, whose career spanned 60 years and whom Said describes in the following terms:

Tahia Carioca [was] the greatest dancer of the day, performing with a seated male singer, Abdel Aziz Mahmoud, around whom she swirled, undulated, gyrated with perfect, controlled poise, her lips, legs, breasts more eloquent and sensually paradisiacal than anything I had dreamed of or imagined in my crude auto-erotic prose. I could see on Tahia's face a smile of such fundamentally irreducible pleasure, her mouth open slightly with a look of ecstatic bliss tempered by irony and an almost prudish restraint. . . . She danced for about forty-five minutes, a long unbroken composition of mostly slow turns and passes, the music rising and falling homophonically, and given meaning not by the singer's repetitive and banal lyrics but by her luminous, incredibly sensual performance (*Reflections on Exile*, 1999: 193).

He adds:

Eastern dancing, as Tahia practiced it, shows the dancer planting herself more and more solidly in the earth, digging into it almost, scarcely moving, certainly never expressing anything like the nimble semblance of weightlessness that a great ballet dancer conveys. Tahia's dancing suggested (vertically) a sequence of horizontal pleasures, but also paradoxically communicated an elusiveness and a kind of grace that cannot be pinned down on a flat surface. . . . One never felt her to be part of an ensemble—as in kathak dancing, say—but always as a solitary, somewhat perilous figure moving to attract and at the same time repel men and women (Ibid., 25).

It is probably too much to say of Tahia that she was a subversive figure, but Said thinks that her meandering, careless way with her relationships with men, her profligacy as an actress whose scripts, contracts (if she had any to begin with), stills, costumes, and the rest suggest how far removed she always was from anything that resembled domesticity, ordinary commercial or bourgeois life, or even comfort of the kind so many of her peers seem to have cared about. She performed within an Arab and Islamic setting but was constantly in tension with it. She belonged to the tradition of الَسَّالِمَة, the learned woman who is also a courtesan, an extremely literate woman who is lithe and profligate with her physical charms. The great thing about Tahia, Said seems to suggest, was that her sensuality, or rather the flicker of it, was so unusual, so attuned to an audience whose gaze in all its raw or, in the case of dance connoisseurs, refined lust, was as transient and unthreatening as she was (Said, 1987).

Within the concert hall, the Prima Donna of the East, the great Koranic reciter and austere singer Umm Kalthoum was reputed to be a lesbian, whose Thursday-evening broadcasts from a Cairo theater were transmitted everywhere between Morocco and Oman. "Having been fed a diet of her music at far too young an age," Said writes "I still find her songs insufferable" (Ibid., 3). But for those who like and believe in such cultural stereotyping, her long, languorous, repetitive lines, slow tempi, strangely retarded rhythms, ponderous monophony, and eerily lachrymose or devotional lyrics stood for something quintessentially Arab. She, who sang with great authority in all the most exacting roles, excelling in the intricate *classical* style of Arabic song (قصيده), carried weight in a way no other female singer had since her arch rival:

> The greatest and most famous singer of the 20th-century Arab world was Umm Kalthoum, whose records and cassettes, fifteen years after her death, are available everywhere. A fair number of non-Arabs know about her too, partly because of the hypnotic and melancholy effect of her singing, partly because in the world-wide rediscovery of authentic people's art Umm Kalthoum is a dominant figure. But she also played a significant role in the emerging Third World women's movement as a pious "Nightingale of the East" whose public exposure was a model not only of feminine conscious-ness but also of domestic propriety. During her lifetime, there was talk about whether or not she was a lesbian, but the sheer force of her perform-ances of elevated music set to classical verse overrode such rumors. In Egypt she was a national symbol, respected both during the monarchy and after the revolution led by Gamal Abdel Nasser (Ibid., 25).

What Said admires in Umm Kalthoum is her majesty, presence, and power of delivery. In her performance, one finds great virtuosity, breadth, and clarity of voice. Said's devotion to the aesthetics of her two-hour performance still strikes a chord many years after her death as the following excerpt shows:

> The first musical performance I ever attended as a very small boy (in the mid-1940s) was a puzzling, interminably long, and yet haunting concert by Umm Kalthoum, already the premier exponent of classical Arabic song. I had no way of knowing that her peculiar rigor as performer derived from an aesthetic whose hallmark was exfoliating variation, in which repetition, a sort of meditative fixation on one or two small patterns, and an almost total absence of developmental (in the Beethovenian sense) tension were the key elements. The point of the performance, I later realized, was not to get to the end of a carefully constructed logical structure—working through it—but to luxuriate in all sorts of byways, to linger over details and changes in text, to digress and then digress from the digression ("Homage to a Belly-Dancer," 1991: xi).

There is an intensity, Said seems to be saying, and a refusal to compromise or cave in to the demands of the concert hall or society at large that constitutes a recog-nized attitude in Umm Kalthoum's lifelong career and that suggests a powerful insubordinate anger. His portrait of her explores with compelling plausibility the idea of an artist at her best. Robed in the black or white gown and head scarf of a devout Muslim woman, Umm Kalthoum radiated the verve and wit that informed her entire personality. Her extraordinary singing career and her power as an icon throughout the Arab world and beyond still resonate many years after her death. Egypt was the capital of that world when it came to such matters as pleasure, the arts of desire, and sociability, and both Tahia and Umm Kalthoum were its representatives.[5]

Said's own knowledge of music is encyclopedic, his taste eclectic. Proud of his achievement as an accomplished pianist, not only does he give recitals for charity and other nonprofit organizations but he deconstructs sonatas and concertos before classes of trained music students. In addition, Said is comfortable with critiquing various opera and orchestral performances and music festivals:

> While it is true that grand opera is essentially a nineteenth-century form, and that our great opera houses now resemble museums which preserve artifacts by Wagner and Verdi for twentieth-century spectators, it is also a fact that some of the nineteenth-century repertory was already reactionary in its own time, whereas some was musically and theatrically revolutionary. In either case, however, nineteenth-century performances maintained vital contact with the cultural and aesthetic practice of the time: composers like Verdi, Wagner and Puccini were often around to influence what was done to their work, audiences and performers usually understood the language in which the opera was sung, and in the main, a musical idiom was shared by all concerned.

Said ends with this remark:

> Very little of this obtains today. . . . The problem . . . comes from the Italian repertory which, aside from Rossini, who was a genius, is mostly made up of second-rate work. The very prominence of a grotesque like Pavarotti is itself an indictment of the repertory that suits him so well. Such singers have reduced opera performance to a minimum of intelligence and a maximum of overpriced noise, in which almost unbelievably low standards of musicality and direction. This is an environment inhospitable to ideas or aesthetic conceptions (1986: 648).

It is tempting to see in Said a frustrated concert pianist, a man who but for the grace of God would be traveling around the world from concert hall to concert hall and recording studio to recording studio. What is clear though is that it is playing music that gives Said the greatest pleasure:

> So in the case of the Brahms variations I found myself playing them with (for me) an unusual commitment to Brahms's music, in part because as I played I found myself recollecting with poignant nostalgia the voice and

even the pianistic gestures of an old teacher, Ignace Tiegerman. . . . I remember asking him then whether he "really" liked Brahms, my tone indicating the perhaps jejune doubts and vacillations about Brahms that I felt even as he played the piece so convincingly. Yes, he said, but only if you really know about him, nodding at his hands.

This wasn't connoisseurship or blasé familiarity. It suggested a whole tradition of teaching and playing that entered into and formed my own relationship with Tiegerman, as it must have between him and his colleagues and friends in Europe. Out of that emerged a capacity for giving life to a piece in the performance, a capacity dependent on knowing a composer through a structure of feeling (*Musical Elaborations*, 1991: 90–91).

In his discussion of Tiegerman's use of variation, Said points to some important differences with both traditional and modern uses. The Brahms variation is the technical means for the development of the novelistic or epic figures that appear in his music as identical but ever changing.

Music permeates most of Said's work; it is a vital factor. Not surprisingly, Said fixes on that most fascinating and ambiguous of all contemporary pianists, Glenn Gould, who gradually came to shun public performance in preference for the recording studio. As if compensating for not giving public performances, Gould developed from modern technology what amounts to another kind of performance space—as instanced by his musically illustrated radio lectures, writings, and films.[6] Indeed, many of Gould's eccentric gestures can be seen as a response to the tired routine and unthinking consensus that ordinarily support the concert performance. In his unique way, Gould, the eccentric performer, refused to give up the values of music. Said returns now and again to his much-admired Gould, who for him attempted, both through the genius of his playing and his decision to give up the routinized existence of a touring artist, to integrate his music with the world—without giving up its "re-interpretive, reproductive" aspect. This is the "Adornian measure of Gould's achievement," Said notes, "and also its limitations, which are those of a late capitalism that has condemned classical music to an impoverished marginality and anti-intellectualism sheltered underneath the umbrella of 'autonomy'" (*Musical Elaborations*, 1991: 95). It is communication that Said sees as central to the culture industry, to the mass-produced and popular construction of aesthetic media. No matter how subtle or sophisticated the intentions of a composer, his or her music becomes, in Said's analysis, part of the culture industry or, at the very least, one of its fellow travelers.

The most obvious expression of Gould's *Klavierradikalismus*, his piano radicalism, was his abandonment of the concert platform. Not that he was the first or the last great pianist to stop giving concerts: Horowitz and Michelangeli retreated for long stretches, and Eileen Joyce gave them up altogether. But Gould did not retire only to make a triumphant return at some later point, nor did he give up merely for personal reasons and disappear into private life. His refusal to play in public was an expression of principle, a rejection of what he felt to be a false and dead form of music-making in favor of a higher artistic mission, which he believed could better be pursued in the recording studio. In this respect, Gould fully understood the problems of his historical position. "[He] . . . was that almost impossible creature," Said observes, "both a pianist of staggering talent and a man of effortlessly articulate opinions, some so arguable as to seem merely quirky, others profoundly insightful and intelligent. His work invariably offers musical and intellectual satisfactions encountered in the performances of no other contemporary musician" ("Glenn Gould and the Metropolitan Museum," 1987: 534). Like Gould, in his approach to the history of music as well as to musical interpretation, Edward Said is able, like no other musician and/or music critic of his age (with the exception of Charles Rosen, a lesser critic, perhaps, but a greater pianist) to think radically and for himself. He confronts the pieces of music themselves, instead of through the preconceptions and musical clichés of his time. This has led him to reject almost all nineteenth-century piano music after Beethoven, to view Wagner with distrust, and to admit to his personal canon only a fraction of the output of Mozart. Said argues for his aesthetic from a number of angles, but it is best understood as the aesthetic of a dedicated and passionate polyphonist. For him, music is polyphony, and to the extent that musical style developed away from polyphonic values, he rejects it. Hence his "blind spot" for music between Bach and Wagner, his championing of preclassical composers such as Sweelinck, Gibbons, and Byrd, and his love of the late romantics (especially Strauss) and Schoenberg, Berg, and Webern.

Auden said of Rimbaud that verse was a special illness of his ear, and one could say of Said that polyphony was a special illness of his inner ear, an almost pathological specialization in his way of thinking, perhaps even a condition of his psyche. His passionate commitment to musical polyphony sets him at odds with the culture of the concert hall and the classical music business. The musical repertoire best suited to that culture, because specifically written for it, is one in which polyphonic values are expressed in favor of drama and virtuoso display. Said finds this music uninteresting and aesthetically corrupted by the functions it is designed to fulfill: nothing better embodies this corruption than the piano concerto. Here we touch on the political dimension of Said's musical aesthetic. For in the piano concerto he sees not only crudeness of form (he thinks the sonata allegro overrated) but a dramatization of the aspect of human behavior that he dislikes most—competitiveness: the piano competing with the orchestra, the pianist strutting the stage as artist hero, vanquisher of orchestras and audiences, master not of musical control but of crowd control. By contrast, the polyphonic music that Said so loves presents an image of equality in formal relations and democracy among participating voices, an image, if you like, of a human set-up in which the competitive stress of the piano business (symbolized by the virtuoso piano concerto) would have no part.

Said's love of polyphony is a love of musical thinking (the pianist, he once said, echoing Gould, plays the piano, not with his fingers, but with his mind), and if he rejects music of slight polyphonic content, this is because such music requires of the player a lesser degree of mental attention. This brought him into direct conflict with the main tradition of piano playing as it has developed since the end of the eighteenth century, a tradition in which mechanical—digital— virtuosity has been the chief technical goal. Said acknowledges this contradiction. Since the concert hall is no place to nurture the subtleties of polyphony, either acoustically or ideologically, the pianist should abandon it for playing in private. Since the piano repertoire is mainly full of antipolyphonic music, the pianist should abandon it for Bach and Schoenberg. And since the conventions of piano technique are musically mindless, he should abandon them for a technique based on thinking. Said's distaste for traditional pianistic virtues—beautiful sound, sensuous texturing, subtle or not so subtle coloration of tone—led him to cultivate an austere, bright, "unpianistic" sound in his own playing. He seeks out instruments that would maximize the clarity of voicing within polyphonic structures and insists on regulating these instruments in ways that gray the piano technique. His views on the role of polyphony in Western music would be correct had he not himself possessed in such a high degree the skill of polyphonic playing, the skill, as Glenn Gould would have it, of playing the piano. But it is the presence of Said's personality in his playing, the note of total commitment that is to be heard in it, that gives it its special power. Said's aesthetic is uncompromisingly puritanical and austere, yet his playing is never cold or dispassionate. It is dynamized by an exultant energy and conveys to the listener the tactility of the music as it is produced by fingers that are thinking.

For Said, without the ability to be radical, to call into question the established certainties of the classical music canon and its institutions, a performer of this music in the early twenty-first century cannot properly interpret it. Unfamiliar music (medieval and Renaissance music and contemporary works) does not demand this kind of radicalism, but the classics of the concert hall can easily become a grinding bore without it. Or, to put this another way, a performer who does not, as Gould did, question the purpose of playing the classical music canon, who is not aware of how the pieces can lose their meaning in the process of constant repetition, who does not entertain the possibility that the commercial institutions of music making create a context in which he can no longer effectively communicate—such a performer cannot develop an aesthetic through which the familiar can once again be heard as new.

As locus classicus Said uses Gould's deliberate refusal to make his legendary 1955 recording of Bach's *Goldberg Variations* the basis for his new interpretation (1981). Gould did not listen to it again until three or four days before the first session in the studio. He makes his point with unerring aptness in the following excerpt:

> I found that it was a rather spooky experience. I listened to it with great pleasure in many respects. I found, for example, that it had a real sense of humor, [. . .] and I found that I recognized at all points really the finger-prints of the party responsible. I mean from a tactile standpoint, from a purely mechanical standpoint my approach to playing the piano you know really hasn't changed all that much over the years. It's remained quite stable, static some people might prefer to say. . . . But, and it is a very big "but," I could not recognize or identify with the spirit of the person who made that recording. It really seemed like some other spirit had been involved.[7]

For Said, perhaps the most telling contrast between the two performances occurs in the final stretch from variations 25 through 30. In 1955, Gould subjects the grief-stricken 25 to a slower, more searching tempo, restores the emotional balance with the radiant *figurae* of the next four variations, and drinks heartily through the combined peasant strains of the quodlibet. The aria reprise confirms his *bonheur de vivre*. The 1981 recording of variation 25 is poised but more sad than despairing; hence, less emotional distance is covered through the next four variations. Curiously, the two bumptious tunes of variations 30 unfold tentatively. This approach makes little sense till the Goldberg aria returns (Said, 1987: 534).

Gould had a rare and astonishing talent for doing one thing brilliantly and suggesting that he was also doing something else at the same time. Hence his predilection for *contrapuntal* forms or, on a slightly different note, his eccentric habit of playing the piano, conducting, and singing or his way of being able to quote musically more or less anything at any time. "In a sense," Said observes, "Gould was gradually moving toward a kind of untheatrical and anti-aesthetic *Gesamtkunstwerk*, or universal artwork, a description which sounds ludicrous and contradictory" (ibid., 535). Where Gould could approach Mozart through his unique Gouldian perspective and find, according to his own lights, much that was wanting in much of Mozart and therefore a beauty in what pleased him, other pianists' trust in the composer's infallibility leaves them little room for maneuver between the familiar rites of Mozart worship: Mozart as fresh but urbane, unaffected but ironic, aloof but intimate, and so on. Where Gould could write jacket notes for his recording of the *Appassionata* dismissing the work as pompous and overrated or could sigh wistfully that he had "tried very, very hard to develop a convincing rationale for the *Emperor* Concerto," other pianists only intone of these works that they have "spacious grandeur." Where Gould could contemplate the possibility that the concert hall was destroying his capacity to be the musician he wanted to be, other pianists can only fuss about the etiquette of program planning.[8] Few pianists playing the classical music canon today interpret

it in the light of a coherent aesthetic, which is why most (with the notable exception of survivors from an earlier generation, like Artur Balsam or Mieczyslaw
Horszowski) sound as though they are simply repeating, rather than re-creating,
the music they play. Gould's strength, Said writes, is that he

> always seemed to achieve a seamless unity between his fingers, the piano
> and the music he was playing, one extending into the other until the three
> became indistinguishable. It was as if Gould's virtuosity finally derived its
> influence from the piece and not from a residue of technical athleticism
> built up independently over the years. Pollini has something of this quality,
> but it is the wonderfully intelligent exercise of his fingers in polyphonic
> music that separates Gould from every other pianist. Only a great Bach
> organist communicates in the same way (Ibid., 536).

Or, to put it differently, the particulars have a momentum in the direction of the
ensemble. For the most part they become what they are because of their relation
to the whole. In themselves they are relatively unspecific, like the basic proportions of tonality, and tend to be amorphous.

The question of whether there is a musical style emerges when Gould or Said
plays and/or writes about music in works such as *Musical Elaborations*, a remarkably
rich and entertaining book. Performance, which now extends from "authentic"
plainsong to Berlioz and Wagner played on period instruments, is an interesting
phenomenon that has become the single most characteristic aspect of our serious
musical life. It is a development that has taken place with astonishing speed over the
past quarter of a century. This success could not have been achieved without the
work of scholars, instrument-builders, enthusiasts, and pioneers dating back more
than a century. Now that it has gone beyond the innocent revival of music that
everyone had forgotten, to strike at the roots of how we perform the music that
everyone knows or seems to know, the question of authenticity rouses the strongest
feelings among musicians—who justifiably feel that traditional performing styles are
being implicitly challenged and even radicalized (Nigel Kennedy's bravura is a case
in point)—and raises questions about the museum culture of our day, our lack of
commitment to emergent composers and music, and our escape into the distant
past. With its claim that the past knows best, the classical music establishment
appears to attack the very idea of cultural continuity and development.

According to Said, classical music enthusiasts have always been open to accusations of arrogance, of claiming that their way to perform is the only way, of
being *effete*. Does a reliance on history somehow remove from the musician the
need to perform with passion and involvement? In the days of Roger Norrington's
Beethoven, John Eliot Gardiner's Handel and Nikolaus Harnoncourt's Mozart,
such an accusation may seem outdated, but some of the variations that Said has

demonstrated show that in the past the claim was certainly justified. When Erwin Bodky wrote in a program note for concerts of his Cambridge Society for Early Music in Boston, Massachusetts, in the 1950s, he declared:

> Classical . . . music was a highly aristocratic art and restraint governed even the display of emotion. . . . This deprives concerts of Classical music of the atmosphere of electricity which, when present, is one of the finest experiences of the modern concert hall. Who seeks but this may stay away from our concert series. We want to take this opportunity, however, to thank our artists for the voluntary restraint in the display of their artistic capabilities which they exercise when recreating with us the atmosphere of equanimity, tranquillity and noble entertainment which is the characteristic feature of Classical music.[9]

This statement goes against the grain of what Said presents us with in *Musical Elaborations*. The essay argues two principal points, and they remain somewhat at odds with each other. The first is a dutiful act of loyalty to the fashionable notion that works of art must be removed from the sphere of aesthetics for subjection to cultural-historical analysis. The most illuminating writing about music, Said states, is "humanistic" rather than merely aesthetic or technical. It must have its various roles in society and in history; its relation to the discourses of political power must be strenuously investigated, just as literature is nowadays primarily a matter for "cultural studies" and routinely submits to ideological or psychoanalytic analysis. Said argues at length with Adorno, who practiced the same critique, though before it became the vogue, with magisterial strength and gloomy inclusiveness. Said, deferential but still his own man, characteristically points out that to treat modern music as a reflection or portent of the world's present or impending ruin is actually a Eurocentric view, which, with unconscious colonialist arrogance, is assumed to apply universally.

Said knows far too much about music to believe that the musical canon is, in common with the literary one, a White male bourgeois fraud. Any interpreter approaching the classical music canon in the early twenty-first century is faced with an interpretative language distended with cliché: the result of the same works having been repeated over and over again (Kermode, 1994). The concert platform is the scene of these repetitions, the place where the classical music canon is done to death night after night and year after year. Like Glenn Gould who stopped playing in public, Said plays in privacy in order to stamp his performance with individuality and intimacy. The subject matter of his transgressive sonata (in chapter 3) is, roughly, the experience of music in solitude, of private performance and properly creative listening. This is far more interesting, and it establishes the right of Said's narrative to be taken more seriously than if it had offered nothing but a Foucauldian exercise in musical "archaeology" or a renegotiation between musical and other discourses.

Said's second principal subject, though still classifiable as cultural criticism, is his study of the conditions of modern performance—for instance, the alienating social arrangements of the concert hall. "Performances of classical music," he rightly observes, "are highly concentrated, rarefied and extreme occasions. . . . Performance is thus an inflected and highly determined point of convergence where the specific and the general come together" (ibid., 17). Or worded differently, performance is a feat quite distinct from composing, which it has in large measure displaced from public interest. Nowadays sharply differentiated from composers, performers are also clearly marked as separate from their audiences. Most members of the audience play no instrument, cannot get to know music by playing piano transcriptions as they once did, and in any case could not hope to play the way the pianist does, so they observe him or her in an alienated but reverential ignorance, much as they might a pole vaulter. This is true as the most effective deterrent to concert going is the nonsense in which all, performers and audience alike, feel obliged to participate, perhaps to establish that elusive rapport—the absurd, ritually prolonged applause, the ceremonial entrances of leader and conductor, the marching off and on to stage, the standing up and sitting down, reaching its farcical nadir in the yelling, stamping foolery of the Proms. Along with Adorno, Gould, and others, Said laments that social and technological developments have gone far toward ruining classical music by making it available in this way or in recorded performance, invariant and therefore falsifying. He also deplores the musical pollution of our aural environment, the "demotion of music to commodity status" (ibid., 72). However, he dislikes the way musicologists barricade themselves behind abstruse textual analysis, not risking the more "humanistic" approach, which places music in social and psychological settings. It sometimes appears that he wants music to suffer all the pains that literature is currently undergoing. This is conscientious, but it seems strikingly at odds with the preferred inwardness of his own experience of music; and it makes for a certain apparent confusedness of exposition (Kermade, 1994).

It is not easy to grasp the structure of the Wellek Lectures right away; listening to them for the first time must have been strenuous, despite the help of musical illustrations. Said talks about a great many things, digresses, honors his critical commitments, and returns, with some relief, to music proper. "So there is a continuous struggle between an intense private love of music," Frank Kermode remarks, "and a conviction that the modern way of treating the discourses of art as underprivileged in relation to other discourses ought to be applied to music as to everything else" (1991: 3). Hence the stress on professional performance. Said pays handsome tribute to Toscanini and Gould among others. He has to weigh against their admired interpretative skills the fact that they, in different ways, conspire in the maintenance of a social order: "Toscanini giving performances appropriate to the sponsorship of a giant industrial concern, Gould abjuring the concert hall but making that very gesture an index of apartness and a permanent part of his performance" (ibid., 98). Said most approves of works that transgress social norms or musical norms socially imposed—for example, *Così fan tutte* and Bach's *Canonic Variations' on Von Himmel hoch*, the latter because it is so enormously and gratuitously in excess of the "pious technical sententiousness" of the chorale.

For Said, performance is a fundamental prerequisite of all true music. Examples abound, but the one that most characterizes his attachment is the final lecture, an account of what it was like to listen to Alfred Brendel playing the Brahms *Piano Variations, Opus 18*, a work he was not familiar with, though he at once realized its connection with the *String Sextet* in *B* flat. He subtly distinguishes between that experience and the experience of listening, in the same recital, to the Diabelli *Variations*, a work Said knows well so that during its performance he was attending to Brendel's interpretation rather than to the music itself, as he had done with the Brahms. The other instance is that of Gould's performance of *contrapuntal* pieces and variations. Said speaks of a one-hour program Gould devoted to the fugue that comprised selections from Bach's *Well Tempered Clavier*, the last movement of Beethoven's *Sonata* in *A* flat major (*Opus 110*) and a daemonic rendition of the last movement of Paul Hindemith's *Sonata No. 3*, "a fine piece hardly ever played in concert today because of the intellectual cowardice of most contemporary musicians" ("The Vienna Philharmonic," 1987: 533). The program of variations climaxed with performances of Webern's *Variations* and Beethoven's *Sonata* in *E major* (*Opus 109*).

> Gould linked the two by a brilliant highlighting of the structural finesse and expressive detail in both works—a considerable achievement, since the pieces are written out of diametrically opposed aesthetics, one exfoliative and elaborate, the other concentrated and crabbed. The program also included a severely restrained performance of a Sweelinck organ, which I first heard during a Gould recital in 1959 or 1960. I was struck then, and again watching the film, by the way Gould disappears as a performer into the work's long complications, providing an instance of what he called "ecstasy," the state of standing outside time and within an integral artistic structure (Ibid., 534).

The greater the autonomy of an artwork from social or institutional imperatives, the more precisely will its formal constitution depict the structure and conflicts of the society in which the artist lives and works. Aesthetic form, the artwork's perceptual frame, is, as a product of consciousness, shaped by the social objectivity that mediates all consciousness; thus the more the artwork relies on its own autonomous form rather than trying to depict social reality, the more distinctly will this reality and its antagonisms appear in cipher in the work's perceptual arrangements and the tensions they engender. "It is as a dynamic totality, not as a series of images that great music becomes an intrinsic theater of the world" (Adorno, 1984: 76). The Said argument easily asserts its status as something more than a pertinent example of interpretation.

The death of interpretation, Michel Foucault argues in *Dits et écrits*, is the belief that there are signs of something, that is to say, some hidden essence waiting for us at the end of our interpretative journeys; the "life of interpretation, on the contrary, is to believe that there are only interpretations" (1994: 322). Modern, critical knowledge of classical music is certainly a hermeneutic of depth; but that should not be construed as a search for deep structures; rather, we must realize the full analytic impact of what Nietzsche saw: that "interpretation has . . . become an *infinite* task." Said's interpretative variations, as I read them, consist in holding every interpretandum *to be already an interpretation*. He reminds one of the Jazz pianist Keith Jarret, polyphonic, *contrapuntal*, variational. But Said effected this technique largely by hybrid means, through the affirmation of a heterogeneous tradition that encompasses not only musicology but also opera, aesthetics, theory. It is because of this state of mingling between music and literature that Said has such a clear grasp of the nature of music that he can see the differences from, as well as the similarities to, text/performance. His musical critical career contains analyses of works by Bach, Mozart, Beethoven, Verdi, Rossini, Richard Strauss, Stravinsky, Chopin, and many others that are completely comprehensible to the layman yet at the same time musically acute. This is so because, we sense, he has himself spent long hours weighing and balancing temporal sequences against each other, without theoretical preconceptions, but solely in order to achieve his own ends in private moments.

Said's admirable clarity about the "life of interpretation," in Foucault's phrase, stems at least in part from his awareness of the fact that the late-twentieth-century interpretation of music, far from being a natural phenomenon, consists of man-made objects, objects, moreover, that are made according to a very limited set of possibilities. Said is aware that we cannot simply object to the results of a performance, but he asks why we should not make use of the fact that works of music are not monuments in themselves but compositions that throw as much light as possible on the experience of life. At times, he raises questions that have no easy answers.

> How far can one go in transforming a work, and what is it about the work itself that appears to permit some changes but not others? Why are ideological notions about authenticity or fidelity to a text allowed to rule performance standards, and what is it about Mozart's operas [for example] in particular . . . that inspires the conservatism of some viewers and the

enthusiasm of others when the works are staged with startlingly new, even shocking force? (*Musical Elaborations*, 1991: 16).

But this is not merely a critic's awareness of an artistic problem: the notion of a work as being filled with "life" has cultural and existential as well as aesthetic dimensions. Commenting on what he calls "an outsider's interpretation" of Mozart's *Don Giovanni*, Said notes:

> Peter Sellars's choice of the drug scene, with a darkened stage and frequently indistinguishable figures, struck me as shatteringly, chillingly pertinent. Don Giovanni's love life is as romantic as a dingy subway platform inhabited by outcasts and misfits who lie in wait for the occasional trick; the attitude of the confirmed junkie shooting up every time he gets a chance is perfectly comparable to the driven rake in his view of women. And Sellars portrayed it ("Maestro for the Masses," 1987: 319).

At such moments it becomes the duty of the musically gifted critic to reveal the cultural roots of wholehearted performances—even though such performances may lack money and stars. "For its part," Said concludes,

> music criticism is now effectively the report of attendance at concerts that are really evanescent happenings, unrepeatable, usually unrecordable, non-recuperable. And yet in the interesting recharting of intellectual undertakings attempted by what has been called cultural studies, certain aspects of the musical experience can be understood inclusively as taking place within the cultural setting of the contemporary West (Ibid., 320).

A music that is truly social (and, therefore, socially true), in Said's analysis, is one in which the elements manifest sociality and temporality in their relations with each other. A composition, for Said, is thus an interdependent whole, a developing process, a becoming. It has history within it and is transformed by outer historical movement in which it participates. The receiver can only appreciate such a process through actively and sympathetically participating in its development, from the inside, as it were; this demands from the receiver—to borrow a phrase from Polanyi—an "indwelling." Any such indwelling presupposes a concentrative and absorbed mode of listening in which no element, be it a rhythm, a melody, or a phrase, takes precedence over the developing totality.

Music and opera performance are, of course, arts of interpretation. Yet it is not plausible to expect a pianist playing a Beethoven sonata or an opera director staging *Wozzek* to produce creative misreadings of these works. Most musical performance is still held in by mimetic norms. The pianist tries to play as exactly as possible what he or she thinks Beethoven actually wrote, in the order that he wrote it, first movement first, last movement last. Similarly, opera productions, although they give the director considerable leeway, must still respect character and plot. It would be impossible to do *Aida* without an Aida even though impresarios today do present *Aidas* and *Toscas* and *Siegfrieds* without Aidas, Toscas, and Siegfrieds. Directors and audiences (to say nothing of singers and dancers) retain a common realistic expectation of what the intactness of a piece is; otherwise there would be no opera, and no paying audience. So it has been the case that musical revivals have tended to be conservative, trying to get back to some lost or forgotten original. The vogue for early music played on original instruments, the revival of *bel canto* repertoire and style, all these have embodied not just the idea of recuperation but an usually unstated ideology of authenticity. The musical results are often satisfying. But it is not generally noted that even so apparently harmless and "correct" a notion as faithfulness to an original is itself already an *interpretation*, in which a slew of unverifiable entities (the composer's intention, the director's method, an original sound) are set up and bowed to as if they were facts of life. Take as an illustration Said's comment on two productions of *Così fan tutte*: the 1951 Metropolitan Opera production directed by Alfred Lunt and the Peter Sellars' production staged in New York in the late 1980s.

> *Così fan tutte* was the first opera I saw when I came to the United States as a schoolboy in the early 1950s. The 1951 Metropolitan Opera production was directed by renowned theater figure Alfred Lunt, and, as I recall, much celebrated as a brilliant yet faithful English-language rendition of an elegant opera that boasted an excellent cast . . . and a fastidiously executed conception as an eighteenth-century court comedy. I remember a lot of curtseying, many lace hankies, elaborate wigs, and acres of beauty spots, much chuckling and all-round good fun, all of which seemed to go well with the very polished, indeed even superb singing by the ensemble ("*Così fan tutte* at the Limits," 1997: 95–96).

Of Sellars's production, Said writes:

> The great virtue of this production [staged . . . at the now defunct PepsiCo Summerfare in Purchase, New York] was that Sellars managed to sweep away all of the eighteenth-century clichés. As Mozart had written the opera while the ancient régime was crumbling, Sellars argued, they should be set by contemporary directors at a similar moment in our time—with the crumbling of the American empire alluded to by characters and settings, as well as by class deformations and personal histories that bore the marks of a society in crisis. Thus Sellars's version of . . . *Così fan tutte* takes place in Despina's Diner, where a group of Vietnam veterans and their

girlfriends hang out, play games, and get frighteningly embroiled in feelings and self-discoveries for which they are unprepared and with which they are incapable of dealing (Ibid.).

It is rewarding, Said goes on to say, to see *Così fan tutte* staged not only as a farce but also as a shrewdly calculating and inventive piece of conventional provocation insofar as the opera's strange lightheartedness hides, or makes light of, an inner system that is quite severe and amoral in its workings. This view, he explains, displays a universe short of any redemptive or palliative schemes, whose one law is motion and instability expressed as the power of libertinage and manipulation. Said explains the director's choice with the searching statement that "no one but Sellars has attempted such a full-scale revisionist interpretation of [this] opera, which remain[s] in the repertory as essentially courtly, classical, eighteenth-century opera" (ibid., 95). He finds Sellars's straying beyond the appointed limits attractive and daring.

Said also points out that there is another, more exigently contemporary and practical reason for interpreting Mozart as Sellars does:

> Consider that Sellars himself is the product of a culture with no continuous and independent opera tradition. Until now mainstream American opera production has derived mainly from Europe, and a boring *verismo* (i.e., mimetic) Europe at that. For such a tradition to work here you need money and stars, neither of which are handily available. Sellars's means are therefore modest. His singers in *Così* were young and of average (even mediocre) voice, with the women in general better than the men. What they lacked in musical polish, they more than made up for in physical agility; many arias were sung by characters rolling around on the stage, with results in pure vocal production that were not always satisfying. . . . In fact, so strong was Sellars's conception of his singers as functionaries in his productions that you can only imagine them singing for him ("Maestro for the Masses," 1987: 320).

The great virtue of Sellars's production, Said adds, is that it can provide some direct insight into Mozart's motives as to why he composed the opera in the first place.

> Almost immediately, they put you in touch with what is most eccentric and opaque about Mozart, the obsessive patternings in the opera, patternings that have little to do with showing that crime does not pay or that the faithlessness inherent in all human dealings must be overcome before true union can occur. Mozart's characters in *Così fan tutte* can be interpreted not as individuals with definable characteristics but as figures driven by forces

outside themselves that they do not comprehend and make no effort to examine. This opera, in fact, Said concludes, is about power and manipulation that reduce individuality to a momentary identity in the vast rush of things. There is very little room in it for providence, or for the heroics of charismatic personalities. Compared with Beethoven, who worked tirelessly to paint a free world where music escapes the shackles of tyranny, Mozart depicts a Lucretian world, in which power has its own hunger, undomesticated by considerations of either piety or verisimilitude (1997:98).

II

Writing about music has served as an escape from polemical politics, a way of moving from the mundane realm to the aesthetic, from social and\or ideological issues to a personal relation with various operas, recitals, and orchestral performances. Having spent a lifetime dealing with the complexity and subtlety of literature and music, Said turns his attention to discovering some basic secrets about aesthetics and the relationship between operatic as opposed to symphonic sound and silence. His love for what Aaron Copland called *"la forme fatale"* (i.e., opera) has led him to cooperate with Daniel Barenboim and the Chicago Symphony Orchestra on a production of *Fidelio*. His project as *dramaturg* for a 2000 Berlin production of *Les Troyens* supports the claim made here: having persuaded us that المـعرفه قـوّه (knowledge is power), he now wants to convince us of the moral dimension of a musical construction and of the aesthetics that is the basis of anything truly creative and liberating. Surely these same insights must ultimately prove of value in the making of a free self. Speaking of a concert Barenboim conducted in Jerusalem in April 1998, Said writes: "After his concert, in front of a packed house, he dedicated his first *encore* to the Palestinian woman who had invited him to dinner the night before and who was present that evening. I was surprised to see the audience, made up entirely of Israeli Jews (she and I were the only Palestinians), respond to his noble dedication with enthusiastic applause" ("La Palestine n'a pas encore disparu," 1998: 5). In the interview Said conducted with Barenboim in Jerusalem, the Argentine pianist and conductor regretted that the fifty years of Israeli statehood represented fifty years of suffering for the Palestinian people. In the end, "he made it clear," Said reports, "that he was in favor of a Palestinian state" (ibid.).

The company Said keeps is well tuned to iconoclasm, for Barenboim is none other than the brilliantly audacious conductor and pianist who in November 1989 led the Berlin Philharmonic Orchestra to commemorate the transition (*Wende*) that had occurred in German politics after the fall of the Iron Curtain by performing Beethoven's *First Piano Concerto* and *Seventh Symphony*, which East Germans experienced "as in a dream."[10] It was in the cause of Beethoven that Barenboim undertook a mammoth task: the complete cycle of Beethoven symphonies and piano concertos over six concerts in London's Royal Festival Hall during May 1998. "I have been nearly 50 years on the stage—I gave my first concert in 1950; my father, who was my teacher, never allowed me to repeat a piece more than twice in the same season, so it really increased my repertoire at a very young age. . . . I played the cycle of Beethoven when I was 15, so I have lived with these pieces for 40 years."[11] Barenboim says that Beethoven sets him free. His approach is to bring an acute sense of focus to the music, built on long familiarity with the scores and the sense of freedom acquired by technical mastery. That Said should choose to coconduct with Barenboim and/or write on *Fidelio* can in itself be understood as a stand against domination, for Beethoven's only opera can be seen as a symbol of liberation and the triumph of good over evil. Perhaps with the signing of Oslo I and Oslo II, which Said opposed, the liberation of Palestine had only reached the first act; only if total decolonization and democracy for all are achieved, only if Palestinian citizens all over the world have the possibility of returning home and voting freely to elect their leaders would Said feel it appropriate to quote Florestan and Leonore from act 2 of *Fidelio*—"*O namenlose freude*" and "*inaussprechlich süsses glück*," sung by the liberatea, prisoners, and soloists, finale.[12]

Nowhere is Said's partiality for Beethoven more amply demonstrated than in the following comment in which he compares *Fidelio* to *Così fan tutte*:

> *Fidelio* can also be interpreted as a terrific counter-blow to *Così fan tutte*, an important antecedent and part of the past that Beethoven is working with. On the one hand, he incorporates the disguises, if not the malice of *Così*: on the other, he uses unmasking to assert the bourgeois ideal of matrimonial fidelity. Memory in *Così fan tutte* is a faculty to be done away with in the pursuit of pleasure: in *Fidelio* it is a vital part of character ("On *Fidelio*," 1997: 25).

From this inclination comes the intense energy of *Fidelio*, expressed in its frequent reference to justice, fidelity, and conjugal love. Less a dramatic representation of redemptive love than an enactment of various principles (loyalty, conjugal bliss, and hatred of tyranny), *Fidelio* is based on Jean Nicolas Bouilly's play *L'Amour conjugal*. Originally finished in 1806, the opera was not successful until eight years later, when Beethoven shortened it considerably and changed its name from *Leonore* to *Fidelio*. The composer's admiration for the French Revolution (from which in a sense his text for the opera was borrowed) pays little heed to actual revolutionary life; what he achieves is the much more special advantage of using a political motif to get beyond politics altogether and beyond history as well. "Indeed," Paul Robinson notes, "one might even argue that linking the opera's liberationist theme to the events of the Revolution violates its universalist spirit and thereby diminishes it" (1993: 80). Ernst Bloch has made the inspired claim that *Fidelio* is an apocalyptic work oriented to the future; thus the famous trumpet call releasing Florestan from Pizarro's dungeon just after Leonore has made herself known is the "*tuba mirum spargens sonum*, pronouncing the saviour's arrival." By the end of the opera, Bloch continues, "Beethoven's music has proved itself to be militant-religious, the dawning of a new day so audible that it seems more than simply a hope. . . . Thus music as a whole stands at the farther limits of humanity, but at those limits where humanity, with new language and haloed by the call to achieved intensity, to the attained world of 'we,' is first taking shape."[13] I suppose it is gargantuan egoism on Beethoven's part to pretend that he was capable of going beyond humanity into the realm of timeless principle. But his egoism, his carefully constructed subjectivity, his aesthetic norms are all part of an attempt to rise out of the particular, the historical, the political. Early romantic art is full of this disenchantment with the worldly, even in supposedly political works; it is interesting not because it is humanistic as it pretends but precisely because its aims are to depoliticize. "Still *Fidelio*'s overall effect is extremely powerful," Said reminds us. "It is as if some other, deeper force moves the work and in a subterranean way compels it forward, from the darkness of the prison into the light of day. Its theme is undoubtedly the very constancy and heroism which are the hallmark of Beethoven's middle-period style, and which are premised on the need to celebrate, indeed proclaim jubilantly, the virtuous love of men and women, the victory of light over darkness, and the defeat of injustice and treachery" ("From Silence to Music," 1997: 80). In other words, what is needed, Said maintains, is for a spiritual regeneration of society to arise from genuine rational cooperation in social production. Beethoven's world is but a reflection of the alienated and impoverished consciousness of society, which would seek to recover at a sensuous level what it has lost through instrumentality. But such a unification has no basis in social reality; there are no means to achieve it in anything but appearance. Genuine liberation would have demanded the rational control of the labor process in the cause of freedom, but this was not possible for Beethoven: his totality was no real totality but the fragmented world of the individual pretending to be totality.[14]

Insofar as an opera or a symphony in performance establishes the illusion of an autonomous work of music independent of the context within which it was created, it is difficult, in view of our present-day knowledge of this context, as Said amply demonstrates in "The Empire at Work: Verdi's *Aida*," to experience the stage illusion it strives for without also feeling aware of the often unresolved social and cultural tensions underlying it. To grapple with these tensions, Said suggests what he calls a "contrapuntal interpretation."[15] This is how he describes it at work in *Così fan tutte*:

> Mozart's use of counterpoint gives the music added substance, so that in
> the A-flat Canon in the second act's finale one experiences not only a

remarkable sense of rigor, but also a special ironic expressiveness well beyond the words and the situation. For, as the lovers have finally worked their way around to the new reversed pairing, three of them sing polyphonically of submerging all thought and memory in the wine they are about to drink, while only one, Guglielmo, remains disaffected—he had greater faith in Fiordiligi's power to resist Ferrando, but he has been disproved—and he stands outside the canon; he wishes that the women (*"queste volpi senza amore"*) would drink poison and end the whole thing. It is as if Mozart wanted the counterpoint to mirror the lovers' embarrassment in a closed polyphonic system (*"Così fan tutte* at the Limits," 1997: 102).

The counterpoint can also be an alternative in the form of a double awareness that experiences the work (of literature, music, art) while at the same time viewing it within the *context* in which it was born: text and context are intertwined, their histories overlap. Take *Aida* as an example. On the one hand, the audience hears the opera "itself" in all its musical and dramatic splendor, and, on the other, it remains aware of a whole cast of characters "outside" the opera who instigated and helped shape its composition and production. The following material, which cannot be overlooked but systematically has been, is intertwined with the birth of *Aida*.

Opera came to Egypt in 1841 when an Italian touring company presented a season in Alexandria, the country's most cosmopolitan city, where many Europeans, mostly Italians, had settled and where the Egyptian court spent the summer months. By the 1860s, opera was being presented in Cairo. It was found pleasing, and in 1869 Khedive Ismail decided to construct a new opera house in Cairo to mark the opening of the Suez Canal. Two Italian architects, Avoscani and Rossi, were commissioned to design the theater in the traditional horseshoe style to seat 850, with two boxes for the khedive and two other closed ones for his حريم (*har'eem*). The theater was inaugurated on 1 November 1869, not as is so often stated with *Aida*, but with *Rigoletto*. The glittering gala audience included the French Empress Eugenie, Franz-Josef of Austria, the prince of Holland, the crown prince of Prussia and Ferdinand de Lesseps, the French engineer who had built the Suez Canal. British royalty was not present. Britain was represented by its ambassador to Constantinople, Egypt in theory still being part of the Ottoman Empire. So the new opera house had few, if any, connections with the British, particularly so after 1882 when the British became the real rulers of the country, and Sir Evelyn Baring, the British agent, laid down his doctrine that British administrators should not mix socially with the natives. Thus the Cairo Opera House was never associated with British colonialism, probably a good thing (Lindenberger, 1998: 165).

After the opening of his new canal and opera house, Ismail declared, "Egypt is now part of Europe." The first season continued with *Il barbiere, Trovatore, Traviata, Ernani, Lucia, elisir d'amore, Ballo in maschera, Faust,* and *Favorita* (both sung in Italian), *Il deserto*, the Italian version of Felicien David's *Le désert*, one of the first works to employ Orientalism, Ricci's *Crispino e la Comore*, and *Semiramide*. Verdi's specially commissioned *Aida*, for which he demanded four times what the Paris Opera had paid him for *Don Carlos*, joined the repertory at the end of the second season on 24 December 1871, and since that time has never ceased to be the most popular opera with Egyptians, being performed almost every season at the Cairo Opera and in 1912 receiving its first open air performance at the foot of the pyramids. Said explains the motives behind the opera's composition:

> In the simple, intense, and above all authentically "Egyptian" scenarios by Mariette, Verdi perceived a unitary intention, the imprint or trace of a masterly and expert will that he hoped to match in music. At the time when his career had been marked with disappointments, unfulfilled intentions, unsatisfying collaborations with impresarios, ticket sellers, singers—the Paris premiere of *Don Carlos* was a recent, still smarting instance—Verdi saw a chance to create a work whose every detail he could supervise from beginning sketch to opening night (1993: 116).

For its part, in 1877 the Egyptian company went bankrupt, and the spendthrift Ismail, now hard pressed for money, could not come to its aid. So for the next twenty years there were no more "official" seasons. The void was filled with unofficial seasons both in the opera house itself, let out to impresarios, and at the Garden Theater. One of these seasons was organized by Adolfo Bracale, a cellist who had played in the Khedival Orchestra. He hired a young tenor only recently starting his career, one Enrico Caruso. Alexandria and the Garden Theater, Cairo, thus became the first steps in Caruso's long international career. He sang there two roles for the first time, Enzo in *La Giaconda* and Grieux in *Manon Lescaut*.[17] Official seasons began again at the opera house in 1897 when an Italian impresario, Gianoli, began the first of his six seasons. Puccini came personally to supervise the production of *Madama Butterfly*. In 1907 the first French impresario, Marius Poncet, tried his luck with a season of sixty performances of twenty-four works, including *Aida*, *Trovatore*, and *Lohengrin*, all sung in French, with *Hérodiade*, *Carmen*, *Werther*, and as novelties, *Thaïs*, *Fortunio*, and *Henri VIII*. But the Cairo Opera with its limited capacity of 850 seats was always a difficult theater to run profitably, and in 1923, after the failure of another French season, it was agreed with the Egyptian government that the French would leave to the Italians the task of organizing the opera seasons, while they, the French, would concentrate on the spoken theater. The opera house had from an early date been used for drama, Sarah Bernhardt having played there as early as 1886 and returning in 1908 in Sardou's *Tosca*.[18]

In 1922, with the breakup of the Ottoman Empire, Khedive Faud took the title of king of Egypt and the Khedival Théâtres became Les Théâtres Royaux, French being the official language of the court. By now, operas were being presented in Arabic with Egyptian casts at the Garden Theater, alongside what can best be described as Egyptian operettas by composers such as Sayed Darwish (1892–1923), who is now considered the father of modern Egyptian music. In 1927 Viconte Visconti de Modrone organized a season that included the first performance in Egypt of *Pelléas et Mélisande* (in Italian). Although the season was an artistic success, financial disaster was only avoided when the Italian government came to the rescue with a subsidy, which from then on was granted annually. In 1935 Rosa Raisa headed the company—Italian companies would continue to come up until World War II, often directed by Vincenzo Bellazza. The pattern began again soon after the war was over, continued until 1971, and was hardly affected by the overthrow of the monarchy in 1954 or by Nasser's nationalization of the Suez Canal, which led to the unhappy British and French intervention (Lindenberger, 1998: 168).

Khedive Ismail, technically viceroy to the Ottoman emperor but very much his own ruler within Egypt, which was at that time the most economically progressive part of the empire; Paul Draneht, a Greek Cypriot who had played a key role in negotiating the construction of the Suez Canal by a European consortium and who happened as well to be the impresario of the new opera house for which *Aida* was commissioned; and finally Auguste Mariette, a Frenchman who counts as one of the founding fathers of Egyptology, and who had lived in Egypt since 1850 conducting archaeological excavations played parts.[19] But it was Mariette who concocted the scenario of the opera that was submitted to Verdi, who "could assume," Said observes, "that a wealthy Oriental potentate had joined with a genuinely brilliant and single-minded Western archeologist to give him an occasion in which he could be a commanding and undistracted artistic presence. The story's alienating Egyptian provenance and setting paradoxically seem to have stimulated his sense of technical mastery" (1993: 116), or *power-knowledge-pleasure*, as Michel Foucault would have it.

For Said, no matter how much Verdi and his followers (directors, divas, impresarios) may have thought themselves to be dramatizing the political tensions generated within the *Risogimento*, to the extent that *Aida*, for example, was the product of the committee named above, it served to offer legitimacy and fame (not least of all because of the composer's high status within European culture) to a Near Eastern ruler of a backward and still-subjugated country. Egypt owed its quick rise to the cotton trade, which had temporarily lost its base in North America as a result of the Civil War; following this prosperity and the recent opening of the Suez Canal, the khedive clearly felt the need to display his success in material terms that the Western world could observe. The opera house that he had built in the neo-Renaissance style then fashionable for public buildings in Europe, is a testimony to his self-fashioning as a pro-Western ruler. By building such a structure and situating it strategically at the confluence of Cairo's popular native quarter and the modern, Western-style city he had constructed, he could at once claim the prestige accruing to a European monarch and display his link with an ancient, archeologically reconstructed Egypt that became glorified in Verdi's opera and that contrasted starkly with the bedraggled, still underdeveloped land he had inherited. This is what Said aptly calls the "cultural machinery of spectacles" that operated on both sides of the dividing line of empire (1993: 130). He further observes:

> One must remember, too, that when one belongs to the more powerful side in the imperial and colonial encounter, it is quite possible to overlook, forget, or ignore the unpleasant aspects of what went on "out there." The cultural machinery—of spectacles like *Aida*, of the genuinely interesting books written by travelers, novelists, and scholars, of fascinating photographs and exotic paintings—has had an aesthetic as well as informative effect on European audiences. Things stay remarkably unchanged when such distancing and aestheticizing cultural practices are employed, for they split and then anesthetize the metropolitan consciousness (Ibid., 130–31).

This is undeniably persuasive as far as it goes; Said is correct about the cultural machinery of spectacles, but he cannot explain what causes it. We should remember that Egypt attracted an entire host of curiosities: Orientalists (T. E. Lawrence), writers (Flaubert), Egyptologists (Champollion and Mariette), composers (Verdi and Puccini), musical directors (Manno Wolf Ferrari, Napoleone Annovazzi, and Nicola Rescigno), and singers (Caruso, Zeani, Scotto, Cagniglia, Filippeschi, Bechi, Rina Gigli, Floriana Cavalli, Tagliavini, Guelfi, Bergonzi, Grobbi, Rossi-Lemeni, and Maria Chiara), although one must note that these stars were sprinkled over a fifteen-year period and appeared alongside more workaday Italian singers. Their thrust was to present Egypt to Europe in a variety of ways through archeology (*Description de l'Egypte*), drawings *(Précis du système hiéroglyphique)*, and grand opera (*Aida*) (Robinson, 1993: 133–40). It is what V. Y. Mudimbe rightly termed the "invention of Africa." This dimension eludes Said, who falls short in telling us that Orientalist learning itself was premised on the silence of the native, who was represented by an Occidental expert speaking *ex cathedra* on the native's behalf, presenting that unfortunate creature as an undeveloped, deficient, and uncivilized being who could not represent himself. But just as it has now become inappropriate for White scholars to speak on behalf of "Negroes," it has, not since the end of classical European colonialism, stopped being fashionable or even acceptable to pontificate about the Oriental's (i.e., the Muslim's, or the Indian's, or the Chinese's) "mentality."

III

Said's gift for playing or critiquing music cannot be detached from the milieu in which he grew up insofar as the 1940s Cairo was well tuned to European high art from literature and opera to ballet, recitals and concerts to regular visits of *La Comédie Française* and the Old Vic. Central (the word is slightly skewed when applied to so brash a critic as Said) to his survival, is the withdrawal into self and solitude he experienced as a child, which he describes in these terms:

> My strongest continuous memory as a child was one of being a misfit. I was incredibly shy. I was terribly anxious and nervous about my relations with others, since I was sort of envious of their being Muslim/Egyptian, or Muslim/Palestinian, and I always had this sense of not being quite right. . . . I felt always that I was being made to pay for it in one way or another. I forgot to add an important component to all of this, which is that I always went to English or French schools, so in addition to my problematic Arab identity, there was this other fact of my education where, by the time I was thirteen or so, I knew everything there was to know about English history, let's say, or French history, and next to nothing about the place I was living in. That was the style of education. So it was a perpetual discomfort. My family compensated for this by creating a cocoon around us. We were unusually different and each of us—my four sisters and I—had different kinds of gifts. And so the result was that we lived in a make-believe world that had no relationship (a) to reality and (b) to the history and actuality of the places we were living in (*Out of Place*, 1997: 76).

The core of Said's reading of his otherwise privileged childhood is rooted in the immediacy with which he brings out the irreducible tension between colonial domination and native resistance on the one hand and inclusion/exclusion on the other. If Said comes across as a "misfit," it is because he wanted to prolong that deep *oppositional* thought over a creative lifetime.

One could define genius as the strategic ability to withstand, deflect, and even positively exploit the plethora of impediments that the colonial master has flung at his passive subjects. In "Cairo Recalled," Said describes how he was affected by the foreign imports, otherwise termed "colonial habits," which forced him to achieve a greater intimacy, almost a profound inwardness.[20] Aware of the contradictions of history, Said wields them to deft and often moving effect. Recalling Ignace Tiegerman, and the political changes that were then sweeping through Egypt, Said reminisces:

> Tiegerman was a remarkable phenomenon. In part, I think, his extraordinary gifts were accentuated for me because of how they clashed with the

anomalous background provided by Cairo, where he stood out as a tiny, almost dwarflike and sharp-featured creature with a marked Polish accent and trilingual facility in hybrid versions of French, German, and English (no Arabic at all), imperious in his ways, heedless and yet occasionally apprehensive about the massive political changes in Egypt as it went from its Faroukian degeneracy into the assertive triumphalism of its Arab nationalist phase under Gamal Abdel Nasser. Tiegerman was a profoundly, but attractively, lazy man who ran a conservatory and employed piano and violin teachers with a kind of salonlike languor. He himself was a mercurial teacher, but certainly the most musical and ingenious that I ever encountered (*Musical Elaborations*, 1991: 90–91).

While Said's account of the period brings much that is unfamiliar, it brings little that is unexpected. It is based partly on a perceptive understanding of the idea of music as a mode for thinking through or thinking with the variety of human cultural practices, generously, noncoercively, and, almost in a utopian cast, if by utopian we mean worldly, possible, attainable. Said is convinced that music has the capacity to transgress all human and natural boundaries. He illustrates this breaking down of the boundaries by quoting C. L. R. James, who used to say, "Beethoven belongs as much to West Indians as he does to Germans, since his music is now part of the human heritage" (Said, *Culture and Imperialism*, 1993: xxv). There is something in this claim: Could it not be that the success of Said, the accomplished pianist and music critic, is due to his geographical, linguistic, cultural border crossings? Why do certain elements like "sound" and "silence" remain most vividly in the mind and memory? Can silence take on the function of a heroic self-redefinition in which the arbitrary ending of mortal existence acquires the redemptive trappings of aesthetic closure?

These are some of the questions Said addresses in "From Silence to Sound and Back Again; Music, Literature, and History." Answering them, he displays a side of his critical persona: poised, meditative, private. For Said, now, a genuine historically based aesthetic encourages him to rethink the common wisdom that has accrued over the years about long-familiar works of literature and music. Such an aesthetic would ask him to reframe the questions he posed about these works, to attempt to locate the most appropriate contexts within which to ponder their meanings, their formal properties, and the power they exercise upon him as interpreter. Said speaks ebulliently about the silence and sound of art and their desirability for Shakespeare, Beethoven, Wagner, Mann, Keats, Cage, Césaire, Foucault, and Conrad—that complex and elusive figure who had a strange sort of exilic consciousness.

The truth is that Conrad's prismatic sense of dislocation and above all, skepticism, especially the skepticism about identity and settled existence, seems to have attracted Said to the Polish writer. Here is how he puts it in a passage from "From Silence to Sound":

> I have chosen this interrelated series of representation of sound and silence for its rather dramatic coherence, although I have emphasized in it the precariousness and vulnerability to silence, of musical sound. In its instrumental form music is a silent art; it does not speak the denotative language of words, and its mysteriousness is deepened by the fact that it appears to be *saying something*. Verbal representations of musical significance necessarily stress the opposition between sound and nonsound, and in the cases I have been discussing, they try to establish a continuity of sorts between them (*Musical Elaborations*, 1997: 11–12).

As an essential component of art, Said seems to hint, sound symbolizes the difficulty but also the opportunity offered by the realm of the aesthetic. He takes the example of Sheherazade "who must continue to tell Shahriar the stories that while away the night and stay the sentence of death imposed on all the king's wives. The continuous sound of the human voice functions as an assurance of the continuity of human life; conversely, silence is associated with death" (ibid., 7). In making the effort, renewed each night, to keep silence outside the circle of sound, Sheherazade produces the text for the narrative voice-over as well as the theme and the pretext of *The Arabian Nights*; in order to elude death, she spoke, telling stories into the early morning, in order to postpone the day of reckoning that would silence the narrator. "This she does," Said adds, "in the course of her immensely long narration: we learn from the concluding frame that she has had three sons whom she brings to Shahriar as a way of inducing mercy in him. She is successful, and the couple and their children live on happily ever after" (ibid.). In the process, the narrative power quickly turns into political power, and the battle of *author*ity involves a deadly contest for *author*ship. Both Shahriar and Sheherazade vie to impose their version of events on the raw material of storytelling, sound, and silence.

Silence, which is required by the structure of classical music and literature, becomes an instrument, even an emblem, of a crowning triumph almost to be desired. In tragedy, at least, it is clear. Anthony's resolve to "be / A bride-groom in my death, and run into't / As to a lover's bed" (Shakespeare, 1989: IV.xxvi.99–101) finds its complement in the final, overwhelming intention that Cleopatra has for the same project: "To do that thing that ends all other deeds / Which shackles accidents and bolts up change" (ibid., V.ii.5–6). Perhaps reinventing at this pitch demands, as Octavius Caesar reluctantly admits, nothing less than a bedlike monument, a place of extinction that is also a site of generation, its embrace simulating the encounter it situates so closely that "no grave upon the earth shall clip in it / A pair so famous" (ibid., V.ii.353–54). Hamlet, whom Said quotes, calls death the "undiscovered country," but perhaps the deftness of that description masks a fatal insouciance. True, it is not really possible for us to "discover" extinction in the sense of gaining actual experience of the phenomenon of silence. But, as Michael Neill points out, human beings do imagine dying, and in the process they inevitably invent a notion of silence capable of matching their presuppositions (1997: 179). To that extent, death could be said to be something that each one individual discovers for himself or herself. As a result, nobody just dies. The icy hand may descend everywhere and indiscriminately, but it does so in specific cultural and historical contexts. In all communities, a high degree of political, economic, and linguistic mediation invariably attends the event that is usually also intensely ritualized. He explains: "There is above all the scandal of a different language, then a different race and identity, a different history and tradition: what this results in is the suppression of difference either into complete invisibility and silence, or its transformation into acceptable, but diametrically opposite identity" (ibid., 16). The result is that only human beings "suffer death" in the form of a subjugation to imperatives molded by their own collective imaginations, customs, and traditions. And if death is culturally determined, it is also historically specific and thus altogether a more complicated matter than Hamlet or anyone else allows.

Certainly, the "crisis" about death, which is at the center of Said's concern, is a quarry worthy of the alert, meticulous scholarship he brings to bear on the question of silence. Said speaks of Conrad's *Heart of Darkness* as "silence's purest model." Marlow's narrative, indeed Marlow's voice, is all we have as the tale unfolds. Not only are the Africans in the tale limited to indecipherable sound and one or two bursts of substandard speech, but even the commanding figure of Kurtz is forever silenced by the nurturing, reassuringly enigmatic sound of Marlow's narrative. "'We live,' he says, 'as we dream, alone.' Silence is transmuted into distance" (Said, "From Silence to Sound," 1997: 21). Said concludes by noting that Conrad was not the only one to be possessed by the topic. In fact, a good deal of artistic creation could be seen as an instrument by which every culture sets out to discover and map new meaning for both sound and silence (i.e., life and death).

The need to reinvent silence springs from a changed experience of life. One of the prices exacted for the development of the sustaining sense of individuality and distinctive "inwardness" that we take so much for granted is a burgeoning horror of personal extinction. As dying comes to be seen as the cancellation of a unique selfhood, so death acquires its own unmistakable identity, no longer vaguely outlined or cloudily envisioned, but brutally personalized, literally given a face. Death becomes "a threatening Other, or a morbid anti-self—the one we are each born to meet, an uncanny companion we carry with us through life, a hidden double who will discover himself at the appointed hour" (Neill, 1997: 312). But death has another characteristic: its shamefulness. The "Dance of Death," in which the impartial, unselective leveler summons all ranks of society to cavort with him to the grave, can bring only humiliation to an intensely hierarchical culture, wedded to the comforting complexities of class and status. The fact that death scandalously degrades and unbearably "vilifies" (that is, removes social distinction from) the body is nothing less than mortifying. Hamlet's knock-down conclusion that "Imperious Caesar, dead and turn'd to clay / Might stop a hole to keep the wind away" (Shakespeare, 1989: V.i. 208–09) has an edge of genuine anxiety that the play sharply whets.

In art, if not in life, death could become a powerfully individuating event, something that surfaces memorably in Mozart's letter to his father in the final period of the latter's life, on 4 April 1787: "As death is the true goal of our existence," he writes, "I have formed during the first few years such close relations with this best and truest friend of mankind, that his image is not only no longer terrifying to me, but is indeed very soothing and consoling! . . . Death is the key that unlocks the door to our true happiness. I never lie down at night without reflecting that—young as I am—I may not live to see another day." Said quotes this passage from Mozart in "*Così fan tutte* at the Limits" and adds "death takes the place of Christian reconciliation and redemption, the key to our true, if unknown and indescribable, hope of rest and stability, soothing and consoling without providing anything more than a theoretical intimation of final repose" ("From Silence to Sound," 1997: 106). The idea that each person carries around from birth as a sort of traveling companion, an uncanny, shadowy "double" erupts on the stage (and, I could add, in life) into the horrific specter of the "thing arm'd with a rake" (Webster, 1964: V.v. 6) stalking the Cardinal in *The Duchess of Malfi*, or Othello at the moment of his demise.

In "From Silence to Sound and Back Again," Said speaks

of an independent yet largely subterranean Dionysian component . . . found in the character of Hamlet who cannot speak of what it is that drives him, and it is found more interestingly in Ophelia, who begins to be deranged under the pressure of what she has seen, and can no longer speak of: "T'have seen what I have seen, see what I see!" Thus is she "Divided from herself and her fair judgment, / Without the which we are pictures, or mere beasts." Or there is Iago, who having destroyed Othello is shut up back in himself, defying the injunction to speak and explain: "Demand me nothing; What you know, you know; / From this time forth I never will speak word" (1997: 16).

It may be appropriate to add that it is in the graveyard that the prince of Denmark encounters a version of his own "fell sergeant," the Clown who started grave digging, that "very day that young Hamlet was born" (*Hamlet*, 1989: V.i. 144–45).

Death, ever strict in the arrest, may even take to parading through the streets like a king. Thus Tamberlaine, the very emblem of mortality, sweeps through the world like a pestilential scourge of God, riding "in triumph" over the carcasses of those he has slain. Of course, death ultimately claims Tamberlaine himself, and his growing awareness of his inability to defeat the fate awaiting him forms part of the play's ironic complexity. The undercurrent of Faustian defiance in the face of extinction finally colors our view of Marlow himself, who from time to time, like Ovid (and, I might add, Said), deliberately fosters the irony that, in the depiction of silence brought about by death, the artist can achieve immortality.

Since the issue of "silence," its social and aesthetic outcome or dénouement, inevitably forms part of the broader cultural narrative to which opera makes its distinctive contribution, Said's concern with the way things work out on the stage constantly illuminates more shadowy aspects of society at large. The Protestant revision of the Christian story, with its denial of Purgatory, meant that it was no longer possible for the living to assist the dead.[21] The consequent decay of the vast industry of intercession resulted in a growing complexity of funerals and monuments and the magnification of obsequies in general. The ostentatious funerals of the great constituted a kind of public spectacle with both biographical and political dimensions. They reinforced a complex system of hierarchy and interdependence in a manner that art found impossible to resist and that ultimately became appropriate to emulate. For poets and writers, it became more than a mere conceit to allow that literature and/or music might eventually offer the most enduring monument of all. Said's supple reading of Foucault's *énoncé* amply confirms this idea. He observes, "[I]n Foucault, one can never accede to complete speech or full utterance, or to complete silence, since as students of texts we deal only with language and its representations" ("From Silence to Sound," 1997: 17). Turning in his own later works on dislocation toward an elusive meaning of writing, Said seems intent on sharing not Foucault's idea of *énoncé*, which he finds deterministic, but Beethoven's need for sound, meaning, and restlessness of mind.

"From Silence to Sound" skillfully traces these alternatives of "silence, exile, cunning, withdrawal into self and solitude" through Shakespeare, Mozart, Beethoven, James Joyce, and others, before turning to settle for the "intellectual whose vocation it is to speak the truth to power, to reject the official discourse of orthodoxy and authority, and to exist through irony and skepticism, mixed in with the languages of media, government, and dissent, trying to articulate the silent testimony of lived suffering and stifled experience" (ibid., 21). But this passes too lightly over the fact that silence is bound to appear scandalous to a hubristic culture that believes that nothing can escape its mastery. The true Platonism of our time, the idealist fantasy that seeks to disown material limits altogether, is surely to be found in the postmodern voice and body, that infinitely pliable nonentity that can be pierced, plumped up, scooped out, remolded, and regendered but cannot finally be prevented from turning into garbage. The sacred rituals that used to promise eternal life—burning incense, drinking the blood of the god, slaying a fatted calf—have now become the liturgy of burning off fat, drinking fruit juice, and not eating meat. In Christian theology, what determines whether or not you can embrace death is how you have lived. If you have failed in life to divest yourself for the sake of others, Said seems to hint, you will be trapped like William Golding's Pincher Martin or T. S. Eliot's Cumen Sibyl in a hell that is the inability to die. By the end of Golding's novel, Martin has dwindled to a pair of huge, lobsterlike claws tenaciously protecting his dark center of selfhood from the "black lightning" of God's ruthless mercy. Martin refuses to be picked apart: he is one of the damned who regard themselves as too important to undergo anything as squalid as personal extinction.

W. B. Yeats may not have landed among that select company, but the hair-raisingly blasphemous epitaph he wrote for himself—

> Cast a cold eye
> On Life, on death
> Horseman, pass by! (1987: 45)

—disdains death as a vulgarity fit only for clerks and shopkeepers. It is the martyr's meaning of death-in-life that St. Paul had in mind when he commented that we die every moment. To live selflessly is not to exist in a state of self-dissolution but to behave in a certain style, one that requires keeping your wits about you and having a resilient ego. True self-abnegation is not a matter of political submissiveness or the heady *jouissance* of sexual pleasure but of anticipating one's death by living in the service of others (the oppressed in Said's case). For Said, if silence is what gives shape to sound, it is because it signifies a self-abandonment that is the pattern of the good life. "There is no sound, no articulation that is adequate to what injustice and power inflict on the poor, the disadvantaged, and disinherited. But there are approximations to it, not representations of it, which have the effect of punctuating discourse with disenchantment and demystifications. To have *that* opportunity is at least something" ("From Silence to Sound," 1997: 21).

IV

One has to marvel at people who, like Said, read literature and music in this fashion. But more than his art, it is his life—the only subject of his art—that serves to inspire so many around the world. By now, it is easy to forget how many of us have been all but patented—or lived out most wholeheartedly—by Said, who has been so spendthrift with himself, and so loud in praise of folly, that he has laid himself open to many charges. He disclosed himself to us at various times without reserve and sometimes with flippancy, which may not always have been allowed. Yet to return to his books is to rediscover him as much more complex than either memory or stereotype. For many in the West, he is still a slightly embarrassing presence, the unruly *enfant terrible* who makes a display of himself at the dinner table. Commenting on how in the eyes of some people he has become some kind of oddity, he writes:

> Occasionally, I'd notice that I had become a peculiar creature to many people, and even a few friends, who had assumed that being Palestinian was the equivalent of something mythological like a unicorn or a hopelessly odd variation of a human being. A Boston psychologist who specialized in conflict resolution, and whom I had met at several seminars involving Palestinians and Israelis, once rang me from Greenwich Village and asked if she could come uptown to pay me a visit. When she arrived, she walked in, looked incredulously at my piano—"Ah, you actually play the piano," she said, with a trace of disbelief in her voice—and then turned around and began to walk out. When I asked her whether she would have a cup of tea before leaving (after all, I said, you have come a long way for such a short visit) she said she didn't have time. "I only came to see how you lived," she said without a hint of irony. Another time a publisher in another city refused to sign my contract until I had lunch with him. When I asked his assistant what was so important about having a meal with me, I was told that the great man wanted to see how I handled myself at the table.[22]

In the East, Said is often referred to as "one of those who jump on the bandwagon of patriotism" (1996: 166). Yet combating constructed fictions such as "East" and "West," to say nothing of racialist essences such as "subject races," "Orientals," "Aryans," "Negroes," "imperialism," "nativism," "nationalism" and the like is precisely what endears Said to the have-nots.

Proust once said that every artist has a particular tune (*chanson*) that can be found in almost every sentence of his work: a special cadence, a theme, an obsession, or characteristic key absolutely the artist's own. Glenn Gould's key may be the combination of rhythm and polyphony that informs all his playing. In Said's case, it is an immediately recognizable tension between simple melody and insistent, sometimes explosive and always *contrapuntal* developmental sequences. Said sets the form, as a dramatist sets a play: on a stage, before the audience, and for a discrete span of time. His essays on music reflect his lifelong concern with art (in contrast to reason) as the only humanly available means of expressing wholeness, or more precisely, the longing for a transcendence whose realization represents not only a vain hope but also a potential source of good and/or evil. In Said's thought, violence and myth, evil and death intrude into the world and must be countered by critical means both literary and aesthetic.

For a region long dismissed as primitive, which has been largely interpreted in terms of its tyrannies, wars and injustice, it is both a timely and fortunate corrective to see the first-rate literature and criticism that exist all over Palestine, that most contested of places. Every writer identifies with a special place (بروه for Darwish, القدس for Said), with its own writing (memory) and history (forgetfulness). If some Arab writers still lament the loss of the past (Darwish), their attempt to claim a lost paradise may paradoxically be the attempt for others (Said) to exorcize it from our collective memory. That, at bottom, is the extraordinary intellectual trajectory of Edward Said, one of the most influential people of our time. Wood expresses its importance best: "Criticism is a chance to be taken and Edward Said continues to illustrate its allure and its rewards" (1997: xv). In the upshot, the central theme of Said's life is his restless anxiety, a narcissistic pattern of self-concern and self-immersion that is fed and accentuated by the life of a musical performer's playing and/or writing. In the process, the extremity of being alone, day after day, sooner or later catches up with one, especially if, as in Said's case, the will to control life and body is constantly challenged—not just by the rigors of a performing life, but also by mortality. Speaking of the variations in his illness while writing *Out of Place*, Said writes:

> As I grew weaker, the more the number of infections and bouts of side-effects increased, the more the memoir was my way of constructing something in prose while in my physical and emotional life I grappled with the anxieties and pains of degeneration. Both tasks resolved themselves into details: to write is to get from word to word, to suffer illness is to go through the infinitesimal steps that take you from one state to another. With other sorts of work that I did, essays, lectures, teaching, journalism, I was going across the illness, punctuating it almost forcibly with deadlines and cycles of beginning, middle and end: with this memoir I was borne along by the episodes of treatment, hospital stay, physical pain and mental anguish, letting those dictate how and when I could write, for how long and where ("On Writing a Memoir," 1999: 11).

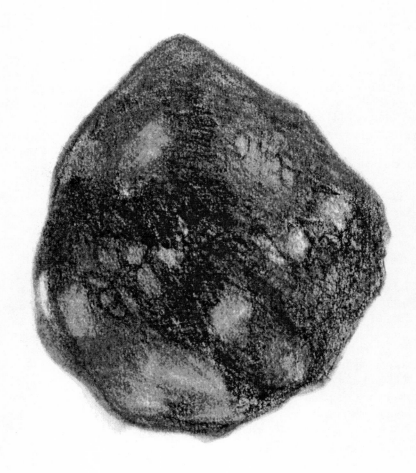

Ahmad Izmer, *Earth; Or, The Entire World as a Foreign Place*, Charcoal on Paper, 28 x 20 cm. © 2002.

CHAPTER SIX

QUITE RIGHT: IN DEFENSE OF EDWARD SAID

> This is how the work of defamation and innuendo proceeds. . . . Weiner
> simply excluded any findings that contradicted his underhanded purpose.
> —Christopher Hitchens, "Whose Life Is It Anyway?," 9.

"A lie can get halfway around the world," Mark Twain once wrote, "before truth has even put its boots on." So it has proved—but only until now—in the matter of Justus Weiner versus Edward Said. Here we approach the crux. Is it seriously proposed that Said's out-of-place early life, spent partly in Jerusalem, partly in Cairo, somehow disqualifies him from speaking as a Palestinian? Is it fine for Weiner, an American Jew transplanted to Israel, to speak as an Israeli, but not for Said, a Palestinian rerooted in New York, to speak for Palestine? What Weiner has in fact done is to hijack a reputation for Zionist ends. For when a distinguished writer, as distinguished as Said, is attacked in this fashion—when his enemies set out not merely to judge his books but to indict him and sully his name—then there is always more at stake than the mere quotidian malice of the world of literature.

It is an irony worth noting by way of a rebuttal that in the summer of 1999 Said found out that his past had been rewritten—that he had not been schooled at the school he attended; that he had not lived in or had been obliged to leave Jerusalem; that he and his family were not refugees from Palestine; that he was a "liar"—by someone of whom he had never heard while attending Daniel Barenboim's master classes in Weimar with ninety Arab and Israeli musicians, including his ten-year-old great nephew, a piano prodigy from Amman. Following the attack, Said who usually exudes calm authority, appeared stung, rummaging through

209

papers to prove he is truly who he says he is, and all the while obviously aware of the bleak absurdity of a situation which forced him to do so (Vulliany, 1999). Disarmingly, Said reveals why he believes he has become the American Right's and/or Zionist's latest bogeyman: "I symbolize the things Zionists are afraid of. I don't believe in partition, and that is why I am dangerous to them."[1] For him, the attack signaled his growing currency within Israel, where he has been more visible championing the cause of reparation, writing and narrating a BBC documentary entitled *Edward Said: A Very Personal View of Palestine*,[2] which was timed to commemorate fifty years of Israeli occupation. Even far-right Israeli Zionists, he now believes, are "less rabid and more in touch with reality" than those who live in the United States. Said, who has long pleaded for both sides to recognize each other's history, rebuffed his enemies' attack in multiple ways. The most sound and unequivocal riposte is *Out of Place*, which stands as a corrective; it rectifies what is amiss. "My parents moved there [to Zamelek] Cairo in 1937, when I was two" (*Out of Place*, 1999: 22). Said goes on to explain that his parents had already lived in Cairo since 1935 but decided that he should be born in Jerusalem: an earlier child, born in a Cairo hospital, had developed an infection and died. To avoid another disaster, his parents decided that he should be born at "home" in Jerusalem, where he was delivered by a Jewish midwife. The home he refers to was the ancestral family home, lived in by his aunt Nabiha and his cousins, now an "upperclass Jewish neighborhood," but prior to 1947 exclusively Palestinian Christian. That "home" was lost in 1948, when Said's aunt and cousins became refugees.

Out of Place is indeed a moving portrait of Said's childhood in Palestine, Lebanon, and Egypt in the cross-currents of the 1940s and 50s. Throughout, Said wittily limns the demands, livens the struggles of exilic life, and hones his voice as a narrator of the instability of displacement. In the process, his words become buoys with which he tries to stay afloat in the world as a man who has endured the hatchet job of Weiner Inc. Justus Weiner's accusations in the neoconservative magazine *Commentary* (September 1999), which had made an effort at slandering Said ten years earlier, when it labeled him "professor of terror," despite his consistent rejection of terrorism or a military solution to the Palestinian-Israeli crisis, are, I believe, an extension of the Zionist-Palestinian conflict masked as an argument against public misbehavior. *Commentary* is drenched in the usual hypocrisy about norms of conduct, a tactic employed by publicists who are trying to hide their real agenda. Who appointed Weiner to research Said's past? Milken is the former junkbond dealer who was imprisoned in 1991 for insider trading. He is also the leading donor of "Special Gifts" to the Jewish Center for Public Affairs, which employs Justus Weiner.[3] Suffice it to add that Conrad Black, the former owner of the *Daily Telegraph*, which carried most of the attack in Europe, also owned for a while the *National Post* (Canada) and the *Jerusalem Post*, which supports the right-wing Likud Party of former Prime Minister Binyamin Netanyahu, the man who in 1988 refused to sit in the same studio with Said during a debate on *Night Line*, hosted by Ted Koppel (NBC, New York). His argument was that Said was a terrorist intent on killing him.[4] Said remains scornful of the suggestion that he wields great power in the media: "The mainstream press makes use of you," he says, "when it wants to, as a token or a symbol, but you have no access" ("On Writing a Memoir," 1999: 3). No major American paper, he adds, would publish his response to Weiner, though it appeared in the Arab press, *Al-Hayat*, for which he has written regularly since 1993. It was also published in Hebrew in the Tel Aviv newspaper *Ha'aretz*.

There is definitely more than a hint of exclusion, racism, and xenophobia in some of the language used in Weiner's essay and letter.[5] The critique is marked by a violence of language and mindless destructiveness seldom encountered in literary culture—certainly not at such a level of intensity, not even during violent social revolutions when the slightest ambiguity in the ideological content of a work of art is seized upon as proof of dangerous, subversive sympathies. Weiner even proudly labeled himself a "scholar" and "journalist," the better to place himself beyond any rules of combat or any knowledge of his subject. With rabid Zionist parochialism and self-obsession, Weiner's argument runs as follows: "I cannot state this often enough or emphatically enough, nothing alleged in Said's own rebuttal or by his defenders shakes my findings by as much as an iota" (2000: 11). This by-now discredited charge rests on a misguided critique that could have been launched from some metaphysical outer space, for it shares the delusion of the reality it detests.

The very idea that somebody from Palestine, from the ex-colonial jungle should (1) speak and challenge a colonial power like Israel in such an urgent way and (2) even propose the idea of return and reparation for his people is anathema to Weiner, who adds:

> Let me close, then, by restating my conviction that the cause of peace between Israelis and Palestinians, to which so many of them assert their devotion, is not well-served but—to the contrary—traduced by an attachment to historical ties. The fact is that the "best-known Palestinian intellectual in the world" (as he was recently described on the BBC) made wholesale political use of the supposed circumstances of his childhood, weaving an elaborate myth of paradise and expulsion from paradise out of one or two circumstances and a raft of inventions. That myth has been exposed, and its purveyor has been revealed not as a refugee from Palestine, but as a refugee from the truth. To judge by the way he and his supporters have responded, he, and they, are still on the run (2000: 16).

This is Weiner's defamation of Edward Said. Let us split it into two. There is first Palestine, and there is second the representative of this Palestine. And that representative also happens to be the same individual who opposed the peace process—at least who is held responsible for disputing its content—and therefore has become an ogre to the outspoken "conscience" of Zionism and its doyens.

I will not pursue here the mixed career of Weiner's newly discovered vocation in journalism—the sweeping generalizations, misquotations, and impudence that mask his ignorance of the Said *story*, the cavalier imposition of far-fetched parameters to provide a veneer of study and research—except to mention the gratuitous violence of his approach, in the brutal appropriation of literary material and its gross mutilation.[6] For many readers, both the article and the letter are a frontal attack, the upshot of which is: if everyone in the world must nowadays be a victim of something, Weiner is a self-confessed victim of his own assumptions, which exert their mindless tyranny over him as ruthlessly as Stalin held sway over the kulaks. For him, nothing in the world could count as evidence for our أصاله (identity), since what we gullibly call "the world" is simply a construct of it. He forgets that identity is a constitutive of the self and so cannot be critically questioned by it.

And so it goes, when you are Palestinian, the question of identity becomes a disturbing one even though Mahmoud Darwish makes a legitimate claim: "There is nothing more apparent than the Palestinian truth and the Palestinian right: this is our country, and this small part is a part of our homeland, or real not mythical homeland. This occupation is a foreign occupation, no matter how many titles of divine right it enlists; God is no one's personal possession" (2002: 1). Darwish brings a correct answer to the myth that Palestinians were just a group of nomads living in tents that can easily enough be moved elsewhere. Additionally, the notion that Said has been vocal about the Law of Return of millions of refugees, persistent and compelling in his argument that Israel cannot just go on oppressing an innocent people is even more troubling to Weiner and others. This is the spillover from standing up to a cause, from representing a people anxious to determine their own fate without being pushed over, bullied, or misrepresented. Weiner, who accuses Said of straying from the truth, is mealy mouthed about it. For what is at stake here is the question of *authenticity*, an accusation that goes beyond the words of his labored article to the arbitrary codes and signifiers that define identity, which is the yardstick we use to determine who is and who is not eligible for inclusion in the tribes that are available to us, such as class, religion, race, ethnicity, and region. Identity provides the parameters for describing who we are and often what we can say. The consequences of these issues are far from academic. In Israel a debate is raging over who, for purposes of immigration, qualifies not as a citizen (regardless of race, religion, gender, sexual orientation, elective affinity) but as a Jew. Since the country's law of return was passed in 1950, anyone with even one Jewish grandparent has an automatic right to Israeli citizenship. The number of new Israeli settlers increased from seven thousand in 1977 to two hundred thousand in 2002. With such an influx of new immigrants, new Palestinian land is confiscated and unilaterally converted into Israeli property, robbing thereby the Saids and other Palestinian families of their homes, their land, and their homeland.[7]

"'My Beautiful Old House'" provides for Weiner's assault on the writings of Said, which "raised doubts" about the latter's credentials as a "refugee," thereby discrediting his entire body of work on the Middle East. "I had never had much respect for the intellectual integrity of Professor Said," a spokesman for the former right-wing Israeli government said. "This proves that my suspicions were not groundless."[8] The affront put Said in the Kafkaesque situation of having to brandish documents to prove that he is in fact who he has always been. But there was more at stake, he believes, than his own integrity. "It is an attempt," he notes, "to pre-empt the process of return and compensation for the Palestinians. It is a way of furthering the argument that the Palestinians never belonged in Palestine. . . . If someone like Edward Said is a liar, runs the argument, how can we believe all those peasants who say they were driven off their land?. . . It is part of the attempt to say that none of this actually happened" (2000: 3). Or, put differently, undermine Said's authenticity, went the logic, and you undermine the credibility of the Palestinian cause. Only the desperation of a mercenary hatchet man could produce such a series of constant affronts to people, who like Said, continue to stand on the margins. The burden of representation on people who do emerge from desperate circumstances is a heavy one. But that is no justification for trying to deny the validity of their voice. In the case of Edward Said there is, of course, no such thing as the Palestinian experience but, instead, several Palestinian experiences (family, birth, name, baptism, life, death, burial).

In reference to Weiner the "scholar," however, the fact remains that in publishing his essay, *Commentary* has allowed his lies, insults, abuse, and misinformation to stand. In doing so, both the *soi-disant* self-fashioned "scholar" and "journalist" and the conservative American Jewish monthly have behaved with total professional irresponsibility. It was enough to say, "Edward Said is a liar." Here as usual, Weiner's rather stagey relish for the defamatory posture leads him astray. It prevents him from seeing that a certain capacity for critical self-distancing is actually part of the way we are bound up with the world, not some chimerical alternative to it. His philippic ignores the question of how people come to change, not necessarily for the better, just as it adopts an untenably provincial and puerile view of the relations between a specific identity system and particular bits of evidence. It also suggests that we cannot ask from whence our identity arises because any answer would be predetermined by our sense of belonging.

In academia, you can hammer your colleagues, safe in the knowledge that, since you all subscribe to the same professional rules, it does not really mean a thing. But when a man and a literary journal descend to such contemptible tactics, I believe that both should be universally condemned. That any one should have the power to label a writer and close down his work on a whim is a sign of our imperfect times. That kind of power is pathological, perverse, and obscene. Not even *Commentary* deserves the likes of Weiner. Sadly, he is not alone. There are many other self-proclaimed "critics" and "scholars" who have abused their calling. These pundits' reactionary commitment to universalist progress and the commonality of the intellectual process, too often mask opportunism, sordid self-interest, and plain intellectual will-to-power. Anyone is, of course, free to choose his weapons, but let no one think that the use of any particular weapon is the monopoly of the unprincipled, championed for example by a pompous ass like Daniel Pipes who thinks that "Palestine is a fantasy" and who goes so far as to allow himself to announce quite shamelessly that Said's memoir is a work of "dissimulation."[9] To paraphrase Allan Edgar Poe, a little learning is a dangerous thing, and a lot of it is positively disastrous. It should be noted that Pipes made his name many years ago as an expert on modern Syria and was quickly drafted into service as a cold warrior, applying his old-fashioned philological training to "Islam" and "Arabs" that suited dominant and pro-Zionist standards in U.S. foreign policy in a stream of repetitive essays made up of unrelieved rubbish. That Pipes should be called upon to evaluate Said is an indication not only of how low most people's expectations are when it comes to discussions of "Arabs" and "Islam" but of the wrong ideological fiction in which pseudo-experts such as Daniel Pipes trade, and with which they hoodwink people in general. It is therefore no surprise that Pipes should pollute public discourse with reductive clichés without a trace of skepticism or rigor. The worst part of this method is that it dehumanizes peoples and turns them into a collection of abstract slogans for purposes of aggressive mobilization and bellicosity. This is not at all a matter of rational understanding. The study of other peoples and/or cultures is a humanistic not a strategic or security pursuit. Pipes, like Weiner, mutilates the effort itself and pretends to be delivering truths from on high. Mere dismissal of them as inept zealots will not suffice. It will not explain why the pages of Weiner's essay and letter are drenched with so much bile, why such virulence dominates even his few instances of reasoned criticism, why smear and sneer are substituted for clarity or precision of attack.

As Said has clearly stated in his rebuttal of Weiner's article, these charges are not new to him nor to his readers who feel angered on behalf of all Palestinian refugees. It is anger directed against an assault that is aimed at preventing understanding and reconciliation between the victims and the victims' victims. After all, it is a fact that on 25 November 1935, in the early hours of the morning, a baby boy, named "Edward," was born in Jerusalem. This *droit du sol* alone, in case anyone is in any doubt, is more than enough for Said to stand up for *his* Palestine. It is this authenticity that places him in a privileged position to reclaim his اصالة (birthright). Few writers are as profoundly engaged with their native land as Said, a Palestinian, whose essays seek, by noticing, arguing, rhapsodizing, mythologizing, to write Palestine into fierce, lyrical being. Yet this same Edward Said also writes: "I have always advocated the acknowledgments by each other of the

Palestinian and Jewish peoples' past suffering. Only in this way can they coexist peacefully together in the future" ("One More Chance," 2000: 4). It is startling to find an admission so close to generosity. Yet this perhaps is the only kind of genuineness and/or vision a writer such as Said can afford. That is why his writing makes great noise in the mind, the heart.

Last, and perhaps sadly for those of us who have lived by his example, is that when people "criticize" a man of letters such as Said,

> when they "denounce" his ideas, when they "condemn" what he writes, I imagine them in the ideal situation in which they would have complete power over him. . . . And I catch a glimpse of the radiant city in which the intellectual would be in prison, or, if he were also a theoretician, hanged, of course.
>
> I can't help but dream about a kind of criticism that would not try to judge, but to bring an oeuvre, a book, a sentence, an idea to life; it would light fires, watch the grass grow, listen to the wind, and catch the sea-foam in the breeze and scatter it. It would multiply, not judgments, but signs of existence; it would summon them, drag them from their sleep. Perhaps it would invent them sometimes—all the better. All the better. Criticism that hands down sentences sends me to sleep; I'd like a criticism of scintillating leaps of the imagination. It would not be sovereign or dressed in red. It would bear the lightning of possible storms (Foucault, 1988: 325–26).

Said, a many-sided apparition with an identifiable moral authority in these specialist times, has survived harsh judgments and threats. Hence he exhibits a sort of anxiety that finds expression in innumerable symptoms, some funny, some not. All of life, it seemed, could turn into a performance piece, at least for Said when he decided to rebuff his accusers, which was seen as a defense of what he stands for, of the world he has hoped for decades to argue into being, a world in which Palestinians are able to live with honor and dignity in their own country, indeed, but also a world in which, by an act of constructive forgetting, the past can be worked through and then left in the past so that Palestinians and Jews can begin to think about a different kind of future. In the process, if he comes across as a historical revisionist, chiding his forebears for their Victorian ways and designs and/or his enemies for their intransigence, he is also one of عصبيّة (a tight-knit community), in Ibn Khaldun's formula. Like Palestine herself, this is a community (the Saids, Dirliks, Ghorras, Mirshaks, Fahoums) caught up in a cycle of constant change, bound by its codes of honor and loyalty to one another. *Out of Place* also has a broader metaphysical resonance. "A form of freedom, I'd like to think," Said reminds us "even if I am far from being totally convinced that it is. That skepticism too is one of the themes I particularly want to hold on to. With so many dissonances in my life I have learned actually to prefer being not quite right and out of place" (*Out of Place*, 1999: 295). The memoir, like the last millennium, closes on a note of somber foreboding.

Said, the erstwhile outsider, has now placed himself boldly at the *fons et origo*, claiming a لسان (eloquence) as always already his own from the outset. It is hard to know whether *Out of Place* is the origin or product of transplantation, but in any case Said has dug down to the first stratum of the language and appropriated his birthright in القدس (Jerusalem). As Harold Bloom might just put it, the belated offspring has now installed himself as the founding patriarch. It might be argued that Said's anxious need for this move to be legitimated is a sign of the cultural colonization it aims to overcome. Yet, having reversed his cultural dispossession, he then in a kind of mocking pseudo-Hegelian negation of negation reverses the reversal. In searching for the pitch or enabling note of the work, he finds it in the weighty, big-voiced utterance of some family relatives such as that of his Aunt Nabiha. Having kicked free of Palestine soil into the upper air, he now has the confidence to touch down on it again. The result is a sturdy and intricate reinvention, which betrays its author's poetic dabbling less in its earthiness than in its airiness. It is the canny colloquialisms of certain spoken phrases in Arabic such as *tislamli*, or *mish 'arfa shu biddi 'amal, rouh'ha*, or *khalas* that are most Saidesque, in addition to the smell of the soil of Palestine. If the stark subject matter of "Between Worlds," is redolent the treatment has the mild insouciance of an earlier collection such as *After the Last Sky*. This writer is so superbly in command that he can risk threadbare, throwaway, matter-of-fact phrases such as "of no small importance" or the "best part of the day" (ibid., 175). There at the narrative's core is also equipoise—the radiance of Said's exquisite articulation of exile.

The narrative, as Georg Lukács once observed, requires historical conditions, which the steam engine and the telegraph put paid to (1999: 34). Mechanically reproduced commodities lack the aura of ancient objects, just as the self-conscious fictions of modernity have lost what Žižek calls "attempts to escape the logic of globalism" (1999: 2). But modern objects, typified for Lukács by Charles Bovary's extraordinary, convoluted, visually unpresentable hat, have also shed what seems to us the unalienated candor of material things in *Out of Place*, which exist more as narrative elements than as literary enigmas. In any case, we no longer believe in heroism or that the world itself is story shaped, and we ask of literature a phenomenological inwardness of recent historical vintage. All of this is a signal (mis)fortune for Edward Said, an artist so exquisitely gifted and imaginatively capacious that only a work of mightier scale would answer to his abilities as a غريب (an exile), forced to see himself as marginal, non-Arab, non-American, alienated, and marked on both sides of the cultural divide line. The following paragraph expresses the pain of this exclusion:

> The school [Victoria College] itself was closed for the Friday holiday, but I persuaded the gatekeeper to let us in anyway. As we stood in my old class-

room, which seemed a good deal smaller than I remembered, I pointed out my desk, the teacher's platform from which Griffiths had expelled me, and the little room where we had imprisoned poor old Mr. Lowe.

At that moment a very angry-looking woman wearing a head covering and Islamic-style dress swept into the room demanding to know what we were doing. I tried to explain the circumstances ("Use your charm," said my daughter, Najla) but to no avail. We were trespassers, and as school director she was demanding that we leave immediately. She refused my extended hand, staring at us with a surfeit of nationalist hostility and unbending zeal as we shuffled out, rather cowed by her evident outrage. The British Eton in Egypt had now become a new kind of privileged Islamic sanctuary from which thirty-eight years later I was once again being *expelled* (Said, Ibid., 213; emphasis added).

There it is: to voice rejection and (un)belonging, uncannily, Said locates in the language into which he is metamorphosing himself the precise equivalent to the stroke of local color in the original home (Palestine). The paradox is this: in Joyce, in Nabokov, the polyglot impulse generates a superabundance of stylistic invention; the voices grow more and more voluminous. In Said, the exact opposite occurs; out of an extreme pressure a linguistic nakedness is born. There is a precedent to this paring down in Conrad, whom Said treasures. Yet the sense of a certain routine, of the formulaic, nags: the omission of connective parts of speech, of punctuation; the insistence on the monosyllabic. That cycle race is there, with its circularity and ennui. Said has observed, "This is what dislocation and insecurity breed, this need to hold onto one's position of authority indefinitely, this feeling that one is indispensable. I am torn about this" ("In Arafat's Palestine," 1996: 15). Will his pessimism change, or will it come to be known as a despairing afterward to the emptying of man in early-twenty-first-century globocracy and genocide? It is difficult to say. But how richly, though no less subversively, a Said radiates, darkly perhaps, out of (even) the most laconic of parables.

CHAPTER SEVEN

ON WRITING, INTELLECTUAL LIFE, AND THE PUBLIC SPHERE

> Welcome to the age of Salman Rushdie, Taslima Nasrin and Naguib Mahfouz, whose Nobel Prize did not safeguard him from being stabbed in the streets of Cairo. African intellectuals, like Rachid Boujedra, are forced to live under cover to ensure themselves some degree of safety. It was not colonial power that put Abdellatif Laabi in prison.
>
> Can a writer remain quiet, at least on certain subjects? Writing always comes down to disclosure and therefore dissidence. To submit would mean resignation. Is a writer turned minister still a writer? . . . But here we are straying from decolonization strictly speaking. . . . Together we must find a common, global definition of the contemporary man.
>
> —Albert Memmi, "Dans quelle langue écrire?
> La Patrie littéraire du colonisé," 13.

In the outpouring of studies about intellectuals today there has been far too much defining of the intellectual and not enough stock taken of the plight, *signature*, the actual intervention and *performance*, all of which taken together constitute the very lifeblood of every real intellectual. It seems ironic that no intellectual giants have yet replaced those of the last generation (say, C. L. R. James, Jean-Paul Sartre, or James Baldwin, even though thinkers such as Michel Foucault, Pierre Bourdieu, Iqbal Ahmad, and others have stimulated our thinking). There is no reason to deduce a generational insufficiency. They would be there today if the space for them was open. It has been closed, along with the question that animated the intellectual's first appearance. Those who yesterday might have been traditional intellectuals may tomorrow perform another role, for which as yet there is no clear name. Gramsci foresaw this development when he wrote of a future need for "organic intellectuals," by which he meant that thinkers who belong "organically" to a cultural milieu are able to make articulate representations to their public despite all sorts of barriers. Edward Said, who may fit into the category of organic intellectuals that Gramsci speaks about, remarked some years ago at a conference in Chicago that he wanted to establish a Palestinian state so that he could critically attack it. Today, we are finding out what he really meant.

> In Palestine the situation had deteriorated considerably. Arafat's security police seemed everywhere on the West Bank. He had requisitioned the entire six-storey Ministry of Education for his "presidential" office in Ramallah and in addition caused a demonstration in the city by confiscating several acres for a new personal residence there. Mrs Arafat was spending the summer in Deauville. . . . Thanks to his total control of the Authority's money and the security services he was getting away with murder. Literally. A few days ago a spokesman admitted to having killed seven Palestinians under torture. Hundreds are picked up and detained, so much so that in late July Arafat's men were finding themselves—like Israeli soldiers during the Intifada—shooting at stone-throwing crowds in Nablus and Tulkaram (*The Politics of Dispossession*, 1996: 14).

With reasoned argument fueled by ethical indignation at the present state of affairs in Palestine and compassion for those claiming justice of a government that is supposed to protect them, Said brings his case to the public. In doing so, he articulates the basic impulse that holds him back from a one-sided polemic that can be brought about by simple opposition—between imperialism and nationalism, between internationalist and nativist perspectives. His scathingly critical stance against Oslo I and Oslo II testifies to his unrelenting commitment to the cause of justice. He explains why such agreements are so disadvantageous to the Palestinian people and contends that in the second of these agreements all the Palestinians received was a series of municipal responsibilities in Bantustans dominated by Israel, whereas Israel received official Palestinian consent to continued occupation (Said, Ibid., 1996: 24–27).

In challenging conventional wisdom on the Middle East peace process—the belief that it is an ineluctably good thing, threatened by self-evidently fanatic extremists—Said fulfills Václev Havel's formulation, in *Disturbing the Peace*, of the intellectual's role:

> [T]he intellectual should constantly disturb, should bear witness to the misery of the world, should be provocative by being independent, should rebel against the hidden and open pressure and manipulations, should be the chief doubter of systems, of power and its incantations, should be a witness to their mendacity. For this very reason, an intellectual cannot fit

into any role that might be assigned to him, nor can he ever be made to fit into any of the histories written by the victors (1990: 167).

Naturally, Havel's moral authority in the West is based on the fact that he was faithful to this job description, a fidelity that cost him imprisonment and defamation (ibid., 98). Said has advocated the kind of public intellectual once upheld by Havel. His work has embodied a practice of engaging civil society and confronting state power. He offers a sustained commentary on intellectuals, their duties, opportunities, betrayals, audiences, and choices while making his own case for the engaged intellectual

> as maintaining a state of constant alertness, of a perpetual willingness not to let half-truths or received ideas steer one along. That this involves a steady realism, an almost athletic rational energy, and a complicated struggle to balance the problems of one's own selfhood against the demands of publishing and speaking out in the public sphere is what makes it an everlasting effort, constitutively unfinished and necessarily imperfect (*Representations of the Intellectual*, 1994: 23).

The intellectual is committed to retrieving the forgotten, to making connections among issues previously kept separate, to envisioning alternative courses of individual and collective action and to disputing the official narratives or justifications—what Ignacio Martín-Baró denounced in El Salvador as the reign of the "institutional lie." Said contends that intellectuals who pursue these tasks are not likely to win the accolades of people in powerful places; indeed, they must be able to endure a certain amount of loneliness as the price for refusing to celebrate the status quo. He champions the intellectual as an outsider without ties to the circles of power. He also prefers the idea of the intellectual as *amateur*—one who is passionately committed to ideas, values, and public exchange—rather than the intellectual as calculating professional. Although Said does not draw on theological language, advocates of the preferential option for the poor can easily recognize him as an ally: "I think the major choice faced by the intellectual is whether to be allied with the stability of the victors and rulers or—the more difficult path—to consider that stability as a state of emergency threatening the less fortunate with the danger of complete extinction" (ibid., 35). Or, to put it differently, we must return to basic values and honesty of discussion. This truth leaves only the power of mind and education to do the job that the state has been unable to accomplish except by maiming and killing those who speak out against corruption and injustice. Said is especially illuminating in cataloging the various ways intellectuals betray their vocation to tell the truth and unmask lies. He is highly skeptical of "what is considered to be proper, professional behavior—not rocking the boat, not straying outside the accepted paradigms or limits, making yourself marketable and above all presentable, hence uncontroversial and unpolitical and 'objective'" (ibid., 74). Other dangers include an acquiescent drift toward established authority, political, corporate, or religious; buying into the "cult of the certified experts"; disavowal of options and alignments by taking refuge in allegedly neutral methodologies; and denunciation of abuses in other nations while one excuses or ignores the same policies by one's own government or its allies. There is a striking congruence in his vision regarding the responsibility of intellectuals. At the heart of his work is a commitment to the power of the powerless and a defiance of state authority.

The atmosphere of terror against intellectuals and writers who are deemed an offense to the state needs therefore to be denounced categorically as is the case in *For Rushdie: Essays by Arab and Muslim Writers in Defense of Free Speech*, a collection of essays that appeared in 1993, some years after Rushdie went into hiding. The collection tells not of Gramsci's guerillalike warfare that the intellectual must adopt in order to face the potentate, but of his impotence. And even though it is a dramatic testimony to the courage and resilience of liberal intellectuals and moderate Muslims alike in the face of daily threats, it says that the intellectual is about to become extinct because of either religious intolerance or state repression. Merely to be a signatory to an appeal in favor of Rushdie (like the 127 Iranian "artists and intellectuals" listed in the eleventh piece in the collection) or to write in defiance of the theocratic imperative (like many of 90 other contributors) is to run a very real risk of assassination. In most of the countries where the writers live, censorship is routine and politically justified murder, commonplace. One thing the collection sets straight, though, is that there is a great variety of opinion in the Muslim and Arab world, a passion bordering on desperation for real freedom to expound and question the "unquestionable." The essays are, in a sense, incantations against fear. In the West, the Rushdie affair has been portrayed by many commentators as little more than an issue, but the contributors to this volume disagree: "It is," Jamil Hatmal writes, "not only for him that we take sides—even if he does deserve it—but also for all those like him and like [other murdered and imprisoned intellectuals], and for life itself" (In *For Rushdie*, 1994: 172). To keep quiet is to sell out to cowardice. "How many anonymous Rushdies and people in hiding are there in our cities?" Wassyla Rais-Ali asks (ibid., 250). For them, Rushdie is the core issue in a crisis that extends throughout their culture. As Rabah Belamri announces, Muslim societies face extreme difficulty in effecting any kind of cultural change. "A society," he writes, "that refuses to question its own premises and denies its own artists and writers the opportunity to raise any doubts whatsoever; a society that does not dare to laugh at itself, and seeks to banish all impertinent questions—such a society has no chance at all of ever flowering again" (ibid., 67). The archival record attests to such a claim in an overwhelming fashion.

Said's essay "Against the Orthodoxies" should be singled out, for it raises disturbing questions that have no easy answers. In the bluntest form, one of his questions is where should we draw the line when it comes to the committed intellectual.

> How far should an intellectual go in getting involved? Should one join a party, serve an idea as it is embodied in actual political processes, personalities, jobs, and therefore become a true believer? Or on the other hand is there some more discrete—but no less serious and involved—way of joining up without suffering the pain of later betrayal and disillusionment? How far should one's loyalty to a cause take one in being consistently faithful to it? Can one retain independence of mind and, at the same time, *not* go through the agonies of public recantation and confession? (Said, 263).

The burden is a crushing one. In a sense frankly admitted in these pages, it is too much for Said or any other individual. He has become the best-known spokesman of the Palestinian struggle in the world yet has always been far too honest and honorable to be merely its loudspeaker. As the gross contradictions and failings of the cause have accumulated over thirty years, he has been unable to avoid registering and criticizing them. *The Politics of Dispossession* and *Peace and Its Discontents* read like a memoir, one continuous journey through the agonies and humiliations, have left indelible scars—above all when inflicted, as they so often are, by those "on his own side." The critique of Arab nationalism and Palestinian parochialism is more telling than anything written by Zionists or the American Israeli lobby. And even though Said can afford to bear the role of the intellectual as *emmerdeur* (trouble maker), he has nevertheless paid the price. He is on six death lists at least. He has also paid another price, his illness, which he faces with stoicism: "It's a holding pattern," he says in an interview with David Barsamian. "I have a chronic disease, leukaemia. . . . I try not to think about the future too much. One has to just keep going. . . . I think the big battle is to try to not make it the center of your every waking moment, put it aside and press on with the tasks at hand" (*The Pen and the Sword*, 1994: 170). This is astonishingly brave, to say the least. Said is among those rare individuals in whose life there is coincidence of ideals and reality, a meeting of abstract principle and individual courage.

What of other Third World intellectuals whose development has been stunted within their own countries by autocratic rulers who have degraded the quality of debate on national issues and forced many gifted writers into exile? In some cases, exile has nurtured creativity, giving some of them the political space to reveal the disparity between official rhetoric and reality. But to many it has not been kind. Can Themba and Todd Matshikiza are among the Black South African writers who died abroad in miserable conditions; Okot p'Bitek, the

Ugandan poet, is not the only one who, lacking a connection to the society he longed to write about, drank himself to death.[1] Many have survived, but their talent has suffered. Unable to endure the loneliness and sterility of exile, South African Ezekiel Mphahlele explains his decision to return home after twenty years "as a way of dealing with the phantoms and echoes that attend exile" (1984: 34–35). The dissident intellectual must keep quiet or exile themselves in order to voice their opinions.

In the hope that within the current turmoil sweeping the Third World, there are prospects for spiritual as well as political liberation, exiled Third World writers are increasingly tempted to return home to participate in the future of their countries. But so far, regimes—except for the "happy few" that have promised "change"—seem reluctant to allow the exiles the freedom they had hoped for. Guinean writer William Sassine, recently returned from a lengthy exile in France, has had several manuscripts confiscated, has been the target of aggressive personal threats, and has been prevented from traveling to international conferences and from pursuing his career as a teacher of mathematics, even though there is a dearth of such professionals. His experiences have, naturally, discouraged other exiled Guinean writers from going home (1985: 22). Gilbert Nsangata, the Congolese filmmaker and theater director was forced to leave his country after he ran up against the censorship of a pariah government that tends to marginalize artists and obliterate all creativity. Nsangata found shelter in a City of Asylum of International Parliament of Writers (Sabadell, Spain). Because he contributed to the creation of an Internet web site (www.vietnamesepoetry.com), Vietnamese Linh Dinh got into trouble with the Vietnamese police. The media, as all other channels of dissemination, are under government control. Writers who attempt to cross the line are intimidated by the police with their unexpected visits to their home in search of "proof" to be seized or exercise pressure on their employers at the risk of their losing their jobs. In August 2001, Dinh was forced to make the decision to leave Vietnam. He now lives in a City of Asylum in Tuscany (Italy). Another case in point is the Lebanese journalist Rhagida Dergham, an outstanding Arab woman who has represented the influential Egyptian newspaper, in New York for many years. An excellent reporter and sharp debater on matters pertaining to the Middle East, Rhagida brought credit and credibility to her profession. She was indicted for high treason in her country because she dared to attend a public meeting in Washington and debated Uri Lubrani, an Israeli Mossad operative who was one of the major architects behind the occupation of Southern Lebanon. Pressure for change from below has forced a number of autocrats to accept the principle of democratic accountability and to permit elections. But elections do not in themselves represent profound democratic change. Without respect for freedom of expression and association, without acceptance of the rule of law, and above all, without strong civic associations, it will be difficult to create a tolerant climate where different voices not only emerge but thrive. Mobyem

Mikanza, a playwright living in the then Zaire and cofounder of the Union of Zairean Writers, is skeptical about the impact of "multipartyism" on writers, individually and collectively. Recalling the misuse of culture for political ends by the late Mobuto, he comments in a letter that

> each new party will want to take creators, writers and artists into their service. . . . In the minds of people, democracy is a vague, nebulous concept. Democracy will succeed insofar as everybody seizes clearly its content and requirements, insofar as the whole nation agrees to radically change its mentality, to assume resolutely the true democratic spirit because multipartyism is not necessarily democracy (1977: 5–7).

Repressive Third World governments have long understood that knowledge is power. In order to ensure that writers cannot challenge official versions of events, and in order to deny them opportunities to voice broad grievances, those in control have forced intellectuals to suffer abuse, psychological intimidation, detention, censorship, and the deprivation of material resources. Inadequate literary infrastructures—the lack of libraries, publishing houses, bookshops, and distributors; the prohibitive cost of books; government control over radio and television; poor educational systems—have inhibited intellectual and cultural pursuits and prevented writers from reaching their audiences.[2]

During a reign that lasted more than twenty-five years, former president of Guinea Ahmed Sekou Touré prohibited the publication of any works other than his own. In the determination to limit the free exchange of ideas, some governments have sought to eliminate criticism by forcing writers to tailor their works to conform to government ideology. For writers who fail to toe the line, reprisals are swift and harsh. Ibrahim Mohamed is one of Somalia's best-known poets and one of the principal architects of the written Somali script. In 1973, he was banished to a remote village; for five and a half years, he was not allowed contact with anyone other than the man whose house he lived in. He was also denied reading and writing material. His crime had been to write a series of plays and contribute to ballads that contradicted the government's ideology of "revolutionary socialism" (1996: 34). Some heads of state have hijacked culture in an effort to legitimize illegitimate regimes, while in Cameroon, Togo, Zaire, Tunisia, Indonesia, Morocco, Algeria, Saudi Arabia, Iraq, and elsewhere, countless writers have been forced to provide their services in the name of the "guide," the "helmsman," the "father of the nation." In some instances, though, the elaborate repressive apparatus of the state has stimulated creativity by compelling writers to develop subtle and imaginative ways of bypassing censorship. Jack Mapanje, Malawi's best-known poet, who was released after three-and-a-half years' detention without charge or trial, believes that the draconian measures taken by the Malawi Censorship Board may have inadvertently caused him to write better poems. However, another

Malawian poet, Frank Chipasula, found that fear of informants took a heavy toll on his work. "I used obscurity as a protective mask which became so opaque that sometimes not even my colleagues in my inner circle, the people I sought to reach, could understand the work" (Chipasula, 1986: 23). To put it in anthropological terms, the native informant never relishes competition! It may be tempting to describe the plight of the Third World intellectual as arising from a tortured and disfigured allegiance to some cause for justice. In fact, Third World intellectuals must live with renewed death threats for their opposition to brutality, tyranny, and injustice. They include the Nobel Laureate Naguib Mahfouz, who was stabbed in Cairo in 1994. Mahfouz's stabbing highlights the total bankruptcy of a movement that prefers killing to dialogue, intolerance to debate, and paranoia to real politics. But it is hypocritical now to say of Mahfouz's assailants only that they are crude fanatics who have no respect for intellectual or artistic expression, without at the same time noting that some of Mahfouz's work has already been officially banned in Egypt itself. There is little basic distinction in the end between authorities who reserve the right for themselves to ban, imprison, or otherwise punish writers who speak their minds and those fanatics who, for example, take to stabbing a famous author just because he seems to them to be an offense to their supposed idea of religion.

The attack itself is troubling, suggesting the kind of murderous campaign against intellectuals taking place in Algeria, Turkey, Indonesia, and Iran, to name but a few. Take Ahmad Kasravi, the Iranian secular nationalist murdered in 1946; Faraj Foda, the Egyptian secular writer, assassinated in 1992; Ugar Mumcu, the Turkish secular journalist, blown up in 1993; Tahar Djaout, the Algerian poet and novelist shot four times in the head in 1993; his fellow countryman, Abdelkader Alloula, a brilliant playwright in the tradition of Chekhov, was also shot twice in the head in 1994; Said Sultanpur, a Marxist playwright who managed to escape to Britain after serving a jail sentence under the late Shah, returned to Iran after the revolution, and was shot after being dragged by guards from his wedding party; Shokrallah Paknejad, a democratic socialist imprisoned for eight years by the late shah for supporting the Palestinian resistance movement, was executed in secret; Abdul-Rahman Qassemlu, leader of the secular nationalist movement in Iranian Kurdistan, murdered by Iranian government agents in Vienna in 1988; and the list goes on.[3] I remain convinced, however, that the real problem at the root of these outrageous killings is the general political failure, secular as well as religious, to come to proper terms with democratic politics. That is what the Third World needs today.

The Third World intellectual as spirit in opposition rather than in accommodation is either killed or imprisoned and his or her work censured. Mohammed Chokri, whose oral memoir of his youth in the slums of Tangier was transcribed into English by Paul Bowles as *For Bread Alone*, was unable to find a publisher in Morocco for the Arabic version he wrote when he became literate. His "protest against the vampirism of the rich" appeared in 1980 in a French translation by Tahar Ben Jelloun, two years before Chokri published it himself in Morocco, only to have it banned. This sorry plight in The Maghreb is captured in Albert Memmi's "Dans Quelle lanque écrire? La Patrie littéraire du colonisé," which paints a grim picture of the post-colonial writer who finds himself compelled to help build his or her nation from within as well as speak against corruption and tyranny. He expounds the point with brio and élan:

> After the hardship of colonialism, the exciting turmoil of decolonization, comes the struggle of a growing nation's self assertion. It is not the least troubling of the three. By its very dangers, rebellion is more exhilarating than opposing one's own. Now, presumed free, the writer is faced with new responsibilities: he must take account of the shortcomings of his own people, the injustice of the privileged, the bad habits of his leaders. He must shake up his own appurtenances, which means also fighting against himself. How can he not be seen as the cause of even more disorder. He was once a rebel who stood by his people; now he's suspected of treachery, something that is tougher to live with. It's less painful to be a rebel than a traitor (1996: 12).

Lebanese writer, Hanan al-Shaykh, refusing to defer to religious or social "taboos," found her novel, *Women of Sand and Myrrh*, banned in many Arab countries for its daring portrayal of female sexuality.[4]

According to Elias Khoury, the Lebanese writer and literary editor of the Beirut weekly *Al-Nahar*, with the destruction of Beirut as the center of free press during Lebanon's civil war, much Arab publishing has shifted to Western capitals. The problem of direct state censorship and control of publishing has been compounded by the burgeoning in the past ten or fifteen years of extremist religious groups. Muslim writers have long had death sentences pronounced against them, but the climate of fear worsened in the 1990s, especially in Egypt with the assassination of more than a dozen top intellectuals, including both devout Muslims and resolute secularists. Egyptian Nawal el-Saadawi, imprisoned under Sadaat, said that the government had imposed an unsolicited bodyguard on her.[5] Playwright Karim al-Rawi describes how religious "fundamentalism," known more aptly in Egypt as "political Islam," constantly subverts cultural expression. "Neofascist groups such as the Muslim Brotherhood," he writes, "have with government complicity infiltrated religious institutions including Al-Azhar, the Islamic University in Cairo which has the power to proscribe works. The choice facing many Muslim writers is between falling silent and courting danger, or else succumbing to a creeping self-censorship" (1996: 12). Under the pseudonym Samir al-Khalil, Kanan Makiya attacks Saddam Hussein's Ba'athist regime in *Republic of Fear* and berates the Arab intelligentsia for "moral bankruptcy" in creating a "discourse of silence" around the region's wars and political repression, including genocide against the Kurds. He denounces the "knee-jerk anti-Westernism" of those who prefer to blame others and style themselves as victims rather than face up to their own shortcomings. Makiya preempts the charge that he is "a self-hating Arab who enjoys criticizing Arabs to curry favor with the West." "I write for myself," he flatly answers (1991: x).

The freedom to speak out in exile can no longer be taken for granted, not least since the mainly conservative oil regimes (like Saudi Arabia), which finance Arab presses abroad, attach their own strings to free expression (Halliday, 1996: 27–51). In the United States, Edward Said suggests, to swim against the current of opinion is to risk being condemned to marginality. While it became acceptable to criticize Saddam Hussein when he fell from favor with the Western governments that backed him in his war against Iran, it was more difficult to be heard if you condemned *both* Iraqi *and* U.S. policy during the Gulf War. Yet Said pronounces the two were related: "The Arab world *is* ruled by tyrants, but the U.S. has never supported any struggle for democracy there" (In *For Rushdie*, 1994: 261). The constraints on free speech in the Arab world raise dilemmas for those such as Said voicing criticisms in the West. Emil Habiby, the Palestinian satirist and Israeli citizen whose acceptance in 1992 of the Israeli Prize for literature sparked controversy among Palestinians, notes that Arabs should not be ashamed to "hang their dirty washing on foreign lines," particularly, he adds pointedly, "when they see other people's" (ibid., 167). Others see a danger in reinforcing anti-Arab, anti-Muslim prejudices—along with the policies they serve to justify. In the context of the cultural war against Arabs in the West, Said remarks that "the writer has a responsibility to write with some awareness of the audience and of the consequences of his or her words" (ibid., 262). The writer's role in undermining the "fortification of intolerance on both sides" of the Palestinian-Israeli conflict is stressed by Israeli novelist David Grossman, author of *Sleeping on a Wire*, which deals with Israel's eighteen percent Palestinian minority. The unacceptable price of being a "professional enemy," he observes, is the need to "obliterate others' complexity, to deny legitimacy to their pain, suffering and memory," and in the process, to obliterate part of oneself (1992: 175). Many reject any intimation of symmetry in the conflict, placing "truth" at a higher value than tolerance and reconciliation. For Habiby, the greater intolerance is that of the colonizer and occupying power. The "truth," for many, requires recognition of a distinction between oppressor and oppressed.

I do not think it is an exaggeration to say that once we start to look at what obtains in the Arab world today most of us are fairly appalled by the overall condition of mediocrity and galloping degeneration that seem to have become our lot. In all the significant fields (except for aping the West), we have sunk to the bottom of the heap when it comes to quality of life. We have become an embarrassment, as much for our powerlessness and hypocrisy (for example, vis-à-vis الإنتفاضه [Uprising] for which the Arab states do next to nothing) as for the abysmally poor social, economic, and political conditions that have overtaken every Arab country from Syria to Morocco. Illiteracy, poverty, unemployment, corruption, and unproductivity have increased alarmingly. And whereas the rest of the world seems to be moving in a democratic direction, the Arab world is going the other way, toward even greater degrees of oppression, autocracy, and Mafia-style rule. As a result, more and more of us feel that we should no longer keep silent about this sad state of affairs. Yet one scarcely knows where to begin in trying to ameliorate the situation, although honesty about what we have allowed to happen to ourselves might be a good way to start.

A small number of instances illustrate what I mean more eloquently than lists of facts and figures, all of which, incidentally, would support my case. In the summer of 2001, the Tunisian journalist, spokesperson for the *Conseil National pour les Libertés en Tunisie* (CNLS), founder of the literary journal *Kalima* and the publishing house *Aloès*, Sihem Bensédrine, was arrested and sentenced to prison by a state security court. The arrest took place after she rightly criticized the Baabuan ruling family for its vampirism. She reminded her audience about the Baabuans and the forty thieves (Queen Baabua and her tribe made of numerous brothers, daughters, cousins, sons, sons-in-law, and the list goes on) who when it comes to power and repression make the Marcoses look like amateurs. After all, for no less than twenty of the forty-seven years of independent Tunisian history, there has been a Baabu: Baabu as head of security, Baabu as minister of the interior, Baabu as prime minister, and finally Baabu as president for sixteen years now and still going.[6] Recently Tunis has not felt like the capital of a so-called republic at all, but rather like an old-fashioned *durbar*, a court with *vizirs*, courtesans and *chamchas*. The powerful figures in this court have not been, in many cases, members of the government or of the Tunisian Parliament even though they, too, spend their lives waiting for the bread crumbs to fall from the presidential table. They have, rather, been a motley assortment of minions and scavengers. The country is owned by seven families. Habib Bourguiba is dead; *Vive la République*. No, I am not trying to lay all of modern Tunisia's many ills at the door of the half-made king or that of his queen. Political corruption is one of Tunisia's besetting ills, and there has been plenty of it in the family, but of course it is not all Baabu's responsibility. Nor will the task of cleaning the stables be easy. Yet it is up to intellectuals such as Sihem Bensédrine, Hichem Djait, and Taoufik Ben Brik, another wronged journalist who risked his life by going on a hunger strike so that he could reclaim his passport back. In the end, Ben Brik won the battle thanks to his will not to cave in and determination not to be bullied by a coercive regime that lost faith in the Tunisia-idea. What, centrally, is that idea? It is based on the most obvious and apparent fact about life in a young democracy. For a nation to make any kind of sense, it must found itself on equality, education, and justice for all, not just for those who are drunk with power.

Two prominent intellectuals have been brought low in a country known for its *douceur* and *joie de vivre*, a country that prides itself on the destructive force of its sand/sun/servitude. What appears incontrovertibly abnormal, however, is that the intellectual in Tunisia *la douce* is systematically punished by the state because of his or her fame and his or her criticism of several of the state's policies. The lesson seems to be that if you have the temerity to speak loudly, and if you displease the powers that be, you will be severely cut down. Many countries in the world are ruled by emergency decree. Without exception such rule must be opposed and condemned. There can be no reason short of absolute natural catastrophe to suspend unilaterally the rule of law and the protection of impartial justice. Even the worst criminals in a society of laws are entitled to justice and proportional sentence. The travesty of due process in the Ben Brik and/or Bensédrine case speaks volumes about our current malaise and our sense of distorted priorities when it is assumed that any citizen can be subject to the machinations of power in the Arab world. These cases tell us that our rulers hold that no one is immune from their wrath and that citizens should maintain a permanent sense of fear and capitulation when it comes to authority, whether secular or religious. Hicham ben Abdallah el Alaoui makes the case in astringent terms:

> Not a single democratic government, not a single democratic state in all of the Arab world. While democracy is spreading throughout the rest of the planet, in Eastern Europe, Latin America, Africa, Asia, this shocking situation is aggravating Arab public opinion, which, increasingly urbanized and better educated, is claiming true status as citizens able to fight more effectively against the neo-authoritarianism of state power and the aggression of Islamicist obscurantism (1995: 11).

Or, to put it differently, when the state is transformed from its role as the people's property and becomes instead the possession of a regime or a ruler, to be used as it/he sees fit, we have to admit that as a sovereign people we have been defeated and have entered a phase of advanced degeneration which it may be too late to repair or reverse.

Neither a constitution nor an election process has any real meaning if such suspensions of law and justice can take place with the relative acquiescence of an entire people, especially the intellectuals. What I mean is not just that we do not have democracy but that at bottom we seem to have refused the very concept itself. I became dramatically aware of this reality when I held a post as visiting professor at the University of Tunis I in the mid-1990s. In the spring of 1996, I was invited to conduct a seminar at the University of Hannover (Germany) but was refused permission to leave. I did go to Germany against all the odds and gave my seminar in postcolonial/postmodern literature. Upon my return to Tunisia, I was summoned by the dean, who had come to power thanks to the support from a tribe of half-made instructors and mini-merchants and who had no shame in opening my mail and reading it in my absence. I was asked to explain myself. When I refused to even speak to the man, a friend interceded and arranged for me to meet with the deputy minister of higher education. What transpired was profoundly revealing. When I repeated my comments about my trip to Germany, the deputy, who had an impressive picture of the Big Man towering over him, lost his temper (he happened to be a member of the ruling party) and told me in no uncertain terms that I had no right "to leave Tunisia." When I retorted that I was not a prisoner and that I was after all invited by another university, he barked that I ought to be careful. "We have a file on you," he kept repeating with almost insensate rage.[7] This affront made me realize that I could not live in a country where the University, let alone the ministry of higher education, kept a file on me as if I were a criminal of some sort. Then I understood that these *hommes de poussière* were out to sally my name, spit on my reputation, and murder my thought. So deep has their authoritarianism become that any challenge to it is seen as little short of devilish and therefore unacceptable.

Not for nothing have so many people turned to an extremist form of religion as a result of desperation and the absence of hope. When democratic rights were first abrogated in the early years of Tunisia's independence because there seemed to be genuine security concerns, no one realized that the emergency would continue for half a century while showing no sign at all of abating in the interests of personal freedom. On the contrary, as the security state has become more insecure after all, what Arab state in our world can actually provide its citizens with the kind of security and freedom from fear and want to which they are entitled? The level of repression increases. No one is safe, no one is free from anxiety, and no value is preserved by law.

The Bensédrine and/or Ben Brik case is an amazing act of perversity that suggests how far the concept of the "crime" of speaking against a regime that built a wall of silence around its people has gone. But this should come as no surprise. To Arab governments, sad as it may seem, enlightened opinions are something they feel must be opposed and muzzled, especially if the ruler is displeased. One can understand and even accept that there can be an adversarial relationship between the state and its citizens, but there is now in the entire Arab world a situation of such profound antagonism whereby the individual citizen can be threatened with near-extinction by government, ruler, and native informant, that the entire balance between various interests in the state has lost all meaning. Crime is no longer an objective act, governed by recognized, publicly codified procedures of evidence, trial, punishment, and appeal but has become the prerogative of the state entirely to define and punish at will. At issue is the right to free thought and expression and, underlying that, the right to be free of ludicrously enacted restrictions against individual freedom. The cases I have cited were brought against well-known writers, intellectuals, and journalists who have the resources and connections to draw attention to what was so unjustly done to them. But a whole, mostly hidden, population of possible victims exists in the Arab world at large, against whom similar measures can and have been taken, either individually or collectively. As it spirals into further incoherence and shame, it is up to every one of us to speak up against these terrible abuses of power the way Ben Brik and Bensédrine did and still do. The truth is that all we have left now is the power to tell our story, and unless we exercise that right, the slide into terminal degeneration cannot ever be stopped.

Such a state of affairs is not, however, peculiar to the Arab world. It is rampant in the rest of the Third World, where the state's repressive machine has revealed its true and terrifying face. It deploys a campaign of lies to justify its oppression of writers. Governments have on their conscience systematic torture tactics as in the case of Yashar Kemal, who was imprisoned by the Turkish government for his views on the Kurdish genocide. As a Turkish writer who never wrote a word in Kurdish, Kemal says he is not fighting just for the Kurds but for all the minorities in Turkey, including the Arabs and the Laz people of the Black Sea region. "On the threshold of the twenty-first century, we cannot refuse human rights to any people or ethnic group," he aptly remarked.[8] Other prominent Turkish writers agree with Kemal that the real problem in Turkey is not separatism but the lack of democracy.

Orhan Pamuk, a young popular novelist, followed up Kemal's essay "Campaign of Lies," which appeared soon after a massive Turkish cross-border operation into northern Iraq was launched in 1995 to flush out PKK guerillas entrenched in the Iraqi mountains:

> Everybody knows that the invasion of northern Iraq solves neither the Kurdish issue nor the PKK problem. But the lie is perpetuated. The state, military and media preach that approval of the invasion means patriotism. Defenders of the military solution don't accept that the Kurdish issue is a problem of democracy and that Kurds must have the right to save and develop their own language, culture, and identity according to their own will (1994: ix).

Pamuk is one of many intellectuals who began a campaign of civil disobedience in support of Kemal and other writers who are being persecuted under the controversial article 8 of the antiterrorist law. The campaign, named "Freedom of Thought," now has more than one hundred thousand supporters. Its organizers republished a book of banned articles, previously confiscated by Turkish authorities, that includes Kemal's essay. Its members say they are ready to go to prison along with the authors and publishers who have already been arrested. "When one does something new in Turkey," Pamuk exclaims, "one is perceived as perverse. . . . Turkey is a violent country, intolerant of other religious ethnic or linguistic communities. If Jesus had been a Turkish policeman, he would have been corrupt in less than ten days." The problem with Turkey is that it is on the border between the West and the East. It is constantly torn between modernity and tradition. "I was raised in a community that considered itself Western," Pamuk adds. "The first time I entered a mosque, taking my shoes off made me feel naked. The whole country is suffering from this coming and going between two cultures. It is not necessarily a metaphysical exercise, it could simply be looked at as a domestic problem" (1997: 71). With the rise of Islamicism, corruption, and injustice, Pamuk continues to fight for the Kurds' rights to claim their identity. With the help of other journalists, writers, and intellectuals, he participates in civil acts of disobedience at a cost. According to Turkey's Human Rights Association, as of the end of 1995 there were 166 writers, journalists, publishers, scientists, and civil rights activists in prison, sentenced under the antiterrorism law. Kemal tells us that "today there are over 5,000 people [in Turkey] who are being interrogated for their views" (in Couturier, 1995: C4), a desolate state of affairs, to say the least.

In response to pressure from Western nations to democratize and permit political dissent, Tansu Ciller, prime minister at the time, made repeated promises at home and abroad to ease restrictions on freedom of expression. But her efforts to amend article 8—which outlaws dissemination of ideas or propaganda in any form that aims to "disrupt the unity of the state"—were bogged down in Parliament, by hard-liners in the mainstream conservative parties who staunchly opposed the idea. "Since Turkey has never been a democratic country, [it] has been a huge prison for all of us. A prison that is smaller won't make a difference to me," Kemal noted during a court hearing in 1995, as the Turkish cross-border operation was winding down. After the hearing, his case was adjourned (ibid., C1). Kemal, like a surprising number of other writers and journalists across the Third World, is no stranger to prison. Branded at a young age as a Communist for denouncing the large landholders of the Anatolian countryside, he was arrested in 1950 for alleged Communist propaganda but acquitted at a trial a few months later, according to an autobiographical sketch. "I resumed my public letter-writing, but the landholders, who had already attempted to kill me in prison, made my life a constant nightmare by denouncing me to the police, who would search my house to tatters regularly twice a week for evidence of subversive activity" (In Darnton, 1995: D2). He eventually escaped his persecutors and moved to Istanbul, where he took the pseudonym Yashar and worked as a journalist for a prominent daily, *Cumhuriyet*. Another stint in prison followed after the military takeover of 1971. *Memed, My Hawk*, Kemal's first and perhaps best-known novel, published in 1955, is the tale of Memed, an Anatolian outlaw who takes a lonely stance against his village's all-powerful landowner, Abdi Agha. The novel climaxes with Memed riding into town to confront Abdi:

He entered Deyirmenoluk one day at noon. His face was dark, his eyes hollow, his brow creased. He was bleak as a rock, but there was an obstinate glint in his eyes. It was the first time in a long while that he had entered the village in broad daylight. . . . The women put their heads out of their doors and were watching him with awe. The children walked with him, but some distance behind, fearfully (Kemal, 1996: 17).

With the same determination, Kemal himself confronts his adversaries today, regretting only that he does not have more time: "I am angry with myself because I am seventy-one years old and I have got little time left. I have got fifteen novels to write. This trial has already taken three months from my life" (ibid., 18). What concerns Kemal now is to write and write again. For that, as a citizen, he takes full responsibility.

A death threat to Taslima Nasrin, first issued when her novel *Lajja* was published and swiftly banned in 1993, has recently been renewed by the religious extremists she angered in Bangladesh.[9] The journalist and novelist, formerly a doctor, has now been charged with blasphemy for demanding the revision of القران (The Koran). Nasrin, however, merely recommended the revision of الشر يعه (A'Sharia), the pragmatic laws encoded in the body of Muslim political thought, in order to reclaim equal rights for women. The legal formulations of الشر يعه (A'Sharia) were intended as guidelines for their time and are in no sense immutable, as Muslim feminist theoreticians, among them Leila Ahmed and Fatima Mernissi, have amply illustrated. Muslim women writers have argued for the reform of prevalent norms since the dawn of practical feminism, citing as evidence and support Islam's egalitarian ethical vision.[10] The misuse of Nasrin's statement by political opportunists who are unacquainted with the actualities of Bangladesh, highlights the poignancy of her situation. Rather than reaching her constituency, she has increasingly been cut off from the very audience she has tried to address.

While Kemal and Nasrin were incarcerated without any serious charges being made against them, Tahar Djaout was attacked as he was leaving his home in Bainem to go to his office where he worked on the journal *Ruptures* that he and his friends had launched in 1993. His attackers shot him several times, dragged him from his car, then used it to make their escape. Djaout died after lying for a week in a deep coma. The assassination was generally attributed to the armed branch of the FIS (Front Islamique du Salut). Two days after the attack, two of Djaout's aggressors were shot and killed by police near Notre Dame d'Afrique on the heights above Algiers, and a third was captured. Early newspaper reports quoted the third killer as saying that Djaout's assassination had been ordered because "he was a Communist and wielded a fearsome pen which could have an effect on Muslim sectors" (quoted in Husarska, 1996: D4). Djaout was a victim of the internecine power struggle between the FIS and the FLN (Front de Libération Nationale), a struggle that grew violent after January 1992, when the government aborted elections that seemed to point to an FIS victory (Farman-farmaian, 1995: 48–70).

In a country ravaged by civil war between a corrupt, long-entrenched authoritarian state and a rising fundamentalist movement, Djaout instantly became everyone's symbol: the then liberals hailed him as a voice in revolt while the imams, not impressed by his poetry, denounced him for being secular. In Algeria, these are complicated and bloody matters, near the heart of an intricate cultural war that has claimed the lives of tens of thousands including hundreds of intellectuals—judges, professors, editors, filmmakers, stage directors, doctors, and writers, all of whom were attacked because of their stand against tyranny. The politics of the area is murky, and much speculation goes on about responsibility for some of the killings and about rumored alliances between "strange bedfellows." The headline of an article in the 1 July 1993 issue of the *Wall Street Journal* declared, "Algerians wonder who's really behind [the] recent series of high-profile murders," and as one of the writer's friends stated, Djaout was "apparently killed by the Muslim fundamentalists . . . or by those who would like us to think so" (Couturier, 1993: 1). The fact, however, remains that Djaout is dead as a result of a tragic, senseless act. His premature death represents a great loss for literature, for Djaout was one of the most promising Maghrebian writers of his generation. He was also a gentle and generous man who seemed to be the heir apparent of the Kabyle writer Mouloud Mammeri (killed in a car crash in 1989) and the quiet but committed leader of the collective effort to safeguard the Tamazigh (Berber) identity and cultural values. He was a firm believer in democracy and, in his writing, underlined the dangers represented by religious extremists and the incumbent complacent bureaucracy alike. Whoever eliminated him did not silence his voice. The killing of this fine writer because of his "high profile" outraged the literary world. Articles in major newspapers around the globe decried the act, and in December 1993 the BBC broadcast a program on Djaout and his assassins. The poet Abdellatif Laâbi—no stranger himself to political oppression—wrote an elegy for him:

> L'enfant s'éloigne
> tirant avec une ficelle
> son petit coffre en bois
> Cercueil ou berceau?
> Il ne sait
> Il marche
> parce qu'on lui a parlé de la mer
> comme d'un âge adulte de l'eau et des îles
> comme des villes de cristal
> érigées dans un jardin
> L'enfant s'éloigne
> et sa tête blanchit
> à la vitesse de la rumeur (1994: 34).

(The child walks away
pulling his little wooden box
on a string
Coffin or cradle?
He does not know
He walks
because they talked to him about the sea
as if it were old age about the water and the islands
as if they were crystal cities
built in a garden
The child walks away
his hair graying
with every step)

All these confusions and contradictions I have described are signs of a deeper malaise in an Arab world in a deep crisis.

The shambles of inertia and impotence are correctly expressed in the 2002 Arab Human Development Report:

> There is no Arab democracy, Arab women are uniformly an oppressed majority, and in science and technology every Arab state is behind the rest of the world. Certainly there is little strategic cooperation between them and virtually none in the economic sphere. As for more specific issues like policy toward Israel, the U.S. and the Palestinians, and despite a common front of embarrassed hand-wringing and disgraceful powerlessness, one senses a frightened determination first of all not to offend the U.S., not to engage in war or in a real peace with Israel, not ever to think of a common Arab front even on matters that affect an over-all Arab future and security. Yet when it comes to the perpetuation of each regime, the Arab ruling classes are united in purpose and survival skills. . . .
>
> There is thus no strong moral center in the Arab world today. Cogent analysis and rational discussion have given way to a fanatical ranting, concerted action on behalf of liberation has been reduced to suicidal attacks, and the idea if not the practice of integrity and honesty as a model to be followed has simply disappeared. So corrupting has the atmosphere exuded from the Arab world become that one scarcely knows why some people are successful while others are thrown in jail.[11]

When we (Arabs) mistake puerile acts of defiance for real resistance, and when we assume that know-nothing ignorance is a political act (when in fact it is nothing of the sort), and when we shed all dignity and clamor for Western patronage and attention, surely our sense of pride and self-respect is in tatters. We have for so long been deprived of a sense of participation and citizenship by our rulers that most of us have lost even the capacity of understanding what personal commitment to a cause bigger than ourselves might mean. Who has not cringed at the memory of the murder of Kuwaiti writer, journalist and publisher, Hidaya Sultan al-Salem in April 2001? Hidaya was brutally killed because she campaigned hard against corruption and for women's suffrage. Kuwait's fundamentalist-tribal alliance did not mourn Hidaya. Apart from its successful antisuffrage campaign, it banned the publication of "licentious" books by two of al-Salem's female allies, Aalia Shuaib and Laila al-Uthman.[12]

Another no less fine Third World intellectual—a man whose name never weighs more heavily than when it is unspoken—is the fervent and most articulate champion against tyranny in Southeast Asia, Pramoedya Ananta Toer.[13] Both Toer and al-Salem are, in a sense, part of the same project. Few figures on the scene share as many presuppositions and preoccupations as they do even though they are geographically far apart. Theirs is a sectlike feeling in its fervor. They both sought militancy as the mode and *rage de rigueur* while holding their pens with clenched fists and knew that change, radical change, is not about niceties of style anyway. Toer's identity card is stamped with two typewritten letters that speak volumes about his life: "ET," for Ex-Tapol, a former political prisoner. It is a label shared by nearly 1.4 million Indonesians believed arrested in the aftermath of the abortive 1965 coup, or at least by those who survived their imprisonment. Today, he is an ex-detainee who still lives as an outcast, a nonperson within his homeland. Samizdat copies of his books circulate among students; he is never quoted in newspapers; a rare public mention came with the recent sentencing of two young men arrested for possessing and selling copies of his works. Lately, the National Human Rights Commission has started trying to erase the stigma, but former prisoners have little confidence it will succeed, especially at a time when charges are circulating of a new Islamist threat to Indonesia. The aged survivors of the Indonesian gulag are dying in increasing numbers. "If what the Human Rights Commission is doing actually happens, it will be too late because we're all old and have had to endure great hardship in struggling through our lives," Toer observes. "Many have died because they couldn't make a living" (Quoted in Gogwilt, 1996: 153). In this writer's understanding, therefore, the opposite of concealing is defiance, the act of standing up and resisting under the will of a power that one perceives as unjust and unreasonable.

On 6 February 1995, his seventieth birthday, Toer launched the first Indonesian-language version of his memoir of ten years in a penal colony on a remote Buru island, where he was among fourteen thousand prisoners. *Nyanyi Seorang Bisu* (*Silent Song of the Mute*) is a Bahasa translation of the original Dutch-language *Lied van een Stomme*.[14] It appeared in the same year Indonesia celebrated fifty years of independence, perhaps a fitting time to face the past. But because Toer's works are banned in Indonesia, he was unsure whether the government would permit the book to be sold openly. "I'm optimistic the government will allow me to go ahead, but if it's banned it doesn't matter," he said in an interview. "For me, [banning] would be an honor" (Quoted in McBeth, 1995: 27). Such defiance probably explains why Toer was among the first batch of prisoners to be shipped to Buru in 1969 and among the last to be released from the malaria-ridden island a decade later. Although his records are incomplete, Toer names 268 who died of brutality, disease, starvation, and suicide. No one is known to have successfully escaped from Buru. Toer claims that about forty inmates who staged a mass breakout into the surrounding wilderness in 1974 either died of starvation or were hunted down and killed. "In the beginning, we all thought we were meant to die one by one because the treatment was so bad," he recalls of his arrival in Buru in 1969. "But after about five years, conditions gradually began to improve because of international pressure" (Quoted in Scott, 1990: 26). He credits his eventual release to then United States President Jimmy Carter. Toer has stubbornly refused to be silenced, even though the then Suharto regime was unrelenting in the suppression of his books. The attorney general stated that the Buru novels are "poisonous and very possibly could create unrest" (Feldman, 1990: 27). In 1988 he was given the PEN Freedom-to-Write award.

Toer spent more than seventeen of his seventy-three years in prison and has lived for the past decade under city arrest in Jakarta. His problems began under the colonial administration of the Dutch, when he worked as an editor at the *Voice of Free Indonesia* and paid with a stint in prison for his pains. With independence, Pramoedya Aranta exchanged one set of troubles for another. Although not a Communist, the author had visited Beijing in 1956; four years later, having taken the unpopular stand of defending Indonesia's Chinese minority in *The History of the Chinese in Indonesia*, he fell afoul of the Indonesian government. When a group of radical officers mounted a coup in 1965, which failed, thousands of left-wing activists were incarcerated, Toer among them.[15]

He is thus not simply a symbol of a persecuted writer but of a writer who confused literature and politics and who in the process lost his independent voice. This is an important distinction. Now he has become simply the victim. While the orthodoxy of the day has changed, the lack of independent voices continues. For there is a pre-Buru island Toer and a post-Buru one. He was a romantic nationalist, determined to establish an Indonesia in his own· image through literature, and failing that, through revolution. He entwined his literary and political fancies. Then the dream turned into a nightmare in 1965, when the army took over the government, eventually replacing Sukarno with Suharto. Toer was put behind bars, and the romantic became a disillusioned utopian. Cleaving to his version of himself as a man altered by Buru, he himself explains that his historical novels also drew on his disillusionment with politics: "Being detained in Buru gave me a strong sense of the rights of the individual. I came to the conclusion that I was wrong; I no longer think Politics is the commander. For me now, culture is the commander" (Quoted in Gogwilt, 1996: 158). But beyond his fancies and his failed revolutionary politics, Toer's contribution has been a lively and long-lasting addition to world dissident literature. His theme is the creation of a voice that is bent on challenging the order of things. He has ridiculed the Javanese myths and legends approvingly taught to every school child as a stultify-ing form of power worship. He has, perhaps even more heretically, kicked against the received wisdom on the genesis of the nationalist movement against the Dutch. And especially in his later writing from Buru, he turned to Indonesian history in his fiction, creating a rich world around a character based on the neg-lected figure of Tirto Adhisurjo, a journalist who founded a nationalist "freedom group" in 1909.

In 1996, Toer, when asked to change his attitude toward the government, replied: "When you return my books, then I will change my attitude," referring to his library, which was confiscated after his 1965 arrest. His books and notes ended up at the market as fish wrap. And although the authorities have forbid-den him to travel in his homeland, he does so whenever he pleases: "I've tried to ignore the city arrest as much as I can. If I obeyed those regulations, I would be nothing better than cattle in a pen" (ibid., 155). After his release from Buru, he was ordered to report at regular intervals to the military authorities, but in 1992 he publicly announced that he would no longer do so. He could not, however, attend the ceremonies for the prize (the 1995 Ramón Magsaysay Award) he was given in Manila; his wife had to accept it on his behalf. Like his works, which not only speak subtly about oppression but have managed, against all odds and with great pain, to transcend the oppressor's power to silence, Toer has found an audience in lands far beyond his own. That is at bottom his gift for escaping into history; he has produced what Wole Soyinka once called "prodigies of spleen."

There is certainly a strictly political and/or religious foundation for such anathema against writers and intellectuals such as Kamal, al-Sultan, Toer, and others who jeopardize their lives for the sake of justice. But in the end, the out-come of the conflict between potentate and intellectual will be determined more by what happens to the intellectual within the country where he or she lives. If there is any hope of a cultural breakthrough, one that goes beyond the minority of the brave, then it may well come from those intellectuals who feel like exiles at home. That is, of course, precisely what current calls to order are designed to fore-stall. Perhaps the rhetorical question with which Scheherazade ends *The Arabian Nights* is yet to be answered: "What finer sound is there than a human being singing against cruelty, against hatred?" (1992: 411). For the roll call of great, persecuted writers and intellectuals—Linh Dinh, Gilbert Nsangata, Gao Er Tai, Nuruddin Farah, Alia Mamdouh, Nawal el-Sadawi, Mahmoud Darwish, Mouna Naim, Leila Shahid, and others come to mind—is a stark reminder that if you tell the truth you are in serious trouble. And yet if you see the truth and keep quiet, you begin to die.

The upshot is that the dissident writer's position is a terrible one. The effort to find an artistic medium adequate enough to voice one's opinion against injustice and corruption has proven costly, especially in the Third World, where writers are constantly imprisoned, maimed, burned, hanged. The Algerian record is particularly appalling.[16] The only way out of the impasse is to reach for those distressed writers who live under repressive regimes so that they can find safe haven elsewhere. A brilliant example of an organization that helps is to be found in the International Parliament of Writers (IPW). Based in France, the IPW was set up in 1993 by Jacques Derrida, Hélène Cixous, Mahmoud Darwish, Bei Dao, Salman Rushdie, Wole Soyinka, the late Pierre Bourdieu, among others, in the wake of the Rushdie *fatwa* and the growing incidence of similar attacks on writers. On 3 February 1994, the IPW issued its declaration of independence. "Our Parliament of writers exists to fight for oppressed writers and against all those who persecute them and their work, and to renew continually the declaration of independence without which writing is impossible; and not only writing, but dreaming; and not only dreaming, but thought; and not only thought, but liberty itself" (Rushdie, 2000: 91). Rushdie, who wrote and read the text in public, is well suited for the role of the first president of the IPW. He also knows that his case is not a special one, that the sheer number of writers who currently live under a death sentence is staggering.

In addition to its scientific journal, *Autodafé*, which helps give a voice to those displaced writers, peoples, and experiences that have been silenced, the IPW came up with the idea of providing cities of refuge for writers forced to live in exile. There is now a flourishing network, hosting writers from many countries, writing in many languages. By 1995, seven towns—Almeria, Berlin, Caen, Gothenburg, Stavanger, Strasbourg, and Valladolid—had declared themselves asylum cities, and there are now many more (thirty-five cities in total), including one in Mexico and surprisingly, Las Vegas. The Pompidou Center in Paris has received many writers, and Barcelona has been active and hospitable. The cities are required to provide refuge for one year to a writer nominated through the IPW. Refuge includes accommodation for the writer's family, a measure of legal and social integration, access to libraries and cultural events, and efforts to offer a public platform and contacts with translators. It also involves a modest financial grant for subsistence.[17]

Fathered by the IPW and published once a year in eight languages simultaneously, *Autodafé* is a literary magazine that offers valuable and at times disturbing reports on the state of literary freedom and censorship in the world at the beginning of the twenty-first century. Evidence of the project's success may be found in the pages of the first two issues of the journal.[18] Many of the contributors have been its beneficiaries. A Cuban dissident has found a home in Sabadell in Spain, an Afghan poet is housed near Paris, a Turkish novelist lives in Stockholm, and poet and novelist Syl Cheney-Coker from Sierra Leone is writing about the tragedy of his country in an asylum city in the United States. Albanian writer Bashkin Shehu, who wrote a darkly comic essay on the reading habits of former dictator Enver Hoxha, called "The Dictator's Library," was offered asylum in Barcelona in 1991 and has since decided to settle there.[19]

Barcelona and Paris are pleasant places to be, by any standards, and have attracted literary exiles for many decades. Other places may appear more challenging. The Chinese poet Bei Dao's *Journal of a Traveler* describes his many wanderings, from Berlin to Oslo to Stockholm to Aarhus to Leiden to Paris to Ypsilanti and Ann Arbor, both in Michigan, to California.[20] The travel narrative is in turn sad, poignant, comic, bleak, and brave, and some of his comments on his hosts are far from anodyne. There were some terrible moments of loneliness and depression, but Bei Dao cannot rest from travel. He needs it, and it needs him. His story offers an entertaining and sharply observed account of the life of an itinerant and finally successful poet on the poetry-reading circuit, from early days reading to eager thousands in China in the 1980s before Tiananmen Square to drunken nights in Stockholm and Copenhagen to an evening in Belfast in 1993, in a theater surrounded by troops patrolling with automatic weapons—a grim reminder of another oppression.

In a breathtaking essay on literature and suffering, Hélène Cixous writes:

> Each time there is a reckoning more or less lucid more or less right which spurs on hunts, hunter and hunted down. A reckoning and an excitement. I want to be rejected just enough, as is fitting for a writer. Even so one is not going to ask for a visa just to write without risk or palpitations of the heart. But on the other hand I am not going to claim that I would like to be in prison, that I would want to be a Wei Jing Cheng and lose all my teeth and years, I would prefer to be and keep all my teeth. . . .
>
> I have no desire to live for years with bodyguards and in my entrails not the noble tragic fear but human jitters nausea.
>
> Who would want to be persecuted? But on the other hand what writer would want to give up their rights to persecution including exile, bereavement, solitude? Not me, nor any of those I have met. . . .
>
> The nostalgia of the worst, that's what makes you write. Uninterrupted solitude dictates the one to one dialogue. . . .
>
> The cruel obstetrics of what is called literary creation: a big bang, a short-lived madness, a three day cut that's enough for all the time of time. Because "literature" is this very long scratching of wounds the remainder; the crime de la crème over and over. . . .
> Writing exists for the worst (2000: 105–09).

Cixous's account is subtle and linguistically complex; it describes what comes across as a sense of survivor guilt—when so many have paid a high price for their art or their testimony, what do the lucky owe to the unlucky?

The answer to the question posed here may be found in the daring and courageous trip the IPW took in March 2002, following an invitation from one of its
members—namely, Mahmoud Darwish, who was denied permission by the Israeli
government to come to the United States to receive a prize given to him by an
American university. The aim of the visit was to break the isolation in which
Darwish and other Palestinian writers and artists found themselves after the
obese war-monger Ariel Sharon ordered the Israeli Army to invade the West
Bank and to establish a personal connection between them and the international
community of writers. The Palestinian poet spoke movingly in honor of the
visit, describing it as a symbolic way of inscribing Palestine in the culture of the
world. "Your courageous visit during this monstrous siege is one form of breaking
the siege. Your presence here makes us feel no longer isolated. With you we realize
that the international conscience, which you honorably represent, is still alive and
capable of protesting and taking the side of justice. You have assured us that
writers still have a valuable role to play in the battle for freedom and in the fight
against racism." Darwish then addressed the guests about the ravages of war on
syntax: "War has brought sclerosis to our language. Our poems have been more
pulverized than our streets. We are constantly driven to dramatize our poetry. Yet
we must resist military meter and find a cadence which is not that of drum rolls."
He concluded in weary irony: "When we gaze at the stars we see helicopters.
The only postmodern thing here is the Israeli army" (2002: 2). There is no denying the force of Darwish's words, which are inscribed in the struggle of a people
living in a closed world, a world without exits, a world where "death is all, death
alone has value," as Octavio Paz would have it.

The aim of both Parliament and the journal is international. *Autodafé* and the
IPW do not, however, support nationalism, though they give voice to many nations
as well as appeal to a hospitality of giving that does not fear to confront the ghosts
and open up paths across to the living word. The rallying cry is that literature
belongs to all of us and has no frontiers. We can read across the boundaries and
draw on a common heritage. All things in the world do homage to Varlam Chalamov, who died in 1982 after enduring labor camps and psychiatric hospitals
and long years of censorship and whose testimony is captured with force in
"Athenian Nights," which describes life in the gulag and evokes the formula for
happiness proposed by Thomas More in his *Utopia*. The four fundamental
pleasures of man, More says, are eating, fornication, urination, and defecation.
Chalamov acknowledges these needs, all four of which were denied or frustrated
in gulag conditions, but adds a fifth—notably, "The need for poetry, overlooked
by Thomas More" (2001: 17). The poetry readings he helped to organize in the
prison hospital wards were a form of survival and salvation.

Only in this way, Chalamov's way, can the dissident writer and/or artist uphold
the traditional role he or she has had as the voice of integrity and courage, speaking
out against those in power. "It is a lonely condition, yes," Said affirms, "but it is

always a better one than a gregarious tolerance for the way things are" (1996: 133). It is more than an urge to make sense or to make sense artfully. It is more than a desire to watch other intellectuals manage to refigure the world. It is making sure that the intellectual is not imperiled by the absence of a hospitable community. Securing that kind of peace is of great importance to those who, like Chalamov, Darwish, Said, and others, are able to illuminate even the stormiest of human prospects with a serene, revelatory light that shows us not only the obligatory two sides to every question, but the often overlooked third dimension as well. To have *that* opportunity is at least something for "[t]here is no ivory tower that can keep reality from beating at the walls," another no less committed writer, Nadine Gordimer notes. "In witness," she goes on to add, "the imagination is not irreal but rather, the deeper reality. Its exigence can never allow compromise with conventional cultural wisdom, and what Milosz calls 'official lies.' The intellectual of no compromise, Edward Said, asks who, if not the writer, is 'to elucidate the contests, challenge and hope, to defeat the imposed silence and normalized quiet power?'" (2002: 5). For Said, a writer's highest calling is to bear witness to the evils of conflict and injustice. And that is when the telling image is vividly enacted. In the age of migrants, curfews, identity cards, refugees, exiles, massacres, camps, and fleeing civilians, his voice represents the poet's mouth that is not silent but rather outspoken and defiant, a mouth that does not fear to face its oppressors implacably. When it comes to the idea of resistance, one must surely as a stout Derridean take stock of the role played by the displaced and deracinated who have responded in different ways to their historical moment in answerably ambitious terms; and it is these, therefore, who, in raising the most searching questions about modern civilization, are able to produce the finest literary art.

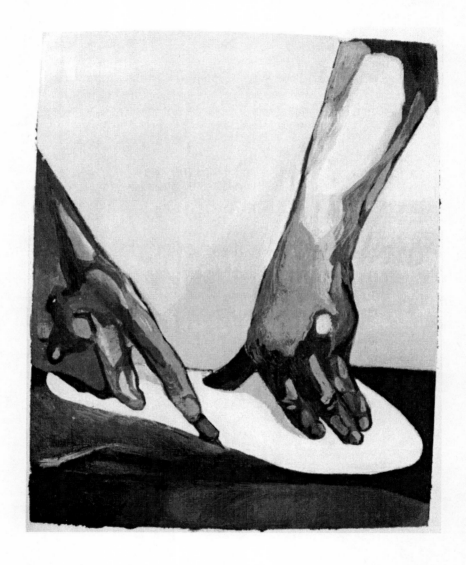

Ahmad Izmer, *being There/Being there: The Palestinian Diaspora*, Acrylic on Paper, 29 x 37 cm. © 2002.

CHAPTER EIGHT

SÄ-ĒD' DATA BASE 1966–2002

I am Adam of the two Edens, I who lost Paradise twice.
—Mahmoud Darwish, *Unfortunately, It Was Paradise*, 32.

To the extent that it is important to know anything about a writer's life aside from his work, it is probably important to know about Edward Said that in the following short passage he speaks poignantly about belonging. "What must it be like to be completely at home?" he asks and answers with equal aplomb. "I don't know. I suppose it's sour grapes that I now think it's maybe not worth the effort to find out" (*More Writers and Company*, 78). Said's idiosyncratic wit and the papery dry prose style he has developed to deliver it are both on display here. But the wit slices deeper when one begins to understand that Said is, in fact, a strange composite. Palestinian American, born Edward William Said, pronounced "*sä ēd*"; left Palestine as a child when his family sought what they thought would be temporary refuge in Egypt during the turmoil that led up to Israel's declaration of independence and the Israeli-Arab war of 1948. After the war, when Israel refused to allow Palestinians who had fled to return to their homes, Said became one of hundreds of thousands of Palestinians made refugee. Said's parents were Palestinian Christian: his father from Jerusalem, his mother from Nazareth. "My father was born in Jerusalem," Said observes, "as were his parents, grandparents, and all his family back in time to a distant vanishing point, he was a child of the Old City" (*After the Last Sky*, 14). "My guess was that both their families had converted in the 1870s or 1880s, my father's from the Greek Orthodox church, my mother's from the Greek Catholic, or Melkite. The Saids became stolidly Anglican, whereas my mother's family—slightly more adventurous—were Baptists many of whom later studied or taught at places like Baylor and Texas A & M" (*Cairo Recalled*, 24).

245

1911: "In 1911 my father," Said adds, "fresh out of school, ran away from Jerusalem to avoid being drafted to fight for the Turks in Bulgaria. He found his way to the United States and during World War I enlisted in the air force in the belief that perhaps a unit would be sent to fight Ottomans in Palestine. He ended up in France—wounded and gassed" (*Cairo Recalled*, 24).

1916: The Sykes-Picot agreement is signed. It is the basis for many of the Arab national states as we know them today—Iraq, Syria, Lebanon, Jordan, Palestine.

1932: Marriage of Wadie A. Said and Hilda Musa Marmoura. They set up house in Jerusalem. Hilda Musa Marmoura was born and lived in Nazareth. A town hall document certifies that when Hilda Marmoura married Wadie Said, they had to register the wedding, and together they went to the Palestine Government Mandatory office where an official (an Englishman) ripped up Hilda Marmoura's passport while adding: "You'll travel on your husband's passport. . . . Your place is going to be given to a Jewish emigrant to Palestine." Said recalls the incident with bitter irony, "[H]er identity was, just by the simple act of tearing up a piece of paper, taken away from her by a foreigner. And she lived through the consequences of that for thirty years" (*The Voice of a Palestinian in Exile*, 42).

1933: Ignace Tiegerman, a tiny Polish Jewish gnome of a man arrives in Cairo from Poland. He would become Said's music teacher and friend.

1935: Edward Said, the son of Wadie A. Said (who changed his name to William to fit his new identity) and Hilda Musa Marmoura is born on 1 November 1935 in Jerusalem, in Mandatory Palestine. "The facts of my birth," he writes, "are so distant and strange. It has to be about someone I have heard of rather than about someone I know" (*In Arafat's Palestine*, 13).

—At the age of two, Said, along with parents, moves to Cairo where his father runs a branch of the Palestine Educational Company, a thriving book business jointly owned with his Uncle Boulos. In the years to come, they would travel back to the extended family home in Jerusalem and to the Lebanese mountain town of Dhour el-Shweir.

1938–42: Although a resident of the affluent town Talbiya, Said attends the Ghezira Preparatory School (GPS) and St. George School in East Jerusalem. In 1942, Said spends the summer holiday in Ramallah with his family. He writes: "I recall it as a leafy slow-paced and prosperous town of free-standing villas largely Christian in population, served by a well-known Friends High School" (*In Arafat's Palestine*, 14).

1946: Wadie Said returns to Palestine as an American citizen.

1947: Said spends the last few weeks in Palestine before leaving it for good. "I had to traverse three of the security zones instituted by the British to get to St. George's School in East Jerusalem from my home in Talbiya," he reminds us. "And by February 1948 Talbiya was in the hands of the Haganah, the Jewish underground" (*Palestine, Then and Now*, 50).

1948: Israel is established; Palestine is wiped out, shattered, dismantled, destroyed by the Zionists.

—Said's last cousin, Martin Buber, abandons the Saids' family house in West Jerusalem.

—In September, Said enrolls in Victoria College (Cairo).

1949–51: Said goes to Victoria College, is expelled, readmitted briefly, then advised to look for another school. In 1950, the Israeli government passes the Absentee Property Law, which forbids Edward Said and his family and 750,000 other Palestinians from ever returning, if they had left their homes in what is now Israel before 1 September 1948. Under this law, an "absentee" includes anyone who is "a legal owner of any property situated in the area of Israel" who "left his ordinary place of residence in Palestine for a place outside Palestine before 1 September 1948" and who finds himself or herself in any country that was then at war with Israel. The law applies even if the refugees were in no way involved in the conflict. The Saids had left Talbiya and sought refuge in Egypt, which was at war with Israel. As a result, Said and his sisters and cousins were effectively dispossessed of their home.

—King Hussein's grandfather, Abdullah, is murdered outside the al-Aqsa mosque in Jerusalem. He is shot down by a Palestinian Arab gunman because Jordan has just annexed the West Bank.

1952: Said is sent off to boarding school in the United States (Mount Hermon School, Massachusetts). "I felt a tremendous blow. Mount Hermon was an austere place, a Puritan place" (*Hard Talk: Interview*, 1997).

—In Egypt, Gamal Abdel Nasser and his free officers overthrow the reign of King Farouk and assume power. "My experience of Nasserism," Said intones, "was one which you might say was already mediated and slightly distanced by a political ideology, which in a certain sense Nasser brought. That is what Nasser in fact introduced, not only into the lives of people in the Middle East but into my own life" (*Edward Said: A Critical Reader*, 228).

1956: Egypt is invaded by Britain, France, and Israel. King Farouk waddles off to Europe as the last reigning member of an Albanian-Turkish-Circassian dynasty that had begun with the considerable éclat of Muhammad Ali in 1805.

1957: Said graduates with a bachelor of arts degree from Princeton; receives Phi Beta Kappa award.

1958: Is awarded the Woodrow Wilson Fellowship at Harvard.

—Attends the Bayreuth Festival (Vienna, Austria). "So stunning was the impression on me of those ten days," he observes, "that I have never wished to return for fear of spoiling it" (*The Nation*, 30 August 1986: 151).

—President Eisenhower sends the Marines into Lebanon to protect it from "Communism."

1959–61: Teaching position in General Education at Harvard University.

1960: Master's degree in English literature from Harvard.

—Farid Haddad, one of Said's closest friends, and to whom *The Question of Palestine* is dedicated, is beaten to death by Nasser's secret police.

1961: Egypt and Syria fail to unify.

1961–63: Resident tutor in history and literature, Adam House, Harvard University; wins Bowdoin Prize.

1963: The Saids, a family of seven resident in Cairo for three decades, leave the city. "'Since Cairo,'" Said notes, "I have often said to my mother, 'since Cairo,' being for both of us the major demarcation in my life and, I believe, in hers. . . . Part of the city's hold over my memory was the clearness of its nearly incredible divisions, divisions almost completely obliterated by Gamal Abdel Nasser. . . . While I was growing up in it in the 1940s, a decade earlier, however, its Arab and Islamic dimensions could be ignored and even suppressed, so strong was the hold over the city of various European interests, each of which created an enclave within all the others. Thus there was, of course, British Cairo, whose center was the embassy in Garden City and whose extensions covered academic, juridical, military, commercial, and recreational activities. French Cairo was there too, a useful foil and opposition for its historic colonial competitor, found in schools, salons, theaters, ateliers" (*Cairo Recalled*, 20).

1963–65: Instructor of English at Columbia University.

1964: Graduates with a Ph.D. in English literature from Harvard. The Palestinian Liberation Organization is created.

1965–67: Assistant professor of English at Columbia University.

—Israel pulls together the Arab and Israeli parts of Jerusalem, East Jerusalem and its people lead segregated lives, hemmed in by the increasing number of Israeli Jews who have taken up residence there. The disparity in power; the differences in culture, language, and tradition; and the accumulated hostilities of the past century, keep Jews and Arabs apart. The role of ideology and state politics among the charter group—the Jewish population—is a dominant factor in this social process.

1966: Visits Ramallah, part of the Jordanian West Bank, for a family wedding.

1967: The Arab-Israeli June War changes the entire map of the Arab Middle East. Israel attacks Egypt, Syria, and Jordan, occupies the Sinai region, East Jerusalem, the Gaza Strip, and the Golan Hights. The war ends with the (*Nakbah*) defeat of the Arabs. For the first time, Israel, which had been confined largely to the small boundaries of the state, had overflowed into Jordan taking the West Bank and Gaza, the Sinai, and the Golan Heights.

—Ignace Tiegerman—Said's music teacher—dies. "I was his piano student at the outset and, many years later, his friend," Said remembers with poignancy. "Tiegerman died in 1967, a few months after the June War" (*Cairo Recalled*, 32).

1967–68: Fellow at the Center for Advanced Study at the University of Illinois.

—The battle of Karameh sees a Zionist force faced with solid resistance from a

Palestinian guerilla group. It also marks the beginning of Said's emergence as an intellectual political activist.

1969: Said wins prize for best essay by the National Council of the Arts. Arafat becomes president of the PLO.

1970: "Black September" Palestinians flee to Lebanon—years of resistance begin.

1971: Wadie Said dies. "One episode," Said recalls, "from those days in the early Seventies provided disquieting indications of the troubles that were to come. After my father died in 1971, we planned to bury him according to his wishes in the mountain village he had loved since 1942. He was well known there and had been a benefactor of Dhour-el-Shweir in many ways. Most of the friends he had in Lebanon after he moved there in 1963 were men and women from the village. Yet when it came to buying a tiny bit of land in one of the local graveyards we had a grotesque time, the still angry memory of which prevents me from recounting it in detail. Suffice it to say that we were unable to conclude an agreement with any of the Christian churches in Dhour except one, and when that one accepted our offer we got so many telephone bomb threats as to end our plan completely. I realized that my father was an outsider, a Palestinian (*ghareeb*), a stranger, was the euphemism, and no matter how jolly they were when he was alive, the residents wouldn't tolerate his long-term presence after he had died" (*After the Last Sky*, 172).

—Said's mother would remain in shattered Beirut until her death. "My widowed mother valiantly hangs on all alone in her West Beirut house, quite sensibly focussed on the problems of her health, the failures of electricity and telephone service, the difficulties of getting help, the collapsing Lebanese pound" (*After the Last Sky*, 170).

1972–73: Receives Guggenheim Fellowship.

—On leave in Beirut. "I spent my first complete year in Beirut during 1972–73, and my still vivid recollection of that year is marked by a sense of how every-thing seemed possible in Beirut then—every kind of person, every idea and identity, every extreme of wealth and poverty—and how the incoherence of the whole seemed to abate and even disappear in either the pleasures or the agonies of the moment, a scintillating seminar discussion or a horrendously cruel Israeli raid on South Lebanon" (*After the Last Sky*, 172).

—Thanks to the Marxist Mikhail Hanna, Said meets with Jean Genet, the cele-brated French novelist, in Said's apartment in New York's Upper West Side. Speaking of the encounter, Said writes: "At first I thought he [Hanna] was joking since for me Genet was a giant of contemporary literature, and the likelihood of his paying me a visit was about as probable as one from Proust or Thomas Mann. 'No, Hanna said, I'm really serious; could we come now?' They appeared fifteen minutes later and stayed for several hours" (*Peace and Its Discontents*, 81).

—In Yom Kippur War Israel again defeats Egypt advancing to within one hundred

Kilometers from Cairo and thirty-six kilometers from Damascus. Arab countries limit oil exports.

1975: The Lebanon civil war starts. It pits the various sects, the Palestinians, and a number of Arabs and foreign powers against each other. The Americans refuse to speak with the PLO's representatives because Israel and Henry Kissinger have inserted a clause in the Sinai II agreement that stipulated that the United States will not deal with the PLO *unless* they meet certain conditions, which would in fact effectively eliminate them.

1976: Said is presented with the Lionel Trilling Award, Columbia University.

—Hanna Mikhail sacrifices his life in order that the principles and goals of the "Palestinian Revolution" (as it was then called) could be safeguarded and realized.

1977: A visit to Cairo lasts five days only. Too unhappy and too sick at heart to stay any longer, Said leaves with no wish to return.

1978: Director, NEH Summer Seminar on Literary Criticism.

—President Carter presides over the drafting of the Camp David agreement, which is signed by Israeli Prime Minister Begin and Egyptian President Sadat. The treaty was rejected by most Arab countries.

Orientalism comes out.

1979: The Iranian Revolution marks a new order in the Middle East. Israel signs a peace treaty with Egypt, handing back Sinai but keeping the Gaza Strip.

—*Orientalism* (1978), first turned down by a publisher, is now runner-up in the criticism category of the National Book Critics Circle Award.

—Visiting professor of humanities at Johns Hopkins University.

1981: Senior Fellowship, National Endowment for the Humanities.

—After Sadat's assassination and Israel's attacks on PLO and Syrian forces in Lebanon, Israel invades the Golan Heights.

1982: Chair of the doctoral program in comparative literature at Columbia University.

—Israel invades Lebanon. The Palestinians are no longer welcome there. They are put out to sea in boats distancing them from their land of origin. Officially the Palestinian link with Lebanon is severed in late August, when the PLO, led by Yasser Arafat, evacuates the city where it has been besieged by Israeli armies for three months.

—The invasion costs more than 17,500 lives, including the hundreds of Palestinians who are murdered at Sabra and Chatila camps. The murderers, Christian Lebanese militiamen, have been sent into the camp by the Israelis.

— Syrian President Hafaz Assad ruthlessly suppresses the Islamic uprising in the city of Hama. This makes him the only Arab leader to use military force to crush Fundamentalism.

—The Israeli army enters West Beirut and carts off documents and files from the Palestinian Research Center, before flattening the building. A few days later came the massacres of Sabra and Chatila.

1983: Sabra and Chatila massacres are revealed to the world.

1984: Said visits the former mayor of Jerusalem and his wife, in exile in (Amman) Jordan.

1984–85: René Wellek Award in literary theory; American Comparative Literature Association; visiting professor in the Department of Comparative Literature at Yale University; T. S. Eliot Lectures, University of Kent, Canterbury.

—Called a "Nazi" by the Jewish Defence League; his university office is set on fire.

—Israel raids PLO headquarters in Tunis: seventy people are killed. Israel withdraws from Lebanon but keeps control over twelve-mile-wide "security zone" in the south.

1986: Joseph Warren Beach Memorial Lecture, University of Minnesota; Messenger Lectures, Cornell University; Tamblyn Lectures, University of Western Ontario; Northrop Frye Chair at the University of Toronto.

—Said had hoped to take a trip to the West Bank and Gaza. He notes: "Some Israeli friends had promised to check the feasibility of this and to get me some assurances that I would be admitted, that I could move about safely, that I could leave when I wished. I had then planned to add a conclusion [to *After the Last Sky*] after my return. The idea was to have rounded out the photographs with the result of a direct encounter in Palestine with Palestinians, and with Israelis. But I still await conclusive news, and this uncertainty, I believe, is probably more congruent with my anomalous position, which is itself a reflection of the political ambiguities in which we are all caught" (*After the Last Sky*, 165–66).

1987: Janet Lee Stevens Award, University of Pennsylvania; William Matthews Lectures, Birbeck College, University of London.

—The Intifada, surely one of the most extraordinary uprisings in modern history, takes the world by surprise. What is interesting about the Intifada, among other things, is that it actually is a galvanizing Palestinian process for self-determination. As part of the uprising, Palestinian men and women take matters to resolve their difficult lives under Israeli military occupation into their own hands. Many would pay with their lives.

1988: Henry Stafford Little Lecture, Princeton University; Sears Lecture, Purdue University.

—Meets with Mahmoud Darwish, Palestine national poet, and the Lebanese writer Elias Khoury for the first time in six years at Algiers, to attend the meetings of the Palestine National Council (PNC). Darwish writes the Declaration of Statehood, which Said helps to redraft and translate into English. Along with the Declaration, the PNC approves resolutions in favor of two states in historical Palestine, one Arab, one Jewish, whose coexistence would assure self-determination for both peoples.

— Exiles, a BBC 2-six-part series features artists and writers who are exiled. The group includes Josef Skvorecky, the Czechoslovak novelist; Eric Fried, the

Austrian poet; Miriam Makeba, the South African singer; and Edward Said, the Palestinian scholar and literary theorist.

—Naguib Mahfouz is awarded the Nobel Prize for literature, the first Arab ever to be given the award.

—Abu Lughud and Said meet with Shultz in the State Department.

—Under the peace deal, King Hussein surrenders Jordan's claim to the West Bank. PNC renounces the armed struggle and accepts UN resolutions on allocation of land.

1989: Said becomes Old Dominion Foundation Professor in the humanities at Columbia University;

—Holds The Bayard Dodge Distinguished Visiting Professor—American University in Cairo, Cairo University.

—Lectures at Ain Shams University and gives the René Wellek Memorial Lectures, University of California-Irvine, George Antonius Lecture, Oxford University, and the First Annual Raymond Williams Memorial Lecture in England.

1990: Hilda Said dies. "My major, most painful regret is that—as the dedication of this book indicates—my mother died during its final preparation," Said observes. "It is to my mother's own wonderful musicality and love of the art that I owe my earliest interest in music. Over the years she has always been interested in my playing, and together we have shared many musical experiences. I am more sorry than I can say that, regardless of its flaws, she did not live to read this book and tell me what she thought" (*Musical Elaborations*, xi).

1991: T. B. Davie Academic Freedom Lecture, University of Cape Town; Edison Lecture, University of California, San Diego; Wilson Lecture, Wellesley College.

—Said withdraws from the PNC after serving as a member since 1977. He continues, however, to be involved in the affairs of Palestine.

—Finds himself writing a letter to his deceased mother, from the urge to make sense of his frenetic but seemingly ebbing life.

—George Bush launches Operation Desert Storm.

—President Bush declares that the Gulf War victory opens a "window of opportunity" for peace. Talks on key issues at Madrid Conference, begins the process that leads to the Oslo accords.

1992: University professor of English and comparative literature at Columbia University; Amnesty Lecture, Oxford University; Camp Lectures, Stanford University; Bertrand Russell Peace Lectures, McMaster University.

—Accompanied by his family, Said visits Palestine. It is his first visit since leaving East Jerusalem as a boy in late 1947.

—Emil Habibi, the Palestinian satirist and Israeli citizen, is awarded the Israeli Prize for literature.

—Baruch Goldstein, an Israeli terrorist, kills twenty-nine Palestinian worshippers in a Hebron mosque. Goldstein enters the mosque in Israeli army uniform carrying an Israeli army service rifle.

—Diagnosed by his doctor, Kanti Rai, as having leukemia, Said undergoes several medical treatments.

1993: D.H.L. at Birzeit University; Lord Northcliffe Lectures, University College, London; Wolfson Lecture, Wolfson College, Oxford University; Reith Lectures, BBC. "There is no equivalent for the Reith Lectures in the United States," Said writes, "although several Americans, Robert Oppenheimer, John Kenneth Galbraith, John Searle, have delivered them since the series was inaugurated in 1948 by Bertrand Russell. I had heard some of them over the air—I particularly remember Toynbee's series in 1950—as a boy growing up in the Arab world, where the BBC was a very important part of our life; even today phrases like 'London said this morning' are common refrain in the Middle East. They are always used with the assumption that 'London' tells the truth. Whether this view of the *BBC* is only a vestige of colonialism I cannot tell. I was therefore very honored to be offered the opportunity by Anne Winder of the BBC to give the 1993 Reith Lectures. . . . But almost from the moment that the announcement of the lectures was made by the BBC in late 1992 there was a persistent, albeit relatively small chorus of criticism directed at it for having invited me in the first place. I was accused of being active in the battle for Palestinian rights, and thus disqualified for any sober or respectable platform at all" (*Representations of the Intellectual*, ix–x).

—In April, Said gives duet recitals with the Lebanese pianist Diana Takiedine, in Washington and New York.

—Oslo I is signed.

—On September 13, Arafat and Rabin shake hands in front of the White House. Said, who is invited to participate in the ceremony, refuses to attend. "The fashion-show vulgarities of the White House ceremony," he remarks, "the degrading spectacle of Yasir Arafat thanking everyone for the suspension of most of his people's rights, and the fatuous solemnity of Bill Clinton's performance, like a 20th-century Roman emperor shepherding two vassal kings through rituals of reconciliation and obeisance: all these only temporarily obscure the truly astonishing proportions of the Palestinian capitulation" (*The Morning After*, 3).

—What is noteworthy about Arafat's Declaration of Principles is that the Palestinians who, like the Saids, lost their homes are dismissed in a single word, buried deep in article 5 of the agreement, which states that "permanent status negotiations"—to begin "as soon as possible"—will cover "remaining issues: Jerusalem, refugees, settlements, security arrangements, borders, relations and cooperation with other neighbors, and other items of common interest." Squeezed between Jerusalem and Jewish settlements, the "refugees" are a "remaining issue."

—The Israeli Army is responsible for the killing of 120 civilians and for driving 300,000 more refugees onto the road during a week-long bombardment of Southern Lebanon. An Israeli tank fires approximately ten shells filled with hundreds of "freshettes"—three-inch-long steel arrows—around the town of Nabatea, killing 7 civilians, 2 of them young girls.

—Knesset lifts the ban on contacts with the PLO, and Israel formerly recognizes the organization. Oslo agreement signed at the White House. Said is invited but refuses to attend.

1994: Said is awarded an honorary doctorate at the University of Chicago, receives the Lionel Trilling Award, Columbia University; Picasso Medal (UNESCO); delivers Kane Lecture, Ohio State University; gives the Gamini Salgado Lecture, University of Exeter; Olin Lecture, Cornell University; Honnold Lectures, Knox College.

—Speaks on "Arafat vs. Mandela" at an African Democratic Congress (ADC) Meeting.

—President Bill Clinton visits Gaza and the West Bank.

—Rabin, Peres, and Arafat receive Peace Prizes. Before the Nobel committee awards the prizes, one member resigns from his post, objecting to the awarding of the Peace Prize to Arafat on the grounds that the PLO leader had been a "terrorist."

—The Jordanian-Israeli peace treaty is signed at Wadi Araba.

—Naguib Mahfouz, the Egyptian Nobel Laureate, is stabbed by Muslim extremists in the streets of Cairo.

—Said begins working on his memoir, *Out of Place,* at the same time as he starts chemotherapy treatment.

—Israel-PLO agreements give Palestinians a first taste of self-rule since 1967. The deal calls for Israeli withdrawal but allows the army to stay in Jewish settlements in the Gaza Strip. Arafat returns to Gaza to rapturous welcome and takes charge of the Palestinian Authority. Israel-Jordan peace treaty is signed.

1995: Delivers "Palestine Authority and Occupation" at Tufts University.

—PLO charter scraps the call for Israel's destruction. Interim agreement on West Bank and Gaza Strip—Oslo II is signed. Israeli Prime Minister Izhak Rabin is assassinated by a student after peace rally.

—Sakakini Cultural Center is created in Ramallah.

1996: Visits Ramallah in March. "Today," Said observes, "it is the West Bank capital of the Palestinian Authority set up under Yasir Arafat as a direct result of the Israeli-PLO negotiations. Most of its Christian residents have been replaced by Muslims; it has considerably increased in size and is now full of office buildings, shops, restaurants, schools, institutes, and taxis, all catering to "al-Dafah," or "the Bank" as it is known.

—Invited by his son, Wadie, who works as a volunteer at an NGO, the Democracy and Workers' Rights Center (DWRC), to visit him in Palestine. He seizes the opportunity. "At the wheel," Said informs us, "Wadie seemed to have the native's sense of known, familiar space. It was the first time in our lives that I felt I was in his hands: I needed the feeling since I often felt disoriented and at a loss" (*In Arafat's Palestine*, 15).

—Yasser Arafat is elected president of Palestine.

—Israel shells the UN positions in Lebanon, killing ninety-six people.

—Benjamin Netanyahu is elected prime minister of Israel.

—Security forces reporting to Yasir Arafat seize all of Said's books from all bookstores in the Palestinian Autonomous Zones in Gaza and the West Bank. The sale of these books is forbidden back there and in Palestinian bookstores in East Jerusalem. A petition is spearheaded by Ronald Harwood, president of International PEN; Anne Hollander, president of PEN American Center; and Karen Kennerly, executive director of PEN American Center. The text reads as follows: "Edward Said is one of the most prominent, influential and admired of cultural critics. In particular, his writings about the Palestinian experience have been an essential instrument in shaping opinions in the United States, the United Kingdom, Europe and the Middle East that are favourably informed about the Palestinian cause. We therefore urge you in your own interests as well as in the interests of people everywhere to reaffirm his right to be heard in the areas where an effort has been made to silence him." The letter is signed by Adonis, K. Anthony Appiah, Paul Auster, Niels Barfoed, Mahmoud Darwish, Jacques Derrida, Gamal al-Ghitani, Allen Ginsberg, Günter Grass, David Grossman, Naguib Mahfouz, Kenzaburo Oe, Orhan Pamuk, Richard Poirier, Anton Shammas, Susan Sontag, Jean Stein, William Styron, Gore Vidal, Torsten Wiesel, and Saadi Youssef.

—Delivers "Authority and Transgression in Opera" at Cambridge University.

—Participates with Terry Eagleton and Camille Paglia in a debate on current literary theory.

—Tours India delivering lectures.

—Elected to serve for a term of three years, Arafat repeatedly postpones calling a new election, which would almost certainly present a serious challenge to his authority and popularity.

1997: Gives "Opera Opposed by Opera: *Così fan tutte* and *Fidelio*," at the Modern Language Association (MLA) meeting in Toronto.

—Joins a group of Palestinian writers, including Mahmoud Darwish, Gharib al-Askalani, Zaki al-Ileh, Azzedine al-Manacirah, Samih al-Qassim, Liana Badr, Riyad Beïdas, Sahar Khalifa, Elias Sanbar, Anton Shammas, and Fadwa Touqan, who read from their works, participate in round-table discussions and debates, and give public lectures in fifteen French cities as well as Brussells.

—Serves as second vice president for the MLA.

1998: Cooperates with Daniel Barenboim and the Chicago Symphony Orchestra on a production of *Fidelio*.

—Speaks about his own life and Joseph Conrad's at New York Public Library.

—Visits Gaza, the Occupied Territories, and Jerusalem, where he films *Edward Said: A Very Personal View of Palestine* for the BBC about the conditions of Palestinians two years after the signing of Oslo I and Oslo II. The film airs on 10 May.

—Travels to Dubai in the United Arab Emirates to receive Sultan Owais Prize in honor of his life's work. The Owais Prize, named after a wealthy Arab businessman, is the premier literary prize of the Arab world. Said is the only American to have received the honor.

—Lectures at the Third International Sabeel Conference on Liberation Theology on "The Challenge of the Jubilee," in Bethlehem.

—Meets with the Argentinian-born conductor and pianist Daniel Barenboim, who happened to be in Jerusalem at the same time. Interviewed by Said, Barenboim delcares that he supports a fully fledged Palsetinian state. (See Edward Said, "La Palestine n'a pas disparu," *Le Monde Diplomatique* [May 1998]: 1, 5.)

—At the MLA meeting in San Francisco, Said participates with Stephen Greenblatt, Rey Chow, and Homi Bhabha in a debate called "Globalizing Literary Study."

—With his Doctor, Kanti Rai (to whom with Said's wife Mariam *Out of Place* is jointly dedicated), reveals that Said has a rare form of leukemia, which has not responded to more than four years of chemotherapy and radiation. "It was depressing; my blood counts were astronomical," Said says. In the summer, he put himself through a grueling twelve-week clinical trial for an experimental drug treatment "in a Long Island Jewish hospital, by an Indian doctor, where all the nurses were Irish."

—Clinton holds meetings with Prime Minister Netanyahu and Chairman Arafat to revive the peace process. In October the Wye River Memorandum is signed. Clinton promises substantial new aid for the Palestinian Authority. On a visit to Palestine, Clinton witnesses a Palestinian Council vote "fully and forever" rejecting conflict with Israel.

1999: Elected MLA's first president, Said presents the MLA Prize for a distinguished bibliography, the William Riley Parker Prize, the James Russell Lowell Prize, the MLA Prize for a first book, the Kenneth W. Mildenberger Prize, the Mina P. Shaughnessy Prize, the MLA Prize for independent scholars, the Katherine Singer Kovacs Prize, the Howard R. Mararo Prize, and the Aldo and Jeanne Scaglione Prize for Italian literary studies, the Aldo Jeanne Scaglione Prize for French and Francophone literary studies, the Aldo and Jeanne Scaglione Prize for Germanic languages and literatures, and the Aldo and Jeanne Scaglione Prize for a translation of a literary work.

—Participates in "The Word: The London Festival Literature" (19–28 March). Reads with Tony Hanania, who launches his novel *Unreal City*. Discusses the role and engagement of the writer in society and political life with Nadine Gordimer and the preeminent Israeli novelist David Grossman. Gives a lecture titled "*Al Kalima*—or the 'Word' in Arabic: Where the World Meets the Word." This lecture addresses the globalization of literary study.

—On the eve of the publication of his keenly anticipated memoir of youth, *Out of Place*, a small right-wing New York magazine, *Commentary*, alleges that Said had through "30 years of carefully crafted deception" fabricated a childhood in Palestine so as to invent himself as a "living embodiment of the Palestinian cause." Justus Weiner's argument crumbles under even the mildest scrutiny, since much of it rests on his refusal to accord Said the right to call his time in Palestine "forma-tive," because his relatively affluent family had been able to move frequently among Palestine, Egypt, and Lebanon until 1948. Yet the spurious scholarship of this argument did not prevent newspapers from giving weight to its claims. Said found himself denounced as a liar and a fraud. *The Wall Street Journal* labeled him "The False Prophet of Palestine." "You feel tremendous anger when you read those lies," Said comments. "But I've trained myself to use a steely cold resolve to fight back rationally and calmly—though it's made easier by friends."

—*Out of Place*, the most intimately personal of his twenty books to date, and a "conscious effort at a more literary form," covers his life up to the early 1960s and forms a "record of a lost world." The initial spur of the memoir, commissioned in 1989, was personal grief: "My mother was dying [of cancer] at the time and I thought, there's an end to a special part of my life."

—Addresses a large crowd at the Institute of Contemporary Arts in London.

—Lectures at the Fifth International Conference for "The Scenarios of Pales-tine" at Birzeit University, Bethlehem.

—Visits Lebanon with his family and friends. In the course of the trip Said and his family take the opportunity to visit the evacuated "security zone" recently occupied by Israeli forces. Like many Arabs, the Saids shudder at the horrors of Khiam prison, built by Israel and used for the incarceration and (subsequently admitted) torture of Palestinian and Lebanese captives. Then the Saids drive to a deserted border post, abandoned by Israeli troops, and now crowded with festive Lebanese who are exuberantly throwing stones at the heavily fortified border. In competitive paternal emulation of his son, Said pitches a stone and is pho-tographed in the act of so doing. He is stunned at the consequences. Throw a rock at a border fence, and if you are a Palestinian called "Edward Said," you will be the object of viciously hostile articles in the media, you will face a campaign to be fired from your tenured job at Columbia, and your invitation from the Freud Institute and Museum in Vienna for a long-standing engagement to deliver the annual Freud lecture there in May 2001 will be canceled.

2000: In late July 2000, Said is invited by the director of the Freud Institute and Museum in Vienna. The invitation will be rescinded on 8 February 2001.

—Attends the Cheltenham Festival of Literature (October) in England organ-ized by Sarah Smyth.

—Following the publication of *Culture et impérialisme* in France, Said partici-pates in a panel organized by *Le Monde Diplomatique* and hosted by L'Institut du Monde Arabe.

—A visit by the right-wing opposition leader Ariel Sharon to Jerusalem's Al-Aqsa mosque compound, Islam's holiest shrine, sparks the spiral of violence. A terrified Mohammed al-Durrah, aged twelve, shelters beneath his father's arm from the Israeli Army who are shooting at random in Netzarim. Moments later, the boy lies dead.

—Said receives the year 2000 Anisfield-Woolf Book Award for non-fiction; the Mortion Dauwen Zabel Award in Literature conferred by the American Academy of Arts and Letters.

—In October, an Israeli army helicopter fires missiles in downtown Ramallah, killing civilians who are harmlessly going about their daily lives. A police station is smashed to rubble.

—Israel withdraws from South Lebanon after nearly two decades of ruthless occupation during which 20,500 civilians were killed. The Peace Summit at Camp David ends in failure. As clashes mount, Arafat meets Barak in Paris but refuses to sign an agreement, insisting on an international inquiry into the bloodshed. The UN is unanimous in condemning Israel's "excessive" use of force, but the United States abstains.

2001: Al-Aqsa Intifada begins in September following a provocative visit to Al-Harem A-Charif by Ariel Sharon.

—On 11 September, terror hits New York and Washington. Thousands of innocent people die as a result of the carnage.

—In late November, Ariel Sharon orders the murder of the Hamas leader Mahmoud Abu Hanoud, an act designed to provoke Hamas into retaliation and thus allow the Israeli army to resume the slaughter of innocent Palestinians.

—Said is awarded the Zoot Lannan Literary Award for Lifetime Achievement.

—Said—with Daniel Barenboim—is recognized in Spain through the Prince of Asturias Award for Concord—Spain's peace prize.

—Arafat is forbidden by Sharon to attend Christmas services in Bethlehem.

—During the night of 5 December, the Israeli army, a fabled beast by now, enters the five-storey offices of the Palestinian Central Bureau of Statistics in Ramallah and carries off the computers, as well as most of the files and reports, thereby effacing virtually the entire record of collective Palestinian life.

—Yasir Arafat is barred from attending the emergency meeting of the Islamic conference foreign ministers on 10 December in Qatar; his speech is read by an aide.

—A new secular nationalist bloc is formed. It includes Drs. Haidar Abdel Shafi, and Mustapha Barghouti, and Ibrahim Dakkak; Professors Ziad Abu Amr, Mamdouh al-Aker, Ahmad Harb, Ali Jabrawi, Fouad Moughrabi; Legislative Council members Rawiya al-Shawa and Kamal Shirafi; writers Hassan Khadr, Mahmoud Darwish, Raja Shehadeh, Rima Tarazi, Ghassan al-Khatib, Naseer Aruri, Elia Zureik, and Edward Said. In mid-December, the bloc issues a collective statement calling for Palestinian unity and resistance and the unconditional end of the Israeli occupation.

2002: In January, Marwan Barghouti is arrested, detained, interrogated, and brutalized by the Israeli army following a press conference he held with about twenty Europeans in East Jerusalem.

—In February, the French writer Hélène Cixous forwards a petition to the International Parliament of Writers. It is written by Lichael Kustow, an English dramatist, and is intended for writers and artists who wish to support Israeli soldiers refusing to serve in Israel's occupied territories.

—In March, a delegation of writers that includes Wole Soyinka, Russell Banks, Breyten Breytenbach, Bei Dao, Vincenzo Consolo, Juan Goytisolo, Christian Salmon, and José Saramago travels to Ramallah to meet the besieged Mahmoud Darwish. In the evening, Kamilia Jubran sings as part of the welcome extended to the delegation and is accompanied by Sabreen, a Palestinian group with sketches by comedians belonging to al-Kasaba. The delegation meets Abdallah Tayeb, the president of the Association of Writers in Gaza. Tayeb has been confined to Gaza since 1987 by the Israeli Army

—The International Parliament of Writers sends an appeal for peace in Palestine. More than five hundred signatories from more than thirty countries have signed the appeal, including Chinua Achebe, Adonis, Gamal Alghitany, Margaret Atwood, Paul Auster, Amiri Baraka, André Brink, Francis Ford Coppola, Anita Desai, Assia Djebar, Ariel Dorfman, Margaret Drabble, Edouard Glissant, Nedum Gürsel, Ted Honderich, Michael Holroyd, Eduardo Manet, Javier Marias, Carlos Monsivais, Augusto Montersso, Toni Morrison, Alvaro Mutis, Marie Ndiaye, Michael Ondaatje, Harold Pinter, Salman Rushdie, Charles Simic, Cornel West, and others.

—Tanks roll into Jenin (where the demolition of the refugee camp by Israelis, a major war crime, is never investigated because cowardly international bureacrats such as Kofi Annan back down when Israel threatens) fire upon and kill children, but that is only one drop in an unending flood of Palestinian civilian deaths caused by deranged and bloodthirsty Israeli soldiers. Palestinians are all "terrorist suspects."

—In April, the UN Security Council gives unanimous backing to the fact-finding team that is to visit the Jenin refugee camp to determine if a massacre was perpetrated on the civilian population by the Israeli army. Under pressure from the Israeli lobby, the team never leaves New York.

—In May, the Bush administration calls for a total ban on all of illegal Israeli settlements building while Israeli tanks and machine guns pound the Arab village of Beit Jala outside Bethlehem. More than five hundred people are brutally killed by the Army.

—In June, *The Accused* is aired on BBC1. The program demonstrates the involvement of Ariel Sharon in the Sabra and Chatila massacre of more than two thousand men, women, and children. According to the former chief prosecutor to the International Tribunal for Yugoslavia, Richard Goldstone, Ariel Sharon should face trial for war crimes in connection with the 1982 massacre.

—Today the Palestinians are locked up in 220 ghettos controlled by the Israeli army; Merkava tanks and American-supplied Apache helicopters and F-16s mow down people, houses, olive groves, and crops on a daily basis.

—Said spends more than three months in the hospital. The treatment he has to undergo takes its toll: painful procedures, blood transfusions, endless tests, draining fatigue, and recurrent infection, days and days of unproductive time spent staring at the ceiling.

—In October, Said is awarded the degree of Doctor Honoris Causa at the Lustrum Ceremony on the 50th Anniversary of the Institute of Social Studies, The Hague, The Netherlands.

BOOKS (by Said)
1966
Joseph Conrad and the Fiction of Autobiography (1966; rprt. Cambridge: Harvard University Press, 1968).
1975
Beginnings: Intention and Method (New York: Basic Books, 1975; New York: Columbia University Press, 1985; London: Granta Books, 1997).
1978
Orientalism (New York: Pantheon, 1978; New York: Vintage, 1994, with New Afterword).
1979
The Question of Palestine (New York: Times Books, 1979; New York: Vintage, 1992).
1980
Literature and Society, ed. (Baltimore: Johns Hopkins University Press, 1980).
1981
Covering Islam: How the Media and the Experts Determine How We See the Rest of the World (New York: Pantheon, 1981; New York: Vintage, 1996).
1983
The World, the Text, and the Critic (Cambridge: Harvard University Press, 1983).
Said et al., A Profile of the Palestinian People (Chicago: Palestine Human Rights Campaign, 1983).
1986
After the Last Sky: Palestinian Lives, photographs by Jean Mohr (New York: Pantheon, 1986).
1988
Blaming the Victims: Spurious Scholarship and the Palestinian Question, ed. with Christopher Hitchens (New York: Verso, 1988).
1990
Nationalism, Colonialism, and Literature (Minneapolis: University of Minnesota Press, 1990).
1991
Musical Elaborations (New York: Columbia University Press, 1991).
1993
Culture and Imperialism (New York: Knopf, 1993; New York: Vintage, 1994).
Peace in the Middle East (New York: New Press, 1993).

1994

Representations of the Intellectual (New York: Pantheon, 1994; New York: Vintage, 1996).

The Politics of Dispossession: The Struggle for Palestinian Self-Determination, 1969–1994 (New York: Pantheon, 1994; New York: Vintage, 1995).

1995

Peace and Its Discontents: Essays on Palestine in the Middle East Peace Process (New York: Vintage, 1995; New York: Vintage 1996).

1998

Entre guerre et paix (Paris: Gallimard, 1998).

1999

Out of Place: A Memoir (New York: Knopf, 1999).

2000

Reflections on Exile and Other Essays (Cambridge: Harvard University Press, 2000).

2001

Power, Politics, and Culture (New York: Pantheon, 2001).

2002

Parallels and Paradoxes, with Daniel Barenboim, (New York: Random House, 2002).

VIDEO RECORDINGS AND FILMS
1973

The Arabs Today: Alternatives for Tomorrow, co-ed. with Fuad Suleiman (Columbus, Ohio: Forum Associates, 1973).

1974

Arabs and Jews: Possibility of Concord, co-author with Daniel Berrigan and Israel Shahak (Association of Arab-American University Graduates, 1974).

1976

Two Studies on the Palestinians Today and American Policy, co-author with Ibrahim Abu-Lughod (AAUG, 1976).

1978

Reaction and Counter-Revolution in the Contemporary Arab World (AAUG, 1978).

The Arab Right Wing (AAUG Information Paper, 1978).

The Idea of Palestine in the West (MERIP Reports, 1978).

1979

The Palestine Question and the American Context (Beirut, Lebanon: Institute for Palestine Studies,1979).

Edward Said [Sound Recording PLO Series], (Los Angeles: Pacifica Tape Library, 1979).

1980

Writers in Conversation [Videorecording], (International Writers, 1980).

1983
A Profile of the Palestinian People, with others, (Palestine Human Rights Campaign, 1983).
1986
The Shadow of the West [Videorecording], (London: VATV Production, in Association with KUFIC Films, B.V., 1986).
1989
Edward Said's Challenge (Israel and Palestine Report, 1989).
1998
Edward Said: A Very Personal View of Palestine (broadcast in England on May 17, 1998).
2001
Self and Others. Produced by Salem Brahimi. Wamip Films. Al-Jazeera. 2001.

ARTICLES (BY SAID)
I have collected here, with their original titles, any articles that do not appear either in Said's books or in essays collected by others. They include reviews, journalistic, and scholarly essays.

"A Configuration of Themes," *The Nation* 30 May 1966.
"A Sociology of Mind," *Partisan Review* (Summer 1966).
"A Labyrinth of Incarnations," *Kenyon Review* (January 1967).
"Levi-Strauss and the Totalitarianism of Mind," *Kenyon Review* (March 1967).
"Endgames," *Book Week* 30 April 1967.
"Vico, Autodidact, and Humanist," *The Centennial Review* (Summer 1967).
"Sense and Sensibility," *Partisan Review* (Fall 1967).
"Beginnings," *Salmagundi* (Fall 1968).
"Swift's Tory Anarchy," *Eighteenth-Century Studies* (Fall 1969).
"Philology of *Weltliteratur*," trans. with Mariam Said, *Centennial Review* (Winter 1969).
"Amateur of the Insoluble: E. M. Cioran," *Hudson Review* (Winter 1969).
"Narrative: Quest for Origins and Discovery of the Mausoleum," *Salmagundi* (Spring 1970).
"A Palestinian Voice," *The Middle East Newsletter* (October–November 1970).
"A Standing Civil War," *Hudson Review* (Winter 1970).
"Notes on the Characterization of a Literary Text," *MLN* 85 (December 1970).
"Linguistics and the Archaeology of the Mind," *International Philosophical Quarterly* (March 1971).
"Les Palestiniens face aux responsabilités de la défaite," *Le Monde Diplomatique* (October 1971).
"*Abecedarium Culturae*: Structuralism, Absence, Writing," *TriQuarterly* (Winter 1971).

"What Is Beyond Formalism?" *MLN* 86 (December 1971).

"Al-Tamunu' wa al-Tajanub wa al-Ta'aruf," *Mawaqif* (March 1972).

"Eclecticism and Orthodoxy in Criticism," *Diacritics* (Spring 1972).

"Al-Yasar al-Amriki wa al-Qadaya al-Filastiniyyah," *Shu'un filistiniyyah* (April 1972).

"Michel Foucault as an Intellectual Imagination," *Boundary 2* (Summer 1972).

"Two without a Context," *The New York Times Book Review* 10 December 1972.

"A Response to Ihab Hassan," *Diacritics* (Spring 1973).

"United States Policy and the Conflict of Powers in the Middle East," *The Journal of Palestine Studies* (Spring 1973).

"Arabs and Jews," *The New York Times* Op-Ed Page, 14 October 1973.

"Getting to the Roots," *American Report* 26 November 1973.

"The Text as Practice and as Idea," *MLN* (December 1973).

"An Ethics of Language," *Diacritics* (Summer 1974).

"Maxime Rodinson's *Islam and Capitalism*," *The New York Times Book Review* 10 November 1974.

"Conrad: The Presentation of Narrative," *Novel: A Forum on Fiction* (Winter 1974).

"An Open Letter to the Israelis," *Newsweek International* 12 December 1974.

"Chomsky and the Question of Palestine," *Journal of Palestine Studies* (Spring 1975).

"Contemporary Fiction and Criticism," *TriQuarterly* (Spring 1975).

"Harold Bloom, *A Map of Misreading*," *The New York Times Book Review* 13 April 1975.

"The Text, the World, the Critic," *The Bulletin of the Midwest Modern Language Association* (Fall 1975).

"Raymond Schwab and Romance of Ideas," *Daedalus* (Winter 1976).

"Between Chance and Determinism," *TLS* 6 February 1976.

"Vico on the Discipline of Bodies and Texts," *MLN* 91 (October 1976).

"Arabs, Islam and the Dogmas of the West," *The New York Times Book Review* 31 October 1976.

"Roads Taken and Not Taken in Contemporary Criticism," *Contemporary Literature* (Summer 1976).

"Under Western Eyes," *TLS* 10 December 1976.

"Orientalism," *The Georgia Review* (Spring 1977).

"Palestinians," *The New York Times* Op-Ed Page 6 October 1977.

"Israel and the Controversial Palestinians," *Boston Globe* 27 December 1977.

"Rhetorical Questions," *New Statesman & Society* 12 May 1978.

"The Problem of Textuality: Two Exemplary Positions," *Critical Inquiry* (Summer 1978).

"Whose Islam?" *The New York Times* Op-Ed Page 29 January 1979.

"Islam, Orientalism and the West: An attack on Learned Ignorance," *Time Magazine* 16 April 1979.

"The Acre and the Goat," *New Statesman & Society* 11 May 1979.

"Palestinian Prospects Now," *Worldview* (May 1979).

"An Exchange on Deconstruction and History," *Boundary 2* (Fall 1979).

"Reflections on Recent American 'Left' Literary Criticism," *Boundary 2* (Fall 1979).

"The Palestinian Mission," *The New York Times* Op-Ed Page 19 November 1979.

"Zionism from the Standpoint of Its Victims," *Social Text* (Winter 1979).

"Tourism among the Dogs," *New Statesman and Society* 18 January 1980.

"Literary Lives," *The New York Times Sunday Book Review* 8 March 1980.

"Edward Lane—A Study of his Life and Work and of British Ideas of the Middle East in the 19th Century,"*Middle East Journal* (Spring 1980).

"The Palestine Question and the American Context," *Arab Studies Quarterly* (Spring 1980).

"Iran and the Media: Whose Holy War?" *Columbia Journalism Review* (March-April 1980).

"Islam through Western Eyes," *The Nation* 26 April 1980.

"Bitter Dispatches from the Third World," *The Nation* 3 May 1980.

"Looking beyond the Autonomy Talks," *Newsday* 18 May 1980.

"Crossing the Barrier," *New Statesman and Society* 17 June 1980.

"Responses to 'Carter and the Jews'-I," *New Leader* 11 August 1980.

"What's in the Future for the Palestinians?" *New Society* (December 1980).

"Inside Islam: How the Press Missed the Story in Iran," *Harper's Magazine* (January 1981).

"Grey Eminence," *LRB* 5–9 March 1981.

"Palestinians in the U.S.," *Manchester Guardian* 23 March 1981.

"A Changing World Order: The Arab Dimension," *Arab Studies Quarterly* (Spring 1981).

"The Arabs Should Face Their Real Priorities," *The New York Times* Op-Ed Page 21 June 1981.

"The Death of Sadat," *Los Angeles Times* Op-Ed Page 11 October 1981.

"Among the Believers," *New Statesman and Society* 16 October 1981.

"Expectations of Inferiority," *New Statesman and Society* 16 October 1981.

"Reflections on Palestinian Self-Determination," *The Nation* 5 December 1981.

"Lord Kim," *Inquiry* 7 and 21 December 1981.

"Susan Sontag's *God That Failed*," *Soho* 24 February–2 March 1982.

"Blind Alleys on the Road to a Satisfactory Peace," *Manchester Guardian* 24 March 1982.

"Adding to the Mythology—Reply," *The Nation* 5 May 1982.

"Begin's Zionism Grinds On," *The New York Times* Op-Ed Page 11 June 1982.

"Perhaps, a Stiffening of Palestinian Will," *Los Angeles Times* 20 June 1982.

"L'Ignorance américaine," *Le Monde* 16 July 1982.

"Response to Bernard Lewis," *The New York Review of Books* 12 August 1982.

"Opponents, Audiences, Constituencies and Community," *Critical Inquiry* (Fall 1982).

"Idea of Palestine Hounds Zionists," *The Times* 8 September 1982.

"'Purifying,' Israelis Called It," *The New York Times* Op-Ed Page 29 September 1982.

"Travelling Theory," *Raritan* (Winter 1982).

"Bursts of Meaning: *Another Way of Telling*," *The Nation* 4 December 1982.

"From the Ashes of Beirut," *New Statesman and Society* 17–24 December 1982.

"The Music Itself: Glenn Gould's Contrapuntal Vision," *Vanity Fair* (May 1983).

"Losses in Lebanon," *The New York Times* Op-Ed Page 10 June 1983.

"A New Literature of the Arab World," *LRB* 7–20 June 1983.

"The Deprivation," *al-Karmel* (Summer 1983).

"Egyptian Rites," *The Village Voice* 30 August 1983.

"Literature as Values," *The New York Times Sunday Book Review* 4 September 1983.

"*Hanna K*: Palestine with a Human Face," *The Village Voice* 11 October 1983.

"Solidly behind Arafat," *The New York Times* Op-Ed Page 15 November 1983.

"Profession Despise Thyself: Fear and Self-Loathing in Literary Studies," *Critical Inquiry* (Winter 1983).

"Secular Criticism," *Raritan* (Winter 1983).

"Palestinians in the Aftermath of Beirut: A Preliminary Stocktaking," *Journal of Palestine Studies* (Winter 1983).

"The Making of a Writer," *The New York Times Sunday Book Review* 11 December 1983.

"Jackson's Heresy Is Arguing That Arabs Have a Case," *Los Angeles Times* Op-Ed Page 8 January 1984.

"Our Lebanon," *The Nation* 18 February 1984.

"Permission to Narrate," *Journal of Palestine Studies* (Spring 1984).

"Michel Foucault, 1927–1984," *Raritan* (Fall 1984).

"The Future of Criticism," *MLN* 99 (September 1984).

"The Mind of Winter: Reflections on a Life in Exile," *Harper's Magazine* (September 1984).

"Seeing through the Story," *TLS* 12 October 1984.

"Reflections on Exile," *Granta 13* (Winter 1984).

"In the Shadow of the West," *Wedge* (Winter/Spring 1985).

"Himself Observed," *The Nation* 2 March 1985.

"La Critique littéraire avancée et le monde extérieur," *Critique* (May 1985).

"Who Would Speak for the Palestinians?" *The New York Times* 24 May 1985.

"The Fall of Beirut," *LRB* 4 July 1985.

"Orientalism Reconsidered," *Cultural Critique* (Fall 1985).

"An Ideology of Difference," *Critical Inquiry* (Fall 1985).

"Neglected Fiction," *TLS* 18 October 1985.

"Conspiracy of Praise," *The Nation* 19 October 1985.

"How Not to Get Gored," *LRB* 21 November 1985.

"The Enduring Romance of the Pianist," *Harper's Magazine* (November 1985).

"Beirut Elegy," *Harper's Magazine* (January 1986).

"Afdal Tariqah li Ikhtiraq al-Aql al-Amriki," *Al-Majalla* 5 February 1986.

"Michael Walzer's *Exodus and Revolution*: A Canaanite Reading," *Grand Street* (Winter 1986).

"Al-Jami'at al-Amrikiyyah wa al-Alam," *Al-Majalla* 12 March 1986.

"Al-I'lam al-Amriki wa al-Sultah," *Al-Majalla* 23 April 1986.

"Intellectuals in the Post-colonial World," *Salmagundi* (Spring-Summer 1986).

"America in Libya," *LRB* 8 May 1986.

"Tankar om exil," *Ord och bild* 1 (1986).

"Dreams of Omniscience," *TLS* 30 May 1986.

"The Essential Terrorist," *The Nation* 14 June 1986.

"Al-I'lam al-Amriki wa al-Mu'aradah," *Al-Majalla* 26 June 1986.

"Terrorism: How the West Can Win," *The Nation* 7 July 1986.

"Bada'il min Amriki al-Rasmiyyah," *Al-Majalla* 30 July 1986.

"Pomp and Circumstance," *The Nation* 30 August 1986.

"Thalathat Wujuh li Amrika," *Al-Majalla* 9 September 1986.

"The Horizon of R. P. Blackmur," *Raritan* (Fall 1986).

"The Burdens of Interpretation and the Question of Palestine," *Journal of Palestine Studies* (Fall 1986).

"Al-Sabr al-Arabi," *Al-Majalla* 15 October 1986.

"On Richard Strauss," *The Nation* 25 October 1986.

"Reticences of an Orientalist," *The Guardian* 21 November 1986.

"On Palestinian Identity: A Conversation with Salman Rushdie," *New Left Review* (November/December 1986).

"Al-Siyasah al-Thaqafiyyah," *Al-Majalla* 3 December 1986.

"Die Walküre, Aida, X," *The Nation* 6 December 1986.

"Books and the Arts: Our Holiday Lists," *The Nation* 27 December 1986.

"The Scholars, the Media and the Middle-East," *Journal of Palestine Studies* (Winter 1987).

"The Imperial Spectacle ('*Aida*')," *Grand Street* (Winter 1987).

"Al-Arab fi Amrika: Kharitah Musahhahah," *Al-Majalla* 5 February 1987.

"Music and Feminism," *The Nation* 7 February 1987.

"Interpreting Palestine," *Harper's Magazine* (March 1987).

"Maestro for the Masses," *The New York Times Book Review* 8 March 1987.

"Azmat Za'amah," *Al-Majalla* 11 March 1987.

"A Jew without Jewishness," *The Guardian* 13 March 1987.

"Middle Age and Performers," *The Nation* 14 March 1987.

"Cairo Recalled," *House and Garden* (April 1987).

"Limadha Ta'mal Qillah min al-Amrikiyyin al-Arab li Hisab al-Sihyuniyyah," *Al-Majallah* 29 April 1987.

"The Vienna Philharmonic: The Complete Beethoven Symphonies and Concertos," *The Nation* 9 May 1987.

"Khayarat Amriki," *Al-Majalla* 17 June 1987.

"Muhakamat Barbi wa Musamahat Isra'il," *Al-Majalla* 22 July 1987.

"Irangate—A Many Sided Story," *Journal of Palestine Studies* (Summer 1987).

"*The Barber of Seville* and *Don Giovanni,*" *The Nation* 26 September 1987.

"Asbab al-Taraju' al-Arabi," *Al-Majalla* 30 September 1987.

"L'Irangate, une crise aux multiples facettes," *Revue d'études palestiniennes* (Fall 1987).

"Bemerkungen zum Selbstverstaendnis der Palaestinenser," *Ethnologica* 13 (1987).

"Shaja'at Siyasah Kharijiyyah Muflasah," *Al-Majalla* 28 October 1987.

"Glenn Gould and the Metropolitan Museum," *The Nation* 7 November 1987.

"U.S. Media Portrays Palestinians as Terrorists," *The Guardian* 14 November 1987.

"Al-Istishraq wa al-Sihuniyyah," *Al-Majalla* 2 December 1987.

"Miami Twice," *LRB* 10 December 1987.

"The Media and Cultural Identity: National Authority or Exilic Wandering?" *Europeans and Arabs in Dialogue 3* 17 December 1987.

"Qissatuna Allati La Ya'rifuha al-Alam," *Al-Majalla* 30 December 1987.

"Spurious Scholarship and the Palestinian Question," *Race and Class* (Winter 1988).

"Some Satisfactions for the Palestinians," *The New York Times* 8 January 1988.

"Last Dispatches from the Border Country: Raymond Williams 1921–1988," *The Nation* 14 February 1988.

"Alexander the Brilliant," *LRB* 18 February 1988.

"Al-I'lam al-Gharbi wa Isa'at Tawdif al-Arqam," *Al-Majalla* 2 March 1988.

"Through Gringo Eyes: With Conrad in Latin America," *Harper's Magazine* (April 1988).

"What Camus Forgot Too: André Gide's Adventures in North Africa," *Conde Nast's Traveler* (April 1988).

"Wedding in Galilee and Friendship's Death," *The Nation* 28 May 1988.

"The Voice of a Palestinian in Exile," *Third Text* (Spring/Summer 1988).

"Arafat Agenda," *New Statesman and Society* 15 June 1988.

"Al-Qadiyyah al-Filastiniyyah fi Intikhabat al-asah al-Amrikiyyah," *Al-Majalla* 17 August 1988.

"How to Answer Palestine's Challenge?" *Mother Jones* (September 1988).

"Aqlam Isra'iliyyah Tantaqid al-Tarikh al-Isra'ili al-Muzawwar," *Al-Majalla* 28 September 1988.

"Identity, Negation and Violence," *New Left Review* (September/October 1988).

"News of the World," *Village Voice Literary Supplement* (October 1988).

"Al-Intifadah al-Filastiniyyah wa Wasa'il al-I'lam," *Al-Majalla* 27 November 1988.

"Ma Dakhal Isra'il fi Ja'izat Najib Mahfouz," *Al-Majalla* 6 November 1988.

"Giulio Cesare," *The Nation* 14 November 1988.

"Goodbye to Mahfouz," *LRB* 8 December 1988.

"Palestine Agenda," *The Nation* 12 December 1988.

"Marhalat al-Jaza'ir wa ma Ba'daha," *Al-Majalla* 21 December 1988.

"Farval till Mahfouz," *Ord och Bild* 4 (1989).

"Representing the Colonized: Anthropology's Interlocutors," *Critical Inquiry* (Winter 1989).

"Ta'ammulat Nihayat al-Am," *Al-Majalla* 11 January 1989.

"Uqdah Tarikiyyah fi al-Ilaqat al-Kharijiyyah al-Amrikiyya," *Al-Majalla* 15 February 1989.

"Lawrence Doesn't Do Arabs any Favors," *Wall Street Journal* 21 February 1989.

"Bluebeard's Castle" and "Erwartung," *The Nation* 6 March 1989..

"Al-Tahawwul min Halat al-Harb ila Halah Ukhra," *Al-Majalla* 22 March 1989.

"*The Satanic Verses* and Democratic Freedoms," *The Black Scholar* (March/April 1989).

"'*Falstaff*: Daniel Barenboim Conducts," *The Nation* 10 April 1989.

"Intiba'at an Misr," *Al-Majalla* 26 April 1989.

"*The Black Jacobins*: Toussaint L'Ouverture and the San-Domingo Revolution," *New Left Review* (May/June 1989).

"C.L.R. James: A Life Beyond the Boundaries," *New Left Review* (May/June) 1989.

"Wasa'il al-I'lam," *Al-Majalla* 7 June 1989.

"Tartibat Mu'aqqatah," *Al-Majalla* 14 June 1989.

"Extreme Occasions," *The Nation* 26 June 1989.

"Sanctum of the Strong," *The Nation* 10 July 1989.

"Afkar min Wahy Murur Mi'atay Am ala al-Thawrah al-Faransiyyah," *Al-Majalla* 25 July 1989.

"Sira al-Thaqafat," *Al-Majalla* 29 August 1989.

"Sanctum of the Strong," *The Nation* 2 September 1989.

"Peter Sellar's Mozart," *The Nation* 18 September 1989.

"Min Beirut ila al-Quds' Kitab Murib an al-Sharq al-Awsat," *Al-Majalla* 10 October 1989.

"Palestine and Israel in the U.S. Arena," *Middle East Report* 5-6 (1989).

"The Orientalist Express: Thomas L. Friedman Wraps up the Middle East," *The Village Voice* 17 October 1989.

"Sahatan Muhimmatan li Taqrir al-Masir," *Al-Majalla* 14 November 1989.

"Uprising," *The Weekend Guardian* 16–17 December 1989.

"Andras Schiff at Carnegie Hall," *The Nation* 25 December 1989.

"Al-Hurriyah wa al-Muqawamah," *Al-Majalla* 26 December 1989.

"Al-Ilaqah al-Khassah Bayna al-Mufakkir wa al-Afkar," *Al-Majlla* 30 December 1989.

"Third World Intellectuals and Metropolitan Culture," *Raritan* (Winter 1990).

"*Kim*: The Pleasures of Imperialism," *Raritan* (Winter 1990).

"Khawatir min Wahy Nihayat al-Aqd," *Al-Majalla* 9 January 1990.

"The Need for Self-Appraisal," *Al-Fajr* 5 February 1990.

"An Nelson Mandela wa Akharin," *Al-Majalla* 13 March 1990.

"Richard Strauss," *The Nation* 19 March 1990.

"Narrative, Geography and Interpretation," *New Left Review* (March–April 1990).

"Isham al-Arab fi al-Thaqafah al-Alamiyyah," *Al-Majalla* 3 April 1990.

"Al-Tis'inat wa Ma ba'dhaha," *Al-Majalla* 8 May 1990.

"Cairo and Alexandria," *Departures* (May/June 1990).

"Taghyir Kabir fi al-Ra'y al'Amriki," *Al-Majalla* 5 June 1990.

"Wagner and the Met's Ring," *The Nation* 18 June 1990.

"On Jean Genet's Late Works," *Grand Street* (Summer 1990).

"Figures, Configurations, Transfigurations," *Race and Class* (July/September 1990).

"Al-Hiwar Lam Yufid Munaddamat al-Tahrir wa La al-Wilayayt al-Muttahidah," *Al-Majalla* 8 August 1990.

"Tragically, a Closed Book to the West," *The Independent on Sunday* 12 August 1990.

"Fuelling the Arab Fire Next Time," *The Observer* 12 August 1990.

"Behind Saddam Hussein's Moves," *Christian Science Monitor* 13 August 1990.

"Saddam Husayn Wahdahu Saddada Darbah Murwi'ah ila al-Intifadah al-Filastiniyyah," *Al-Majalla* 5 September 1990.

"Arabesque," *New Statesman and Society* 7 September 1990.

"A propos de la guerre du Golfe," *Peuples meditérranéens* 7–12 (1990).

"Homage to a Belly-Dancer," *LRB* 13 September 1990.

"Embargoed Literature," *The Nation* 17 September 1990.

"Heroes of Muscular Judaism," *The Washington Post Book World* 23 September 1990.

"Shah of Blah Rules OK," *The Independent on Sunday* 23 September 1990.

"The Intellectuals and the War," *Middle East Report* 7-8 (1991).

"Arabs Surrender to a War Psychosis," *The Observer* 6 January 1991.

"Opera Productions: *'Der Rosenkavalier, House of the Dead, Doctor Faust*,'" *The Nation* 7 January 1991.

"A Tragic Convergence," *The New York Times* 11 January 1991.

"Ignorant Armies Clash by Night," *The Nation* 11 February 1991.

"The Splendid Tapestry of Arab Life," *Los Angeles Times* 17 February 1991.

"An American and an Arab Writes on the Eve of the Iraqi-Soviet Peace Talks," *LRB* 7 March 1991.

"Les derniers écrits de Jean Genet," *Revues d'études palestiniennes* (Printemps 1991).

"In the Name of Prejudice," *Index on Censorship* 4/5 (1991).

"A Plan for Palestinian Self-Determination," *The Washington Post* 17 March 1991.

"Style and Stylessness: *Elektra, Semiramide, Katya, Kabanova*," *The Nation* 6 May 1991.

"Living among the Palestinians," *The Washington Post Book World* 3–9 June 1991.

"Reflections on Twenty Years of Palestinian History," *Journal of Palestine Studies* (Summer 1991).

"The Politics of Knowledge," *Raritan* (Summer 1991).

"Patriotism," *The Nation* 15 July 1991.

"Alfred Brendel: Words for Music," *The Washington Post Book World* 18 August 1991.

"Art and National Identity: A Critic's Symposium," *Art in America* (September 1991).

"Razón moral y dedicación," *El País* 31 October 1991.

"Opera and Cultural Politics," *The Nation* 11 November 1991.

"*Die Tote Stadt, Fidelio, The Death of Klinghoffer*," *The Nation* 11 November 1991.

"On Board the 'Fiona,'" *LRB* 19 December 1991.

"Our Holiday Lists," *The Nation* 30 December 1991.

"Peace in the Middle East," *Journal of Communication Inquiry* (Winter 1992).

"There Is an Obvious Flaw in U.S. Peace Role," *Al-Fajr* 6 January 1992.

"Wagner, Nazism and the Israeli Soul," *The New York Times* 12 January 1992.

"Uncertainties of Style," *The Nation* 9 March 1992.

"Paulin's People," *LRB* 9 April 1992.

"The Anglo-Arab Encounter," *TLS* 19 June 1992.

"Iphigenia at Aulis and *The Bacchae*," *Grand Street* (Summer 1992).

"The New World Order and Middle East Peace," *The Guardian* 30 September 1992.

"Musical Retrospection," *The Nation* 26 October 1992.

"Palestine, Then and Now: An Exile's Journey through Israel and the Occupied Territories," *Harper's Magazine* (December 1992).

"Nationalism, Human Rights, and Interpretation," *Raritan* (Winter 1993).

"Arabs and Americans: Toward the Twenty-First Century," *Mideast Monitor* (Winter 1993).

"Hudud al-Ta'awin bayna al-Filastiniyyin wa al-Isra'ilyyin," *Al-Hayat* 7 January 1993.

"Summer Music Festivals," *The Nation* 25 January 1993.

"The Bard Festival," *The Nation* 25 January 1993.

"The Importance of Being Unfaithful to Wagner," *LRB* 11 February 1993.

"The Wreck of Nations," *The Washington Post Book World* 21 February 1993.

"Orientalism and After," *Radical Philosophy* (Spring 1993).

"The Phony Islamic Threat," *The New York Times Magazine* 21 June 1993.

"Man al-Mas'ul an al-Madi wa al-Mustaqbal?'" *Al-Hayat* 12 September 1993.

"Intellectual Exile: Expatriates and Marginals," *Grand Street* (Fall 1993).

"Arafat's Deal," *The Nation* 20 September 1993.

"The Morning After," *LRB* 21 October 1993.

"Jean Genet: The Miracle of Prose," *The Washington Post Book World* 14 November 1993.

"Retour au pays," *Revue d'études palestiniennes* (Winter 1993).

"Haqa'iq, Haqa'iq, Mazid Min al-Haqa'iq," *Al-Hayat* 10 December 1993.

"On Mahmoud Darwish," *Grand Street* (Winter 1994).

"Music as Gesture," *The Nation* 17 January 1994.

"Al-Istimar ala Hadha al-Hal," *Al-Hayat* 18 January 1994.

"Influences," *New Statesman and Society* 21 January 1994.

"Mufaraqat Amrikiyyah," *Al-Hayat* 2 February 1994.

"Haqa'iq Marirah an Ghazzah," *Al-Hayat* 3 March 1994.

"Gods That Always Fail," *Raritan* (Spring 1994).

"Further Reflections on the Hebron Massacre," *LRB* 7 April 1994.

"The Bernard Lewis Case," *Al-Hayat* 22 April 1994.

"Hal Sar al-salam fi al-Mutanawal?" *Al-Hayat* 6 May 1994.

"The Symbols and Realities of Power," *Al-Ahram Weekly* 9 June 1994.

"*Les Troyens,*" *The Nation* 27 June 1994.

"Winners and Losers," *Al-Ahram Weekly* 30 June 1994.

"At Miss Whitehead's," *LRB* 7 July 1994.

"The American 'Peace Process,'" *Al-Ahram Weekly* 4 August 1994.

"Identity, Authority, and Freedom: The Potentate and the Traveler," *Boundary 2* (Fall 1994).

"Tahrir al-Aql Awwalan," *Al-Hayat* 16 September 1994.

"A Cold and Ungenerous Peace," *Al-Ahram Weekly* 29 September 1994.

"*Hamas* Paves the Way for a New *Intifada,*" *Los Angeles Times* 20 October 1994.

"Violence for a Good Cause," *Al-Ahram Weekly* 27 October 1994.

"Victimes consentantes," *Le Monde Diplomatique* (Novembre 1994).

"Changes for the Worse," *Al-Ahram Weekly* 24 November 1994.

"Two Peoples in One Land," *Al-Ahram Weekly* 22 December 1994.

"The Palestinian Case against Arafat," *The Washington Post* 25 December 1994.

"Symbol versus Substance: A Year after the Declaration of Principles," *Journal of Palestine Studies* (Winter 1995).

"Orientalism, an Afterward," *Raritan* (Winter 1995).

"Sober Truth about Israel and Zionism," *Al-Ahram Weekly* 26 January 1995.

"East Isn't East: The Impending End of the Age of Orientalism," *TLS* 3 February 1995.

"What Is Islam?" *New Statesman and Society* 10 February 1995.

"Memory and Forgetfulness," *Al-Ahram Weekly* 23 February 1995.

"Contra Mundum," *LRB* 9 March 1995.

"New World Orders for Old," *al-Ahram Weekly* 6 April 1995.

"The American Media on a Spree," *Al-Ahram Weekly* 4 May 1995.

"Child's Play," *The New Yorker* 13 May 1995.

"Taking the First Step," *Al-Ahram Weekly* 25 May 1995.

"al-Quds: Qissat Istilâb Arabiyyah," *Al-Hayat* 7 August 1995.

"al-I'tidhârât wa al-Ta'widât: Kam wa Ilâ Matâ?" *Al-Hayat* 26 August 1995.

"Projecting Jerusalem," *Journal of Palestine Studies* (Fall 1995).

"Bach's Genius, Schumann's Eccentricity, Chopin's Ruthlessness, Rosen's Gift," *LRB* 21 September 1995.

"Cry Palestine," *New Statesman and Society* 10 November 1995.

"On the Concealed Side," *TLS* 1 December 1995.

"Jabra Ibrahim Jabra: A Kindly Sage," *Al-Ahram Weekly* 29 December 1995.

"A Configuration of Themes," *The Nation* 30 May 1996.

"Fantasy's Role in the Making of Nations," *TLS* 9 August 1996.

"In Arafat's Palestine," *LRB* 5 September 1996.

"An Intifadha against Betrayal, Despair," *Los Angeles Times* 2 October 1996.

"The Real Meaning of the Hebron Agreement," *Journal of Palestine Studies* (Spring 1997).

"Theater, Opera, and Society: The Director's Perspective," *Grand Street* (Summer 1997).

"In the Chair," *LRB* 17 July 1997.

"*Così fan tutte* at the Limits," *Grand Street* (Fall 1997).

"From Silence to Sound and Back Again: Music, Literature, and History," *Raritan* (Fall 1997).

"An Orgy of Racist Fantasy and Sexual Peeping Tom-ism," *Al-Ahram* 5 September 1997.

"Bombs and Bulldozers," *The Nation* 8 September 1997.

"On *Fidelio*," *LRB* 30 October 1997.

"Between Worlds," *LRB* 7 May 1998.

"La Palestine n'a pas encore disparu," *Le Monde Dipolomatique* (May 1998).

"An Orphaned People," *The Nation* 4 May 1998.

"Daniel Barenboim and Edward Said: A Conversation," *Raritan* (Summer 1998).

"Fifty Years of Dispossession," *Harper's Magazine* (October 1998).

"On Writing a Memoir," *LRB* 29 April 1999.

"Really, Now—What's Next?" *Al-Ahram* 16 June 1999.

"The Treason of the Intellectuals," *Al-Ahram* 30 June 1999.

"John McEnroe Plus Anyone," *LRB* 1 July 1999.

"Private Planes, Power and Privilege," *Al-Ahram* 28 July 1999.

"Refusal to Surrender Quietly," *Al-Ahram* 11 August 1999.

"Defamation, Zionist Style," *Al-Ahram* 26 August 1999.

"I Left Cairo for What I Felt Was My American Banishment," *The Observer* 29 August 1999.

"Hey, Mister, You Want Dirty Books?" *LRB* 30 September 1999.
"Leaving Palestine," *New York Books Review* (September 1999).
"Paying the Price for Personal Politics," *Al-Ahram* 6 October 1999.
"By Birth or by Choice?" *Al-Ahram* 13 October 1999.
"In Memory of Tahia," *LRB* 28 October 1999.
"Millennial Reflections: Heroism and Humanism," *Al-Ahram* 12 January 2000.
"How Long Can Waiting Work?" *Al-Ahram* 2 February 2000.
"The Right of Return, at Last," *Al-Ahram* 16 February 2000.
"A Truly Fragile Identity," *Al-Ahram* 29 March 2000.
"Jean-Paul Sartre and the Arabs," *Dawn* 14 May 2000.
"A New Kind of Thriller," *Dawn* 24 May 2000.
"Israel Needs Realism to Find Its Way in an Arab World," *LA Times* 31 May 2000.
"My Encounter with Sartre," *LRB* 1 June 2000.
"The Landscape of Opposition," *Al-Ahram* 14 June 2000.
"Magic Thought and Wishful Thinking," *Al-Ahram* 5 July 2000.
"Dark at the End of the Tunnel," *Al-Ahram* 26 July 2000.
"One More Chance," *Al-Ahram* 9 August 2000.
"A Voice Crying in the Wilderness," *Al-Ahram* 30 August 2000.
"Problems of Neoliberalism," *Al-Ahram* 13 September 2000.
"American Zionism—the Real Problem," *Al-Ahram* 27 September 2000.
"The Special Relationship: The Arabs and the United States," *CCAS* 5 October 2000.
"More on American Zionism," *Al-Ahram* 11 October 2000.
"Double Standards," *The Guardian* 12 October 2000.
"The End of Oslo," *The Nation* 13 October 2000.
"American Zionism," *Al-Ahram* 8 November 2000.
"The Cruelty of Memory," *New York Review of Books* 30 November 2000.
"The Tragedy Deepens," *Al-Ahram* 13 December 2000.
"Palestinians Under Siege," *LRB* 14 December 2000.
"American Elections: System or Farce?" *Al-Ahram* 27 December 2000.
"Scoundrel Times Indeed," *Al-Ahram* 29 December 2000.
"Trying again and again," *Al-Ahram* 17 January 2001.
"Too Much Work," *Al-Ahram* 7 February 2001.
"Where Is Israel Going?" *Al-Ahram* 14 February 2001.
"The Only Alternative," *Al-Ahram* 7 March 2001.
"Freud, Zionism, and Vienna," *Al-Ahram* 21 March 2001.
"Time to Turn to the Other Front," *Al Ahram* 4 April 2001.
"These Are the Realities," *Al-Ahram* 25 April 2001.
"Thinking about Israel," *Al-Ahram* 3 May 2001.
"Defiance, Dignity, and the Rule of Dogma," *Al-Ahram* 23 May 2001.
"Enemies of the State," *Al-Ahram* 27 June 2001.
"Sharpening the Axe," *Al-Ahram* 11 July 2001.
"The Price of Camp David," *Al-Ahram* 25 July 2001.

"Innocents Face Endless Cruelty without End," *The Guardian Unlimited* 12 August 2001.

"Occupation Is the Atrocity," *Al-Ahram* 16 August 2001.

"Propaganda and war," *Al-Ahram* 6 September 2001.

"Islam and the West Are Inadequate Banners," *The Guardian* 16 September 2001.

"The Public Role of Intellectuals," *The Nation* 17 September 2001.

"The Desertion of Arafat," *New Left Review* 17 September 2001.

"Collective Passion," *Al-Ahram* 26 September 2001.

"Backlash and Backtrack," *Al-Ahram* 3 October 2001.

"The Clash of Ignorance," *The Nation* 22 Ocotober 2001.

"Suicidal Ignorance," *Al-Ahram* 21 November 2001.

"Naguib Mahfouz and the Cruelty of Memory," *CounterPunch* 16 December 2001.

"Israel's Dead End," *Al-Ahram* 26 December 2001.

"A Living Idea," *Al-Ahram* 27 December 2001.

"Is Israel More Secure Now?" *CounterPunch* 4 January 2002.

"Emerging Alternatives in Palestine," *CounterPunch* 14 January 2002.

"The Screw Turns, Again," *Al-Ahram* 6 February 2002.

"Committed Scholar: Pierre Bourdieu (1930–2002)," *Al-Ahram* 14 February 2002.

"Thoughts about America," *Al-Ahram* 6 March 2002.

"What Price Oslo?" *Al-Ahram* 14 March 2002.

"Thinking Ahead," *Al-Ahram* 4 April 2002.

"What Israel Has Done," *Al-Ahram* 18 April 2002.

"Palestinian Elections," *Al-Ahram* 13 June 2002.

"One Way Street," *Al-Ahram* 11 July 2002.

"Punishment by Detail," *Al-Ahram* 8 August 2002.

"Disunity and Factionalism," *Al-Ahram* 15 August 2002.

"Low Points of Powerlessness," *Al-Ahram* 2 October 2002.

"Israel, Iraq, and the United States," *LRB* 10 October 2002.

"Europe versus America," *Al-Ahram* 14 November 2002.

"Immediate Imperatives," *Al-Ahram* 19 December 2002.

CHAPTERS CONTRIBUTED (BY SAID) TO BOOKS

"Record and Reality," in *Approaches to Twentieth Century Novel*, ed. John Unterecker (New York: Thomas Crowell, 1965).

"The Arab Portrayed," in *The Arab-Israeli Confrontation of June 1967: An Arab Perspective*, ed. Ibrahim Abu-Lughod (Evanston: Northwestern University Press, 1970).

"Beginnings," in *The American Literary Anthology*, ed. George Plimpton et al. (New York: Viking Press,1970).

Introduction, *Three Tales*, by Joseph Conrad (New York: Washington Square, 1970).

"The Palestinian Experience," in *Reflections on the Middle Eastern Crisis*, ed. Herbert Mason (The Hague and Paris: Mouton and Co., 1970).

"Molestation and Authority in Narrative Fiction," in *Aspects of Narrative*, ed. J. Hillis Miller (New York: Columbia University Press, 1971).

"*Abecedarium Culturae*: Structuralism, Absence, Writing," in *Modern French Criticism*, ed. John Simon (Chicago: Chicago University Press, 1972).

"On Originality," in *Uses of Literature*, ed. Engel Monroe (Cambridge: Harvard University Press, 1973).

"Arabic Prose and Prose Fiction Since 1948: An Introduction," in Halim Barakat, *Days of Dust*, trans. Trevor LeGassick (Wilmette, Illinois: Medina, 1974).

"Arabs and Jews," in *Settler Regimes in Africa and the Arab World: The Illusion of Endurance*, ed. Ibrahim Abu-Lughod et al. (Wilmette, Illinois: Medina, 1974).

"Notes on the Characterization of a Literary Text," in *Velocities of Change: Critical Essays from MLN*, ed. Richard Macksey (Baltimore; Johns Hopkins University Press, 1974).

"Arab Society and the War of 1973: Shattered Myths," in *Middle East Crucible: Studies on the Arab-Israeli War of 1973*, ed. Naseer Aruri (Wilmette, Illinois: Medina Press, 1975).

"On Repetition," in *English Institute Essays*, ed. Angus Fletcher (New York: Columbia University Press, 1976).

"Can Cultures Communicate? Round Table," in *Arab and American Cultures*, ed. George Atiyeh (Washington, D.C.: American Enterprise Institute for Public Policy Research, 1977).

"Renan's Philological Laboratory," in *Art, Politics, and Will*, ed. Anderson Quentin et al. (New York: Basic Books, 1977).

"Roads Taken and Not Taken in Contemporary Criticism," in *Directions for Criticism*, ed. Murray Krieger et al. (Madison: University of Wisconsin Press, 1977).

"Rashid Hussein," in *The World of Rashid Hussein: A Palestinian Poet in Exile*, ed. Kamal Boullata et al. (American-Arab University Graduates, 1979).

"Islam, the Philological Vocation, and French Culture: Renan and Massignon," in *Levi della Vida Memorial Award Volume*, ed. Malcom Kerr (Los Angeles: University of California Press, 1980).

"Text, Ideology, Realism," in *Literature and Society*, ed. Edward Said (Baltimore: Johns Hopkins University Press,1980).

"The Formation of American Public Opinion on the Question of Palestine," in *Palestinian Rights: Affirmation and Denial*, ed. Ibrahim Abu-Lughod (Welmette: Medina, 1982).

"Opponents, Audiences, Constituencies, and Community," in *The Politics of Interpretation*, ed. W. J. T. Mitchell (Chicago and London: Chicago University Press, 1982); rprt. in *The Anti-Aesthetic: Essays on Postmodern Culture*, ed. Hal Foster (Port Townsend, Washington: Bay, 1983); rprt. in *Modern Literary Theory: A Reader*, ed. Philip Rice et al. (London: Arnold, 1989).

"Reflections on Recent American 'Left' Literary Criticism," in *The Question of Textuality: Strategies of Reading in Contemporary American Criticism*, ed. William Spanos et al. (Bloomington: Indiana University Press, 1982).

"The Text, the World, the Critic," in *Textual Strategies: Perspectives on Post-Structuralist Criticism*, ed. Josué Harari (Ithica: Cornell University Press, 1979) 161–89; rprt. in *The Horizon of Literature*, ed. Paul Hernadi et al. (Lincoln: University of Nebraska Press, 1982).

"The Experience of Dispossession," in *The Shaping of an Arab Statesman: Abd al-Hamid Sharaf and the Modern Arab World*, ed. Patrick Seale (London: Quartet, 1983).

"The Music Itself: Glenn Gould's Contrapuntal Vision," in *Glenn Gould: Variations*, ed. John McGreevy (New York: Doubleday, 1983).

"Bursts of Meaning," in *Twentieth Century British Literature, Vol. I*, ed. Harold Bloom (New York: Chelsea House, 1985).

"Foucault and the Imagination of Power," in *Foucault: A Critical Reader*, ed. David Hoy (Oxford: Blackwell, 1986).

"An Ideology of Difference," in *Race, Writing and Difference*, ed. Henry Louis Gates Jr. (Chicago: University of Chicago Press, 1986).

"Secular Criticism," in *Critical Theory since 1965*, ed. Hazard Adams et al. (Tallahasse: Florida State University Press, 1986).

Introduction, *Kim*, by Rudyard Kipling (New York: Penguin, 1987).

"Palestine and the Future of the Arabs," in *Arab Nationalism and the Future of the Arab World*, ed. Hani Faris (Belmont: Association of Arab-American Graduates, 1987).

"Michel Foucault, 1927–1984," in *After Foucault: Humanistic Knowledge, Postmodern Challenges*, ed. Jonathan Arac (New Brunswick and London: Rutgers University Press, 1988).

"The Problem of Textuality: Two Exemplary Positions," in *Twentieth Century Literary Theory: A Reader*, ed. K. M. Newton (New York: St. Martin Press, 1988).

"Intifada and Independence," in *Intifada: The Palestinian Uprising against Israeli Occupation*, ed. Zachary Lockman et al. (Washington: Middle East Research and Information Project, 1989).

"Jane Austen and Empire," in *Raymond Williams: Critical Perspectives*, ed. Terry Eagleton (Boston: Northern University Press, 1989) 150–64; rprt. in *Contemporary Marxist Literary Criticism*, ed. Francis Mulhern (London: Longman, 1992).

"Media, Margins and Modernity: Raymond Williams and Edward Said," in *The Politics of Modernism: Against the New Conformists*, ed. Williams Raymonds (London Verso, 1989).

"Michael Walzer's *Exodus and Revolution*: A Canaanite Reading," in *Performance and Reality: Essays from Grand Street*, ed. Ben Sonnenberg (New Brunswick & London: Rutgers University Press, 1989).

"Yeats and Decolonization," in *Remaking History: Discussions in Contemporary Culture*, ed. Barbara Kruger et al. (Dublin: Bay, 1989); rprt. in *Nationalism, Colonialism and Literature*, ed. Terry Eagleton (Minneapolis: University of Minnesota Press, 1990).

"American Intellectuals and Middle East Politics," in *Intellectuals, Aesthetics, Politics, and Academics*, ed. Bruce Robbins (Minneapolis: University of Minnesota Press, 1990).

"Literacy and Liberation: The Palestinians," in *Literacy and Liberation: Report of the WUS Annual Conference 1990* (World University Service, 1990).

"Reflections on Exile," in *Out There: Marginalization and Contemporary Cultures*, ed. Russell Ferguson et al. (Cambridge: MIT Press, 1990); *One World: Many Cultures*, ed. StuartHirschberg (New York: Macmillan, 1992); rprt. in *Writings from America's Many Cultures* (second edition), ed. Jerome Beaty et al. (New York: Norton, 1994).

"*The Satanic Verses* and Democratic Freedoms," in *The Rushdie File*, ed. Lisa Appignanesi *et al* (Syracuse: Syracuse University Press, 1990).

"Travelling Theory," in *Raritan Reading*, ed. Richard Poirier (New Brunswick: Rutgers University Press, 1990).

"Zionism from the Standpoint of Its Victims," in *Anatomy of Racism*, ed. David Goldberg (Minneapolis: University of Minnesota Press, 1990).

"Literature, Theory, and Commitment," in *Crisscrossing Boundaries in African Literatures*, ed.Kenneth Harrow *et al* (Zimra: 1991).

"Orientalism Reconsidered," in *Europe and its Others*, ed. Peter Hulme et al. (Colchester: University of Essex Press, 1985) 14–27; rprt. in *Literature, Politics and Theory*, ed. Francis Barker et al. (London: Methuen, 1986); rprt. in *The Contemporary Study of the Arab World*, ed. Earl Sullivan et al. (Edmonton: University of Alberta Press, 1991); rprt. in *Pós-Modernismo E Politica*, ed. Heloisa Buarque de Hollanda (Rio de Janeiro: Rocco, 1991).

"Europe and Its Others: An Arab Perspective," in *Visions of Europe: Conversations on the Legacy and Future of Europe*, ed. Richard Kearny (Dublin: Wolfhound Press, 1992).

Forward, in *The Performing Self: Compositions and Decompositions in the Languages of Contemporary Life*, by Richard Poirier (New Brunswick: Rutgers University Press, 1992).

Forward, in *Thoughts on a War*, ed. Phyllis Bennis et al. (Edinburgh: Canongate, 1992).

"On Linkage, Language, and Identity," in *The Gulf War Reader: Histories, Documents, Opinions*, ed. Micah al-Sifry et al. (New York: Times Books, 1992).

"Contre les Orthodoxies," in *Pour Rushdie: Cent intellectuels arabes et musulmans pour la libertéd'expression*, ed. Abdallah Anouar et al. (Paris: Editions la Découverte, 1993); rprt. in *Til Rushdie* (Narway: Cappelen, 1994); rprt. in *For Rushdie: Essays by Arab and Muslim Writers in Defense of Free Speech*, ed. Abdallah Anouar et al., trans. Kevin Anderson and Kenneth Whitehead (New York: George Braziller, 1994).

"Expanding Humanism," in *Wild Orchids and Trotsky*, ed. Mark Edmundson (New York: Penguin Books, 1993).

"Figures, Configurations, Transfigurations," in *New Historical Literary Study: Essays on Reproducing Texts, Representing History*, ed. Jeffrey Cox et al. (Princeton: Princeton University Press, 1993) 316–30.

"Imperialism and After: Europe, the US and the Rest of Us," in *A Window of Europe: The Lothian European Lectures 1992*, ed. Geraldine Prince (Edinburgh: Canongate Press, 1993).

"Nationalism, Human Rights, and Interpretation," in *Freedom and Interpretation: The Oxford Amnesty Lectures 1992*, ed. Barbara Johnson (New York: Basic Books, 1993).

"The New World Order and Middle East Peace," in *Altered States: A Reader in the New World Order*,ed. Phyllis Bennis et al. (New York: Olive Branch Press, 1993).

"Peace in the Middle East," in *Open Fire*, ed. Ruggiero & Sahulka (New York: The New Press, 1993).

"The Politics of Knowledge," in *Debating P.C.: The Controversy Over Political Correctness on College Campuses*, ed. Paul Berman (New York: Dell, 1992); rprt. in *Race, Identity and Representation in Education*, ed. Cameron McCarthy et al. (New York & London: Routledge, 1993); rprt. in *Falling into Theory: Conflicting Views on Reading Literature*, ed. David Richter (Boston; Bedford Books, 1994).

"Travelling Theory Reconsidered," in *Critical Reconstructions of Fiction and Life*, ed. Robert Polhemus et al. (Stanford: Stanford University Press, 1994).

"Not All the Way to the Tigers: Britten's *Death in Venice*," in *On Mahler and Britten: Essays in Honor of Donald Mitchell on His Seventieth Birthday*, ed. Philip Reed (Woodbridge: Boydell Press, 1995).

Preface, *Politics and Revelation: Mawaradi and After*, by Hanna Mikhail (Edinburgh: Edinburgh University Press, 1995).

"On Lost Causes," in *The Tanner Lectures on Human Values*, ed. Grethe B. Peterson (Salt Lake City: University of Utah Press, 1997).

INTERVIEWS with SAID
The following are interviews given by Edward Said at different times and in different locations. Some of them have been edited and have appeared in books and/or journals.

"Interview," *Diacritics* (Fall 1976).

"Palestinian Prospects Now," *Worldview* (May 1979).

"L'Orient, fantasme de l'Occident," *Le Monde* 7-8 December 1980; rprt. in *Entretiens avec le Monde*, 4 (Paris: La Découverte/Le Monde, 1984).

"Edward Said's Review of Western Coverage of the Islamic World," *New Haven Advocate* 11 November 1981.

"In the Shadow of the West," *Wedge* (Winter/Spring 1985).

"An Interview with Edward Said," *Critical Texts* (Winter 1986).

"Edward Said: An Exile's Exile," *The Progressive* (February 1987).
"Edward Said," in *Criticism and Society* (New York: Methuen, 1987); rprt. in *Al-Quds al-Àrabi* 14 May 1993.
"Interview: Edward Said," *Red Bass* 12 (1987).
"Orientalism Revisited: An Interview with Edward Said," *MERIP* (January–February 1988).
"Interview," *Hug* [Denmark] 52 (1988).
"American Intellectuals and the Middle East Politics: Interview with Edward Said," *Social Text* (Fall 1988).
"The Need for Self-Appraisal," *Al-Fajr* [Egypt] 5 February 1990.
"A Formula for More Husseins: An Interview with Edward Said," *L.A. Weekly* 31 August–6 September 1990.
"Arabesque," *New Statesman and Society* 7 September 1990.
"In the Shadow of the West: An Interview with Edward Said," in *Discourses: Conversations in Postmodern Art and Culture* (1990).
"L'Irak n'est pas un désert," *Le Nouvel Observateur* 21–27 février 1991.
"Coming Weeks Very Decisive in Palestinian History: Interview with Edward Said," *Al-Fajr* [Egypt] 15 April 1991.
"Orientalism Revisited: Interview with Edward Said," *Blast* (Fall 1991).
"Criticism, Culture, and Performance: An Interview with Edward Said," in *Interculturalism and Performance: Writings from PAJ* (1991).
"Les douleurs de la géographie," *Gulliver* (September 1991).
"There Is an Obvious Flaw in U.S. Peace Role," *Al-Fajr* [Egypt] 6 January 1992.
"An Interview with Edward Said," *Z Magazine* (February 1992); rprt. in *For Palestine* (New York: Writers and Readers, 1993).
"Interview," *Herald* [Pakistan] (February 1992).
"Interview," *Al-Fajr* [Egypt] June 29 1992.
"Interview," *Harbour* (Fall 1992).
"Interview," *Knack* 20 October 1992.
"Interview," *Al-Hayat* [Egypt] 19 March 1993.
"Orientalism and After," *Radical Philosophy* (Spring 1993).
"An Interview with Edward Said," *Boundary 2* (Spring 1993).
"Interview," *Babelia: Revista de Cultura* [Spain] 19 June 1993.
"Interview," *Il Manifesto* [Italy] 11 July 1993.
"Peoples' Rights and Literature: An Interview with Edward Said," *Alif* 13 (1993).
"Al-Ma`rifah wa al-Hurriyyah," *Al-Mulhaq* [Egypt] 7 August 1993.
"Edward Said," *Queen's Quarterly* (Fall 1993).
"Interview," *Lies of Our Time* (September 1993).
"Interview," *Corriere Della Sera* [Italy] 10 September 1993.
"Interview," *Wochenpost* [Germany] 16 September 1993.
"Al-Tatawwur al-Fikri wa al-Siyasi `inda Edward Said," *Al-Siyasah al-Filas-tiniyyah* (Winter/Spring 1994).
"Interview," *Il Manifesto* [Italy] 1 April 1994.

"Interview," *Newsweek International* 18 July 1994.
"The Intellectuals and the War: Interview," *Middle East Report* July/August 1991; rprt. in *Al-Adab* June/July 1994.
"What Is Islam?" *New Statesman and Society* 10 February 1995.
"Making a Cause to be Reckoned with," *Jerusalem Post* 6 March 1998.

ARTICLES ABOUT SAID
From a colossal number of articles, essays, reviews, I made stringent and at times difficult selections.

M. Abaza et al., "Occidental Reason, Orientalism, Islamic Fundamentalism," *International Sociology* (1988).
Walter Abish, "The Writer-To-Be: An Impression of Living," *Sub-Stance* (1980).
Rifaat Abo-el-Haj, "The Social Uses of the Past: Recent Arab Historiography of Ottoman Rule," *International Journal of Middle East Studies* (May 1982).
M.H. Abrams, "How to Do Things with Texts," *Partisan Review* (Fall 1979).
Gerald Ackerman, "Gérome's Oriental Paintings and the Western Genre Tradition," *Arts Magazine* (March 1986).
Aijaz Ahmad, "Between Orientalism and Historicism: Anthropological Knowledge of India," *Studies in History* 7 (1991).
Susan Aiken, "Dinesen's 'Sorrow-Acre': Tracing the Woman's Line," *Contemporary Literature* (Summer 1984).
Deniz Akaril, "The Long Peace," *Middle Eastern Studies* (January 1995).
Jalal Sakid al-Azm, "*Orientalism* and Orientalism in Reverse," *Khamsin* (5:1981).
Larry Alderink, "Pauline Text as Drama of Salvation," *Helios* (Spring 1986).
Edward Alexander, "Professor of Terror," *Commentary* (August 1989).
Margaret Alexiou, "Modern Greek Studies in the West: Between the Classics and the Orient," *Journal of Modern Greek* (May 1986).
R. Amitaipress, "Orientalism, the West, and the Academy," *TLS* 31 March 1995.
Hugh Amory, "Apologetics," *Commentary* (July 1974).
Bernadette Andrea, "Columbus in Istanbul: Ottoman Mappings of the 'New World,'" Genre (Spring–Summer 1997).
Brian Appleyard, "Reflections from the Tightrope," *The Independent* (23 June 1993).
David Apter, "The New Mytho/Logics and the Specter of Superfluous Man," *Social Research* (Summer 1985).
Jonathan Arac, "The Function of Foucault at the Present Time," *Humanties in Society* (Winter 1980).
———, "Romanticism, the Self and the City: The Secret Agent in Literary History," *Boundary 2* (Fall 1980).
———, "The Arnoldian Prophecy: Making Critical History," *Boundary 2* (Spring 1984).

L. Arenilla, "Orientalism: The Orient as Created by the West," *Futuribles* 44 (1981).

Alexander Argyros, "The Seam of the Trace," *Boundary 2* (Winter 1982).

Paul Armstrong, "The Hermeneutics of Literary Impressionism: Interpretation and Reality in James, Conrad, and Ford," *Centennial Review* (Fall 1983).

———, "Reading, Representation, and Realism in *The Ambassadors*," *American Studies* (Winter 1986).

———,"Play and Cultural Differences," *Kenyan Review* (Winter 1991).

Lida Aronne, "El mito contro el mito: narración e ideografía en '*El otono del patriarca*,'" *Revista Iberoamericana* (April–September 1986).

Phlip Arrington et al., "Prologues to What Is Possible: Introductions to Metadiscourse," *College Composition and Communication* (October 1987).

Nina Athanassoglou, "Un tableau d'inspiration phillénique à Saint-Omer," *La revue du Louvre et des musées de France* 1(1982).

G. Atiyeh, "Ibn Khaldun in Modern Scholarship: A Study in Orientalism," *Journal of Near Eastern Studies* 46 (1987).

Douglas Atkin, "A(fter) D(econstruction): The Relations of Literature and Religion in the Wake of Deconstruction," *Studies in the Literary Imagination* (Spring 1985).

Timothy Bahti, "Vico, Auerbach, and Literary History," *Philosophical Quarterly* (Spring 1981).

Mieke Bal, "Force and Meaning: The Interdisciplinary Struggle of Psychoanalysis, Semiotics, and Aesthetics," *Semiotica* 63 (1987).

Frank Baldanza, "Opera in Conrad; 'More Real than Anything in Life,'" *Studies in the Literary Imagination* (Spring 1980).

Richard Barnet et al., "U.S. Foreign Policy in the Middle East," *Journal of Palestine Studies* 10 (1980).

J. Barry, "The Textual Body: Incorporating Writing and Flesh," *Philosophy Today* (Spring 1986).

Susan Bazargan, "'*Oxen of the Sun*': Maternity, Language, and History," *James Joyce Quaterly* (Spring 1985).

George Behlmer, "The Gypsy Problem in Victorian England," *Victorian Studies* (Winter 1985).

Leornard Bell, "Artists and Empire: Victorian Representations of Subject People," *Art History* (March 1982).

James Bennett, "Plot Repetition: Theme and Variation of Narrative Macroepisodes," *Papers on Language and Literature* (Fall 1981).

Homi Bhabha, "The Other Question: The Stereotype and Colonial Discourse," *Screen* (November–December 1983).

———, "Of Mimicry and Man: The Ambivalence of Colonial Discourse," *October* (Spring 1984).

———, "Signs Taken for Wonders: Questions of Ambivalence and Authority under a Tree Outside Delhi, May 1817," *Critical Inquiry* (Autumn 1985).

Rashmi Bhatnagar, "Uses and Limits of Foucault: A Study of the Theme of Origin in Edward Said's '*Orientalism*,'" *Social Scientist: Monthly Journal of the Indian School of Social Sciences* (July 1986).

Zarko Biblija, "The Fuss over Islam," *Harper's Magazine* (March 1981).

Willem Bijlefeld, "Controversies around the Qur'anic Ibrahim Narrative and Its 'Orientalist' Interpretation," *Muslim World* (April 1982).

Peter Bishop, "Jung, Eastern Religion, and the Language of the Imagination," *Eastern Buddhist* (Spring 1984).

Daniel Bivona, "Alice the Child-Imperialist and the Games of Wonderland," *Nineteenth Century Literature* (September 1986).

Jeannine Blackwell, "Fractured Fairy Tales: German Women Authors and the Grimm Tradition," *Germanic Review* (Fall 1987).

John Blair, "Structuralism, American Studies, and the Humanties," *American Quarterly* (Summer 1978).

Marc Eli Blanchard, "The Critique of Autobiography," *Comparative Literature* (Spring 1982).

Morton Bloomfield, "Stylistics and the Theory of Literature," *New Literary History* (Winter 1976).

Martin Bock, "The Sensationalist Epistemology in Conrad's Early Fiction," *Conradiana* 1 (1984).

———, "Conrad's Voyages of Disorientation: Crossing *The Shadow Line*," *Conradiana* 2 (1985).

Frederic Bogel, "Deconstructive Criticism: The Logic of Derrida's Difference," *Centrum* (Spring 1978).

Philip Bohlman, "The European Discovery of Music in the Islamic World and the 'Non-Western' in Nineteenth Century Music History," *Journal of Musicology* (Spring 1987).

David Bond, "Jean-Luc Benoziglio and the Self-Conscious Text," *French Forum* (January 1984).

Ronald Bond, "'Dark Deeds Darkly Answered': Thomas Becon's Homily against Whoredom and Adultery, Its Contexts, and Its Affiliations with Three Sheakespearean Plays," *Sixteenth Century Journal* (Summer 1985).

Chris Bongie, "Fathers and Sons: The Self-Revelation of Flaubert and Celine," *Romantic Review* (November 1986).

William Bonney, "Joseph Conrad and the Betrayal of Language," *Nineteenth Century Fiction* (September 1979).

James Boon, "An Endogamy of Poets, and Vice Versa: Exotic Ideals in Romanticism/Structuralism," *Studies in Romanticism* (Fall 1979).

Wayne Booth, "'Preserving the Exemplar': Or, How Not to Dig Our Own Graves," *Critical Inquiry* (Spring 1977).

———, "Freedom of Interpretation: Bakhtin and the Challenge of Feminist Criticism," *Critical Inquiry* (Fall 1982).

Paul Bové, "Cleanth Brooks and Modern Irony: A Kierkegaardian Critique," *Boundary 2* (Spring 1976).

———, "The Image of the Creator in Beckett's Postmodern Writing," *Philosophy and Literature* (Spring 1980).

———, "Mendacious Innocents, Or, the Modern Genealogist as Conscientious Intellectual: Nietzsche, Foucault, Said," *Boundary 2* (Spring 1981).

———, "In Defense of Edward W. Said: Editorial," *Boundary 2* (Winter 1991).

———, "Hope and Reconciliation: A Review of Edward Said," *Boundary 2* (Summer 1993).

Daniel Boyarin et al., "Toward a Dialogue with Edward Said," *Critical Inquiry* (Spring 1989).

Jonathan Boyarin, "Reading Exodus into History," *New Literary History* (Summer 1992).

Robert Boyers, "Confronting the Present," *Salmagundi* (Fall 1981).

Sibel Bozdogan, "*Orientalism* and Architectural Culture," *Social Scientist: Monthly Journal of the Indian School of Social Sciences* (July 1986).

Patrick Brantinger, "Anti-Imperialism, Racism, Or Impressionism?" *Criticism* (Fall 1985).

———, "Victorians and Africans: the Genealogy of the Myth of the Dark Continent," *Critical Inquiry* (Fall 1985).

Richard Braverman, "Locke, Defoe, and the Politics of Childhood," *English Language Notes* (Spetember 1986).

Germaine Brée, "Gide et l'histoire," *L'Esprit créateur* (Fall 1975).

Victor Brombert, "Opening Signals in Narrative," *New Literary History* (Spring 1980).

Marilyn Brown, "The Harem Dehistoricized: Ingres's 'Turkish Bath,'" *Arts Magazine* (June 1987).

Marshall Brown, "The Pre-Romantic Discovery of Consciousness," *Studies in Romanticism* (Fall 1978).

Michael Brown, "The Viability of Racism: South Africa and the United Sates," *Philosophical Forum* (Winter–Spring 1986–87).

Obed Brown, "Creations and Destroyings: Keats's Protestant Hymn, the '*Ode to Psyche*,'" *Diacritics* (Winter 1976).

———, "The Errant Letter and the Whispering Gallery," *Genre* (Winter 1977).

Susan Bryan, "Reauthorizing the Text: Jefferson's Scissor Edit of the Gospels," *Early American Literature* (Spring 1987).

Diana Brydon, "New Approaches to the New Literatures in English," *Westerly: A Quarterly Review* (September 1989).

James Bunn, "The Aesthetics of British Mercantilism," *New Literary History* (Winter 1980).

Joan Burbick, "The Irony of Self-Reference: Emily Dickinson's Pronominal Language," *Essays in Literature* (Spring 1982).

Edmund Burke, "Islam and World History: The Contribution of Marshall Hodgson," *Radical History Review* 39 (1987).

Israel Burshatin, "The Moor in the Text: Metaphor, Emblem, and Silence," *Critical Inquiry* (Fall 1985).

Abena Busia, "Miscegenation as Metonymy: Sexuality and Power in the Colonial Novel," *Ethnic and Racial Studies* (July 1989).

Joseph Buttigieg, "The Exemplary Worldliness of Antonio Gramsci's Literary Criticism," *Boundary 2* (Fall–Winter 1982–83).

William Cain, "The Institutionalization of the New Criticism," *MLN* (December 1982).

———, "The Humanities in Higher Education: A Reply to William Bennett," *Michigan Quarterly Review* (Fall 1985).

———, "Theory and Practice in Contemporary Criticism," *CEA Critic* (Winter 1986/Summer 1987).

Lionel Caplan, "'Bravest of the Brave': Representations of 'The Gurkha' in British Military Writings," *Modern Asian Studies* 25 (1991).

Alberto Cardin, "Primer etnólogo moderno?" *Los Cuadernos del Norte* (March–April 1985).

Helen Carr, "The Myth of Hiawatha," *Literature and History* (Spring 1986).

Robert Caserio, "Paracriticisms, Postmodernism, and Prophecy," *Boundary 2* (Fall 1976).

Robert Casillo, "Dirty Gondola: The Image of Italy in American Advertisements," *Word and Image* (October-December 1985).

E. L. Cerronilong, "*Orientalism*, the West and the Academy," *TLS* 24 February 1995.

Khadija Chaker, "Uncovering *Covering Islam*: A Critical Analysis of Anti-Islamic Forces," *Al-Ittihad* (April–June 1982.

A. Chan, "Orientalism and Image Making," *Journal of Ethnic Studies* 9 (1981).

James Chandler, "Romantic Allusiveness," *Critical Inquiry* (Spring 1982).

Xiaomei Chen, "Occidentalism as Counterdiscourse: 'He Shang' in Post-Mao-China," *Critical Inquiry* (Summer 1992).

François Chevaldonne, "Globalization and Orientalism: The Case of TV Serials," *Media, Culture, and Society* (April 1987).

Jerome Christensen, "Byron's Career: The Speculative Stage," *ELH* (Spring 1985).

———, "Hume's Social Composition," *Representations* (Fall 1985).

Kathleen Christison, "The Arab in Recent Popular Fiction," *Middle East Journal* (Summer 1987).

William Ciamurro, "Judgment and Rhetoric in *La horoa de todos*," *Journal of Hispanic Philology* (Winter 1982).

Jean-François Clément, "Journalistes et chercheurs des sciences sociales face aux mouvements islamistes," *Archives des sciences sociales des religions* (January–March 1983).

James Clifford, "On Ethnographic Surrealism," *Comparative Studies in Society and History* (October 1981).

―――, "On Ethnographic Authority," *Representations* (Spring 1983).

John Coates, "Metaphor and Meaning in the Towers of Trebizond," *Durham University Journal* (December 1987).

Alexander Cockburn, "Beat the Devil: One Hand Clapping," *The Nation* 23 April 1988.

―――, "The Kach Hit List," *The Nation* 31 December 1990.

―――, "The Tel Aviv Bombing," *The Nation* 7 November 1994.

Robert Davis Con, "Theorizing Opposition: Aristotle, Greimas, Jameson, and Said," *L'Esprit créateur* (*The Creative Mind*) (Été 1987).

S. Cooper, "Materialist Orientalism: Marx, Asiatic Mode of Production, and India," *Journal of Contemporary Asia* 20 (1990).

Jacques Couland, "Recherches arabes et islamiques aujourd'hui," *La Pensée* (September–October 1981).

John Cushman Jr., "Shultz Will Make New Mideast Trip: Revived Peace Quest Doesn't Signal Any Breakthrough," *The New York Times* 27 March 1988.

Michael Dalby, "Nocturnal Labors in the Light of Day," *Journal of Asian Studies* 39 (1980).

R. Dasenbrock, "Word-World Relations: The Work of Charles Altieri and Edward Said," *New Orleans Review* (Spring 1985).

Gautam Dasgupta, "The Mahabharata: Peter Brook's Orientalism," *Performing Arts Journal* 3 (1987).

Michael Davidson, "'From the Latin Speculum': The Modern Poet as Philologist," *Contemporary Literature* (Summer 1987).

Robert Davis, "Theorizing Opposition: Aristotle, Greimas, Jameson, Said," *L'Esprit Créateur* (Summer 1987).

Joan DeJean, "Fictive Performances: Oriental Music in Alexander Dumas' *The Count of Monte Cristo*," *Asian Music* 1 (1979).

Thomas DeLoughry, "Professor and Advocate of Palestinians—and Cultural Awareness," *Chronicle of Higher Education* 1 June 1988.

Barbara De Mille, "An Inquiry into Some Points of Seamanship: Narration as Preservation in *Heart of Darkness*," *Conradiana* 2 (1986).

Walter Denny, "Orientalism in European Art," *Muslim World* (January 1983).

Terrence des Pres, "On Governing Narratives: The Turkish-American Case," *Yale Review* (Summer 1986).

Philip Dodd, "History or Fiction: Balancing Contemporary Autobiography's Claims," *Mosaic* (Fall 1987).

Eugenio Donato, "'Here, Now'/ 'Always, Already,'" *Diacritics* (Summer 1976).

Terry Eagleton, "Nationalism, Colonialism, and Literature," *James Joyce Quarterly* (Spring 1991).

Joe Earle, "The Taxonomic Obsession: British Collectors and Japanese Objects, 1852–1986," *Burlington Magazine* (December 1986).

Hasan Eaton, "Reflections on Edward Said's *Covering Islam*," *Islamic Quarterly* 29 (1985).

Barbara Eckstein, "What Humanists Help America to Forget," *Literary Review* (Summer 1985).

Richard Eder, "Edward Said: Bright Star of English Lit. and P.L.O.," *The New York Times* 22 February 1980.

———, "Edward Said Speaks: The Palestinian Peace Process," *New Indicator: San Diego's Progressive Bi-Weekly* 6–20 February 1980.

Robert Edwards, "The Book of the Duchess and the Beginnings of Chaucer's Narrative," *New Literary History* (Fall 1981).

Fouzi el-Asmar, "The Portrayal of Arabs in Hebrew Children's Literature," *Journal of Palestine Studies* (Fall 1986).

Robert Elbaz, "Autobiography, Ideology, and Genre Theory," *Orbis Litterarum* 197 (1983).

Dorice Elliott, "Hearing the Darkness: The Narrative Chain in Conrad's *Heart of Darkness*," *English Literature in Transition* 2 (1985).

Joseph Escovitz, "Orientalists and Orientalism in the Writings of Muhammad Kurd Ali," *International Journal of Middle East Studies* (February 1983).

Ghazi Falah, "The Frontier of Political Criticism in Israeli Geographic Practice," *Area* (March 1994).

———, "Living Together Apart: Residential Segregation in Mixed Arab-Jewish Cities in Israel," *Urban Studies* (June 1996).

N. N. Feites, "The Moment of Pickwick, or the Production of a Commodity Text," *Literature and History* (Fall 1984).

John Fekete, "Literature and Politics/Literary Politics," *Dalhousie Review* (Spring–Summer 1986).

Maurizio Ferraris, "L'etnologia bianca. Deconstruzione e scienze umane," *Aut Aut* (May–June 1984).

Hartmut Findrich, "Orientalismus und Orientalismus: Berlegungen zu Edward Said, Michel Foucault, und westlichen 'islamstudien,'" *Welt des Islams* 28 (1988).

Guido Fink, "Mark Twain: In fondo al pozzo," *Paragone* (August 1983).

Karl Fink, "Goethe's *West östlicher Divan*: Orientalism Restructured," *International Journal of Middle East Studies* 14 (1982).

Stanley Fish, "Profession Despise Thyself: Fear and Self-Loathing in Literary Studies," *Critical Inquiry* (Winter 1983).

Robert Fisk, "Reading Between the Middle East Lines," *Times* (27 December 1980).

———, "Arafat's Betrayal," *LRB* 23 February 1995.

———, "Who Will Speak for the Palestinians?" *Times* (16 May 1985).

Patrick Flanagan, "Orientalism," *Journal of Contemporary Asia* 16 (1986).

Barbara Foley, "The Politics of Deconstruction," *Genre* (Spring–Summer 1984).

Susan Fraiman, "Jane Austen and Edward Said: Gender, Culture, and Imperialism," *Critical Inquiry* (Summer 1995).

Catherine Gallagher, "Politics, the Profession, and the Critic," *Diacritics* (Summer 1985).

Arran Gare, "Understanding Oriental Cultures," *Philosophy East and West* (July 1995).

Henry Louis Gates Jr., "Said as Music Critic," *Raritan* (Summer 1993).

Ernest Gellner, "The Mightier Pen?" *TLS* 19 February 1993.

Rolf Goebel, "Kafka's Orientalist Rhetoric: China, the Middle East, India," *Journal of the Kafka Society of America* (June–December 1991).

Philip Goldstein, "The Politics of Literary Theory," *Style* (Spring 1993).

James Goode, "A Good Start: The First American Mission to Iran, 1883–1885," *Muslim World* (April 1984).

Robert Gooding, "The Drama of Nietzsche's *Zarathustra*: Intention, Repetition, Prelude," *International Studies in Philosophy* 20 (1988).

Michael Gora, "Who Paid the Bills at Mansfield Park?" *The New York Times Book Review* 28 February 1993.

David Gordon, "Orientalism," *Antioch Review* (Winter 1982).

Juan Goytisolo et al., "From Count Julian to Makbara: A Possible Orientalist Reading," *The Review of Contemporary Fiction* (Summer 1984).

———, "In the Gods of the Eden: Marrakesh, Bruce Lee and the Twilight World of the Matinee Idler," *TLS* 23 December 1994.

Oleg Grabar, "Orientalism: An Exchange," *The New York Review of Books* 12 August 1982.

Gerald Graff, "Politics, Language, Deconstruction, Lies, and the Reflexive Fallacy: A Rejoinder to W. J. T. Mitchell," *Salmagundi* (Winter–Spring 1980).

D. Grafflin, "Orientalisms's Attack on *Orientalism*," *Bulletin of Concerned Asian Scholars* 15.3 (1983).

Grewgious, "Used Books," *Critical Quarterly* (Winter 1994).

Robert Griffin, "Ideology and Representation: A Response to Edward Said," *Critical Inquiry* (Spring 1989).

Hilel Halkin, "Whose Palestine? An Open Letter to Edward Said," *Commentary* (May 1980).

R. Hammami et al., "Feminist Orientalism and Orientalist Marxism," *New Left Review* 170 (1988).

Barbara Harlow, "Cairo Curiosities: E. W. Lane's Account and Ahmad Amin's Dictionary," *Journal of the History of Ideas* (April–June 1985).

———, "History and Endings: Ghassan Kanafani's *Men in the Sun* and Tawfiq Salih's *The Duped*," *Minnesota Review* (Fall 1985).

Ihab Hassan, "Polemic," *Diacritics* (Fall 1972).

Scott Heller, "After '*Orientalism*': Exploring the Complicity of Literature and Empire," *Chronicle of Higher Education* (May 19, 1993).

Bob Hodge, "Language and War: Orientalism in the 'Mother of Battles,'" *Journal of the South Pacific Association for Commonwealth Literature and Language Studies* (May 1992).

Anne Christine Holmlund, "Displacing Limits of Difference: Gender, Race, and Colonialism in Edward Said and Homi Bhabha's Theoretical Models and Marguerite Duras's Experimental Films," *Quarterly Review of Film and Video* (May–October 1991).

Albert Hourani, "The Road to Morocco," *The New York Review of Books* 8 March 1979.

Irving Howe, "History and Literature: Edward Said's *Culture and Imperialism*," *Dissent* (Fall 1993).

Marvin Howe, "For Edward Said, Shultz Session Proved Collegial and Constructive," *The New York Times* 28 March 1988.

Craig Howes, "Hawaii through Western Eyes: Orientalism and Historical Fiction for Children," *The Lion and the Unicorn* (April 1987).

Robert Hughes, "Envoy to Two Cultures," *Time Magazine* 21 June 1993.

Ronald Inden, "Orientalist Constructions of India," *Modern Asian Studies* (July 1986).

———, "In Defense of Edward W. Said," *Boundary 2* (Spring 1991).

Bogumil Jewsiewicki and V. Y. Mudimbe, "For Said: Why Even the Critic of Imperialism Labors under Western Skies?" *Transition* 63 (1994).

Robert Blair Kaiser, "Bantam's Khomeini Book Stirs Dispute," *The New York Times* 28 March 1980.

Robert Kapp, "Introduction to Review Symposium of Edward Said's *Orientalism*," *Journal of Asian Studies* (May 1980).

E. D. Karampetsos, "Stratis Tsirkas and the Arabs," *Journal of Modern Greek* (May 1984).

Percy Kemp, "Le Nouvel orientaliste," *L'Esprit* (May–June 1983).

M. Kerr, "Orientalism: The Orient as Created by the West," *International Journal of Middle East Studies* 12 (1981).

Diana Knight, "Barthes and Orientalism," *New Literary History* (Summer 1993).

Rhoda Koenig, "Limp Lit," *The New Yorker* 1 March 1993.

David Kopf, "Orientalism, Poetry, and the Millennium," *Pacific Affairs* 58 (1985).

———, "A Macrohistoriographical Essay on the Idea of East and West from Herodotus to Edward Said," *Comparative Civilizations Review* 15 (1986).

Mark Krupnick, "Edward Said: Discourse and Palestinian Rage," *Tikkun* (November–December 1989).

Jacques Langlais, "Science de la religion et cultures orales: Pour une approche renouvelée," *Sciences Religieuses: Revue Canadienne* (1983).

Dan Latimer, "The Politics of Literary Theory: An Evanston Memoir," *Southern Humanities Review* (Spring 1984).

Gwendolyn Layne, "Orientalists and Literary Critics: East Is East, West Is West, and It Is in the Professional Interest of Some to Keep It That Way," *Western Humanities Review* (Summer 1982).

James Lehmann, "Polemic and Satire in the Poetry of the Maimonidean Controversy," *Prooftexts* (May 1981).

K. Lennon, "Gender and Knowledge," *Journal of Gender Studies* (July 1995).

John Leonard, "Novel Colonies," *The Nation* 22 March 1993.

Bernard Lewis, "The Question of *Orientalism*," *The New York Review of Books* 24 June 1982.

Deborah Linderman, "Pepe le Moko and the Discourse of Orientalism," *Literature and Psychology* 42 (1996).

Luce López, "Makbara: Juan Goytisolo's Fictionalized Version of 'Orientalism,'" *The Review of Contemporary Fiction* (Summer 1984).

J. Lukacs, "The Legacy of Orwell: A Discussion," *Salmagundi* (Spring–Summer 1986).

Donald Lyons, "Presences and Absences in Edward Said's *Culture and Imperialism*," *Commentary* (July 1994).

John MacKenzie, "Occidentalism: Counterpoint and Counter-Polemic," *Journal of Historical Geography* (July 1993).

Colin MacKinnon, "Talking Back: '*Orientalism*' and the Orientals," Humanties Report (February 1982).

Robert Markand, "Conversations with Outstanding Americans: Edward Said," *Christian Science Monitor* 27 May 1997.

Mustapha Marrouchi, "The Critic as Dis/Placed Intelligence: The Case of Edward Said," *Diacritics* (Spring 1991).

———, "Rootprints," *The Dalhousie Review* (Spring 1997).

———, "Counternarratives, Recoveries, Refusals," *Boundary 2* (Summer 1998).

Catherine Martin-Gimelli, "Orientalism and the Ethnographer: Said, Herodotus, and the Discourse of Alterity," *Criticism* (Fall 1990).

Nivedita Menon, "Orientalism and After," *Public Culture* (Fall 1993).

Thomas Metcalf, "Architecture and the Representation of Empire: India, 1860–1910," Representations (Spring 1984).

Peter Meyer, "Tombs and Dark Houses: Ideology, Intellectuals and Proletarians in the Study of Contemporary Indian Islam," *Journal of Asian Studies* (May 1981).

J. Hillis Miller, "Beginning with a Text," *Diacritics* (Fall 1976).

Richard Minear, "Orientalism and the Study of Japan," *Journal of Asian Studies* (May 1980).

W. J. T. Mitchell, "The Golden Age of Criticism: Seven Theses and a Commentary," *LRB* (25 June 1987).

———, "The Ethics of Form in the Photographic Essay," *Afterimage* (January 1989).

———, "In the Wilderness," *LRB* 8 April 1993.

Chandra Mohanty, "Under Western Eyes: Feminist Scholarship and Colonial Discourse," *Boundary 2* (Spring/Fall 1984).

Bart Moore-Gilbert, "Kipling and Orientalism," *The Modern Language Review* (January 1989).

Klaus Naumann, "Der imperiale Blick," *Die Zeit* 2 December 1994.

Jack Newfield, "Well Said," *The Nation* 16 November 1985.

Hilton Obenzinger, "The Heart of the Matter," *Journal of Palestine Studies* 9 (1980).

Daniel O'Hara, "Criticism Wordly and Otherwordly: Edward W. Said and the Cult of Theory," *Boundary 2* (Spring/Fall 1984).

Zakia Pathak et al., "The Prisonhouse of Orientalism," *Textual Practice* (Summer 1991).

Marjorie Perloff, "Ca(n)non to the Right of Us, Ca(n)non to the Left of Us: A Plea for Difference," *New Literary History* (Spring 1987).

Benita Perry, "Problems in Current Theories of Colonial Discourse," *Oxford Literary Review* 1-2 (1987).

Stuart Peterfreund, "Criticism and Metahistory," *Jewish Thought* (Winter 1982).

Elizabeth Picard, "Political Science, Orientalism and Sociology at Lebanon's Sickbed," *Revue française de sciences politiques* 27 (1977).

Dana Polan, "Film as Language, Film as Power," *East West Film Journal* (June 1988).

David Powers, "Orientalism, Colonialism, and Legal History," *Comparative Historical Review* (July 1989).

Gyan Prakash, "Orientalism Now," *History and Theory* 34 (1995).

Madhava Prasad, "The 'Other' Worldliness of Postcolonial Discourse: A Critique," *Critical Inquiry* (Fall 1992).

Duara Prasenjit, "Knowledge and Power in the Discourse of Modernity: The Campaigns against Popular Religion in Early Twentieth-Century China," *Journal of Asian Studies* 50 (1991).

Mary Louise Pratt, "Edward Said's *Culture and Imperialism:* A Symposium," *Social Text* (Fall 1994).

Mohammad Quadar, "Paternalism and Enlightenment: The Purpose of Third World Studies," *Third World Quarterly* (October 1981).

José Rabasa, "Dialogue as Conquest; Mapping Spaces for Counter-Discourse," *Cultural Critique* (Spring 1987).

A. Rai, "*Orientalism* and the Postcolonial Predicament," *Oxford Literary Review* 16 (1994).

Rajeswari Sunder Rajan, "After '*Orientalism*': Colonialism and English Literary Studies in India," *Social Scientist: Monthly Journal of the Indian School of Social Sciences* (July 1986).

Amal Rassam et al., "Comments on *Orientalism*," *Comparative Studies in Society and History* (October 1980).

Seymour Reich, "Refuting Edward Said," *Harper's Magazine* (June 1987).

Roddey Reid, "Modernist Aesthetics and Familial Textuality: Gide's Straight Is the Gate," *Studies in Twentieth Century Literature* (Summer 1989).

Jane Rendall, "Scottish Orientalism: from Robertson to James Mill," *Historical Journal* (March 1982).

Robert Fernández Retamar, "Calibán revistado," *Casa de las Americas* (July–August 1986).

Hans Peter Rickman, "Strange Encounter," *Contemporary Review* (February 1992).

Joseph Riddel, "Scriptive Fate / Scriptive Hope," *Diacritics* (Fall 1976).

Bruce Robbins,"Homelessness and Worldliness," *Diacritics* (Fall 1983).

——, "The Butler Did It: On Agency in the Novel," *Representations* (Spring 1984).

——, "Poaching off the Disciplines," *Raritan* (Spring 1987).

——, "Secularism, Elitism, Progress, and Other Transgressions: On Edward Said's 'Voyage In,'" *Social Text* (Fall 1994).

Rosanne Rocher, "Orientalism, Poetry, and the Millennium," *Pacific Affairs* (Fall 1985).

Maxime Rodinson, "Fantômes et réalités de l'orientalisme," *Qantara* (Novembre-Décembre 1994).

John Rogers, "Post-Orientalism and the Interpretation of Premodern and Modern Political Identities: The Case of Sri Lanka," *Journal of Asian Studies* 53 (1994).

Mitchell Ross, "Allah and Man at Columbia," *American Spectator* (May 1982).

Michael Rossington, "Shelley and the Orient," *Keats-Shelley Review* (Fall 1991).

Matthew Rothschild, "Lenses and Tripods," *The Progressive* (January 1996).

Suzanne Ruggi, "Edward W. Said: Humor, Conviction & Scholarly Agitation," *Jerusalem Times* 20 February 1998.

Kalpana Sahni, "Oriental Phantoms," *Social Scientist: Monthly Journal of the Indian School of Social Sciences* (July 1986).

T. Sarkar, "Orientalism Revisited: Saidian Frameworks in the Writing of Modern Indian History," *Oxford Literary Review* 16 (1994).

Janny Scott, "A Palestinian Confronts Time: For Columbia Literary Critic, Cancer is a Spur to Memory," *The New York Times* 19 September 1998.

Anton Shammas, "Arafat's Types of Ambiguity: A Close Reading of a Historic Palestinian Text," *Harper's Magazine* (March 1989).

Ella Shocaht and Robert Stam, "Shultz Meeting with Edward Said and Ibrahim Abu-Lughod," *Journal of Palestine Studies* (Summer 1983).

A. Silvera, "The Intellectual Origins of the French Expedition to Egypt," *American Historical Review* 94 (1989).

Emmanuel Sivan, "Edward Said and His Arab Reviewers," *Jerusalem Quarterly* 35 (1985).

David Spanier, "Strengths and Weaknesses: On the Lebanese War," *Encounter* (April 1986).

Patricia Springborg, "Politics, Primordialism, and Orientalism: Marx, Aristotle, and the Myth of the Gemeinschaft," *American Political Science Review* (March 1986).

Michael Sprinker, "The National Question: Said, Ahmad, Jameson," *Public Culture* (Fall 1993).

Sara Suleri, "The Secret Sharers," *Voice Literary Supplement* 8 June 1993.

Edward Sullivan, "Mariano Fortuny y Marsal and Orientalism in Nineteenth-Century Spain," *Arts Magazine* (April 1981).

Heather Sutherland, "Symposium on Edward Said's *Orientalism*," *Journal of Asian Studies* (May 1980).

Suzanne Trimel, "Faculty Profile: Edward Said," *Columbia University Record* 24 April 1998.

Katie Trumpener, "Rewriting *Roxanne*: Orientalism and Intertextuality in Montesquieu's *Lettres persanes* and Defoe's *The Fortunate Mistress*," *Stanford French Review* (Summer 1987).

A. Tuck, "On Nietzsche and Orientalism," *New Ideas in Psychology* 7 (1989).

Bryan Turner, "From Orientalism to Global Sociology," *Sociology* (November 1989).

Aram Veeser, "Edward Said," *Minnesota Review* 30 (1988).

Giorgio Vercellin, "Fine della storia, storia orientale e orientalistica," *Studi Storici* 32 (1991).

Ed Vulliamy, "Disarming—and Dangerous?" *The Observer* 29 August 1999.

M. Wahba, "An Anger Observed," *Journal of Arabic Literature* 2 (1989).

Jo Ann Wein, "Delacroix's 'Street in Meknes' and the Ideology of Orientalism," *Arts Magazine* (June 1983).

Justus Reid Weiner, "'My Beautiful Old House' and Other Fabrications by Edward Said," *Commentary* (September 1999).

Harold Weiss, "The Genealogy of Justice and the Justice of Genealogy: Chomsky and Said vs. Foucault and Bové," *Philosophy Today* (Spring 1989).

J. Welwood, "Turning East: The Promise and Peril of the New Orientalism," *Journal of Transpersonal Psychology* 9 (1977).

Harold Wershow, "The Fuss Over Islam," *Harper's Magazine* (March 1981).

Hayden White, "Criticism as Cultural Politics," *Diacritics* (Fall 1976).

Leo Wieseltier, "Exchange on Orientalism," *New Republic* 180 (1979).

Ernest Wilson, "Orientalism: A Black Perspective," *Journal of Palestine Studies* 10 (1981).

George Wilson, "Edward Said on Contrapuntal Reading," *Philosophy and Literature* (October 1994).

Michael Wood, "Lost Paradises," *The New York Review of Books* 3 March 1994.

Elia Zureik, "Arab Youth in Israel: Their Situation and Status Perceptions," *Journal of Palestine Studies* (Spring 1974).

CHAPTERS IN BOOKS ON SAID

Aijaz Ahmad, "Orientalism and After: Ambivalence and Metropolitan Location in the Work of Edward Said," in *In Theory: Classes, Nations, Literatures* (London and New York: Verso, 1992).

Sadiq Jalal Al-Azm, "Orientalism and Orientalism in Reverse," in *Forbidden Agendas: Intolerance and Defiance in the Middle East* (London: Al Saqi Books, 1984).

Aziz al-Azmah, "The Articulation of Orientalism," in *Orientalism, Islam, and Islamicists*, ed. Assaf Hussain et al. (Brattheboro, Vermont: Amana Books, 1984).

Rukmini Bhaya-Nair, "Fictional Selves, Empire's Fictions: The Poets of John Company," in *Tropic Crucible Self and Theory in Language and Literature*, ed. Ranjit Chatterjee (Singapore: Singapore University Press, 1984).

Patrick Brantlinger, "Rule of Darkness: Said, *Culture and Imperialism*," in *Macropolitics of Nineteenth Century Literature: Nationalism, Exoticism, Imperialism* (Philadelphia: University of Pennsylvania Press, 1991).

Tim Brennan, "Places of Mind, Occupied Lands: Edward Said and Philology," in *Edward Said: A Critical Reader*, ed Michael Sprinker (Cambridge, Mass.: Blackwell, 1992).

Paul Brown, "'This Thing of Darkness I Acknowledge Mine,': *The Tempest* and the Discourse of Colonialism," in *Political Shakespeare: New Essays in Cultural Materialism*, ed. Jonathan Dollimore and Alan Sinfield (Ithaca: Cornell University Press, 1985).

Partha Chatterjee, "Their Own Words? An Essay for Edward Said," in *Edward Said: A Critical Reader*, ed. Michael Sprinker (Oxford: Blackwell, 1992).

James Clifford, "On *Orientalism*," in *The Predicament of Culture: Twentieth-Century Ethnography, Literature, and Art* (Cambridge: Harvard University Press, 1988).

Jonathan Culler, "Political Criticism," in *Writing the Future*, ed. David Wood (London: Routledge, 1990).

Richard Fox, "East of Said," in *Edward Said: A Critical Reader*, ed. Michael Sprinker (Oxford: Blackwell, 1992).

Ralph Gasché, "Hegel's Orient or the End of Romanticism," in *History and Mimesis*, ed. Irving Massey et al. (Albany: State University of New York Press, 1983).

Jan Gorak, "Edward Said and the Open Canon," in *The Making of the Modern Canon: Genesis and Crisis of a Literary Idea* (London: Athlone and Atlantic Highlands, 1991).

M. A. R. Habib, "Said, Edward William," in *A Dictionary of Cultural and Critical Theory*, ed. Michael Payne (Cambridge, Mass.: Blackwell, 1996).

Barbara Harlow, "The Palestinian Intellectual and the Liberation of the Academy," in *Edward Said: A Critical Reader*, ed. Michael Sprinker (Oxford: Blackwell, 1992).

Nobar Hovsepian, "Connections with Palestine," in *Edward Said: A Critical Reader*, ed. Michael Sprinker (Oxford: Blackwell, 1992).

Abdul JanMohamed, "Worldliness-without-World, Homelessness-as-Home: Toward a Definition of the Specular Border Intellectual," in *Edward Said: A Critical Reader*, ed. Michael Sprinker (Oxford: Blackwell, 1992).

Frank Joostens, "Schaven ann de zwarte: Koloniaal discours in *het Vlaams-Afrikaanse tijdschrift Band* (1942-1960),"
———. *Restant: Tijdschrift voor Recente Semiotische* (1991).
John Kucich, "Edward W. Said," in *Modern American Critics Since 1955*, ed. Gregory S. Jay (Detroit, Mich.: Gale Research, 1988).
Günter Lenz, "Edward Said (1935–)," in *Contemporaries in Cultural Criticism*, ed. Hartmut Heuermann et al. (Frankfurt: Verlag, 1991).
David Lodge, "Edward Said," in *Modern Criticism Today: A Reader*, ed. David Lodge (London: Longman, 1988).
Bart Moore-Gilbert, "Edward Said: *Orientalism* and Beyond," in *Postcolonial Theory: Contexts, Practices, Politics* (London: Verso, 1996).
Benita Parry, "Overlapping Territories and Intertwined Histories: Edward Said's Postcolonial Cosmopolitanism," in *Edward Said: A Critical Reader*, ed. Michael Sprinker (Oxford: Blackwell, 1992).
Dennis Porter, "Orientalism and Its Problems," in *The Politics of Theory*, ed. Francis Barker et al. (Colchester: University of Essex Press, 1983).
Ella Shohat, "Antinomies of Exile: Said at the Frontiers of National Narrations," in *Edward Said: A Critical Reader*, ed. Michael Sprinker (Oxford: Blackwell, 1992).
Asha Varadharajan, "Edward Said," in *Exotic Parodies: Subjectivity in Adorno, Said, Spivak* (Minneapolis: University of Minnesota Press, 1995).
Eleanor Wachtel, "Edward Said," in *More Writers and Company* (Toronto: Vintage, 1997).
Robert Young, "Disorienting Orientalism," in *White Mythologies* (London: Routledge, 1990).

BOOKS ON SAID

The following books deal in part with Said. In some of the books, Said himself is a contributor.

Ahmed, Aijaz, *In Theory: Classes, Nations, Literatures*. London: Verso, 1992.
The Anti-Aesthetic: Essays on Postmodern Culture. Ed. Hal Foster et al. New York: New Press, 1998.
Barsamian, David, *The Pen and the Sword*. Toronto: Between the Lines, 1994.
Bivona, Daniel, *Desire and Contradiction: Imperial Visions and Domestic Debates in Victorian Literature*. Manchester: Manchester University Press, 1990.
Bongie, Chris, *Exotic Memories: Literature, Colonialism, and the Fin de Siècle*. Stanford: Stanford University Press, 1991.
Bové, Paul A., *In the Wake of Theory*. Hanover, Wesleyan University Press, 1992.
Brown, Laura, *Ends of Empire: Women and Ideology in Early Eighteenth-Century English Literature*. Ithaca: Cornell University Press, 1993.

Cairns, David, and Shaun Richards, *Writing Ireland: Colonialism, Nationalism and Culture.* Manchester: Manchester University Press, 1994.

Cheng, Vincent, *Joyce, Race and Empire.* Cambridge: Cambridge University Press, 1995.

Chomsky, Noam (with Edward Said and Ramsey Clark), *Acts of Agression.* New York: Seven Stories Press, 1999.

———— (with Edward Said). *The Fateful Triangle: The United States, Israel and the Palestinians.* Boston: South End Press, 1983.

Chopin at the Boundaries: Sex, History and Musical Genre. Ed. Jeffrey Kallberg and Edward Said. Cambridge: Harvard University Press, 1997.

Clifford, James, *The Predicament of Culture: Twentieth-century Ethnography, Literature and Art.* Cambridge: Harvard University Press, 1988.

Edward Said and the Work of the Critic: Speaking Truth to Power, Ed. Paul A. Bové. Durham: Duke University Press, 2000.

The Edward Said Reader, Ed. Moustafa Bayoumi and Andrew Rubin. New York: Vintage, 2000.

Europe and Its Others, Ed. Peter Hulme *et al.* Colchester: University of Essex, 1985.

Evans, Martin J., *Milton's Imperial Epic: "Paradise Lost" and the Discourse of Colonialism.* Ithaca: Cornell University Press, 1996).

Gunn, Giles, *The Culture of Criticism and the Criticism of Culture.* New York: Oxford University Press, 1987.

Guttmann, Allen, *Games and Empire: Modern Sports and Cultural Imperialism.* New York: Columbia University Press, 1994.

Jerusalem Today, Ed. Ghada Karmi and Edward Said. London: Garnet Publishing, 1998.

Kabani, Rana, *Europe's Myths of Orient: Devise and Rule.* Bloomington: Indiana University Press, 1986.

Kim, Ed. Edward Said. New York: Penguin, 1991.

Lewis, Reina, *Gendering Orientalism: Race, Femininity, and Representation.* London: Routledge, 1995.

Lloyd, David, Anomalous *States: Irish Writing and the Post-colonial Moment.* Dublin: Lilliput, 1993.

Lowe, Lisa, *Critical Terrains: French and British Orientalisms.* Ithaca: Cornell University Press, 1991.

Masters of the Universe: NATO's Balkan Crusade. Ed. Tariq Ali. London and New York: Verso, 2000.

Makiya, Kanan, *Cruelty and Silence: War, Tyranny, Uprising, and the Arab World.* London: Gernet, 1994.

Melman, Billie, *Women's Orients: English Women and the Middle East, 1718–1918: Sexuality, Religion and Work.* London: Macmillan, 1992.

Miller, Janet, *Seductions: Studies in Reading Culture.* London and New York: Routledge, 1990.

Mitchell, Timothy, *Colonising Egypt*. Berkeley: University of California Press, 1988.

Mitter, Partha, *Art and Nationalism in Colonial India 1850–1922: Occidental Orientations*. Cambridge: Cambridge University Press, 1994.

Mudimbe, V. Y., *The Invention of Africa: Gnosis, Philosophy, and the Other Knowledge*. London: James Currey, 1988.

Phillips, Kathy J., *Virginia Woolf against Empire*. Knoxville: Tennessee University Press, 1996.

Porter, Denis, *Halted Journeys: Desire and Transgression in European Travel Writing*. Princeton: Princeton University Press, 1991.

The Postcolonial Question: Common Skies, Divided Horizons, Ed. Iain Chambers and Lidia Curti. London and New York: Routledge, 1996.

Pratt, Mary-Louise, *Imperial Eyes: Travel Writing and Trans-culturation*. London and New York: Routledge, 1992.

Qing, Zhaoming, *Orientalism and Modernism: The Legacy of China in Pound and Williams*. Durham:Duke University Press, 1995.

Reflections on Orientalism: Edward Said, Ed. Warren Cohen. East Lansing: Michigan State University Press, 1983.

Revisiting Culture, Reinventing Peace, Ed. Muhammed A. Shuraydi et al. New York: Interlink Publishing Group, 2000.

Edward Said: A Critical Reader, Ed. Michael Sprinkler Oxford: Blackwell, 1992.

Salusinszky, Imre, *Criticism in Society*. New York: Methuen, 1987.

San Juan, E. Jr., *Beyond Postcolonial Theory*. New York: St. Martin's Press, 1998.

Saccco, Joe (with Edward Said), *Palestine*. New York: Fantagraphics Books, 2001.

Sotomayor, Carmen, *Una lectura orientalista de Juan Goytisolo*. Madrid: Fundamentos, 1990.

Spurr, David, *The Rhetoric of Empire: Colonial Discourse in Journalism, Travel Writing, and Imperial Administration*. Durham: Duke University Press, 1993.

Suleri, Sara, *The Rhetoric of English India*. Chicago: University of Chicago Press, 1992.

Selected Subaltern Studies. Ed. Ranajit Guha and Gayatri Spivak. Oxford: Oxford University Press, 1988.

Zhorah J. Sullivan, *Narratives of Empire: The Fictions of Rudyard Kipling*. Cambridge: Cambridge University Press, 1993

Symposium on *Orientalism, Journal of Asian Studies* (May 1980).

Symposium on *Culture and Imperialism, Social Text* (Fall 1994).

Viswanathan, Gauri, *Masks of Conquest: Literary Study and British Rule in India*. New York: Columbia University Press, 1989.

Women and Children First, Ed. Ian Jack et al. Oxford: Granta Books, 1999.

Young, Robert J. C., *White Mythologies: Writing History and the West*. London and New York: Routledge, 1990.

———. *Colonial Desire: Hybridity in Theory, Culture, and Race*, London and New York: Routledge, 1995.

Venice Desired, Ed. Tony Tanner and Edward Said. London: Garnet, 1998.

The War for Palestine: Rewriting the History of 1948, Ed. Eugene L. Rogan and Avi Shlaim. Cambridge: Cambridge University Press, 2001.

Xu, Ben, *Situational Tensions of Critic-Intellectuals: Thinking through Literary Politics with Edward Said and Frank Lentricchia*. New York: Peter Lang, 1992.

Edward Said

Drawing by David Levine. Reprinted with permission from *The New York Review of Books*. Copyright © 1994 Nyrev, Inc.

Notes

Introduction: Edward Said at the Limits

1. See Bryan Turner, *Orientalism, Postmodernism and Globalism* (London: Routledge, 1994), chap. 2 in particular; Perry Anderson, *The Origins of Postmodernity* (London: Verso, 1998); Frederic Jameson, *The Cultural Turn: Selected Writings on the Postmodern, 1983–1998* (London and New York: Verso, 1998); Terry Eagleton, "Allergic to Depths," *LRB* 18 March 1999: 7–8.

2. Bellow paints a picture of resistance to the forces of destruction that continue to dog our times. For more on the subject, see Saul Bellow, *The Dean's December* (New York: Barnes and Nobel, 1998); chap. 5 is markedly interesting.

3. I have already dealt with *Culture and Imperialism* in *Signifying with a Vengeance: Theories, Literatures, Storytellers* (New York: State University of New York Press, 2002): chap. 3 in particular.

4. See Edward Said, "Refusal to Surrender Quietly," *Al-Ahram* Weekly 5–11 August 1999: 3. In the article, Said praises projects such as Across Borders and Museum of Memory.

5. For more on the subject, see Enoch Powell, *Reflections of a Statesman: The Writings and Speeches of Enoch Powell* (New York: Barnes and Noble, 1997): chaps. 2, 3, and 5. See also Charles Glass, *Tribes with Flags: A Dangerous Passage through the Chaos of the Middle East* (London: Grove/Atlantic, 1991): 23–44.

6. Quoted in Horace Wyndham, *Speranza: A Biography of Lady Wilde* (London: 1951): 160. See also Terry Eagleton, *Scholars and Rebels in Nineteenth-Century Ireland* (Oxford: Blackwell, 1999): chap. 4 in particular.

7. In other words, Israel took 78 percent of Palestine in 1948 and the remaining 22 percent in 1967. For more details on the subject, see Phyllis Bennis and Neal Cassidy, *From Stones to Statehood: The Palestinian Uprising* (New York: Olive Branch, 1990); *Intifada: The Palestinian Uprising against Israeli Occupation*, ed., Zachary Lockman and Joel Beinin (Toronto: Between the Lines, 1989); Edward Said, "Palestinians under Siege," *LRB* 14 December 2000: 9–14.

8. The ideas developed in this section are drawn from Fakrul Alam, "Edward Said and the Counter-Discourse of Post-colonial Intellectuals," *Colonial and Post-colonial Encounters*, ed. Niaz Zaman, Firduous Azim, and Shakar Hussein (Dhaka: Vedams Books, 1999): 34–37.

9. I have dealt with this matter in *Signifying with a Vengeance*. See chap. 3 in particular.

10. For more on the subject, see Mustapha Marrouchi, "Exile Runes," *College Literature* (Fall 2001): 88–129.

11. Although this is not the place to summarize Edward Said's life story, it is helpful to remind ourselves that he was born in Jerusalem in 1935 only to be forced to leave the city with his family after Israel annexed Palestine in 1948. From Palestine the Saids moved to Cairo, where he was a student for a while before going to Mount Hermon School in Massachusetts and to the Universities of Princeton and Harvard. After graduating from Harvard, Said began teaching in Columbia. In 1966 he published his first book, *Joseph Conrad and the Fictions of Autobiography*. It is a volume that holds few clues to Said's subsequent work except for the choice of the writer (Conrad has been one of his obsessive interests and is the type of extraterritorial writer that fascinates him) and the decision to go beyond the "literary" works to study the novelist's letters and their position vis-à-vis the fiction. Noticeably, Said showed no interest in Conrad as a novelist of the colonial experience. For more on the subject, see Pal Ahluwalia and Bill Ashcroft, *The Politics of Identity* (London: Routledge, 1997): 45–51.

12. For more on the subject, see Mustapha Marrouchi, "Rootprints," *The Dalhousie Review* (Spring 1997): 67–97.

13. See Timothy Garton Ash, *History of the Present: Essays, Sketches and Despatches from Europe in the Nineties* (London: Allen Lane, 1999) 323–27. Garton Ash adds Balcerowicz to Havel and Geremek.

14. There is a shrewdly entertaining account of the matter in Edward Said, *Representations of the Intellectual* (New York: Pantheon, 1994) 69–70.

15. This nasty episode in Said's life is eloquently narrated in Edward Said, "Freud, Zionism, and Vienna," *Al-Ahram Weekly* 15–21 March 2001.

16. It must be added that *Culture and Imperialism*, despite its many merits, did not have the impact for which it was perhaps intended.

17. Said expounds his view of sound versus silence in "From Silence to Sound and Back Again: Music, Literature, and History," *Raritan* (Fall 1997): 23–45.

18. *Commentary* has axed Said more than once. In 1981 when his book *Out of Place: A Memoir* came out, the monthly journal went on the attack and called him "misfit and deranged." Justus Reid Weinet, "'My Beautiful Old House' and Other Fabrications by Edward Said," *Commentary* (September 1999). The same happened when Said visited Palestine in 1992 and wrote on the plight of the Palesinians under occupation. For more on the subject see Edward Said, "Palestine, Then and Now," *Harper's Magazine* (December 1992): 13–21.

19. I have read "'My Beautiful Old House' and Other Fabrications by Edward Said" with care and attention only to discover how Weiner manages skilfully to bring forward what suits his hogwash thesis and bury everything else that confirms that Said did indeed attend St. George School and that the Saids were well known as an old Palestinian family. At least one of the students who studied with Edward said as much to Weiner, who conveniently failed to mention the fact in his attack. Other errors are to be noted:

Weiner quotes only those who consolidate his slanderous thesis. See Justus Reid Weiner, "'My Beautiful Old House' and Other Fabrications by Edward Said," *Commentary* (September 1999): 23–32.

20. Weiner refused to check his allegations against Said's memoir, *Out of Place*. See Edward Said, "Defamation, Revisionist Style," *Al-Ahram Weekly* 26 August 1999.

21. Piali Roy interviews Edward Said for "Ideas," CBC 23 November 1999: 9:00 P.M.

22. The tragedy of living a meaningless life and being quickly forgotten at the end of it has been so skilfully projected in Said's works that it has become accepted by most of his readers and audiences and, paradoxically, gives much comfort. It takes any guilt out of failure, which is the inevitable fate of us all.

Chapter One: The Intellectual with a Mandate

1. An interesting essay on Said's debt to Williams is to be found in Patrick Brantlinger, "Edward Said and/versus Raymond Williams," in *Edward Said and the Post-Colonial*, ed. Bill Ashcroft and Hussein Kadhim (New York: Nova, 2001): 57–72.

2. There is irony in the fact that the best three cultural critics England produced are not English. Frank Kermode, Raymond Williams, and Terry Eagleton are proud of their Manx, Welsh, and Irish roots. As a result, each one's journey from the periphery to the center, from the working-class outskirts of English culture to its middle- and upper-class core, from outlandish Douglas, Pandy, and Salford to chairs at London, Cambridge, and Oxford, takes on something of an epic air, almost at one with the path from Caliban's cave to Prospero's study.

3. See "Edward Said," in Eleanor Wachtel, *More Writers and Company* (Toronto:Vintage, 1977) 76–77; Edward Said, "Between Worlds," *LRB* 1 May 1998: 3–7. Said elaborates a breathtaking genealogy of his prepolitical life in Jerusalem and Cairo. The essay is moving, at times sad, and full of revelations about a man who was destined to become a polyartist. He is one of these figures whom if he did not already exist, the philistines would need to invent him.

4. "Patriotism," Said adds, "is best thought of as an obscure dead language, learned prehistorically but almost forgotten and almost unused since. Nearly everything normally associated with it—wars, rituals of nationalistic loyalty, sentimentalized (or invented) traditions, parades, flags, etc.—is quite dreadful and full of appalling claims of superiority and pre-eminence. Is theoretical patriotism really that much better?" Edward Said, "Which Country?" *The Nation* 15–22 July 1991: 116.

5. D. H. Lawrence, *Poems* (London: Duckworth, 1976): 81; David Ellis gives a perspicacious reading of some of Lawrence's poems in his *D. H. Lawrence: Dying Game 1922–30* (Cambridge, Mass.: Cambridge University Press, 1998): 45–106.

6. For an excellent analysis of the problem of famine in Gaza and the West Bank, see Robert Fisk, "The Palestinians Believe They Have Nothing to Lose by Fighting On," *The Independent* 30 October 2000: 1–4.

7. Edward Said, *The World, the Text, and the Critic* (Cambridge, Mass.: Harvard University Press, 1983) 29. "It is an undoubted exaggeration to say," Said notes, ". . . that these essays make absolutely clear what my critical position—only implied by *Orientalism* and my other recent books—really is. To some this may seem like a failing of rigour, honesty, or energy. To others it may imply some radical uncertainty on my part as to what I do

stand for, especially given the fact that I have been accused by colleagues of intemperate and even unseemly polemicism. To still others—and this concerns me more—it may seem that I am an undeclared Marxist, afraid of losing respectability and concerned by the contradictions entailed by the label "'Marxist'" (1983: 28).

8. I have discussed the context of this trope in detail in "Fear of the Other, Loathing the Similar," *College Literature* (Fall 1999): 17–59.

9. See "Bill Gates Is," *Harper's Magazine* (July 2002): 28–29.

10. Edward Said's method of *contrapuntal* analysis has been largely documented in George Wilson, "Edward Said on Contrapuntal Reading," *Philosophy and Literature* (October 1994): 265–73.

11. At the other end of the spectrum, Said praises intellectuals such as Gore Vidal and Noam Chomsky, who oppose oppression of any kind and speak out against all injustices.

12. *Sä-ēd'* Data Base traces the evolution of Said and Palestine from 1935 to 2002.

13. See the dust cover of the American edition of *The World, the Text, and the Critic*.

14. Raymond Williams, *Culture and Society 1780–1950* (London: Chatto and Windus, 1958) 47. Following Williams' crucial and useful distinctions among residual, dominant, and emergent aspects of culture, contradictions can be acknowledged as an indication that dominant ideologies are potentially unstable and never totally effective; hence they may provide the space for radical intervention and change.

15. Nowhere is this view better captured than in Edward Said, *Covering Islam: How the Media and the Experts Determine How We See the Rest of the World* (New York: Pantheon Books, 1981).

16. I am indebted to Sara Suleri for the formulation of some of the ideas I developed here.

17. *The Question of Palestine, The Politics of Dispossession*, and *The End of the Peace Process* easily come to mind.

18. The note is perfectly struck in the following instance, where Said speaks of the his role as member in the PNC in more endearing terms than in the following passage, which celebrates an exhilarating moment in the life of so many Palestinian exiles: "It is an irony and contradiction worth noting by way of an epilogue that Darwish, Khoury and I met together for the first time in six years at Algiers the other week, to attend the meetings of the Palestine National Council. Darwish wrote the Declaration of Statehood, which I helped to re-draft and translate into English. Along with the Declaration, the PNC approved resolutions in favour of two states in historical Palestine, one Arab, one Jewish, whose co-existence would assure self-determination for both peoples. Khoury commented relentlessly, but fondly, as a Lebanese, on what we did, suggesting that perhaps Lebanon might some day be like Palestine. All three of us were present as both participants and observers. We were tremendously moved, of course: yet Darwish and I were worried that our texts were being mutilated by politicians and even more worried that our state was, after all, only an idea. Perhaps the habits of exile and eccentricity could not be changed as far as we ourselves were concerned: but for a short, non-stop talking spell, Palestine and Lebanon were alive in the texts." See Edward Said, "Goodbye to Mahfouz," *LRB* 8 December 1988: 12.

19. Yezid Sayigh, *Armed Struggle and the Search for State: The Palestinian National Movement, 1949–1993* (Oxford: Clarendon, 1998). The major contribution of Sayigh's book is that it presents a mass of new material and an extraordinary detailed and coherent account of the history of the PNM and its relation with its neighbours, especially Lebanon.

20. I am greatly indebted to Charles Glass for the ideas I develop in this section.

21. See *The Pen and Sword: Conversations with David Barsamian*, introduction by Iqbal Ahmed, ed. David Barsamian (Toronto: Between the Lines, 1994): 8.

22. For more details on the subject of expulsion, see Edward Said, *The Question of Palestine* (1979: rprt, New York: Vintage, 1992); *Blaming the Victims*, ed. Edward Said and Christopher Hitchens (New York and London: Verso, 1988): 207–35.

23. Helga Graham, "Saudis Break the Silence," *LRB* 22 April 1993: 6–9; Fred Halliday, *Islam and the Myth of Confrontation: Politics in the Middle East* (London; Tauris, 1996): 34–111 in particular.

24. For more details on the subject, see Alexei Vassiliev, *The History of Saudi Arabia 1745–1994* (London: Saqi Books, 1998); Robert Fisk, "All These Cruel Muslim Regimes Abuse the People of the Middle East," *The Independent* 7 August 2001: 1–3.

25. Said speaks endearingly of Abu Zeid, the Egyptian intellectual who was killed by the fundamentalists. For Said, Abu Zeid represents a rising new critical consciousness within the Arab and Islamic world. See *The Politics of Dispossession* (New York: Pantheon, 1994): 408–09.

26. See, for example, Edward Said, "La Palestine n'a pas disparu," *Le Monde Diplomatique* (May 1998): 1, 5.

Chapter Two: The *Old/New Idiot*: Rereading the Postcolonial Sign

1. It is now granted that Post colonial Theory was born around the same time as the launching of *Orientalism* by Edward Said in 1979. Other pioneers before Said paved the road for the discipline: Frantz Fanon, C.L.R. James, Malcolm X, James Baldwin among others come to mind.

2. Edward Said is one (Raymond Williams, Terry Eagleton, and Frank Kermode also fit in the bill) of the best prizes offered by the builders of Empire. The practical side of this example is that it expanded what is today called "English Literature" as a subject or field of inquiry.

3. For more on the subject, see Julia Kriteva, "Le Sujet en procès," in *Polygone* (Paris: Seuil, 1977): 55–166; Roland Barthes, "The Death of the Author," in *Image-Music-Text*, trans. Stephen Heath (New York: Hill and Wang, 1977): 143–148.

4. *Out of Place*, "Living by the Clock," "Between Worlds," *Reflections on Exile* come easily to mind.

5. Just as Auerbach was dismissed from his university post in Marburg in 1935 "on racist grounds," Said was also nearly dismissed from his post of University professor at Columbia University. See Edward Said, "Freud, Zionism, and Vienna," *Al-Ahram Weekly* 15–21 March 2001: 4; Alexander Cockburn, "Said, Sontag and the Laws of Intellectual Safety," *Left Coast* 17 August 2001: 6.

6. Gilles Deleuze and Félix Guattari, *What Is Philosophy?*, trans. Hugh Tomlinson and Graham Burchell (New York: Columbia University Press, 1994. I am indebted to Deleuze and Guattari for the formulation of some of the ideas I expound on in this section.

7. After 9/11, anyone with an Arab or Muslim name is usually made to stand aside for special attention during airport security checks. There have been many reported instances of discriminatory behavior against Arabs, so that speaking Arabic or even reading

an Arabic document in public is likely to draw unwelcome attention. Arabic is also synonymous with terrorism. The line of misrepresentation is so reductive and so hostile to the history, society, and culture of the region.

8. For an elaborate view on the subject, see Jasper Hopkins, *Nicholas of Cusa's Dialectical Mysticism: Text, Translation, and Interpretive Study of de Visione Dei* (New York: Arthur J. Press, 1985). Hopkins develops a suggestive introduction to the idea of the "Idiot."

9. Said has elaborated on his method of (*inventio*) in "Globalizing Literary Study," *PMLA* January 2001: 64–68. For more on the New Idiot, see Gilles Deleuze and Félix Guattari, *Qu'est-ce que la philosophie* (Paris: Les Éditions de Minuit, 1991): 45–49.

10. On the Idiot (the uninitiated, private, or ordinary individual as opposed to the technician or expert) in his relationships with thought, see Nicholas of Cusa, *The Idiot*, trans. of *Idiota* [1450]; London: 1650).

11. Thomas Kuhn, *The Structure of Scientific Revolutions* (Chicago: University of Chicago Press, 1996). Chap. 1 in particular.

12. See also François Jacob, *The Logic of Life: A History of Heredity*, trans. Betty E. Spillmann (New York: Panteon Books, 1973): 50 and passim; Georges Canguilhem, *La Connaissance de la vie* (Paris: Gustave-Joseph Vrin, 1969): 44–63.

13. By shifting the origin of the gaze from a Western male viewer to a native female viewer, Said stresses the circulation and negotiation of the look rather than a unidirectional movement (from white male subject-viewer to indigenous object). The reader is made to identify with the position of the object of the gaze, as well as with the gaze itself, so that the spectacle is no longer exclusively feminine, or the gaze exclusively masculine. For Sartre on the other hand, the gaze is a menace, a threat directed at the Other. It is mobilized to unsettle, so that the subject and object of the gaze appear as relative positions in the symbolic chain rather than as fixed or essential. See Edward Said, *Orientalism* (New York: Vintage, 1989): 23; Jean-Paul Sartre, *Nausea*, trans. Lloyd Alexander (New York: New Directions, 1964): 3.

14. For more on the subject, see *Selected Essays of John Berger*, ed. Geoff Dyer (London: Bloomsbury, 2002).

15. For more on this subject, see Jacques Lacan, "Le Mythe individuel du névrosé ," *Ornicar?* 17/18 (1979): 289–307; *Écrits* (Paris: Seuil, 1966): 213–241.

16. Charles de Baudelaire, *Oeuvres complètes* (Paris: La Pléiade, 1966). "L'amour du mensonge" and "la brune" in particular.

17. France is barely starting to face up to its shady past. The rise of Le Pen and his political party in the 2002-presidential election is a clear indication of the way the French still think of and treat their minorities. That Jacques Chirac was elected with 80% of the total vote was a defeat of his policy to say the least. For he, too, thinks little of "les petits Arabes," as he once called them.

18. See Jacques Lacan, "Anamorphosis," in *The Four Fundamental Concepts of PsychoAnalysis*, ed. Jacques-Alain Miller, trans. Alan Sheridan (New York: and London: W.W. Norton & Company, 1981): 79–91.

19. Jacques Derrida, *Of Hospitality*, trans. Rachel Bowlby (Stanford: Stanford University Press, 2000): 34–41; Catherine Malabou et Jacques Derrida, *La Contre-allée* (Aubenas d'Ardèche: Imprimerie Leienhart, 1999): 23.

20. It is an irony and contradiction worth noting by way of a supplement that during a recent trip to the South of France (Aix-en-Provence to be precise), I dealt with an

unforgivably nasty merchant in an open-air market who wanted to sell me two straw bags at a high price. When I pointed out that the merchant next to him was selling them for much less, he asked his assistant to check if "l'Arabe" was indeed selling them for less. I then told him that the merchant in question was not an Arab and what difference did it make even if he were, at which point he answered by saying: "Ce n'est pas pareil, cher monsieur! Un Arabe, c'est un Arabe, point final!." In other words, an Arab is a "scum." In another instance that took place in a bakery, a six-month-old Arab baby carried by her mother touched the head-scarf of a French woman standing in line to buy bread. The baby's hand was pushed away by the woman, who stormed off muttering in disapproval. On my way back to Canada, a much more pleasant and tolerant country, I kept thinking about both incidents and asking myself: Why should we (the children of people who were once colonized) spend good money to experience meanness and intolerance, not to mention sheer racism and anti-Semitism? No wine, food or landscape is worth that kind of humiliation even if it was not directed at me. It was after all directed at my people, and I am one of them. *Point final.*

21. Said makes the point in "Orientalism, an Afterward," *Raritan* (Winter 1995): 23–41.

22. See Deleuze and Guattari, *What Is Philosophy?*, 163–185. This is a shrewd and daring view of the matter I discuss here.

23. In his stunning book, *The Trial of Henry Kissinger* (London & New York: Verso, 2001), Christopher Hitchens maintains that not only Kissinger is guilty of crimes against humanity but that he was personally involved in the coup that toppled Allende and his government. See chap. 3 in paticular.

24. Deleuze and Guattari make the point with brio in chap. 3 of *What is Philosophy?*.

25. In this respect, the painting stands for the Temporally eternal, the Eternity of becoming according to Nietzsche and the Outside-interior for Foucault and Said, we might add.

26. Much gratitude goes to Sara Suleri for some of the ideas I develop here.

27. *Orientalism* generated an astonishingly productive range of scholarship and interpretation; *Culture and Imperialism* proved to be an equally evocative beginning for revisionary readings of the cultural intersections between literature and empire.

28. Letter no. 15, March 1939, in *Hannah Arendt/Karl Jaspers Correspondence, 1926–1969*, ed. Lotte Kohler and Hans Saner, trans. from the German by Roberta and Rita Kimber (New York & London: Harcourt Brace Jovanovich, 1992): 11.

29. For an insightful view of this matter, see Julia Kriteva, *Hannah Arendt: Life Is a Narrative*, trans. Frank Collins (Toronto: University of Toronto Press, 2001): 7–14.

30. See E. Naville, *Maine de Biran, sa vie et ses pensées* (Paris: 1857): 357.

Chapter Three: My Homeland, the Text

1. I have written on Said the exile elsewhere. See Mustapha Marrouchi, "Rootprints," *The Dalhousie Review* (Spring 1997): 67–97: "The Critic as Exiled Intelligence: The Case of Edward Said," *Diacritics* (Spring 1991): 63–74.

2. Approaching Said as one would any other influential thinker, by locating his ideas in context, does not mean that we should easily dismiss them. His verdict on Israel's subjugation of Palestine is bang-on: he is right to argue that in more ways than one Palestinians

are not just marginals but marginalized. He is also right to claim that more and more Palestinians are now imprisoned and tortured by Arafat and his cronies while simultaneously sustaining corrupt bureaucracy, obedient to Israel and the United States.

3. Said Aburish, *Arafat: From Defender to Dictator* (London: Bloomsbury, 1999): 13–92 in particular.

4. Said's autobiographical works are dispersed but include such essays as "Between Worlds," "Living by the Clock," "Palestine, Then and Now," "Cairo Recalled," and *Out of Place: A Memoir.*

5. A case in point is *Min Al-Manfa, Ana Ohibbak,* and *Memory for Forgetfulness* by Mahmoud Darwish.

6. Eric Auerbach, *Mimesis: The Representations of Reality in Western Literature*, trans. Willard Trask (1953; rprt. Princeton: Princeton University Press, 1968) 44–45.

7. See Seamus Deane, *Reading in the Dark* (New York: Random House, 1998): 17–82 in particular.

8. Fred Halliday, *Islam and the Myth of Confrontation: Religion and Politics in the Middle East* (London: Faber, 1996) 34–66.

9. When Said opposed the signing of Oslo I and Oslo II, he was attacked by Arafat and his acolytes not only for the suffering of his people but also for not understanding the importance of the uprising, which is considered to be the completion of the Palestinian revolution. For Arafat and his followers, because Said resides in America, he therefore cannot really fathom the everyday reality on the terrain. As a result, he should keep his mouth shut. In the end, his books were seized and carried off from all bookstores in Gaza and the West Bank as well as in East Jerusalem. Said is now banned in his own homeland. For a comprehensive view of the problem, see Said, *Peace and Its Discontents*, 147–165.

10. *Blaming the Victims.* 1–19 in particular.

11. Jacques Derrida plays on the expression by introducing *abyme and abime*, abyss. The term originally comes from the heraldic notion of an escutcheon. See his *Post Card*, trans. Alan Bass (Chicago: University of Chicago Press, 1978): 511.

12. Said, *The Pen and the Sword*, 53. Following Said's visit to Palestine, Joseph Papp, the New York producer and director who is widely respected for his commitment to liberal causes, canceled a show by Hakawati, a West Bank theater group.

13. Take the Sabra and Chatila camps as an example, and the idea will be clear enough. The murderers who were Christian Lebanese militiamen had been sent into the camps by the Israelis. See Edward Said, "Permission to Narrate," *LRB* 16 February 1984: 13–17; Robert Fisk, "Arafat's Betrayal," *LRB* 23 February 1995: 15.

14. See Salman Rushdie, "On Palestinian Identity: A Conversation with Edward Said," in *Imaginary Homelands* (London: Granta, 1991) 168.

15. The excerpt is taken from *The Nation* 15/22 July 1991: 116, where Edward Said is asked, along with other intellectuals such as John Rosenberg, Paul Savoy, and Ishmael Reed to define patriotism.

16. On the massacre in Jenin, see Robert Fisk's excellent essay, "Mr Powell Must See for Himself What Israel Inflicted on Jenin," *The Independent* 14 April 2002: 1–5; Marwan Bishara, "Le Cancer des colonies juives," *Le Monde Diplomatique* (June 2002): 15.

Chapter Four: The Site of Memory

1. I am indebted to Ian Baucom for some of the ideas I treat in this section.

2. See the dust-jacket to the American edition where Salman Rushdie praises *Out of Place.*

3. A perspicacious analysis of the "living" is to be found in Michel de Certeau, *The Practice of Everyday Life, Vol. 2: Living and Cooking*, trans., Timothy J. Tomasik (Minneapolis: University of Minnesota Press, 1998: 4.

4. Elsewhere in the memoir Said is sympathetic to the poor. Speaking of a porter in Dhour, he writes: "After an hour and a half at the bank the two of us would go shopping for heavy goods unobtainable in Dhour—wicker baskets, plates and cups, sheets and towels, 20-kilo bags of sugar and rice—and hire one of the numerous barefoot, *sharwal*-suited porters idling on the main tramline to carry them for us. Normally about 120 kilos of these goods were loaded carefully into the porter's long basket, which he strapped to his padded back, with one of the bands going across his forehead; I was afraid it might split open from the pressure" (161).

5. Slavoj Žižek, "The World Turned back to Front," *LRB* 18 March 1999: 6. Žižek is one of the most vocal and thorough critics of Postmodernism and Globocracy.

6. Edward el-Karrat, *City of Saffron*, trans. Frances Liardet (London: Quartet, 1989); *Girls of Alexandria*, trans. Frances Liardet (London: Quartet, 1993).

7. Quoted in *The Atlas of Literature*, ed. Malcolm Bradbury (London: De Agostini Editions, 1996) 211.

8. "*The Book of Ester*," in *The Old Testament* in *The New American Bible* (New York: Catholic Book Publishing Co. 1970) 507.

9. Wicke and Sprinker, "Interview with Edward Said," in *Edward Said: A Critical Reader*, 227.

Chapter Five: The Will to Authority and Transgression

1. Once playing the piano or violin or singing becomes professional, that is, a paying activity, it is hard to fault exceptionally gifted performances. Glenn Gould knew all that perfectly well but tried always to give the impression that he was really all about something else—an ideal of perfected articulation regardless of cost, a self-awareness that defied convention. For more details on piano playing, see Norman Lebrecht, *When the Music Stops: Managers, Maestros, and the Corporate Murder of Classical Music* (New York: Simon and Schuster, 1997).

2. The problem is that music today is as massively organized a White male domain as it was in the past. Without significant exception, peripherals, like women, play a crucial but subaltern role. This is true in almost any random sampling of recent events—operas, recitals, orchestral performances—in which issues of interest to the subaltern are in evidence, but for which critical responses are not likely to be encountered. Ruth Padel's impressively documented study of the female role in opera is an electric, disturbing, and brilliantly provocative work, truly worthy of its subject and an essential companion to a reading of late-twentieth-century classical music. "So far," she writes, "Western tragedy and opera have preferred to express the pain of sexual desertion through a woman's voice. They have also made it the voice of universal solitude." See Ruth Padel, "Putting the Words into Women's Mouths: The Female Role in Opera," *LRB* 23 January 1997: 12.

3. "A month after I was diagnosed I discovered myself in the middle of writing a letter to my mother, who had been dead for a year and a half. Somehow the urge to communicate with her overcame the factual reality of her death, which in mid-sentence stopped my fanciful urge, leaving me slightly disoriented, even embarrassed. A vague narrative urge seemed to be stirring inside me, but I was too caught up in the anxieties and nervousness

of my life with CLL (chronic lymphocytic leukemia) to pay it much attention." Edward Said, "Living by the Clock," *LRB* 29 April 1999: 10.

4. Edward Said, "Cairo Recalled: Growing Up in the Cultural Crosscurrents of 1940s Egypt," *House and Garden* (April 1987): 32.

5. I am indebted to Edward Said for the formulation of some of the ideas I develop in this section. For more on the subject, see Edward Said, *Relections on Exile* (Cambridge Harvard University Press, 2000).

6. See Peter Ostwald, *Glenn Gould: The Ecstasy and the Tragedy of Genius* (London: Norton, 1997) chap. 3 in particular.

7. See Michael Stegemann, "A Kind of Autumnal Repose," in *The Glenn Gould Edition*, trans. Gerry Bramall (Toronto: Sony Classical, 1993): 11.

8. See Edward Said, "In the Chair," *LRB* 17 July 1997: 3–5.

9. See Alan Durant, *Conditions of Music* (London: Macmillan, 1984): 123.

10. For more details on the subject of celebrating freedom in Germany in 1989, see David B. Dennis, *Beethoven in German Politics 1870–1989* (New Haven and London: Yale University Press, 1996): 175–205.

11. Quoted in Graeme Kay, "The Natural," *Music* (May 1998): 24. See also Edward Said, "Daniel Barenboim and Edward Said: A Conversation," *Raritan* (Summer 1998): 4–22.

12. In May 1997, Said gave the new Empson lectures in Cambridge, where he presented "Authority and Transgression in Opera." Said, who has combined his musical career and love for music with a devotion to the cause of liberation, has written music criticism on his own terms and has been rejuvenated rather than defeated by the exercise. Anyone who, like Said, tries to grasp the significance of Beethoven's life and music finds himself faced with a daunting task. The heroic element so central to it resides entirely within human proportions: the life is neither too long nor too short, the oeuvre seems exactly large enough, with clearly defined outlines, periods, and developments. As we enter the nineteenth century, we leave behind composers such as Bach, with his twenty children, his two hundred-plus cantatas, his innumerable instrumental works, and his unendingly complex and inventive counterpoint, Mozart, with his inhuman productivity, his forty-nine symphonies and twenty-one piano concertos, his operas, masses, quartets, trios, and sonatas, all exuding formal perfection and grace; Haydn, with his more than one hundred symphonies and dozens of works in every conceivable genre; or Handel, like Bach in his vast output, exuberant, repetitious, gallant. Such men both express a kind of murmuring anonymity and evoke a distinct aesthetic signature; the net effect is that the twentieth-century listener is awed and mystified, above all unable to identify with musical careers that were fashioned as subaltern structures framed by court and church. For more details on the subject, see Charles Rosen, *The Romantic Generation* (London: Harper-Collins, 1995); John Rosselli, *The Life of Mozart* (Cambridge: Cambridge University Press, 1998); Edward Said, "Bach's Genius, Schumann's Eccentricity, Chopin's Ruthlessness, Rosen's Gift," *LRB* 21 September 1995: 13–15.

Beethoven appeals to musicians such as Said because he is the musical vanguard of what Charles Morazé has called "*les bourgeois conquérants.*" Beethoven's aristocratic supporters were, he believed, his subordinates, not his overlords. Though he was a man of the middle classes, his were the stubborn, almost entrepreneurial successes of a thoroughly worldly individual who rose well above the circumstances of his birth. Everything about his music, from the large cache of sketchbook to the laboriously worked and reworked scores, argues effort and development on a human scale. The difficulties of his life are understandable—illness, debt, loneliness, an unpleasant family, unhappy love affairs, creative blocks—and if we take into account his extraordinary gifts and accomplishments, his artistic achievements as a whole belong to a creaturely realm. They have a dimension no lesser mortal needs to feel is theoretically unattainable. Beethoven's music is vitally committed either to sonata forms or to variation forms, the former dramatic and developmental, the latter, exfoliative and circular; in both instances, his hallmark is work, not sharing insight, and although the so-called late-period style, which so fascinated Adorno and Thomas Mann (and, I could add, Said), alternates between the demonic and the quasietherereal, there is always a healthy modicum of gritty technical effort to be appreciated. A perspicacious view of this topic can be found in Paul Robinson, *Ludwig van Beethoven, Fidelio* (Cambridge: Cambridge University Press, 1996): 7–12; David B. Dennis, *Beethoven in German Politics 1870–1989* (New Haven and London: Yale University Press, 1996): 1–32.

13. Quoted in Richard Kostelanetz, *John Cage (Ex)plain(ed)* (London: Prentice Hall International, 1996): 67.

14. In some instances, Said reminds us of Thomas Mann, who shows in *Doctor Faustus* how the Wagnerian concept of 'leitmotif' can be revealed "to the principle of National Socialism" (1991: 46). Taking Mann literally instead of taking him as the inventor of an imaginatively constructed constitutive symbol, Said perhaps goes beyond the pale, as when he suggests that post-Wagnerian music may represent the catastrophic collapse of a great civilizational achievement. While there is nothing wrong with an imaginative allegorization of such music, like the one Mann gives, it is quite another thing to suggest that this is part of what the real-world music itself means. This is something like reading Hemingway to learn what bullfights really are.

15. Ibid., 18–19, 32, 43, 51, 66–67, 146, 194, 259, and, applied to *Aida*, III, 114, 125.

16. I owe much gratitude to Lindenberger for the formulation of some of the ideas I expound on here. For more on the subject, see Herbert Liudenberger, *Opera in History: From Mouteverdi to Cage* (Stanford: Stanford University Press, 1998).

17. Bryan Turner, *Orientalism, Postmodernism, and Globalism*, 122–23.

18. See Herbert Lindenberger, *Opera in History: From Monteverdi to Cage* (Stanford: Stanford University Press, 1998): 166. I am deeply indebted to Lindenberger for the formulation of some of the ideas I develop in this section.

19. "Auguste Mariette's career is significant for *Aida* in many interesting ways. Although there has been some dispute about his exact contribution to the *Aida* libretto, his intervention has been vindicated definitively by Jean Humbert as *the* important inaugurating one for the opera. Immediately behind the libretto was his role as principal designer of antiquities at the Egyptian pavilion in the Paris International Exhibition of 1887, one of the greatest and earliest displays of imperial potency." See Said, *Culture and Imperialism*, 119.

20. Said speaks of the discipline at Victoria College where he went and how pupils were forbidden to speak any other language except English. Those who were caught speaking a language other than English were severely punished. For more details on the subject, see Said, "Cairo Recalled," 19–21.

21. Stephen Greenblatt deals with the subject in his *Hamlet in Purgatory* (Princeton and Oxford: Princeton University Press, 2001): 102–51.

22. Said, "Between Worlds," 7. Another instance of harassment can be found in his comment on the reception of the 1993 Reith Lectures he gave in England. "I had no idea of the limitations to which I was subject, before I gave the lectures," he writes. "It was

often said by complaining journalists and commentators that I was a Palestinian, and that, as everyone knew, was synonymous with violence, fanaticism, the killing of Jews. Nothing by me was quoted: it was just supposed to be a matter of common knowledge. In addition, I was described in the sonorous tones of *The Sunday Telegraph* as anti-Western, and my writing as focused on 'blaming the West' for all the evils of the world, the Third World especially." For more details on this matter, see Edward Said, *Representations of the Intellectual* (Paris: Pantheon, 1994): xi.

Chapter Six: Quite Right: In Defense of Edward Said

1. Quoted in Ed Vulliany, "Disarming—and Dangerous?" *The Observer Review* 29 August 1999: 2. See also Maya Taggi, "Out of the Shadows," *The Guardian* 12 September 1999: 12–14; Julian Borger, "Friends Rally to Repulse Attack on Edward Said," *The Guardian* 23 August 1999: 7; Christopher Hitchens, "Whose Life Is It Anyway?" *The Nation* 4 October 1999: 9. Nowhere is the attack on Said more disfiguring than in Charles Krauthammer, "The Case of the Suspect Bios," *Time* 4 October 1999: 84. Krauthammer makes his findings fiasco the cornerstone for his edifice of misrepresentations, misreadings, and ultimately his pervert ire.

2. The documentary program was aired by the Public Broadcasting System (on WNET on 5 July 5 1999) under the title *In Search of Palestine.*

3. I have read Weiner, "'My Beautiful Old House'" with care and enthusiasm only to discover how Weiner manages skilfully to bring forward what suits his hogwash thesis and bury everything else, which confirms that Said did indeed attend St. George School, that the Saids were well known as an old Palestinian family. At least one of the students who studied with Edward said as much to Weiner, who conveniently failed to mention the fact in his attack. Other errors are to be noted: Weiner quotes only those whose theses consolidate his own.

4. Piali Roy interviews Edward Said for "Ideas," CBC 23 November 1999: 9–10 P.M. The interview is detailed, sharp, and up to date with Said's views on various topics: peace in the Middle East, the vocation of the intellectual, reparation, the crisis of the Arab intellectual, Arafat.

5. Weiner's language comes across as noisy, vindictive, and pushy. His ideas are put in the conceptual marketplace with all the fervour with which others peddle second-hand Hoovers.

6. There is too much of a cultural sheep or lemming mentality among those who, like Weiner, engage in slanderous misrepresentations of others. In a series of audacious bounds, Weiner refers to Said's memoir, which was originally titled *Not Quite Right,* as "radically revised . . . in favor of the truer one presented in *Out of Place*" (2000: 12).

7. See Gary Younge, "Struggles of the Artist," *The Guardian* 17 January 2000: 3.

8. See Hitchens, "Whose Life Is It Anyway?": 9.

Chapter Seven: On Writing, Intellectual Life, and the Public Sphere

1. Okot p'Bitek, "From Where Did God Get the Clay for Making Things?" trans. T. Lo Liyong, *The Literary Review* (Summer 1991): 559–66; "White Teeth," *Africa Today* 38:2 (1991): 99–100.

2. Albert Memmi, "Dans quelle language écrire? La patrie littéraire du colonisé," *Le Monde Diplomatique* (September 1996): 12; Hichem Ben Abdallah el Aalaoui, "Être citoyen dans le monde arabe," *Le Monde Diplomatique* (July 1995): 11.

3. Mark Huband, *Warriors of the Prophet: The Challenge of Islamic Fundamentalism* (London: Westview, 1998); Mohamed Elhachni Hamdi, *The Politicisation of Islam: A Case Study of Tunisia* (London: Westview, 1998).

4. Set in a "desert state" in the Gulf, the novel is an exploration of female consciousness in an alien, oppressive environment. The fundamentalist ethic and rigid social mores keep the women segregated from the men and suffocatingly close to each other. The novel takes the form of a quartet narrated by four voices: two indigenous women and two outsiders. Each woman interprets and deals with the same set of circumstances differently. Suzanne, an American, is completely out of her depth and uses facile romantic terms to decipher the voracious interest of the men who pursue her. The two local women never question the rules that govern their lives. The wealthier of them, Nur, uses money to circumvent these rules— to buy foreign travel and sex—while the other, Tamr, takes direct action against a particular circumstance, running away from her husband's home when she finds it unbearable and going on a hunger strike to force her brother to allow her to start a dress-making business. Suha, the other outsider, is a Lebanese "modern" woman, accustomed to life in Europe and prewar Beirut. She can find no outlet for her energy in the cramped atmosphere of the "Eldorado of the East" and objects to it. It is her voice that starts and ends the novel. The discoveries she makes about herself in relation to the other women, their usually destructive energy and their sexuality, send her fleeing back to Beirut, preferring the hazards of bullets and bombs in her war-torn country to a life of lust and sloth in the land of sand and myrrh. See Ibrahim Alaoui, "Le portrait d'une romancière aggressée," *Le Monde* 1 June 1989: 12; Hanan al-Shaykh, *The Story of Zahra*, trans. Catherine Cobham (London: Quartet, 1986); *Women of Sand and Myrrh*, trans. Catherine Cobham (London: Quartet, 1989).

5. Quoted in Tahar Ben Jelloun, "Nawal el-Saadawi sous surveillance," *Le Monde* 12 March 1990: 14; Nawal el-Saadawi, *The Circling Song* (London: Atlantic Highlands, 1989); "Veils East and West," *New Statesman and Society* 9 October 1992: 19.

6. King Baabu came to power after staging a bloodless *coup* on November 7, 1987, which has become a sacred public holiday. The number 7 is now a heavenly one: there is a Television Channel called "Channel 7," a boulevard called "Boulevard November 7."

7. As with the efforts to prove I was not welcome in the country of my birth, these assaults have a humorous absurdity to them. In another instance, I was threatened with being jailed by a rather jejune, pompous ass. The reader may accuse me of being pitiless, and above all unjust with the University of Tunis (scores to be settled perhaps). They expelled me from it because I was an '*emmerdeur*'. I, for a while at least, had ensconced myself in it to provoke them, grant them their most urgent wish, always at the limit, to expel me again.

8. Quoted in Kelly Couturier, "The Writer Who Talked Turkey," *The Wahsington Post* 13 June 1995: C4; Yasar Kemal, *Murder in the Market*, trans. Thilda Kemal (London: Collins and Harvill 1979); *Anatolain Tales*, trans. Thilda Kemal (New York: Dodd Mead, 1969).

9. Frederick Edwards, "In Defense of Taslima Nasrin," *The Humanist* (September/October 1994): 42–44; "Taslima Nasrin in Europe," *The Humanist* (March/April 1995): 39; Philippe Le Corre, "Unrepentant Exile," *Far Eastern Economic Review* 24 November 1994: 32; Taslima Nasrin, *The Game in Reverse*, trans. Caroline Wright (New York: George Braziller, 1995).

10. Assia Djebar's *L'Amour, la fantasia* (Paris: Lattès, 1985) deals precisely with the subject of the silenced discourse of women in Algeria. Fatima Mernissi maintains that prohibition of the gaze is as much to protect men from themselves as from women, for *Al-Qur'ān* bears out the notion "that seclusion in Islam is a device to protect the passive male who cannot control himself sexually in the presence of [the] lust-inducing female." See Fatima Mernissi, *Beyond the Veil: Male-Female Dynamics ina Modern Muslim Society*, trans. Ptaricia Geesey (New York: Schenkman, 1975): 83.

11. See an excellent summary of the report in Edward Said, "Disunity and Factionalism," *Al-Ahram Weekly* 15–21 August 2002: 1–5.

12. Aalia Shuaib and Laila al-Uthman came to Hidaya Sultan al-Salem's rescue, but it was too late. For more on the subject of al-Salem's assassination, see Jean-Marie Colombani, "Le mot et l'épée," *Le Monde* 23 May 2001: 3.

13. Pramoedya Ananta Toer, "Surati's Revenge," trans. Max Lane, *Grand Street* (Summer 1993): 140–67; Margaret Scott, "Waging War with Words," *Far Eastern Economic Review* (August 1990): 26–28; Gayle Feldman, "Morrow Gives Voice to Banned Indonesian Novelist," *Publishers Weekly* (9 February 1990): 27.

14. Toer is also the author of *The Fugitive*, trans. Willem Samuels (New York: William Morrow, 1990); *A Heap of Ashes*, trans. Harry Aveling (St. Lucia, Queensland: University of Queensland Press, 1975); *The Buru Tetralogy* comprising *This Earth of Mankind*, trans. Max Lane (New York: William Morrow, 1991); *Child of All Nations*, trans. Max Lane (New York: William Morrow, 1993); *Footsteps*, trans. Max Lane (New York: William Morrow, 1995); *House of Glass*, trans. Max Lane (New York: William Morrow, 1996).

15. See Krishna Sen, *Culture and Society in New Order Indonesia*, ed. Virginia Matheson Hooker (Kuala Lumpur: Oxford University Press, 1993) 123–24. As Noam Chomsky has argued, the murkiness of American involvement in the birth of " New Order" Indonesia is not a thing of the past. The shared official secrets of Indonesia and the United States have helped to shape representations of the "New World Order" as we know it now. See, for example, Noam Chomsky, *Year 501: The Conquest Continues* (Boston: South End, 1993): especially 122–23; *World Orders and New* (New York: Columbia University press, 1994). Tahar Ben Jelloun wrote *L'Homme rompu* as a tribute to Pramoedya Ananta Toer. "Pour lui rendre hommage et lui exprimer mon soutien d'écrivain à écrivain, j'ai écrit *L'Homme rompu*, un roman sur la corruption, calamité aujourd'hui banale aussi bien dans les pays du Sud que dans ceux du Nord." Quoted in Hélène Milliex, "De la corruption," *Nuit blanche* (June July, August 1990): 60.

16. Algerians writers, artists, and intellectuals continue to die by the dozens without a peep from the international community. Many have left the country to find refuge in the West. It is a collective tragedy.

17. For more details on the subject, see Alexie Lorca, "La voix de la conscience," *Lire* (October 2000): 107.

18. A glance at the table of contents of *Autodafé* (issues of 2000 and 2001) confirms the seriousness of its quest.

19. For a fascinating argument about the responsibility of the writer, see Guy Rossi-Landi, "La responsabilité des intellectuels," *Lire* (May 2001): 100.

20. See, especially Sean James Rose, "Les autres n'existent pas," *Lire* (October 2000): 104; Bei Dao, "Journal de mes déménagements," *Autodafé* (Fall 2000): 81–90.

Chapter Eight: Sä-ēd' Data Base 1966–2002

1. I owe much gratitude to Edward Said, who gave me a copy of his curriculum vitae, the Edward Said Archive, Eddie Yeghiayan who maintains the Edward Said bibliography, the UCI Critical Theory Resource, Rice Webscast Archive: Edward Said on the Tragedy of Palestine, and the website www.edwardsaid.org. Dr. Zeinab Astrabani played a crucial role in making sure that I got a copy of Edward's c.v. Thank you wholeheartedly, Dr. Astrabani. They all played a major part in assembling the *Sä-ēd'* Data Base 1966–2002.

Selected Bibliography

Aburish, Said. *Arafat: From Defender to Dictator.* London: Bloomsbury, 1999.

Adorno, Theodor. *Minima Moralia: Reflections from Damaged Life.* Trans. E.F.N. Jephcott. London: New Left Books, 1951.

After Colonialism: Imperial Histories and Postcolonial Displacements. Ed. Gyan Prakash. Princeton: Princeton University Press, 1994.

Ahmad, Aijaz. *In Theory: Classes, Nations, Literatures.* London: Verso, 1992.

Ahmed, Iqbal. "Introduction." In *Edward Said. The Pen and the Sword: Conversations with David Barsamian.* Toronto: Between the Lines, 1994: 7–23.

Alcalay, Ammiel. "Step-Time in the Levant." *The Nation* 20 December 1999: 9–12.

Alexander, Edward. "Professor of Terror." *Commentary* (August 1989): 49–50.

Anderson, Perry. *The Origins of Post-Modernity.* London: Methuen, 1998.

Alaloui, el, Hichom Ben Abdallah. "Être citoyen dans le monde arabe." *Le Monde Diplomatique* (July 1995): 77.

Ali, Agha Shahid. "Ghazal I: For Edward Said." *TriQuarterly 100* (Spring 1998): 24–26.

Al-Shaykh, Hanan. *The Story of Zahra.* Trans. Catherine Cobham. London: Quartet, 1986.

Al-Rawi, Karim. "L'Écrivain encerclé." *Le Novel Observateur* 15 Janvier 1996: 12–14.

The Arabian Nights. Trans. Husain Haddawy. New York: Knopf, 1992.

Ash, Timothy Garton. *History of the Present: Essays, Sketches and Despatches from Europe in the Nineties.* London: Allen Lane, 1999.

Ashcroft, Bill and Ahluwalia. *The Plitics of Identity.* London: Routledge, 1977.

The Atlas of Literature. Ed. Malcolm Bradbury. London: De Agostini Editions, 1996.

Auerbach, Eric. *Mimesis: The Representations of Reality in Western Literature.* Trans. Willard Trask. 1953; rprt. Princeton: Princeton University Press, 1968.

Autodafe. New York: Seven Stories Press, 2000.

Autodafe. New York. Seven Stories Press, 2001.

Barthes, Roland. *Camera Lucida.* Trans. Richard Howard. New York: Farrar, Straus, and Giroux, 1981.

———. *Leçon.* Paris: Seuil, 1978.

———. *Image-Music-Text.* Trans. Stephen Heath. New York: Farrar, Strauss, and Giroux, 1977.

———. *Le Dgré zéro de l'écriture*. Paris: Seuil, 1953.

Baucom, Ian. *Out of Place: Englishness, Empire, and The Locations of Identity*. Princeton: Princeton University Press, 1999.

Baudelaire, Charles. *Oeuvres complètes*. Paris: La Pléiade, 1966.

Bayoumi, Moustapha and Rubin, Andrew. "Introduction." In *The Edward Said Reader*. New York: Vintage, 2000: i-xi.

Bellow, Saul. *The Dean's December*. New York: Harper and Row, 1982.

Benda, Julien. *The Treason of the Intellectuals*. Trans. Richard Aldington. New York: Pantheon, 1969.

Ben Jelloun, Tahar. *Le Racisme expliqué à ma Fille*. Paris: Seuil, 1994.

———. "Nawal Saadawi sous Surveillance." *Le Monde* 12 March 1990: 14.

Bennis, Phyllis and Cassidy, Neal. *From Stones to Statehood: The Palestinian Uprising*. New York: Olive Branch, 1990.

Benrabeh, Mohamed. "La Purification ethnique." *Télérama hors/série* (March 1995): 36–39.

Berger, John. *Selected Essays of John Berger*. Ed. Geoff Dyer. London: Bloomsbury, 2002.

Berques, Jacques. "Au-delà de l'Orientalisme: Entretien avec Jacques Berques." *Qantara* 13 (October, November, December 1994): 27–28.

Bhabha, Homi. *The Location of Culture*. London and New York: Routledge, 1994.

———. "Culture's Between." *Artforum* (September 1993): 167–68; 211–12.

———. "Double Visions." *Artforum* (January 1992): 85–89.

———. *Nation and Narration*. London and New York: Routledge, 1990 .

"Bill Gates Is?" *Harper's Magazine* (July 2002): 28–29.

Bishara, Marwan. "Le Cancer des colonies juives." *Le Monde Diplomatique* (June 2002): 15.

Blaming the Victims: Spurious Scholarship and the Palestinian Question. Eds. Edward Said and Christopher Hitchens. London and New York, 1988.

Bergson, Henry. *The Two Forms of Memory*. Trans. Nancy Margaret Paul and W. Scott Palmer. London: George Allen, 1962.

Borger, Julian. "Friends Rally to Repulse Attack on Edward Said." *The Guardian* 23 August 1997: 7.

Boucenne, Pierre. "André Glucksmann/Interview." *Écrire, lire et parler*. Paris: Laffont, 1985: 34–49.

Brantlinger, Patrick. "Edward Said and/ versus Raymond Williams." In *Edward Said and the Post-Colonial*. Eds. Bill Ashcroft and Hussein Kadhim. New York: Nova, 2001): 57–72.

Brennan, Timothy. "The Illusion of a Future: *Orientalism* as Travelling Theory. " *Critical Inquiry* 27:3 (Spring 2001): 90–122.

Chamalov, Varlam. "Athenian Nights." *Autodafé* (2001): 153–65.

Chevrier, Jacques. "L'Univers romanesque de William Sassine." *In Les Mots de la terre: géographie et littératures francophones*. Roma: Bulzoni, 1998: 211–31.

Chinweizu. *The West and the Rest of Us: White Predators, Black Slavers, and the African Elite*. New York: Pantheon, 1975.

Chipasula, Frank. *Nightwatcher, Nightsong*. Peterborough: Peter Green, 1986.

Chomsky, Noam. *World Orders and New*. New York: Columbia University Press, 1994.

———. *Year 507: The Conquest Continues*. Boston: South End, 1993.

Cixous, Hélène. "Obstétriques cruelles." *Autodafé* (2000): 105–18.

Cixous, Hélène, and Mireille-Calle-Gruber. *Rootprints: Memory and Life Writing*. Trans. Eric Prenowitz. London: Routledge, 1997.

———. "My Algeriance: In Other Worlds, to Depart Not to Arrive from Algeria." *Tri-Quarterly* (Fall 1997): 250–69.

Clark, Caryl. "Forging Identity: Beethoven's 'Ode' as European Anthem." *Critical Inquiry* (Summer 1997): 789–807.

Cockburn, Alexander. "Said, Sontag, and the Laws of Intellectual Safety." *Left Coast* 17 August 2001: 4–7.

———. "The Attack on Said." *Counterpunch* 1 September 1999: 14–21.

Columbani, Jean-Marie. "le Mot et l'épée." *Le Monde* 23 May 2001: 3.

Colonial and Postcolonial Encounters. Eds. Niaz Zaman *et al*. Dhaka: Vedams Books, 1999.

Conversations with V.S. Naipaul. Ed. Feroza Jussawalla. Jackson: University Press of Mississipi, 1997.

Corm, Georges. "L'Occident a planté les graines de la violence." *L'Express* 27/2/2003: 60–63.

Couturier, Kelly. "The Writer Who Talked Turkey." *The Washington Post* 13 June 1995: C4.

———. "Algerians Wonder Who's Really Behind the Recent Series of High-Profile Murders." *Wall Street Journal* 1 July 1993: 34.

cummings, e. e. "Thanksgiving." In *Complete Poems, 1904–1962*. Ed. George J. Firmage. New York: Liverlight Publishing, 1994: 65–69.

Coste, Philippe. "Pourquoi Bush veut aller jusqu'au bout." *L'Express* 6/3/2003: 47–53.

Dao, Bei. "Le Journal of mes déménagements." *Autodafé* (Fall 2000): 81–90.

Daruton, John. "A Prophet Test the Honor of his Own Country." *The New York Times International* 14 March 1995: D2.

Darwish, Mahmoud. *Memory for Forgetfulness*. Trans. Ibrahim Muhawi. Berkeley: University of California Press, 1995.

———. "We Have an Incurable Malady: Hope." *Autodafé* (2002): 34–41.

Deane, Seamus. *Reading in the Dark*. New York: Random House, 1998.

De Certeau, Michel. *The Practice of Everyday Life*. Trans. Timothy J. Tomasik. Minneapolis: University of Minnesota Press, 1998.

De Cusa, Nicholas. *The Idiot*. Trans. *Of Idiota*. [1450] London: 1650.

Deleuze, Gilles and Guattari Félix. *What is Philosophy?* Trans. Hugh Tomlinson and Graham Burchell. New York: Columbia University Press, 1994.

———. *Anti-Oedipus: Capitalism and Schizophrenia*. Trans. Robert Hurley, Mark Seem, and Helen R. Lane. New York: Viking, 1977.

Dennis, David B. *Beethoven in German Politics 1870–1989*. New Haven and London: Yale University Press, 1996: 175–205.

Derrida, Jacques. *États d'âme de la psychanalyse: adresse aux états généraux de la psychanalyse*. Paris: Galilée, 2000.

———. "Living On: Border Lines." In *Deconstruction and Criticism*. Ed. Harold Bloom. New York: Seabury, 1979: 111–27.

———. "The Supplement of Copula: Philosophy before Linguistics." In *Textual Strategies: Perspectives in Post-Structuralist Criticism*. Ed. Josué V. Harari. Ithaca: Cornell University Press, 1979: 82–121.

———. *Le Monolinguisme de l'autre la prothése d'origine.* Paris: Galileé, 1996.

———. *Of Grammatology.* Trans. Gayatri Chakravorty Spivak. Baltimore: Johns Hopkins University Press, 1979.

———. *Of Hospitality.* Trans. Rachel Bowlby. Stanford: Stanford University Press, 2000.

———. *The Post Card: From Socrates to Freud and Beyond.* Trans. Alan Bass. Chicago: University of Chicago Press, 1978.

Descartes, René. *Meditations and Other Metaphysical Writings.* London: Penguin, 2000.

Dirlik, Arif. "Placing Edward Said: Space Time and the Traveling Theorist." In *Edward Said and the Post-Colonial.* Eds. Bill Ashcroft and Hussein Kadhim. New York: Nova, 2001: 1–31.

———. *The Postcolonial Aura: Third World Criticism in the Age of Global Capitalism.* Boulder, Co.: Westview, 1997.

Diski, Jenni. "Entitlement." *LRB* 18 October 2001: 21–22.

Djebar, Assia. *L'amour, la fantasia.* Paris: Lattès, 1985.

Durant, Alan. *Conditions of Music.* London: Macmillan, 1984.

Eagleton, Terry. "Allergic to Depths." *LRB* 18 March 1999: 7–8.

———. *Scholars and Rebels in Nineteenth-Century Ireland.* Oxford: Blackwell, 1999.

El-Karrat, Edward. *Girls of Alexandria.* Trans. Frances Liardet. London: Quartet, 1993.

———. *City of Saffron.* Trans. Frances Liardet. London: Quartet, 1989.

Edward Said: A Critical Reader. Ed. Michael Sprinker. Oxford: Blackwell, 1992.

Edwards, Frederick. "In Defense of Taslima Nasrin." *The Humanist* (September/October 1994): 42–44.

El-Aalaoui, Hichem ben Abdallah. "Être citoyen dans le monde arabe." *Le Monde Diplomatique* (July 1995): 9–11.

Eagleton, Terry. "*Newsreel History.*" *LRB* 12 November 1998: 8–10.

———. "Spaced Out." *LRB* 24 April 1997: 22–23.

Ellis, David. *D. H. Lawrence 1922–30.* Cambridge, Mass.: Cambridge University Press, 1998.

Eloquent Obsessions: Writing Cultural Criticism. Ed. Marianna Torgovnick. Durham: Duke University Press, 1995.

Fanon, Frantz. *The Wretched of the Earth.* Trans. Constance Farrington. New York: Grove, 1964.

Feldman, Gayle. "Morrow Gives Voice to Banned Indonesian Novelist." *Publishers Weekly* 9 February 1990: 24–26.

Farman, Abonali. "Fear of the Bread." *Transition* (Fall 1995): 48–70.

Fineman, Joel. "The History of the Anecdote: Fiction and Fiction." In *The New Historicism.* Ed. H. Aram Veeser. New York and London: Routledge, 1989: 49–76.

Fish, Stanley. "The Ignorance of Our Warrior Intellectuals." *Harper's Magazine* (July 2002): 33–40.

Fisher, Clive. *Cyril Connolly: A Nostalgic Life.* London: Macmillan, 1995.

Fisk, Robert. "Sharon's Strategy Aimed at Destroying Arafat's Security Infrastructure." *The Independent* 4 April 2002: 4–5.

———. "Mr. Powell Must See for Himself What Israel Inflicted on Jenin." *The Independent* 14 April 2002: 1–5.

———. "All These Cruel Muslim Regimes Abuse the People of the Middle East." *The Independent* 7 August 2001: 1–3.

————. "The Palestinians Believe They Have Nothing to Lose by Fighting On." *The Independent* 30 October 2000: 1–4.

————. "Arafat's Betrayal." *LRB* 25 February 1995: 15.

For Rushdie: Essays by Arab and Muslim Writers in Defense of Free Speech. Trans. Kevin Anderson and Kenneth Whitehead. New York: George Brazillier, 1994.

Foucault, Michel. *Dits et écrits 1954–1988. Vol.: III.* Paris: Gallimard, 1994.

————. "The Masked Philosopher." In *Politics, Philosophy, Culture: Interviews and Other Writings 1977–1984.* Ed. Lawrence D. Kritzman. London and New York: Routledge, 1988: 324–30.

————. "Contemporary Music and the Public." Trans. John Rahn. In *Perspectives of New Music* (Fall/Winter 1985): 6–18.

————. *The Order of Things: An Archeology of the Human Sciences.* New York: Pantheon, 1970.

————. *Language, Counter-Memory, Practice: Selected Essays and Interviews by Michel Foucault.* Ed. with intro. Donald F. Bouchard and Sherry Simon. Ithaca, N.Y.: Cornell University Press, 1977.

————. *Surveiller et punir: naissance de la prison.* Paris: Gallimard, 1975.

Freire, Paul. *Cultural Action for Freedom.* Cambridge, Mass.: Havard Educational Review and Center for the Study Development and Social Change, 1970.

————. *Letters to Cristina: Reflections on my Life and Work.* New York: Routledge, 1996.

Fukuyama, Francis. *The End of History.* New York: Harper Collins, 2002.

Gathering Seaweed: African Prison Writing. Ed. Jack Mapanje. Oxford; Portsmouth, N.H.: Heinemann, 2002.

Gilsenan, Michael. *Lords of the Lebanese Marches: Violence and Narrative in an Arab Society.* London: Tauris, 1995.

Glass, Charles. "Iraq Must Go!." *LRB* 3 October 2002: 12–14.

————. "On Palestine." *LRB* 21 February 2002: 36–37.

————. *Money for Old Rope: Disorderly Compositions.* London: Pan Books, 1992.

————. *Tribes with Flags: A Dangerous Passage through the Chaos of the Middle East.* London: Grove/Atlantic, 1991.

Gogwilt, Chris. "Pramoedya's Fiction and History: An Interview with Indonesian Novelist Pramoedya Ananta Toer." *The Yale Journal of Criticism* (Spring 1996): 143–57.

Gordimer, Nadine. "Testamanet of the Word." *The Guardian* 15 June 2002: 12–14.

Graham, Helga. "Saudis Break the Silence." *LRB* 22 April 1993: 6–9.

Gramsci, Antonio. *Studies in Socialist Pedagogy.* Ed. Theodore Mills and Bertell Ollman. New York: Monthly Review, 1978.

Gramsci, Antonio. *Selections from the Prison Notebooks.* Trans. Quintin Hoare and Geoffrey Nowell Smith. New York: International Publishers, 1971.

Greenblatt, Stephen. *Hamlet in Purgatory.* Princeton and Oxford: Princeton University Press, 2001.

Grossman, David. *Be My Knife.* Trans. Vered Almog and Maya Gurantz. New York: Farrar, Straus, and Giroux, 2002.

Haddad, Malek. "La Révolution a-t-elle été trahie?" In a Special Issue of *Le Nouvel Observateur* titled *La Guerre d'Algérie: 30 Ans Après* (1992): 62.

Hadrawi, Ibrahim Mohamed. "La plume et le sabre." *Lire* (March 1996): 30–36.

Halliday, Fred. *Islam and the Myth of Confrontation: Religion and Politics in the Middle East.* London: Faber, 1996.

Hamdi, Mohamed Elhachmi. *The Politics of Islam: A Case Study of Tunisia*. London: Faber, 1996.

Hannah Arendt/Karl Jaspers. *Correspondence 1926–1969*. Ed. Lotte Kohler and Hans Saner. Trans. Roberta and Rita Kimber. New York and London: Harcourt, 1992.

Hawi, Khalil and Naimy, Nadeem. *From the Vineyards of Lebanon*. Syracuse: Syracuse University Press, 1992.

Havel, Václav. *Disturbing the Peace: Conversations with Hvízdala*. New York: Knopf, 1990.

Hatmal, Jamil. "And Also For Them." In *For Rushdie: Essays by Arab and Mislum Writers in Defense of Free Speech*. Trans. Kevin Anderson and Kenneth Whitehead. New York: St. Martin Press, 1994: 172–74.

Hass, Amira. "Les Israéliens qui rêvent de 'transfert'." *Le Monde Diplomatique* (February 2003): 23.

Hayford, Elizabeth. "*After the Last Sky*: A Review." *Library Journal* (December 1986): 32–38.

Heaney, Seamus. "Exile Runes." *LRB* 20 April 1989: 12.

Hitchens, Christopher. *The Trial of Henry Kissinger*. London and New York. Verso, 2001.

———. *Why Orwell Matters*. New York: Basic Books, 2002.

———. "Preface." In *Edward Said, Peace and Its Discontents: Essays on Palestine in the Middle East Process*. New York: Vintage, 1996: xiii–xxiii.

Howe, Irving. *Celebrations and Attacks: Thirty Years of Literary and Cultural Commentary*. New York: Horizon, 1979.

Huband, Mark. *Warriors of the Prophet: The Challenge of Islamic Fundamentalism*. London: Westview, 1998.

Husarska, Anna. "Why So Many Journalists Die in Algeria?" *The Globe and Mail* 17 August 1996: 12.

Hugeux, Vincent. "Les Irakiens depuis 8000 ans au coeur de l'Histoire." *L'Express* 27/2/2003: 53–59.

Hull, Margaret Betz. *The Hidden Philosophy of Hannah Arendt*. London & New York: Routledge, 2002.

Intifada: The Palestinian Uprising against Israeli Occupation. Ed. Zachary Lockman and Joel Benin. Toronto: Between the Lines, 1989.

Issues of Death: Mortality and Identity in English Renaissance Tragedy. Ed. Michael Neill. Oxford: Oxford University Press, 1997.

Jacoby, Russell. "Marginal Returns: The Trouble with Post-Colonial Theory." *Lingua Franca* (September/October 1995): 30–38.

———. *The Last Intellectuals: American Culture in the Age of Academe*. New York: Noonday, 1989.

JanMohammed, Abdul. "The Economy of Manichean Allegory: The Foundation of Racial Difference in Colonialist Literature." In *Race, Writing, and Difference*. Ed. Henry Louis Gates Jr. Chicago: University of Chicago Press, 1985.

Kagan, Robert. "L'Amérique doit mener la politique des forts." *L'Express* 6/3/2003: 54–57.

Joyce, James. *A Portrait of the Artist as a Young Man*. New York: Everyman, 1991.

Khalil, Samir. *Art, Vulgarity, and Responsibility in Iraq*. London: André Deutsch, 1991.

Khatibi, Abdelkebir. "A Colonial Labyrinth." *Yale French Studies* 2:83 (1993): 19–24.

———. *Maghreb pluriel*. Paris: Denoel, 1987.

Kay, Graeme. "The Natural." *Music* (May 1998): 24–27.

Kemal, Yasar. *Memed, My Hawk.* Trans. Edouard Roditi. London: Writers and Readers, 1981.

———. *Murder in the Ironists Market.* Trans. Thilda Kemal. London: Collins and Harxill, 1979.

———. *Anatolian Tales.* Trans. Thilda Kemal. New York: Dodd Mead, 1969.

Kermode, Frank. "Off the Edge." *LRB* 7 November 1991: 11.

Khalil, Samir. *Republic of Fear: The Inside Story of Saddam's Iraq.* New York: Pantheon, 1990.

Kostelanetz, Richard. *John Cage (Ex)plain(ed).* London: Prentice Hall International, 1996.

Kramer, Lawrence. *Music as Cultural Practice, 1800–1900.* Berkeley: University of California Press, 1990.

Krauthammer, Charles. "The Case of the Suspect Bios." *Time* 4 October 1999: 84.

Kristeva, Julia. *Hannah Arendt: Life is a Narrative.* Trans. Frank Collins. Toronto: University of Toronto Press, 2001.

———. "Le Sujet en procès." In *Polygone.* Paris: Seuil, 1977. 41–58.

Laâbi, Abdellatif. "La Différence." *Lire* (October 1994): 34.

Lacan, Jacques. *Ecrits.* Paris: Seuil, 1966.

———. "Le Mythe individuel du nevrosé." *Ornicar?* 17/18 (1979): 289–307.

———. *The Four Fundamental Concepts of Psycho-Analysis*, Ed. Jacques-Alain Miller. Trans. Alan Sheridan. New York and London: W. W. Norton, 1981.

Lagarde, Dominique et Salün, Tangi. "Le grand écart des régimes arabes." *L'Express* 3/4/2003: 18–19.

Laroui, Abdallah. The Crisis of the Arab Intellectuals. Berkeley: University of California Press, 1976.

Lawrence, D. H. *Poems.* London: Duckworth, 1976.

Le Corre, Philippe. "Unrepentent Exile." *Far Eastern Economic Review* 24 November 1994: 32–37.

———. "Les 6 géants de l'armement américain." *L'Express* 27/3/2003: 75.

Lebrecht, Norman. *When the Music Stops: Managers, Maestros, and the Corporate Murder of Classical Music.* New York: Simon and Schuster, 1997.

Levinson, Jerrold. *Music, Art, and Metaphysics: Essays in Philosophical Aesthetics.* Ithaca, N.Y.: Cornell University Press, 1990.

Lewis, Bernard. "The Question of Orientalism." *The New York Review of Books* 24 June 1982: 44–49.

Lindenberger, Herbert. *Opera in History: From Monteverdi to Cage.* Stanford: Stanford University Press, 1998.

Lorca, Alexie. "La Voix de la Conscience." *Lire* (October 2000): 92–109.

Loomba, Ania. "Overworlding the Third World." *The Oxford Literary Review* 13 (1991): 37–61.

Louis Bouilhet: Lettres à Gustave Flaubert. Ed. Maria Capello. Paris: CNRS, 1996.

Lukács, Georg. *History and Class Consciousness: Studies in Marxist Dialectics.* Trans. Rodney Livingstone. London: Merlin Press, 1971.

MacKenzie, John. *Orientalism: History, Theory, and the Arts.* Manchester: Manchester University Press, 1995.

Lalabou, Catherine and Jacques Derrida. *La Contre-allée.* Aubenas d'Ardèche: Imprimerie Lienhart, 1999.

Larkin, Philip. *Collected Poems.* New York: Farrar, Straus and Giroux, 1991.

Marrouchi, Mustapha. *Signifying with a Vengeance: Theories, Literature, Storytellers*. New York: SUNY Press, 2002.

———. "Exile Runes," *College Literture* (Fall 2001): 88–129.

———. "Fear of the Other, Loathing the Similar." *College Literature* (Fall 1999): 17–59.

———. "Rootprints." *The Dalhousie Review* (Spring 1997): 67–97.

———. "The Critic as Exiled Intelligence: The Case of Edward Said." *Diacritics* (Spring 1991): 63–74.

Marx, Karl. *Texts on Method*. Trans. Terrell Carver. New York: Barnes and Noble, 1975.

Maya, Taggi. "Out of the Shadows." *The Guardian* 12 September 1999: 12–14.

Mcbeth, John. "Prisoners of History." *Far Eastern Economic Review* 16 February 1995: 27–29.

McCarthy, Patrick. *Albert Camus: A Critical Study of His Life and Work*. London: Hamish Hamilton, 1982.

McLaren, Peter. *Critical Pedagogy and Predatory Culture*. New York: Routledge, 1995.

McClary, Susan. *Feminine Endings: Music, Gender, and Sexuality*. Minneapolis: University of Minnesota Press, 1991.

Memmi, Albert. "Dans quelle langue écrire? La patrie littéraire du colonisé." *Le Monde Diplomatique* (September 1996): 11–12.

Merod, Jim. "Sublime Lyrical Abstractions." *Boundary 2* (Summer 1998): 117–45.

Mernissi, Fatima. *Beyond the Veil: Male-Female Dynamics in a Modern Muslim Society*. Trans. Patricia Geesey. New York: Schenkman, 1975.

———. *Le Harem politique: Le Prophète et les femmes*. Paris: Albin Michel, 1988.

Mikanza, Mobyem. *Procès à Malala: Théâtre*. Kinshasa: Presses Africaines 1977.

Milliex, Hélène. "De La Corruption." *Nuit blanche* (June, July, August 1990): 60–67.

Mitchell, W. J. T. "Panic of the Visual: A Conversation with Edward W. Said." *Boundary 2* (Summer 1998): 4–23.

———. "The Ethics of Form in the Photographic Essay." *Afterimage* (January 1989): 9–14.

Moore-Gilbert, Bart. *Postcolonial Theory: Contexts, Practices, Politics*. London: Verso, 1997.

Morrison, Toni. "On 'the Radiance of the King.'" *The New York Review of Books* 9 August 2001: 9–11.

Mphahlele, Ezekiel. *Bury Me at the Marketplace: Selected Letters of Es'kia Mohahlele, 1943–1980*. Johannesbourg, Skotaville 1984.

Mudimbe, V. Y., and Boumil Jewsiewicki. "For Said: Why Even the Critic of Imperialism Labors Under Western Skies." *Transition* 63 (1994): 34–50.

Mukerjee, Baharati. *Jasmine*. London: Penguin, 1989.

Nasrin, Taslima. *The Game in Reverse*. Trans. Carolyne Wright. New York: George Brazillier, 1992.

Nietzsche, Frederik. *Das Philosophenbuch: Theoretische Studien*. Paris: Aubier-Flammarion, 1969.

———. *The Will to Power*. Trans. Walter Kaufman and R.J. Hollingdale. New York: Vintage, 1968.

Neill, Michael. *Issues of Death: Mortality and Identity in English Rennaissance Tragedy*. Oxford: Oxford University Press, 1997.

Nora, Pierre. "Between Memory and History: Les Lieux de Mémoire." Trans. Marc Roudebush. *Representations 26* (Spring 1989): 7–25.

The Old Testament in The New American Bible. New York: Catholic Book Publishing Co., 1970.

Oliver, Roland. *The African Experience.* London: Routledge, 1992.

Ostwald, Peter. *Glenn Gould: The Ecstasy and the Tragedy of Genius.* London: Norton, 1997.

Padel, Ruth. "Putting the Words into Women's Mouths: The Female Role in Opera." *LRB* 23 January 1997: 10–13.

Pamuk, Orhan. The Black Book. Trans. Guneli Gun. New York: Farrar, Straus and Giroux 1994.

Pamuk, Orhan. "L'Hérétique." *Le Point* 27 September 1997: 71–73.

p'Bitek, Okot. "From Where Did God Get the Clay for Making Things?" Trans. T. Lo Liyong. *The Literary Review* (Summer 1991): 559–66.

Pathak, Zakia, Sawati Sengupta, and Sharmila Purkayastha. "The Prisonhouse of *Orientalism*." *Textual Practice* (Summer 1991): 195–218.

The Pen and the Sword: Conversations with David Barsamian. Intro. Iqbal Ahmad. Ed. David Barsamian. Toronto: Between the Lines, 1994.

Porter, Dennis. "Orientalism and Its Problems." In *The Politics of Theory.* Ed. Francis Barker et al. Colchester: University of Essex Press, 1983.

Postman, Neil. *Amusing Ourselves to Death: Public Dicourse in the Age of Show Business.* New York: Penguin, 1985.

Powell, Enoch. *Reflections of a Statesman: The Writings and Speeches of Enoch Powell.* New York: Barnes and Noble, 1997.

Ramonet, Ignacio. "Illégale aggression." *Le Monde Diplomatique* (April 2003): 1.

Rich, Adrienne. *An Atlas of the Difficult World: Poems 1988–1991.* New York: Norton, 1991.

Rieff, David. *Going to Miami: Exiles and Refugees in the New America.* London: Bloomsbury, 1987.

Ricoeur, Paul. *La Mémoire, l'histoire, l'oubli.* Paris: Seuil, 2000.

Robbins, Bruce. "Edward Said's Culture and Imperialism: A Symposium." *Social Text* (Fall 1994): 2–14.

Robinson, Paul. "Is Aida an Orientalist Opera?" *Cambridge Opera Journal* 5 (1993): 133–140.

———. *Ludwig van Beethoven, Fidelio.* Cambridge: Harvard University Press, 1983.

Rodinson, Maxime. "Fantômes et réalités de l'Orientalisme." *Qantara* 13 (October, November, December 1994): 13–15.

Rose, Sean James. "Les Autres n'existent pas." *Lire* (October 2000): 99–105.

Rosen, Charles. *The Romantic Generation.* London: Harper Collins, 1995.

Rosseli, John. *The Life of Mozart.* Cambridge: Cambridge University Press, 1998.

Rossi-Laudi, Guy. "La Responsabilité des intellectuels." *Lire* (May 2001): 94–102.

Roy, Piali. "Ideas." CBC 23 November 1999: 9–10 P.M.

Rushdie, Salman. "Une Déclaration d'indépendence." *Autodafé* (2000): 90–93.

———. "On Palestinian Identity: A Conversation with Edward Said." In *Imaginary Homelands: Essays and Criticism 1981–1991.* London: Granta, 1991: 166–87.

Saadawi, Nawal. *The Circling Song.* London: Atlantic Highlands, 1989.

———. "Veils East and West." *New Statesman and Society* 9 October 1992: 19.

Said, Edward. "Diary." *LRB* 17 April 2003: 39.

———. "The Appalling Consequences Are Now Clear." *CounterPunch* 22 April 2003: 1–8.

———. "'We Know Who 'We' Are." *LRB* 17 October 2002: 23–25.

———. "Disunity and Factionalism." *Al-Ahram* 15–21 August 2002: 1–5.

———. "Freud, Zionism and Vienna." *Al-Ahram Weekly* 15–21 March 2001.

———. *Power, Culture, and Politics.* New York: Pantheon, 2001.

———. *Reflections on Exile and Other Essays.* Cambridge: Harvard University Press, 2000.

———. "In Memory of a Belly-Dancer." *LRB* 28 October 1999: 25.

———. "Refusal to Surrender Quielty." *Al-Ahram Weekly* 5–11 August 1999: 3.

———. "Living by the Clock." *LRB* 29 April 1999: 8–12.

———. "Defamation, Revisionist Style." *Al-Ahram Weekly* 26 August 1999.

———. *Out of Place: A Memoir.* New York: Knopf, 1999.

———. "Between Worlds." *LRB* 7 May 1998: 3–5.

———. "La Palestine n'a pas encore disparu." *Le Monde Diplomatique* (May 1998): 5–7.

———. "Daniel Barenboim and Edward Said: A Conversation." *Raritan* (Summer 1998): 3–24.

———. "In the Chair." *LRB* 17 July 1997: 3–6.

———. "On *Fidelio.*" *LRB* 30 October 1997: 25–27.

———. "From Silence to Sound and Back Again: Music, Literature, and History." *Raritan* (Fall 1997): 21–40.

———. "*Così fan tutte* at the Limits." *Grand Street* (Fall 1997): 95–107.

———. *Peace and Its Discontents: Essays on Palestine in the Middle East Peace Process.* New York: Vintage, 1996.

———. "Bookless in Gaza." *The Nation* 23 September 1996: 6–7.

———. "Orientalism: An Afterward." *Raritan* (Winter 1995): 32–59.

———. "Bach's Genius, Schumann's Eccentricity, Chopin's Ruthlessness, Rosen's Gift." *LRB* 21 September 1995: 13–15.

———. *The Pen and the Sword: Conversations with David Barsamian.* Toronto: Between the Lines, 1994.

———. *The Politics of Dispossession: The Struggle for Palestinian Self-Determination, 1969–1994.* New York: Pantheon, 1994.

———. "Against the Orthodoxies." In *For Rushdie: Essays by Arab and Mislum Writers in Defense of Free Speech.* Trans. Kevin Anderson and Kenneth Whitehead. New York: St. Martin Press, 1994: 260–62.

———. *Culture and Imperialism.* New York: Knopf, 1994.

———. "On Mahmoud Darwish." *Grand Street* 48 (1994): 101–11.

———. *Representations of the Intellectual.* New York: Pantheon, 1994.

———. "The Importance of Being Faithful to Wagner." *LRB* 11 February 1993: 11–13.

———. "Palestine, Then and Now: An Exile's Journey through Israel and the Occupied Territories." *Harper's Magazine* (December 1992): 47–51.

———. *Musical Elaborations.* New York: Columbia University Press, 1991.

———. "Identity, Authority, and Freedom: The Potentate and the Traveller." *Transition* 54 (1991): 12–32.

———. "Which Country?" *The Nation* 15–22 July 1991: 116.

———. "War in the Gulf." *LRB* 7 March 1991: 7–8.

———. "Cairo and Alexandria." *Departures* (May/June 1990): 1–15.

———. "Yeats and Decolonization." In *Nationalism, Colonialism and Literature.* Intro. Seamus Deane. Minneapolis: University of Minnesota Press, 1990: 69–99.

———. "Homage to a Belly-Dancer." *LRB* 13 September 1990: 7–9.

———. "Alexander the Brilliant." *LRB* 18 February 1988: 17.

———. *Blaming the Victims: Spurious Scholarship and the Palestinian Question.* Ed. Edward Said and Christopher Hitchens. New York and London: Verso, 1988.

———. "The Voice of a Palestinian in Exile." *Third Text* (Spring/Summer 1988): 23–41.

———. "Goodbye to Mahfouz." *LRB* 8 December 1988: 10–13.

———. "Miami Twice." *LRB* 10 December 1987: 3–6.

———. "Cairo Recalled: Growing up in the Cultural Cross Currents of 1940s Egypt." *House and Garden* (April 1987): 32–45.

———. "*The Barber of Seville, Don Giovanni.*" *The Nation* 26 September 1987: 320–26.

———. "Glenn Gould at the Metropolitan Museum." *The Nation* 7 November 1987: 534–38.

———. "*Die Walküre, Aida, X.*" The Nation 6 December 1986: 648–51.

———. "Orientalism Reconsidered." In *Literature, Politics, and Theory.* Ed. Francis Barker et al. Colchester: University of Essex Press, 1986.

———. With Jean Mohr. *After the Last Sky: Palestinian Lives.* New York: Pantheon, 1986.

———. "An Ideology of Difference." *Critical Inquiry* (Fall 1985): 38–58.

———. "The Mind of Winter: Reflections on Life in Exile." *Harper's Magazine* (September 1984): 47–55.

———. *The World, the Text, and the Critic.* Cambridge: Harvard University Press, 1983.

———. "Secular Criticism." In *The World, the Text,, and the Critic.* Cambridge: Harvard University Press, 1983: 1–31.

———. "Opponents, Audiences, Constituencies, and Community." *Critical Inquiry* (Spring 1982): 23–39.

———. *Orientalism.* New York: Vintage, 1979.

———. *Covering Islam: How the Media and the Experts Determine How We See the Rest of the World.* New York: Pantheon, 1981.

———. "From the Ashes of Beirut." *New Statesman and Society* 17–24 December 1977: 20.

———. "Interview." *Diacritics* (Fall 1976): 29–40.

———. *Beginnings: Intention and Method.* New York: Columbia University Press, 1975.

Salusinszky, Imre. *Criticism in Society: Interviews.* New York: Methuen, 1987.

San Juan, Jr., E. *Beyond Postcolonial Theory.* New York: St. Martin's, 1998.

Sartre, Jean-Paul. *Nausea.* Trans. Lloyd Alexander. New York: New Directions, 1964.

St. Hugo of, Victor. *Didascalicon.* Trans. Jerome Taylor. New York: Columbia University Press, 1961.

Selected Essays of John Berger. Ed. Geoff Dyer. London: Bloomsbury, 2002.

Sayigh, Yezid. *Armed Struggle and the Search for State: The Palestinian National Movement, 1949–1993.* Oxford: Clarendon, 1998.

Scott, Margaret. "Waging War in Words." *Far Eastern Economic Review* (August 1990): 26–28.

Sen, Krishna. *Culture and Society in New Order Indonesia.* Ed. Virginia Matheson Hooker. Kuala Lumpur: Oxford University Press, 1993.

Shakespeare, William. *The Complete Works.* Ed. Stanley Wells and Gary Taylor. Oxford: Clarendon, 1989.

———. *Women of Sand and Myrrh.* Trans. Catherine Cobham. London: Quartet, 1989.

Sorin, Gerald. *Irving Howe: A Life of Passionate Dissent.* New York: New York University Press, 2002.

Soyinka, Wole. *The Open Sore of a Continent: A Personal Narrative of the Nigerian Crisis.* Oxford: Oxford University Press, 1996.

Sprinker, Michael. "Introduction." In *Edward Said: A Critical Reader.* Ed. Michael Sprinker. Oxford: Blackwell, 1992: 1–5.

Spivak, Gayatri Chakravorty. *A Critique of Postcolonial Reason: Toward a History of the Vanishing Present.* Cambridge: Harvard University Press, 1999.

———. "The Rani of Simur: An Essay in Reading the Archives." *History and Theory* 24:3 (1985): 247–72.

Stegemann, Michael. "A Kind of Autumnal Repose." In *The Glenn Gould Edition.* Trans. Gerry Bramall. Toronto: Sony Classical, 1993: 45–71.

Stora, Benjamin. "Guèrre d'Algérie: les mémoires blessées." *L'Express* 23 December 1988: 56–61.

Subotnik, Rose. *Deconstructive Variations: Music and Reason in Western Society.* Minneapolis: University of Minnesota Press, 1996.

———. *Developing Variations: Style and Ideology in Western Music.* Minneapolis: University of Minnesota Press, 1991.

Suleri, Sara. "The Secret Sharers: Edward Said's Imperial Imagination." *The Village Voice* (June 1993): 7–8.

Taggi, Maya. "Out of the Shadows." *The Guardian* 12 September 1999: 12–14.

Theory, Sport and Society. Ed. Joseph Maguire. Amsterdam; Boston: JAI, 2002.

Thompson, Edward. *The Other Side of the Medal.* New Delhi: Sterling Publishers, 1989.

Todd, Olivier. *Albert Camus: Une vie.* Paris: Gallimard, 1995.

Tolstoy, Leo. *War and Peace.* New York: Modern Library, 1950.

Tomalin, Claire. *Jane Austen: A Biography.* New York: Knopf, 1998.

Tower, Pramoedya Ananta. "Surati's Revenge." Trans. Max Lane. *Grand Street* (Summer 1993): 140–67.

———. *The Fugitive.* Trans. Willem Samuels. New York: William Morrow, 1990.

———. *A Heap of Ashes.* Trans. Harry Aveling. St. Lucia, Queensland: University of Queensland Press, 1975.

———. *This Earth of Mankind.* Trans. Max Lane. New York: William Morrow, 1991.

———. *The Buru Tetralogy.* Trans. Max Lane. New York: William Morrow, 1991.

———. *Child of All Nations.* Trans. Max Lane. New York: William Morrow, 1993.

———. *Footsteps.* Trans. Max Lane. New York: William Morrow, 1995.

Turner, Brian. *Orientalism, Postmodernism, and Globalism.* London: Routledge, 1994.

Vassiliev, Alexei. *The History of Saudi Arabia (1745–1994).* London: Saqi Books, 1998.

Vico, Giambattista. *The New Science.* Trans. Thomas Goddard Bergin and Max Harold Fisch. Ithaca: Cornell University press, 1968.

Viswanathan, Gauri. *Masks of Conquest: Literary Study and British Rule in India.* New York: Columbia University Press, 1989.

Vulliany, Ed. "Disarming and Dangerous?" *The Observer Review* 29 August 1999: 2.

Wa Thiong'o, Ngugi. *Decolonizing the Mind: The Politics of Language in African Literature.* London: 1986.

Wachtel, Eleanor. *More Writers and Company.* Toronto: Vintage, 1977.

Waller, David. *Rwanda: Which Way Now?* Oxford: Oxfam, 1993.

Ward, Ibrahim. "L'ordre américain, coûte que coûte." *Le Monde Diplomatique* (April 2003): 20–21.

Waters, Lindsay. "In Responses Begins Responsibility." *Boundary 2* (Summer 1998): 34–44.

Webster, John. *The Duchess of Malfi*. Ed. Elizabeth M. Brennan. London: Ernst Benn Limited, 1964.

Wicke, Jennifer and Sprinker, Michael. "Interview with Edward Said." *In Edward Said: A Critical Reader*. Oxford: Blackwell, 1992: 221–65.

Weiner, Justus Reid. "'My Beautiful Old House' and Other Fabrications by Edward Said." *Commentary* (September 1999): 23–32.

West, Cornel. "The New Cultural Politics of Difference." In *Out There: Marginalization and Contemporary Cultures*. Ed. Russell Ferguson et al. Cambridge: MIT Press, 1990: 19–36.

Williams, Raymond. *Culture and Society 1780–1950*. London: Chatto and Windus, 1958.

Williams, Sassine. *Le Zéhéros n'est pas n'importe qui*. Paris: Présence Africaine, 1985.

Wilson, George. "Edward Said on Contrapuntal Reading." *Philosophy and Literature* (October 1994): 265–73.

Wilson, Jonathan. "A Very English Story." *The New Yorker* 6 March 1995: 96–106.

Wood, Michael. "Introduction." In *Beginnings: Intention and Method*, by Edward Said. 1975; rprt. London: Granta, 1997.

———. "Lost Paradises." *The New York Review of Books* 3 March 1994: 44–47.

Wyndham, Horace, Speranza. *A Biliography of Lady Wilde*. London: Metheun, 1987.

Yasar Kemal on his Life and Art. Eds. Trans. Eugene Lyons Hébert and Barry Tharaud. Syracuse, N.Y.: Syracuse University Press, 1999.

Yeats, W. B. *The Early Poetry*. Ithaca: Cornell University Press, 1987.

Younge, Gary. "Struggles of the Artist." *The Guardian* 17 January 2003: 3.

Young, Robert. "Disorienting Orientalism." In *White Mythologies: Writing History and the West*. London and New York: Routledge, 1990: 119–41.

Žižek, Slavoj. "The World Turned Back to Front." *LRB* 18 March 1999: 4–7.

———. "You May!" *LRB* 18 March 1999: 1–6.

Index